China's Rural Areas

The prosperity of China's people has advanced very much in recent decades. However, in many respects China is still a developing country, and this is especially true of rural areas where economic progress has not been as marked as in urban areas and where many people still live in relative poverty. The Chinese government recognizes that more hard work is needed in order to improve prosperity in the countryside. This book provides a systematic and comprehensive analysis of the situation in China's rural areas, assesses the effectiveness or otherwise of current policies, and puts forward proposals for further development. Subjects covered include the changing population profile of rural areas, land ownership, agricultural improvements, and local self-government.

China Development Research Foundation is one of the leading economic think tanks in China, where many of the details of China's economic reform have been formulated. Its work and publications therefore provide great insights into what the Chinese themselves think about economic reform and how it should develop.

Routledge Studies on the Chinese Economy

Series Editor
Peter Nolan
Director, Centre of Development Studies;
Chong Hua Professor in Chinese Development; and
Director of the Chinese Executive Leadership Programme (CELP),
University of Cambridge

Founding Series Editors
Peter Nolan, University of Cambridge and
Dong Fureng, Beijing University

The aim of this series is to publish original, high-quality, research-level work by both new and established scholars in the West and the East, on all aspects of the Chinese economy, including studies of business and economic history.

57 **China's Exchange Rate Regime**
    China Development Research Foundation

58 **China's WTO Accession Reassessed**
    China Development Research Foundation

59 **US–China Relations in the Twenty-first Century**
    A Question of Trust
    Michael Tai

60 **Understanding China**
    The Silk Road and the Communist Manifesto
    Peter Nolan

61 **Being Middle Class in China**
    Identity, Attitudes and Behaviour
    Ying Miao

62 **Governing the Commons in China**
    Yan Zhang

63 **The Economic Cycle and the Growth of the Chinese Economy**
    Li Jianwei

64 **China's Rural Areas**
    Building a Moderately Prosperous Society
    China Development Research Foundation

China's Rural Areas

Building a Moderately
Prosperous Society

China Development
Research Foundation

Routledge
Taylor & Francis Group

LONDON AND NEW YORK

CDRF 中国发展研究基金会
China Development Research
Foundation

First published 2017
by Routledge

2 Park Square, Milton Park, Abingdon, Oxfordshire OX14 4RN
52 Vanderbilt Avenue, New York, NY 10017

Routledge is an imprint of the Taylor & Francis Group, an informa business

First issued in paperback 2019

British Library Cataloguing-in-Publication Data
A catalogue record for this book is available from the British Library

Library of Congress Cataloging-in-Publication Data
A catalogue record for this book has been requested

ISBN: 978-1-138-70500-5 (hbk)
ISBN: 978-0-367-88732-2 (pbk)

Typeset in Times New Roman
by Apex CoVantage, LLC

Contents

List of figures   ix
List of tables   xi
List of boxes   xiii
China Development Report 2013/14 project team   xv
Foreword   xvii
Acknowledgements   xix

Introduction   1

1 The epic task of "building a moderately prosperous
   society in an all-round way" in rural parts of China   7

   The atypical dichotomy between urban and rural areas and
       how this pattern developed in China 8
   Rural development strategy in China from a historical
       perspective 10
   Key tasks and challenges as we seek to establish all-round
       moderate prosperity in rural areas 14
   The basic pathway toward building an all-round moderately
       prosperous society in rural areas 18

2 Changes in the geographic distribution of China's rural
   population and in the allocation of its labor resources   22

   Number, geographic distribution, and structure of China's
       rural population in the year 2020 23
   China's rural labor force in the year 2020 30
   Three pathways for dealing with changes in the rural
       population and labor force 40

3 Furthering reform of China's land system and granting greater property rights to rural residents   44

The evolution of China's land system, its primary
characteristics, and its main problems 45
Pushing forward on the reform of the property-rights
[ownership] system that governs rural land in China
by undertaking the critical step of confirming and certifying
ownership rights 51
Actively promoting the transferability of contractual
operating rights to farmland 55
Reforming the management system that governs rural
homestead sites ["residential-use land"] 60
Models that explore putting collectively owned
construction-use land on the market 67
Deepening reform of the system that governs land
requisitions [expropriations] 71
Being proactive in exploring how to reform the system
that governs collectively owned property rights 75

4 Achieving a balance in the supply and demand for grain in China and ensuring food safety in terms of the quality of food   84

The resource constraints that limit China's grain production 85
The supply and demand for grain and trend lines 88
Changes in global supply and demand for grain and its
impact on China 91
The situation with respect to food safety and establishing
a regulatory system that addresses the situation 95
Implementing the new national food security strategy 100

5 Changing the operating systems that apply to Chinese agriculture and speeding up agricultural modernization   113

Overall framework of the "new-style agricultural
operating system" 113
The necessity and the urgency of setting up a
new-style agricultural operating system 116
The current status of new-style agricultural operating
systems and problems 119
The overall rationale for developing a new-style
agricultural operating system and basic requirements 129

*Key tasks and policy measures in developing the new-style
  agricultural operating system 133*

**6 Increasing the income of farmers and ensuring
    fair distribution of income**   143

*The current situation of farmers' income with respect to the
  objective of setting up a moderately prosperous
  society in an all-round way 144*
*On promoting a further shift of the rural population
  toward cities and speeding up the growth of wage-type
  income among farmers 148*
*Improving agricultural productivity and laying a firm foundation
  for increases in operating income from agriculture 149*
*Increasing the strength of preferential policies for farmers
  and increasing transfer-type income for farmers 152*
*Increasing the forcefulness of poverty-alleviation policies
  and eliminating absolute poverty 157*

**7 Improving China's social security system and
    its systems for providing public services**   164

*Optimize the allocation of educational resources, and
  improve the quality of education in rural areas 165*
*Improve the rural old-age security system, and speed up
  the building of systems that provide services to the elderly
  in rural areas 170*
*Improve the rural healthcare system, and raise levels of
  health among rural residents 175*
*Improve the housing conditions of rural residents and
  ensure that vulnerable populations have a place to live 186*
*Push forward the building of public service facilities in rural
  areas, and improve the living conditions of people
  in rural areas 191*

**8 Promoting innovative ways to involve rural
    communities in self-governance**   198

The current pattern of governance in rural communities 199
*Rural communities and their changing dynamics in the
  current era 217*
Problems in rural governance at the present time 221
*Policy recommendations for creative ways to enable
  governance by rural communities 227*

9 **Strengthening controls over resources and environmental protection, building an "ecological civilization" in the countryside**   235

Main problems facing the building of an "ecological civilization" in the countryside 235
The serious impacts of environmental degradation in rural areas 243
Countermeasures aimed at strengthening management controls over agricultural resources and at rural governance as it relates to the environment 248

10 **Clarifying the responsibilities and accountabilities of governments and increasing support from public finance**   269

The evolution of the relationship between the State and farmers since the founding of the PRC 270
Overall situation with regard to public-finance spending at the current time 284
Main problems with public spending at the present time 291
Policy recommendations with respect to increasing public-finance spending 300

11 **Accelerate reform of the household registration system and promoting the unification of urban and rural development**   307

Accelerate reform of the system that manages household registrations 309
Push forward the process of providing basic public services to all long-term residents of cities 317
Push forward mechanisms that enable the transitioning agricultural population to become "urbanized" 331

Concluding remarks   336
Background reports that were incorporated in this volume   338
References   339
Index   349

Figures

2.1   Changes in China's rural population by province,
      from 2000 to 2010   25
2.2   Changes in the age structure of China's rural population,
      from 2000 to 2010   28
2.3   Comparison of the age structures of the agricultural labor force
      and rural migrant workers   34
2.4   Urban employment and structure between 2001 and 2011, as
      shown by urban residents (light gray) and rural migrant workers
      who have come into the city (dark gray)   35
2.5   Historical comparisons on agricultural productivity   37
3.1   Framework of China's land management system   46
4.1   Comparison of the amount of water used by different sectors
      of China's economy – household use, industrial use, and
      agricultural use – in 1949, 1978, and 2011   86
4.2   Change of monthly income of migrant workers from 2008 to 2013   88
4.3   Total grain production in five countries and their production
      relative to total global grain production   92
4.4   National food safety information platform   109
5.1   Overall structure of the new-style agricultural operating system   115
6.1   Growth of per capita net income of farmers (1978–2013)   144
6.2   Urban and rural income growth   145
6.3   Change of urban/rural income ratio   145
6.4   Income ratio between top and bottom 20 percent households
      in income ladder in rural areas   146
6.5   Comparison of farmers' income growth at two stages in
      the 21st century (annual average growth)   150
6.6   Correlation between price change of farm produce and
      agricultural business income growth of farmers   151
6.7   Ratio of rural nonagricultural employees and nonagricultural
      income   152
6.8   Rural subsistence security standards in different counties/regions
      in 2013   155

6.9	Rate in minimum living allowances for residents of both urban and rural areas in all provinces in the country in the year 2013	156
6.10	Downward trend of rural poverty-stricken population and poverty incidence in China	158
7.1	Gross enrollment rate of senior high schools (2005–2013)	168
7.2	Number of students attending secondary vocational schools and regular high schools (1990–2013)	168
7.3	Maternal mortality rate in China from 1991 to 2012 (1/100,000)	176
7.4	The mortality rate of children under 5 in China from 1991 to 2012	177
7.5	Infant mortality rate from 1991 to 2012	177
7.6	Prevalence rate of sanitary toilets	179
7.7	Change in housing area and quality for rural residents (2001–2012)	187
7.8	The proportion of rural families living in houses built in or before the 1970s in 2010	188
8.1	Changes of the suicide rate in the countryside (1/100,000)	225
9.1	Agriculture-related water consumption in the 21st century	237
9.2	Chemical fertilizer application (net quantity) in the 21st century	239
9.3	Chemical pesticide application in the 21st century	239
9.4	Agricultural film application in the 21st century	240
9.5	Land desertification and sandy lands in China	243
9.6	Annual increment and total number of "cancer villages" in China	246
9.7	Distribution and density of "cancer villages" in China	246
10.1	Financial expenditure on agriculture and percentage, 2003–2012	284
10.2	Agricultural support and protection levels of major countries	293
11.1	Public opinions were solicited concerning the *Management Measures for Residence Permit (exposure draft)* to specify the rights and interests of permit holders	312
11.2	Pie chart showing how the floating population in Chuanfang Community accesses medical assistance	325
11.3	Central and local expenditure structure, 2012	332

Tables

2.1	Average length of time the rural labor force spends on agricultural work: data from 2003 to 2012 (unit: days)	32
2.2	Numbers and types of rural migrant workers	33
2.3	Per capita gross national income in select countries and the percentage of agricultural workers in their labor forces (2011)	39
3.1	Progress in the reform of the property-rights system governing China's rural collectives	76
4.1	Area and price of household contracted land in circulation	87
4.2	Impact of change of agricultural resource factors on yield of major farm produce from 2012 to 2020	89
4.3	Projections of supply and demand for grain in 2020 and actual figures for 2012	90
4.4	China's supply and demand for pork, beef, mutton, chicken, eggs, milk, and aquatic products in 2012 and a projection for 2020	91
4.5	Comparison of total global production of corn, rice, and wheat between 1990 and 2012 and percentages of the total held by each commodity	92
4.6	Global supply and demand for grain since 2000	93
4.7	National institutions responsible for food safety regulation in China and the responsibilities of each	98
4.8	Policy documents that have been issued in China since the start of the 21st century on food safety management	99
5.1	Size of arable land managed by farming households	116
5.2	Development overview of specialized farmer cooperatives from 2008 to 2013	122
5.3	Development overview of agricultural industrialized leading enterprises in recent years	123
5.4	Status of institutions promoting agricultural skills in China at all levels of government, on a nationwide basis, in 2012	125
6.1	Fiscal spending on certain policies intended to benefit farmers	153
6.2	Benefit for different income groups from the mutual-aid funds	163
7.1	Development of the New Rural Cooperative Medical Scheme (NCMS)	176

7.2	The mortality rate of rural residents and diseases as major causes of death in 2012	181
7.3	Funds invested by different departments in the new-countryside construction project of a village in western China	194
7.4	List of main public facilities in villages and townships of Hebei province ranked by the administrative level	194
8.1	Changes in the number and population of administrative villages	207
9.1	Damage to crops due to soil contamination by sewage irrigation, 2000–2005	244
9.2	The eight environmental management systems	251
9.3	Laws and regulations on agricultural resource management and environmental protection	253
9.4	Technological systems for agricultural resource management and rural ecological protection	258
10.1	Supply of public products and services in rural areas in the People's Commune period	272
10.2	Fund sources of public products and public services in rural areas	273
10.3	Incomes and expenditures of township governments	274
10.4	Incomes and expenditures of villages	274
10.5	Revenue and expenditure of central and local finance, 1993–1999	279
10.6	Financial revenue and fund-raising of townships in China, 1996–2000	279
10.7	Burdens on farmers, 1994–1999	280
10.8	Central financial expenditure on Sangong, 2007–2012	286
10.9	Percentages of agricultural added value in GDP in some countries	292
10.10	Financial input in urban and rural primary and middle schools	295
10.11	Medical technicians and hospital beds, urban vs. rural, 2012	295
10.12	Urban–rural gap in medical insurance, 2012	296
10.13	Urban–rural gap in subsistence allowance, 2012	296
10.14	Farmers' burdens in 2013	300
11.1	Landmarks of the reform of the household registration system	310
11.2	Preconditions for settlement in cities	315
11.3	Public school enrollment of migrant children since 2011	318
11.4	Housing of rural farmers in 2013	330

Boxes

2.1   How many more villages are going to disappear?   26

2.2   The caregiving dilemma in China's "oldest" county   28

3.1   Different approaches to using land for industrial, commercial, and residential purposes   49

3.2   Industrial and commercial capital being invested in rural areas   57

3.3   Developing a market in Shanghai for the transfer of contracted operating rights to land   59

3.4   The controversy over "housing that enjoys limited property rights"   62

3.5   The shift of rural homesteads and the policy of tying together land increases and decreases   65

3.6   Administrative measures of Guangdong province regarding the circulation of rights to collectively owned construction-use land   69

3.7   Different opinions about the quantification of collectively owned assets   76

3.8   Pingluo county in Ningxia launches a pilot program to define membership in collective economic organizations   78

3.9   Efforts to quantify assets and turn them into shareholdings in the Minhang district of Shanghai   80

4.1   A case of food poisoning and its causes: "lean meat powder"   96

4.2   Accomplishments in developing rice hybrids   105

4.3   The plan to improve the nutrition of rural children at the age of compulsory education   110

5.1   Experimenting with family farms in the Songjiang district of Shanghai   120

5.2   Land shareholding cooperatives in Sichuan's Zhanqi village, which is in Tangchang town, Pi county   122

5.3   The Wens model for industrializing agriculture: the Guangdong Wens Food Group Co., Ltd.   123

5.4   The Hunan Anbang New-agricultural Technology Co., Ltd.   125

5.5   The mutual aid cooperative of the Moslem population [hui-min] in Mayu town, Rui'an city, Zhejiang province   139

5.6   On micro-loans: the Ri Sheng Long Micro-Credit Companies, Ltd.   140

6.1	Targeting poverty with mutual-aid funds and the results of this kind of poverty alleviation	162
7.1	The poverty-alleviation effects of the government's policies in support of mid-level vocational education	169
7.2	The living conditions of elderly people in Laoying village, Hubei province	173
7.3	Nutrition packets: making a good start on lifelong health	185
7.4	The actions taken by Guizhou province in 2014 to improve living conditions in rural areas	189
8.1	Main efforts to find a way to resolve conflicts between the "two committees" governing towns and villages	209
8.2	The Wukan Incident	212
8.3	College students serve as town officials	216
8.4	The "participatory budgeting" in the township people's congresses of Wenling	230
9.1	The "nine dragons" situation with respect to handling environmental protection in China	249
9.2	The application of compensation requirements to the process of controlling water contamination	255
9.3	Projects to protect agricultural resources and achieve more efficient use of resources	264
9.4	Projects to remediate environmental problems in rural areas and to protect the environment	266
9.5	Projects to restore and protect rural ecosystems	267
10.1	Rural debt	276
10.2	Comprehensive rural reform	281
10.3	The "three subsidies" for agriculture goes to "four subsidies"	285
10.4	Basic infrastructure development in rural areas	287
10.5	Policy options for using public finance to fund comprehensive rural environmental remediation	288
11.1	Draft version asking for opinions on "Management Methods for Residence Certificates"	311
11.2	Shanghai's solution for the problem of education for children of rural migrant workers: public education that is driven by a "double-axle," namely public and private	320
11.3	Night school for rural migrant workers	322
11.4	The health of the floating population and its situation with respect to medical treatment	324
11.5	The systemic arrangements for enabling rural migrant workers to participate in social insurance	327

China Development Report 2013/14 project team

Advisor

Wang Mengkui, former director of Development Research Center of the State Council, chairman of China Development Research Foundation

Project Leader

Lu Mai, secretary general and researcher of China Development Research Foundation

Main Report Authors

Song Hongyuan, director and researcher of Rural Economy Research Center of Ministry of Agriculture
Li Shi, professor of Beijing Normal University Business School

Background Report Authors

Cai Fang, vice president, member and researcher of Chinese Academy of Social Sciences
Zhang Xiaoshan, member and research fellow of Chinese Academy of Social Sciences
Zhang Hongyu, head of Department of Rural Economic System and Management, Ministry of Agriculture
Lv Qingzhe, director of Social Science Statistics Office of Research Institute of Statistical Sciences, National Bureau of Statistics
Li Zhou, director and researcher of Rural Development Research Institute, Chinese Academy of Social Sciences
Liu Shouying, deputy director and researcher of Research Department of Rural Economy, Development Research Centre of the State Council
Wang Sangui, professor of School of Agricultural Economics and Rural Development, Renmin University of China
Zhou Feizhou, professor of Department of Sociology, Peking University
Li Yuanxing, professor of School of Social Development, Central University of Finance and Economics

Wang Xiaoyi, director and researcher of Institute of Sociology, Chinese Academy of Social Sciences

Yu Jianrong, researcher of Rural Development Research Institute, Chinese Academy of Social Sciences

Liu Yanwu, School of Sociology, Wuhan University

Jin Sanlin, researcher of Research Department of Rural Economy, Development Research Centre of the State Council

Zhang Hongkui, Rural Economy Research Center, Ministry of Agriculture

Zhao Hai, Rural Economy Research Center, Ministry of Agriculture

Jin Shuqin, Rural Economy Research Center, Ministry of Agriculture

Hang Jing, Rural Economy Research Center, Ministry of Agriculture

Li Jie, Rural Economy Research Center, Ministry of Agriculture

Feng Wenmeng, director of No. 2 Division and researcher of China Development Research Foundation

Yu Jiantuo, director of No. 2 Division of China Development Research Foundation

Feng Mingliang, Research Department of Rural Economy, Development Research Centre of the State Council

Project Coordinator

Feng Wenmeng, director of No. 2 Division and associate researcher of China Development Research Foundation

Foreword[1]

Building a moderately prosperous society in all respects is an essential stage in China's modernization drive. In 2002, the 16th National Party Congress of the Communist Party of China made a strategic policy decision to build a moderately prosperous society in all respects within the first two decades of the 21st century. This was then reconfirmed by the 18th National Party Congress in 2012. The entire country is currently engaged in the most critical part of this process. It is deepening reform on all fronts and making a concerted effort to push forward the endeavor by advancing the rule of law. Its efforts represent the primary theme of China's current stage of development.

The focus of the effort must be on China's rural areas, given the uneven development of urban and rural parts of the country and resulting social and economic disparities. The world has witnessed remarkable advances in China since the founding of the People's Republic of China, particularly since the reform and opening up process of the past thirty-some years. The rural aspect of the country has changed enormously – hundreds of millions of rural people now have adequate food and clothing, which represents an historic achievement. At the same time, however, it is hard not to recognize that China is still a developing country and still in the initial stages of socialism. Achieving overall modernization will take several more decades of hard work. This is true particularly in the countryside, where progress is clearly lagging behind urban areas and the goal of a moderately prosperous society for all is far from being realized. What's more, many new issues have emerged in recent years in the countryside, given the rapid pace of industrialization and urbanization and the dual issues of the massive migration of rural labor into cities and the aging of the overall population. New challenges include the fact that the amount of arable land in the country is declining, and the number of people actually farming is also declining. Rural towns are being "hollowed out," while ecosystems are being destroyed by environmental pollution. The call for a "moderately prosperous society in all respects" was first put forward over a dozen years ago, but since that time not only has China's economy grown, but its social structure has changed in epic ways. More than half of the population is no longer engaged in farming, and that percentage is rising. The economic contribution of China's rural areas to GDP has notably fallen and continues to fall. At the same time, however, China's real economic power as a country has grown enormously, giving it greater ability to support rural development initiatives. This situation has been the motivation behind the comprehensive research program described in this volume. The program has sought to address the question, "Given new conditions, how can we make sure that we arrive at our goal of a moderately prosperous society for all in the smoothest possible way?" This is a very large topic, requiring concerted attention and conscientious proposals. It forms the subject of this Report.

This is the fifth *China Development Report* to have been put forward by the China Development Research Foundation. Reports prior to this one addressed four different subjects: poverty alleviation, building a social welfare system, urbanization, and the adjustment of population policies. This Report continues to follow the established principles of all previous China Development Reports. It aims to be systematic and comprehensive in analyzing the subject from all perspectives. It looks at the overall situation and the specific tasks that confront rural areas as they establish a moderately prosperous society. Its guiding principle is to promote and push forward the integration of urban and rural areas. To do this, the Report discusses the overarching subject of rural development in terms of ten specific areas. These are: changes in the geographic distribution of the rural population and changes in how labor resources are allocated, reform of the land system, grain production in the country, China's operating system with respect to agriculture, how to increase farmers' incomes, issues of rural social security and public services, rural governance, environmental protection, support from public finance, and reform of the household registration system. These subjects basically cover the full range of issues having to do with the reform of China's rural development at the current stage. The Report analyzes both the current situation as well as past conditions in these categories. It discusses policies now under way, while also recommending reform measures and policy proposals for the future. I personally feel that this Report is highly conscientious in terms of the meticulous research that has gone into it and that its recommendations are constructive.

I hope that the public dissemination of this Report will play a positive role in furthering the creation of an "all-round" moderately prosperous society in rural areas. I hope it will be helpful to readers both inside and outside China as they seek to understand the intent of China's policies with regard to rural development and the processes by which these policies are being carried out.

Wang Mengkui
Chairman, China Development Research Foundation
Former Director, Development Research
Center of the State Council

Note

1 See also Wang Mengkui, *China's Economic Trends as Viewed by Wang Mengkui*. Beijing: CPC Central Party School Press, 2008.

Acknowledgements

After two years of hard work, this Report is finally being released to the public. It concerns a topic of vital importance to China's economic and social development at this stage in the country's history and one that will continue to be important for some time to come. In 2012, the 18th National Party Congress highlighted the strategic goal of creating a moderately prosperous society throughout China by the year 2020. This then pointed the way for policies regarding rural economic and social development. Over the past two years, we have been pleased to see real progress in both regards, with the mobilization of land-system reform and reform of the household registration system. These give us a measure of confidence in the process of achieving all-round moderate prosperity in rural areas. Nevertheless, we are highly cognizant of the fact that it is going to be a monumental task to achieve our rural objectives within the remaining six years. These objectives relate to specific measures of progress in the economic, political, cultural, social, and ecological spheres. Given the size of China and the extent of the gap between urban and rural, achieving all-round moderate prosperity within the time allotted is going to require a concerted focus on priorities, a deepening of reforms, and increased investment of public resources.

China's rural areas have achieved considerable success in economic development over the past thirty-some years, as the country implemented a whole series of reform measures. Policies included such things as "unleashing" the energies of the rural economy in the 1980s, "stabilizing" the economy in the 1990s, and "supporting" rural areas after 2000, that is, paying back the countryside for its earlier contributions. These policies injected considerable energy into both agriculture and rural economies in general. They ensured that the most populous nation on earth could achieve a basically adequate grain supply and absolute food security overall. Meanwhile, the per capita net income of rural residents went from RMB 133.6 in 1978 to RMB 8895.9 in 2013. All of China's several kinds of social security systems began to be implemented in the countryside, while a rural population that numbers in the hundreds of millions emerged from poverty. These things represented monumental changes in the country.

Even as we have achieved certain goals, however, many aspects of China's rural areas have remained limiting factors, the so-called short staves in the bucket that allow it to be filled up only so far. These limiting factors include agricultural output, rural incomes, social security, public services, and social governance. As compared with urban parts of the country, these things have ensured that the situation of a "backward countryside" has not fundamentally changed. Certain things are, however, changing rapidly. "Urbanized" people now account for over one-half of China's population, and the urban component of the population continues to grow. China continues to stride into the ranks of mid- to upper-income countries, even as the aging of the rural population intensifies. The internal as well as external conditions for rural development have undergone fundamental change, given that rural development is now being approached in terms of coordinated urban–rural development. In this new period, the question of how to construct an overall policy framework that can deal with existing problems in rural development, as well as new challenges, has emerged as highly significant in a very real sense.

It is against this backdrop that the China Development Research Foundation [CDRF] launched a comprehensive research project in early 2013, which has now come to fruition with this Report. Completion of the Report was made possible by the hard work of the entire project team, as well as the generous support of a number of experts and scholars. Wang Mengkui, former director of the Development Research Center of the State Council and current chairman of the CDRF provided valuable advice on the overall framework and structure of the Report, as well as important guidance on the contents of each chapter. He carefully reviewed and edited the Report four times, in addition to writing the Foreword, which set the tone for the rest of the volume.

Song Hongyuan, director of the Rural Economy Research Center in the Ministry of Agriculture, and Li Shi, professor of Beijing Normal University, contributed enormously to the Report with their wealth of experience in theory as well as years of implementing policy. Their strong grasp of practical issues, meticulous approach to scholarship, and hard work provided the Report with a strong foundation.

Research on rural affairs is an interdisciplinary field. This Report is therefore the outcome of cooperation among many people in different areas. In order to ensure that it maintained a broad perspective and was also based on solid analysis, the CDRF convened forums for experts in specific fields, as well as a number of meetings to discuss the overall main Report. It asked researchers in both academic and government research institutions, as well as policy implementers in relevant government departments, to write twenty-one background reports on specific subjects. Many of the recommendations and material coming out of these forums and background reports have been incorporated in the main Report. The background reports and their authors are as follows: [Zhang Xiaoshan], *Reflections on Rural Economic and Social Policies over the Past Decade* [Zhang Hongyu], *An Evaluation of Progress in Reaching Moderate Prosperity in Rural Areas, and a System for Quantifying Progress in Terms of Standards and Indicators* [Lv Qingzhe], *A Study of Issues Relating to Development of the Agricultural Industry* [Li Zhou], *Research on Rural Labor-Force Issues* [Cai Fang, Wang Meiyan], *On the Connection between the Rural Land System and Building a Moderately Prosperous Society* [Liu Shouying, Shao Ting], *On Balancing China's Supply And Demand for Grain, and Issues to Do with Food Safety* [Jin Sanlin], *Rural Poverty-Alleviation Policies and Increases in Farmers' Income* [Wang Sangui, Zhang Weibin], *Report on Public Finance and Developing Public Services in Rural China* [Zhou Feizhou, et al.], *Research on Social Issues in Rural China* [Li Yuanxing], *Environmental Issues in the Course of Economic Development in Rural Areas* [Wang Xiaoyi], *Administering Rural Areas in China at the Present Time: Difficulties and Breakthroughs* [Yu Jianrong], *Research on Suicide in Rural Areas* [Liu Yanwu], *Strengthening Basic Infrastructure in Rural Areas* [Wu Zhigan, Li Jie], *Promoting Coordinated Development of Urban and Rural Areas* [Zhang Hongkui, Gao Ming], *Innovations to Do with the operating systems governing agriculture in China* [Zhao Hai, Ma Kai], *Building an "Ecological Civilization" in the Countryside* [Jin Shuqin, Zhang Canqiang], *Clarifying the Duties and the Role of Governments [at Different Levels] in China* [Hang Jing, Gao Qiang], *Forecasting Demographic Changes in China by the Year 2020* [Feng Wenmeng], *Principles behind the Indicator System That Quantifies "Moderate Prosperity," and Understanding Those Indicators* [Yu Jiantuo], and *Rural Governance: Issues and Countermeasures* [Feng Mingliang].

All of the authors of these background reports also participated in discussions at each stage of preparing this Report and made valuable suggestions. It was my honor to be able to work with such an outstanding group of people. I express my heartfelt gratitude to each and every one of the team.

In addition to organizing the reports, the project team carried out field surveys in various parts of the country in order to have an accurate understanding of the current situation as well as ongoing changes in rural areas. Among other places, we visited Nanxiang and Xiangtan counties in Hunan, Ningjin county in Hebei, and Xundian county in Yunnan. Local government departments were enormously helpful as we carried out research in each location.

The CDRF put tremendous amounts of effort into completing this Report, particularly in terms of human resources. A number of people were outstanding in organizing the actual work of the project. They included Feng Wenmeng, Yu Jiantuo, Feng Mingliang, Du Jing, Chen Cheng, Li Fan, Chen Hao, Liu Yang, Du Zhixin, Zhang Jing, Zhao Chen, and Liang Bojiao. These people also undertook to collect materials, do supplementary research, and carry the project through all of the revisions and refinements that came in the latter period. Specifically, Chapter I was revised by Yu Jiantuo, Chapter 2 by Feng Wenmeng, Chapter 3 by Liu Yang and Feng Wenmeng, Chapter 4 by Chen Cheng, Chapter 5 by Chen Cheng and Yu Jiantuo, Chapter 6 by Yu Jiantuo, Chapter 7 by Li Fan, Chapter 8 by Feng Mingliang, Chapter 9 by Chen Hao, Chapter 10 by Du Jing, Chapter 11 by Du Zhixin, and the Concluding Remarks by Feng Wenmeng.

In 2008, the CDRF established a China Policy Research Fund to help support the work of putting out an annual *China Development Report*, as well as to help in carrying out other research projects. In this regard, we wish to extend our great appreciation to the Starr Foundation of the United States for its generous financial support to the China Policy Research Fund. Hony Capital [a Chinese private equity firm] and GIZ of Germany provided generous support for this specific Report.

As this Report goes to press, on behalf of the CDRF, I extend heartfelt gratitude to the project team, all entities involved, and all individuals who participated.

I thank them for their good work and for bringing this project to a smooth and successful conclusion.

Lu Mai
Secretary General
China Development Research Foundation

Introduction

China is currently in the midst of creating a moderately prosperous society "in an all-round way." The goal is to establish such a society by the year 2020, and the process represents an essential step in China's overall drive to modernize the country.

Social and economic development in China is highly uneven, however. An inclusive approach to moderate prosperity must therefore focus on the most difficult areas, which means China's rural areas. This Report is therefore aimed at the situation in rural areas and the tasks that the country faces in building a moderately prosperous society in rural areas.

The terms "moderate prosperity" [*xiao kang*] and "a moderately prosperous society" have been used for quite a long time in China and are now fairly well understood by the Chinese public at large. Due to greater interaction between China and the rest of the world, along with the broadening influence of China in the world, this quintessentially Chinese concept is now gradually coming to be understood by the international community as well.

Historically, the term *xiao kang* was first cited in a passage in the *Book of Songs* [the *Shi Jing*], compiled between the 11th and 6th centuries BCE. The term literally means "small well-being." The author of the passage laments the tribulations that people have endured and hopes for a small respite, a small well-being. As a generalized condition of society, the term is later found in the work called the *Book of Rites* [the *Li Ji*], in a section called *Conveyance of Rites* [*Li Yun*]. This Confucian work dating to the 1st century BCE is the first to apply the idea of *xiao kang* to society at large as a condition that does not yet regain the idealized utopia found in the distant past, known as the Great Harmony, or *da tong*; instead, it is a condition that is achievable in the current realities of the world. That is, property is not owned communally in a "great oneness under heaven," private ownership still exists, but politics are relatively stable given that there are "walls and moats for security and rites to maintain order." The author's description of the unreachable ideal of a great harmony [*da tong*] and hopes for the reality of a moderate prosperity [*xiao kang*] have had an enduring influence on Chinese people down through the ages.

With the passage of time, the concepts embodied in moderate prosperity [*xiao kang*] evolved. The term came to mean that people in general had adequate food and clothing and lived fairly peaceful lives. As China's long history has shown, philosophers and politicians have often plucked what was useful from China's rich trove of cultural legacy to suit the demands of their current situation. They have drawn nourishment from China's classics, even as they altered and enriched them. Kang Youwei, Sun Yatsen, and Mao Zedong all turned the thinking behind *da tong* into pursuit of an ideal society in the future. In contrast, Deng Xiaoping borrowed from the essence of traditional Chinese philosophy and placed a completely new significance on the idea of *xiao kang*, using language that is familiar to all Chinese. He described *xiao kang* as a necessary stage through which China must pass *at the present time* as it casts off poverty and moves toward modernization.

Deng Xiaoping's formulation of "moderate prosperity" and "a moderately prosperous society" was linked to the adjustments in the country's economic development strategy after the start of reform and opening up. As all know, in 1964, the Third National People's Congress brought forth the strategic policy goal called the Four Modernizations. This aimed to realize the modernization of industry, agriculture, science and technology, and national defense by the end of the 20th century. This goal was reiterated at the Fourth National People's Congress in 1975. It expressed the powerful desire of the Chinese people to modernize, and at the time it did indeed serve a positive role in mobilizing people's will to move forward. Actually realizing "modernization" in a short period of time proved impossible, however, in a country as large, economically backward, and populous as China. China's economy developed abnormally fast in the last two decades of the 20th century, but the country to this day cannot be considered modernized. At the conclusion of the Great Cultural Revolution, it became necessary to make major strategic adjustments to economic develop-ment policies if the country was going to continue to push forward its aim of modernizing. Deng Xiaoping was acutely aware of this and highly prescient in foreseeing what was to come.

In December 1979, during a meeting with the Prime Minister of Japan Ohira Masayoshi, Deng Xiaoping expressly noted that China's goal for the end of the 20th century was to realize *xiao kang*, moderate prosperity. He said:

> The kind of Four Modernizations that we aim to realize is a "China-style" of modernization. The concept is different from yours in that it aims for a *xiao kang* kind of living, with *xiao kang* families. Even if we reach this goal by the end of the century, we may still have a low per capita GDP. We will only get to the level of the more prosperous third-world countries through extreme effort, those with a per capita GDP of USD 1,000 for example. And if we do get there, we will still look underdeveloped compared to western countries. All I can say is that, by that time, China will still only be in a condition of what I call "moderately prosperous according to Chinese standards." (Deng Xiaoping, 2001).

Over the next few years, Deng Xiaoping returned to this issue many times, not always in the same words but with basically the same intent. The *xiao kang* that he referred to was different from that of the classics but also different from the vague yearning of people for a better life. Instead, it indicated a precisely defined stage of development in China's process of modernization. He thereby changed China's strategic development goals for the end of the 20th century from "realizing modernization" to "realizing *xiao kang*." This might appear to be "retrogression," but in fact it was a more accurate description of China's actual situation and more in line with a correct positioning of China's strategic development goals. Going from subsistence to modernization in a country as economically underdeveloped as China was going to take a long time. During this time, there were going to be wide disparities in people's standard of living and in social and economic development. During the transition period, achieving *xiao kang* was much more in accord with the standard rules of economic development. It also allowed for the creation of practical and feasible steps along the way to the grand goal of achieving modernization. This allowed for the formulation of more accurate policy guidelines for social and economic development.

In 1987, during the 13th National Party Congress, the Party formulated a three-step development strategy that conformed to Deng Xiaoping's ideas. The first step was to double gross national product over the amount produced in 1980 and to ensure that people were provided with the basic needs of life. The second step was to achieve a second doubling of GNP by the end of the 20th century and to enable people to enjoy a *xiao kang* standard of living, or moderate prosperity. The third step was to reach a GNP per capita that matched developed countries by the middle of the 21st century and to achieve a fairly prosperous standard of living among people together with a basic degree of modernization. This kind of development strategy, which divided the process into discrete steps and specific stages, was correct. It is one of the reasons China was able to achieve such fast growth over the past thirty-some years.

In the twenty-plus years since the Third Plenary Session of the 11th CPC Central Committee, reform and opening up have led to epic changes in China's social and economic landscape. By the end of the 20th century, the first two of these two steps had basically been achieved. At the start of the 21st century, the plans to implement the third strategic step are facing the following two considerations.

On the one hand, China's economic power has markedly increased. By 2000, it had reached a GDP that was six times what it had been in 1980.[1] This exceeded the "doubling twice" expectation and fundamentally changed the long-term problem of material shortages that had stymied economic development and improvement in standards of living. The process of industrialization was accelerating, economic structural issues were being addressed, and the percentage of the population engaged in farming had gone from 70 percent down to 30 percent. Reform of the economic structure had achieved breakthrough progress such that the country had taken the first steps in going from a planned economy to a socialist market economy. People's lives had already gone through two historic "leapfrogging" changes, one in the 1980s, as basic necessities were now being met, and another in the late 1990s, as the population overall achieved a stage of moderate prosperity. Despite the fact that the population had grown by 300 million since the year 1980, the goal of a per capita GDP of USD 850 was achieved as expected by the year 2000. According to standards as defined at the time, more than 85 percent of impoverished people had been lifted out of poverty, which meant that only 3 percent of the rural population as opposed to the previous 30 percent remained in poverty. A comprehensive assessment was done in 2000 by a project team composed of researchers from twelve State agencies including the National Bureau of Statistics, as well as ministries and commissions in state planning, finance, health, and education. They looked at sixteen basic indicators and critical values in terms of five aspects: level of economic development, material goods, population "caliber" or level of education, spiritual [cultural] stimulation, and environment and public health. They found that, on an overall basis, the country had indeed become a moderately prosperous society at the end of the 20th century, with approximately 75 percent of the population leading a moderately good life (Xie Mingguang and Wen Jianwu, 2000). Finally, problems of adequate food and clothing that had plagued the Chinese people for thousands of years had basically been resolved. The dream of generations of people had become a reality. This marked a milestone in the history of China, as well as the starting point in building real "modernization."

On the other hand, China's development was and remains very uneven. Both statistical data and the quite apparent facts of life show that the kind of *xiao kang* prosperity achieved to date in China is at a low level, not inclusive, and highly unbalanced. The reasons are as follows.

First, going from subsistence to modernization is a process that requires many decades, and "moderate prosperity" itself requires a process of going from lower to higher levels. The end of the 20th century marked only the initial step in crossing over the threshold into moderate prosperity. In all respects, the moderate prosperity that has been accomplished to date is still at the lowest levels of quantifiable standards.

Second, even this kind of low-level moderate prosperity has not reached all people in the country. The research of the team mentioned above also noted that, while 75 percent of the population has reached a moderately prosperous life to an initial degree, 25 percent has not. Of this 25 percent, 13 percent are approaching moderate prosperity, while 12 percent are still very far from it. In 2000, more than 30 million people in China's rural areas did not have adequate food and clothing, that is, had not reached the most basic level of subsistence. Another 60 million people were no longer impoverished but were susceptible to falling back into poverty. Meanwhile, in urban areas, more than 20 million people were living below the minimum living standard.

Third, there remain large disparities in income and living standards between developed and underdeveloped regions, urban and rural areas, and different classes in society. Economic aggregates and per capita figures often conceal these differences. The state of affairs is actually quite uneven in many aspects of building a moderately prosperous society. This can be said both in terms of already achieved standards as well as the extent of progress in various spheres.

Such low standards, noninclusive aspects, and uneven progress indicate that China is still at the initial stages of moderate prosperity. It is obvious that a fairly long period of time will be required to reach a moderately prosperous society.

Based on an accurate assessment of China's social and economic conditions, therefore, the Party set forth a strategic policy decision at the 16th National Party Congress in 2002. This aims to gather forces in the first two decades of the 21st century to ensure that a higher level of moderate prosperity actually reaches over 1 billion people in an all-round or inclusive way. Only one concrete figure was presented by the 16th National Party Congress, namely that GDP should quadruple by 2020 over the year 2000. At the same time, the Congress explicitly presented a policy orientation and necessary principles to follow in achieving "a more developed economy, sounder and more complete democracy, more advanced science and technology, more culture, greater social harmony, and better-off lives in general." This goal is in accord with accelerating the drive to modernize the country. The time span between realizing moderate prosperity to an initial degree and achieving basic modernization is expected to run into decades. Establishing the goal of achieving a moderately prosperous society in an all-round way provided an organic link between China's second and third strategic steps in modernization. It provided the start of thinking strategically about how to achieve the third step in a very concrete way and provided tremendous room to develop that process. It has enriched and further developed the three-step conceptualization of a modernization strategy.

China has made relatively smooth progress in both economic and social terms in the early part of the 21st century. In 2007, the 17th National Party Congress announced with considerable confidence that it was reconfirming the goal of achieving moderate prosperity in an all-round way by the year 2020. The aggregate figure for economic growth was indeed expected to quadruple by that year, and the goal was now to quadruple *per capita* income by 2020. The Party's basic policy line, which consists of basic goals and basic measures, was now enriched to include a higher degree of "building up" economic, political, cultural, and social measures of progress.

In 2012, the 18th National Party Congress reinstated the grand goal of building a moderately prosperous society in an all-round way by the year 2020. In addition, however, it also included a focus on improving "ecological awareness" in the basic policy line. The anticipated value for economic growth sees both aggregate GDP and per capita incomes in rural as well as urban areas doubling by 2020 over the year 2010. This indicates two things. First, since economic growth between 2001 and 2010 exceeded the expectation of doubling, the new targets call for a larger aggregate economy. Second, since the target was changed from growth in per capita GDP to growth in per capita income of rural and urban residents, there was new focus on the incomes of rural people. Explicit requirements for rural incomes were built into the plan. The 18th National Party Congress also set forth an explicit policy guideline that called for pushing forward a unified approach to urban and rural development. It called for accelerating the structural incentives for achieving this. Moreover, it presented a set of policies and principles to ensure that the process moved forward. As a result, the vast reaches of China's rural areas are currently engaged in following these guidelines and pushing forward the process of establishing a moderately prosperous society in an all-round way.

This introduction has described the origins of the concept of a "moderately prosperous society." It has placed the intent to establish such a society in the context of China's history and its process of modernization. This is the background for what follows in this Report.

Note

1   China used gross output value of industry and agriculture to measure its economic aggregate for a long time. The country started to use GNP after reform and opening up and replaced GNP with GDP from the 15th National Party Congress in 1997 or slightly earlier. At the time, there was little difference in the amount of GNP versus GDP.

1 The epic task of "building a moderately prosperous society in an all-round way" in rural parts of China

- The atypical dichotomy between urban and rural areas and how this pattern developed in China
- Rural development strategy in China from a historical perspective
- Key tasks and challenges as we seek to establish all-round moderate prosperity in rural areas
- The basic pathway toward building an all-round moderately prosperous society in rural areas

"Building a moderately prosperous society in an all-round way in China's rural areas" is a task of epic proportions and historic significance. It is also the most challenging link in China's overall strategy. Remarkable progress has been made in rural development and in rural people's living standards since the start of reform and opening up, but despite such progress there is still a long way to go in achieving the requirements of "moderate prosperity." China's rural situation contains many obvious "short staves in the bucket" (limiting factors) when it comes to eradicating poverty, improving health, education, and culture, ensuring security, providing for social governance, and protecting resources and the environment. Some 60 percent of China's total population is expected to be urbanized by the year 2020, but that still leaves 40 percent, roughly 500 million people, who live in rural areas. Without including them in moderate prosperity, China will not achieve its goal of nationwide moderate prosperity in an inclusive sense. That is true whether the results are measured in terms of the total number of rural people, or their percentage of the population, or in terms of the interdependency of China's urban and rural areas.

Reaching the grand goal of a moderately prosperous society in an all-round way by the year 2020 will require evaluating the situation in terms of an overarching framework that incorporates a unified approach to urban and rural development. It will require going further in defining strategic priorities for rural reform and development. It will require mobilizing the resources and personnel to accomplish those priorities, as well as refining and being more creative in coming up with policies and measures that promote rural development. In December of 2013, President Xi Jinping spoke to the Central Rural Work Conference and emphasized a more proactive and long-term approach to the issues at hand. He said that if China is to be strong, its agriculture needs to be strong. If it is to be beautiful, its countryside must be beautiful, and if it is to be prosperous, its rural residents must be prosperous.

Any progress in achieving moderate prosperity in the countryside needs to be evaluated and understood from two different perspectives, which could be defined as horizontal and vertical. The horizontal perspective examines the relationship between China's urban and rural areas and takes into account the realities of how their differences came about. The vertical perspective examines rural development strategies and their evolution since the founding of the People's Republic of China but particularly since the start of reform and opening up. This chapter serves as a prologue to the analysis and discussions in subsequent chapters by reviewing the relationship between urban and rural development in China and the evolution of changing strategies. On the basis of that review, it points out the tasks and the challenges facing rural areas as the country seeks to accomplish this historic goal.

1.   The atypical dichotomy between urban and rural areas and how this pattern developed in China

One of the fundamental topics in development economics concerns the issue of how a country can transition from a dual economic structure to a unified economic structure. According to the classical theory of development economics, countries at a stage of economic takeoff suffer from a severe surplus of agricultural labor, from a dual economic structure as defined in terms of urban and rural, and from radically unequal incomes and levels of economic and social development in urban and rural areas. As the economy develops, particularly through a process of modern industrialization and urbanization, the rural labor force shifts toward the industrial sector as the rural population migrates into cities. The result is a constant decrease in the rural population and a decrease in the amount of surplus agricultural labor. At the same time, the disparity in productivity between agricultural and industrial sectors declines, as well as the disparity in wages and incomes between urban and rural inhabitants. As the process continues and the economy develops, the surplus of agricultural labor disappears, together with the development gap between urban and rural. A more unified economic structure begins to develop. This process has been described most particularly by the Lewis dual-economy model, which posits a disappearance of surplus agricultural labor at a point that has come to be called a Lewisian turning point. The classical theory of development economics has focused primarily on economic issues prior to the Lewisian turning point, however. Economic development after that point has received less attention. The reason is that classical theory makes the assumption that an economy will embark on sound growth once the dual-economic pattern has become unified. The disparity between cities and countryside will disappear, markets will allocate resources effectively between urban and rural areas and between agricultural and industrial sectors, production factors will flow freely between urban and rural areas, and urban and rural economies and social structures will mutually interact in ways that promote common development.

The actual situation in China is, however, quite different from these assumptions. First, prior to the Lewisian turning point, China's disparity between urban and rural areas has been monumental and has far surpassed that of most other developing countries on earth.[1] The reason is that China adhered to policies and a governing system that intentionally blocked off the countryside from cities. The household registration system was the primary means by which the rural population and any mobility of the labor force was controlled. There were, therefore, no market mechanisms that could enable resource allocation between urban and rural areas. At the same time, the government's development strategies focused on industry, while slighting agriculture. They placed the priority on urban development and not on rural development. Moreover, even after China reached a Lewisian turning point, the gap between social and economic development in urban and rural areas and between urban and rural incomes remained high. Finally, institutional obstacles to any unification of urban and rural development in China remain firmly in place. Such things as employment opportunities, wages and salaries, social security provisions, public services, and so on remain highly unequal. Rural residents are in an unfavorable position when it comes to development opportunities. Given this situation, it is hard for the kind of sound economic development and unified urban–rural structure that classical development theory posits to make its appearance. If the government does not modify its traditional development strategy, if it continues to place its priorities on cities and industry while slighting agriculture and rural areas, the "divided up" urban–rural dichotomy in China will simply continue.

International experience has shown that, as a country passes through a Lewisian turning point, it also transitions from being a low-income to a middle-income country. It then embarks on the path to becoming a high-income country. International experience also indicates, however, that few countries can smoothly transition to becoming high-income countries, since most fall into what is known as the middle-income trap. Research indicates that many factors may lead a country into this trap, but one factor that all countries in the trap have in common is a wide disparity in incomes (Rozelle, 2012). Over the past thirty years, China's income disparity has notably increased (Li Shi et al., 2013; Li and Sicular, 2014). A major structural factor leading to increased income disparities overall relates to excessive income disparities between urban and rural areas (Li Shi and Luo Chuliang, 2007; Sicular et al., 2007). It will take years before China becomes a high-income country. Among the challenges facing the country in the interim, one of the most important is achieving social fairness while sustaining economic development. Meanwhile, one of the least fair aspects of China's situation, specifically, is the inequality in development opportunities between urban and rural areas. Realizing moderate prosperity in an all-round way in rural areas is therefore a prerequisite for realizing China's social fairness objectives. It also is the necessary policy option if China is to avoid falling into the middle-income trap.

In terms of national considerations, food security is also at stake in this equation. If there is a massive disparity between urban and rural areas and agricultural productivity does not increase once a country reaches a Lewisian turning point, the ongoing shift of agricultural labor to nonagricultural industries will negatively impact agricultural production. This will affect food security. China is just on the verge of entering a post-Lewisian turning point era. China's agriculture will soon be facing not just a shortage of agricultural labor but the severe challenge of radically inadequate labor. It has therefore become imperative to pick up the pace of modernizing agriculture, reforming the "land system," and improving agricultural productivity as a part of creating a moderately prosperous society in rural areas.

2. Rural development strategy in China from a historical perspective

Starting in 1958, the household registration system, among a number of other institutional arrangements, intensified the separation of urban and rural areas in China. In addition, there are tremendous differences between the countryside and cities that fall outside just the dual-economic system and that exacerbate and solidify the formation of a dichotomy in the country. These relate to property rights, the supply of public services, the tax revenue system, and forms of governance.

This situation has been changing since the start of reform and opening up. As the dual economic structure has changed, systems that relate to other aspects of the urban-rural dichotomy have also evolved. These changes can be roughly divided into the following four periods.

1978–1992: Invigorating the rural economy

The countryside is the area that led the way in breaking through the constraints of the planned-economy system in China. This was achieved through what was known as the rural household contract responsibility system. Ownership or property rights to land continued to be held by the collective, but collective economic entities allocated operating rights over that land to individual households. They were allowed to farm these independently. The unified national system by which agricultural goods were purchased also underwent reform as controls were lifted and markets for such goods began to open up. Meanwhile, town-and-village enterprises were also allowed to operate as a supplement to State-Owned Enterprises and became an important component of the national economy as their "status" was confirmed. This propelled the strong growth of such enterprises to the extent that they were generating one-fifth of industrial production in China by 1988, despite the lack of any funding from the State budget or loans from State-owned banks. In addition, restrictions on human movements were relaxed, which spurred greater mobility of the rural population and led to greater concentrations in towns and cities. It can be said that rural areas in China made a major contribution to the country's overall reform by generating a dynamic market-economy force that drove economic growth. "Incremental reform" enabled the growth of a market economy that sprouted outside the bounds of the existing economy. Green light policies allowed the countryside to lead the way in economic growth with a minimum of inputs from public finance. This then became the major feature of government policy in terms of adjusting urban–rural relations during this period in China.

1993–2002: Efforts to stabilize the relationship between urban and rural areas

The reform orientation of China's policies was confirmed in 1993, via a Decision adopted by the Third Plenary Session of the 14th CPC Central Committee. This was called the "*Decision on Various Issues Relating to Establishing a Socialist Market Economy as Determined by the Central Committee of the Communist Party of China.* This marked the policy determination to set up a socialist market-economy structure in the country. During this period, a number of initiatives were beneficial to pushing forward rural economic development and improving rural incomes, including such things as eliminating the requirement to sell a set amount of grain to the government at the minimum price, allowing greater mobility of rural people, and encouraging the growth of town-and-village enterprises. At the same time, however, the State became unable to provide more financial support to rural areas due to several factors. These included the way reform in urban areas entered an important phase of fiscal and tax reform, exchange-rate reform, and State-Owned Enterprise reform. They included the need to hold down inflation within the country and the need to deal with the Asian financial crisis outside the country. As a result, not only were rural reforms left in abeyance, but preferential tax treatment of town-and-village enterprises was eliminated, mobility of rural migrant workers was subjected to demands for greater "order," and various restrictions were reimposed. One of the most critical issues became the extremely tense relationship between local cadres and the masses of rural people. The fixed quotas for grain requisition had been eliminated, but rural residents were now required to hand over an agricultural tax and "two levels" of fees as charged by township- and village-level governments as a way to fund all public goods at the rural level. Such goods included education, as well as grassroots-level governance by local officials.[2] In addition to onerous fees and taxes, rural residents were now subjected to more stringent enforcement of family planning policies. During this period, the central government felt called upon to issue documents to "lessen the load on farmers" nearly every year, which had essentially no effect.

2003–2012: Urban areas start "paying back" to the countryside

China's economy grew rapidly as the country entered the World Trade Organization and as urban reforms were rolled out successfully. This gave the government significantly more leeway to support rural areas. At the same time, the stymied development of the countryside and the growing gap between urban and rural served as a brake on urban development, as well as on the country overall. Based on these changes, the government carried out substantive modifications to its "three agricultures" policies [farmers, farming, and the rural economy]. With respect to rural migrant workers, it shifted from an emphasis on "orderly migration" to "protecting migrant workers." With respect to agriculture, it first carried out regional pilot projects and then ultimately, in 2005, completely eliminated the agricultural tax and the various fees that had been added onto that tax. Instead, agricultural production began to receive direct subsidies from the government. In education, the various fees that had been charged for the nine-year compulsory education program and for textbooks were exempted, and subsidies were extended to students in need (known as the "two exemptions and one subsidy policy"). A cooperative medical system and a subsistence allowance system were set up, and a pension system began to be introduced. New standards were adopted for assistance to impoverished regions, and the country began implementing a new poverty alleviation program. A plan to improve the nutrition of impoverished students in the nine-year compulsory education program began to be implemented. These government-funded policies and measures, aimed at improving rural welfare systems, brought increased public spending to rural areas and very tangible benefits to people. They played an important role in preventing the urban–rural disparity from widening even further. They moderated the conflicts between grassroots administrators and local people and helped stabilize social order in rural areas. Meanwhile, a whole series of agricultural support policies also led to year-on-year annual increases in grain production and helped stabilize the supply of agricultural goods.

Post-2013: Unifying the approach to urban and rural development and building a moderately prosperous society in an all-round way

The critical element in setting up a moderately prosperous society in an all-round way involves a coordinated or overall approach to urban and rural development. The 18th National Party Congress explicitly pointed out that unifying urban and rural development was the fundamental solution to issues involving farmers, farming, and the rural economy. Several hundred million people live in China's vast rural areas; this means that they are the deciding factor in whether or not the country can achieve moderate prosperity for all. In addition, however, China's urban and rural economies are already tightly bound to one another. The importance of rural development therefore takes on major significance since cities can no longer develop in isolation.

First, cities are relying ever more heavily on rural areas for agricultural products. In 2013, China's urbanization rate exceeded 53 percent, and its national income reached the level of upper-middle-income countries. The situation with respect to demand for agricultural goods is very different from a time when farmers were in the majority in the country and the purchasing power of urban residents was limited. In terms of diversity, quantity, and quality, the new forms of demand highlight the importance of agricultural production, especially grain production, to cities. If agriculture cannot modernize sufficiently to ensure that it meets the demands of the majority of China's population who live in cities, this will threaten the social stability of China's cities.

Second, cities in China increasingly rely on a labor force that is made up of young people from the countryside. As urbanization proceeds in China, cities will continue to depend on this supplemental labor force given economic development and the aging of the population. Some 60 percent of students enrolled in the nine-year compulsory-education stage of schooling are in grade schools and middle schools in rural areas. Their early childhood care and preschool development are inadequate, and their levels of nutrition and education are far below those of urban children. This is going to have a serious impact on the caliber of China's urban labor force in the future. Undernourished and undereducated children will not be able to achieve higher levels of attainment and skills. This is eventually going to hold back China's industrial upgrading and its economic restructuring.

Third, urban and rural areas rely on each other in terms of their ecological environment. Rural areas have been the victims of industrial pollution, but they also have generated rural forms of pollution through overuse of chemical fertilizers and pesticides and the lack of effective systems to dispose of all kinds of garbage and domestic waste. Single-source pollution, as well as area-wide pollution, has been the result. Not only do efforts need to be made in environmental and ecological remediation, but local people in rural areas need to participate in and support these efforts, whether they are replanting trees, managing field improvements, restoring polluted water systems and degraded soils, or addressing the most outstanding of environmental problems.

Finally, due to the mobility of China's population, urban and rural people are now tightly linked to one another in many ways. Because of this, grassroots-level governance has an effect on the harmony and stability of the entire society. Rural land disputes are often connected to the process of urban development. Failure to coordinate the interests of both sides may lead to major social problems and conflicts. The percentage of criminal cases that relate to the "floating population" remains consistently high in both urban and rural areas. Within rural areas, small conflicts may lack sufficient mechanisms to handle dispute resolution, leading to repeated petitions to higher levels of authority, or to the intensification of the conflict, or to violence and major incidents. Improving the practical governance capabilities of local areas is imperative. That means expanding participation by the public and integrating modern social governance in an organic way with traditional forms of rural governance. It means allowing for positive feedback loops between government administration that is law-based and self-governance by local people that is also law-based. These must be intrinsic parts of modernizing China's governance capabilities and improving the country's governance systems.

Unifying urban and rural development is therefore not just a matter of social fairness and "helping out" rural areas. It is done to serve the common interests of both sides and to enable the sustainable development of cities that can continue to invest in rural areas, particularly in agriculture, in rural youth, in rural ecosystems and the environment, and in rural society. All of this is done to stimulate the interaction and interpenetration of urban and rural areas. If rural areas are overlooked, this will ultimately hurt cities. It will hold back the development of the country as a whole.

3.   Key tasks and challenges as we seek to establish all-round moderate prosperity in rural areas

The concept of *xiao kang*, moderate prosperity, reflects a more highly developed stage than "adequate food and clothing but not to the point of affluence." Adding the term *all-round* to this concept means that policies focus on universal enjoyment of the benefits of economic development. It means that all the people in the country are able to live with a sense of security and a sense of dignity as the country lays a solid foundation for universal affluence in the future.

Tasks and goals that relate to establishing all-round moderate prosperity need to be measured and monitored so as to ensure coordinated action throughout the country. In various documents, the Party has set forth a number of key indicators and requirements that include such things as economic aggregates, per capita GDP, level of income among citizens, and so on. In addition to these, however, many central government departments, think tanks, international organizations, and local government departments have also proposed sets of indicators and standards for this purpose. The National Development and Reform Commission, the Development Research Center of the State Council, China's National Bureau of Statistics, the United Nations Development Program, and the provincial government of Jiangsu have been particularly active in this regard. The National Bureau of Statistics has created a fairly comprehensive system of standards and indicators after soliciting opinions from central and local departments. From 2007 to 2011, it published annual reports assessing progress on the national and provincial bases.[3] These became highly important as points of reference for both practical work and academic research into the subject.

The various tasks involved in creating an all-round moderately prosperous society have changed somewhat as the process has continued. Standards and indicators provided by both the central government documents and various departments have been modified in a dynamic way according to actual circumstances and internal and external conditions. The emphasis was on economic construction when the call to create a moderately prosperous society was first put forth. By the time of the 18th National Party Congress, the emphasis had broadened to include five main aspects that are incorporated into one overarching goal. The five are economic, political, cultural, social, and ecological progress. Since the speed with which targets have been achieved has surpassed expectations, the goals have been enriched, and the standards for monitoring progress have been constantly upgraded.

The concept of "scientific development" as a national goal has gradually gained universal acceptance in China. As that has occurred, support for the practical realities of achieving all-round moderate prosperity in rural parts of the country has had to undergo profound changes. Newly defined tasks need to be clarified now that are in accord with these changes so that we can address issues with a consensus of opinion and with coordinated policies and integrated resources in the Five-Year Plan that will end in the year 2020. Efforts must carry forward on a number of fronts to achieve moderate prosperity in economic, political, cultural, social, and ecological spheres. Not only is the work complex, but it varies from place to place. Defining results in terms of one unified and inclusive monitoring system is not feasible. What this Report does, therefore, is to propose six key tasks that are based on analysis of the most important but also weakest aspects of rural development right now in the country. It then analyzes the challenges facing those key tasks.

The first task relates to food security. This means ensuring that there is enough grain and enough food supply in the country to satisfy the needs of the entire society in terms of both quantity and quality. In 2013, total grain output in China came to 601.94 million tons. Since this was the tenth consecutive year of increases in production, the foundation for food security in the country is sound in overall terms. However, food security in a country with over 1.3 billion people is something that cannot be taken for granted. To a certain degree, China's increasing output relies on the massive use of such inputs as chemical fertilizers and pesticides. Continuing this practice on a long-term basis presents a severe threat to the sustainability of food production but also to the ecological environment of rural areas. On top of that problem, China's food security faces the dual threat of labor and land shortages, given an aging population and encroaching urbanization. To ensure a positive balance of supply and demand for food over the long term and to raise the country's level of food security, we must go further in reforming a number of relevant systems. These include transforming operating practices in agriculture, changing the system that governs land in rural areas, improving systems that enable innovative scientific and technical applications in agriculture, and changing our agricultural subsidy systems.

The second task relates to income levels and the standard of living in rural areas. It involves steadily increasing these so as to lessen the disparity with urban areas. In 2013, per capita net income of rural residents on a nationwide basis came to RMB 8,895.9. After allowing for inflation, this was 12.8 times the net income of rural residents in 1978. While such an increase in income cannot be regarded as too slow, it still has allowed for an increasing gap in urban–rural incomes. In 2009, urban residents on average had 3.33 times the income of rural residents. The disparity in incomes began to fall back slightly in 2010, and in recent years the disparities that exist within rural areas have also stabilized to a degree. One of China's long-term economic problems has been that incomes overall have grown more slowly than the economy has grown, while rural incomes have grown more slowly than urban incomes. Despite major changes that have occurred in the supply and demand situation for labor, it is not going to be easy to make any fundamental changes to this long-term problem within the next six years. What's more, China is in the midst of a period of "stage shift" in terms of its economic growth rate. As the rate of economic growth declines, it is fairly uncertain whether or not the country can achieve its declared task of doubling per capita net rural incomes by 2020 as compared to 2010. In recent years, the decline in urban–rural income disparities and the easing of increasing disparities within rural incomes can be attributed somewhat to favorable policy factors as well as economic cycles. Maintaining these trends and ensuring that income disparities decline are by no means going to be easy.

The third task relates to social security in rural areas. This involves further improvements to existing social security systems and ensuring that all rural residents have an adequate safety net. At present, the "three main pillars" of social security have already been introduced in rural areas, namely health insurance, social [old-age] pensions, and minimum living allowances. Given the impending problems of a swiftly aging society and major changes in rural communities, however, these systems urgently need upgrading in terms of both scope and level of coverage. Despite remarkable accomplishments in poverty alleviation over the past thirty-some years, China still has more than 80 million people living in poverty in rural areas as defined by China's current standards of measurement. Poverty alleviation therefore remains a formidable task. The coverage of both minimum living allowances and social pensions in the countryside is vastly lower than it is in cities. Standards are also lower, which makes it hard to say that the systems play any real role in furthering equality in the country and maintaining minimum levels of protection. Notable results have been achieved by the "new-style cooperative medical services system," which basically provides coverage for the entire population, but improving the effectiveness of the system and coordinating it over the levels of administration is challenging. Budgets are tightening at all levels of government, given slower economic growth. Governments must do what they can within their fiscal constraints and avoid making excessive promises that exceed their actual capacity to deliver, since this threatens the sustainability of social security systems as a whole as well as macroeconomic stability. At the same time, governments should do everything in their power to ensure that the lives of poor and elderly people do not fall below poverty levels. They must also avoid the phenomenon of people falling into poverty once they get sick and then having no recourse at all.

The fourth task relates to education and healthcare. It involves achieving significant improvement in education and the provision of medical services in rural areas such that levels of health and education among rural people come up to higher standards. The country has consistently increased investment in rural education to the extent that nine-year compulsory education is provided at no cost in rural areas, leading to notable improvements in enrollment. Progress with respect to healthcare has been made in recent years such that China's standing in terms of developing countries on a global basis is fairly good. Such key indicators as the maternal mortality rate, the under-5 mortality rate, the child malnutrition rate, and overall life expectancy place China at fairly good levels relative to other developing countries. Nevertheless, many "weak links" are still apparent in China's rural education and healthcare situation. In education, preschool education is a notable problem. In 2013, on a nationwide basis, the gross enrollment rate in three-year preschool education was 67.5 percent, while in rural areas more than one-third of all preschool age children had no access to such benefits; either families were too poor or the distance between home and township kindergartens was too great. In terms of nutrition, the rate of low-weight children and stunted-growth children in rural areas is three to four times what it is in urban areas. Meanwhile, the situation in rural areas that are defined as impoverished is twice as bad as it is in normal rural areas. In 2010, 20 percent of children under the age of five in impoverished areas experienced such problems as stunted growth, anemia, among other health and nutrition issues. The situation in certain impoverished parts of the countryside is severe. By 2020, the goal is to bring children in such areas up to the 2015 level of education and healthcare of children in normal rural areas. This will mean focusing in particular on work in early childhood development.

The fifth task relates to the system of administering grassroots governance. This involves linking "institutionalized" government with "organized" rural residents such that a new pattern of social governance creates a positive interaction between the two. In order to promote social harmony, the linkage must be effective. The current situation is that the first steps in setting up legal systems for grassroots governance in rural areas have been taken. Systems relating to village-level elections, democratic decision making, and democratic oversight are increasingly being standardized. The trend toward ever less provision of basic public services has been halted. Nevertheless, despite such improvements in the overall context of grassroots governance, the old mode of grassroots governance still prevails due to the processes of marketization and urbanization. This mode relies on administrative power and the monopolization of available resources. It mobilizes action via top-down commands. It cannot satisfy the needs of rural social development. Rural areas continue to exhibit major social problems that are made manifest by the increasing numbers of mass incidents caused by conflicts of interest, by suicides due to social as well as household problems, by the lack of caregiving for elderly people who live alone and for single men without families, by the paucity of any cultural or recreational stimulation, and so on. Addressing these outstanding problems will require innovations in social governance structures. It will require the close cooperation of government and nongovernmental entities, and it will require investment in systems building and cultural infrastructure.

The sixth task relates to water quality and pollution. It involves providing safe drinking water and improved sanitation facilities to address the increasing spread of pollution in the countryside that stems from both single-point and area-wide sources. Major effort must be put to turning this trend around and effectively improving the living environment of rural people. Since the "socialist new countryside" effort was launched in China, the State has increased its investment in improving the habitat for rural people; the percentage of rural residents who now have access to safe drinking water and improved hygienic facilities is on the increase. However, as the report called *Work Report of the State Council on Ensuring the Safety of Drinking Water* makes clear, more than 100 million rural residents still had no access to safe drinking water by the end of 2010, nor did 114,000 rural schools (State Council, 2012). Moreover, "hygienic-standard" toilets in the countryside in China were available to only 72 percent of the rural population in 2012.

This means that almost 73 million rural households with more than 200 million people lacked such toilets.[4] In addition to this, air pollution is spreading from cities to the countryside, while water pollution is entering agricultural areas from neighboring industrial zones. China's soil is increasingly polluted. Many of China's most impoverished areas are located in environmentally vulnerable locations. This intensifies the dilemma that these areas face since economic development leads to environmental damage. The task is monumental if we are to provide safe drinking water for the remaining 100 million people in China who are without it and provide hygienic toilets to the 200 million people in China who still lack such toilets, and if we are to control the ongoing spread of single-point and area-wide pollution and push forward on ecological remediation.

These six key tasks do not encompass the entire process of "creating moderate prosperity in an all-round way in rural areas." Instead, they adhere to the principle of "focusing on outstanding issues, raising the overall level, and ensuring that minimum standards are maintained." Through focused application of resources, and reform of structures and mechanisms, they aim to achieve the strategic goal of achieving moderate prosperity in an all-round way by the year 2020.

4.   The basic pathway toward building an all-round moderately prosperous society in rural areas

To realize these six tasks, it is imperative that China adhere to the development path that is described as "a new type of urbanization and rural modernization." The "new type of urbanization" is a major strategic initiative that has come about in recent years as the result of the experience and the lessons of urbanization to date. Not only is it about how to "urbanize" land properly, but it involves turning rural migrant workers who have migrated to cities into permanent urban residents (CDRF, 2010). Reform of the household registration system is the main precondition for achieving this process as smoothly as possible. This means establishing a unified household registration system by the year 2020 that makes no distinction between urban and rural residents. The core substance of household registration reform involves eradicating the discriminatory treatment of people who are currently classified as having "rural status." It involves reforming the unequal systems and policies that apply to such people, including hiring practices, wage determination, social security, and availability of public services. This means reforming institutional arrangements as well as policy laws and regulations.

Rural modernization cannot be achieved without adjusting existing reform measures and development policies. This Report has concluded that four key areas of reform must be addressed. The first involves transforming China's mode of agricultural production so as to meet the country's goal of food security by ensuring stable levels of output and ongoing increases in output. The second involves reforming the "land system." This includes reforming the administrative system that governs land on which rural people actually have their homes, "residential-use land." This reform is necessary in order to allow for improved allocation of land resources and to meet the goals of stable agricultural output as well as improvement in farmers' incomes. The third involves reforming the system of public finance that pertains in rural areas, as well as the system of financing business. The aim is to set up public finance and financial structures that are more suited to the needs of rural areas so as to assist in rural development and the stable growth of rural economies. It is to ensure the sustainable provision of public services and social security systems. The fourth involves reform of rural systems of governance, including transforming the functions of township governments, standardizing [regularizing] grassroots government operations, and expanding orderly participation by the public in rural social governance so as to increase the degree of self-governance as well as self-servicing. This involves forming decision-making mechanisms that involve the joint interaction of government and community, and forming governance institutions that involve "cogovernance" by officials and the people.

In 2013, the Third Plenary Session of the 18th CPC Central Committee passed a decision supporting the comprehensive deepening of China's reform measures. In 2014, specific policies relating to key issues were passed, including reform of the household registration system, reform of the land transfer system, and reform of China's fiscal and taxation systems. As these are implemented, these key reform policies will have a massive influence on urban and rural economic and social conditions. They will lay the foundation for the stated intent to "unify urban and rural development" in the country. If reform objectives are indeed achieved, the expectation is that some 100 million "people transitioning out of agriculture" will have become permanent urban residents by the year 2020. This requires that an average of more than 16 million people undertake this transition every year. In addition to this figure are the nearly 10 million rural students who graduate from junior middle schools every year; as these children go to college or vocational schools, the great majority of them will also become permanent urban residents. A total figure of some 25 million rural people transitioning to urban residence every year is an indication that the country is on a fast track to what is being described as "a new type of urbanization that is people-centered." Rapid urbanization of this kind will provide new opportunities for all-round prosperity in rural areas, but it will also confront rural areas with the challenge of an accelerated outflow of human resources and other kinds of resources over a certain period of time. This makes it even more necessary to strengthen a unified and balanced approach to urban–rural development. Based on a full awareness of the magnitude of the task of creating all-round moderate prosperity in rural areas, this Report concludes that policy measures during this period of structural reform must include what it calls the "four investments" and "three securities."

Four investments: First, we should increase investments in agricultural infrastructure, as well as other forms of rural infrastructure, so as to improve production and living conditions in rural areas in a comprehensive way, to raise agricultural productivity, and to encourage the effective allocation of factors that can flow freely and smoothly between urban and rural areas. Second, we should increase investments in the human capital of rural areas, particularly in the areas of child nutrition and education. Not only is this necessary in order to deal with the aging of the rural labor force and the process of urbanization, but it relates to the bigger picture of upgrading the caliber of the population overall as China transforms its economic structure. Third, we should invest in environmental protection in rural areas. This means improving the carrying capacity of rural ecosystems, improving the sustainability of urban–rural eco-environments, ensuring greater food safety, improving public health facilities in rural areas, and improving the living conditions for humans in both urban and rural areas. Fourth, we should invest more in community development so as to speed up the process of establishing rural organizations that can help mitigate social conflicts. Rural organizations must be able to contribute to making a more inclusive and stable situation in rural areas.

Three securities: This involves making three specific systems the key components of a social safety net in rural areas, namely the rural minimum living allowance, the social pension system, and healthcare provisions. By 2020, we should have achieved coverage of all people who should be covered, and we should make every effort to ensure that levels of coverage are markedly improved over the base level of 2010.

We should uphold four principles as we implement these policy measures:

> *Comprehensive*: Progress should be made in an all-encompassing way, with every effort to ensure there are no limiting factors, or the so-called short staves in the bucket.
>
> *Coordinated*: All government departments and different parts of the country should implement policies in a unified and coordinated way.
>
> *Equal*: All sectors of society should have equal opportunity to participate in development, and the benefits of development should be enjoyed on an equal basis; that is, no one should be excluded from the process of economic development on the basis of ethnicity, gender, age, urban or rural status, or geographic location in the country.
>
> *Sustainable*: The results of creating a moderately prosperous society in an all-round way should be able to be consolidated and maintained so as to lay a firm foundation for realizing a higher level of development in the future.

These six tasks and four key systemic reforms are intertwined. Each key task requires institutional reform in many areas, and each reform will influence the process of achieving different tasks. This Report therefore divides the overall endeavor into ten specific areas according to the actual realities in rural areas, the demands of the task, and the priorities for institutional reform. These ten areas are: rural demographics and the allocation of labor resources, reform of the rural land system, food security, creating a new form of agricultural operating system, increasing the income of farmers and income distribution issues, social security and the provision of public services, innovative approaches to rural social governance, building an "ecological civilization" in rural areas, reform of the public finance system, and reform of the household registration system. By looking at these ten areas, this Report seeks to analyze the primary challenges confronting the process of "building moderate prosperity in rural areas." On the basis of its conclusions, it makes specific targeted recommendations.

Notes

1 Knight and Song (1999) find, by comparison, that China ranks second in the world in terms of the income gap between urban and rural areas.
2 At the time, rural households were required to pay fees for the provident fund and public welfare fund and an administrative fee to village-level administrations, as well as the educational surtax, family planning fee, militia training fee, rural road construction fee, and favored treatment fee to township governments.
3 In early 2003, the National Bureau of Statistics launched a key project for a statistical monitoring indicator system for building a moderately prosperous society in an all-round way. In 2005, after soliciting opinions from the National Development Research Center and other ministries and commissions under the State Council, the National Bureau of Statistics released the indicator system proposed by the project team and then adjusted and refined it according to feedback from various departments and regions. In 2007, the 17th National Party Congress put forward higher requirements on building a moderately prosperous society in an all-round way, so the National Bureau of Statistics organized experts to discuss and make important changes to the system. In June 2008, in order to facilitate the statistical monitoring in different areas, it issued the Statistical Monitoring Program for Building a Moderately Prosperous Society in an all-round Way, in which the indicator system was composed of twenty-three indicators across six spheres: social development, social harmony, quality of life, democracy and rule of law, as well as environment and resources.
4 National Health and Family Planning Commission. As of 2012, hygienic toilets had been available in 72 percent of rural areas (http://www.chinanews.com/sh/2013/11–19/5522104.shtml).

2 Changes in the geographic distribution of China's rural population and in the allocation of its labor resources

- Number, geographic distribution, and structure of China's rural population in the year 2020
- China's rural labor force in the year 2020
- Three pathways for dealing with changes in the rural population and labor force

Enormous changes have taken place in the number, structure, and distribution of China's rural population since the start of the 21st century. The percentage of this group in the total population has continued to decline given ongoing urbanization. By the end of 2013, the rural population constituted 46.3 percent of China's total population, which was 17.5 percentage points less than it had been in the year 2000. This means that the rural population has been declining by more than one percentage point per year, on average. This decrease in the numbers of rural people can be attributed mainly to people flowing out of the countryside to cities. Since the outflow is primarily made up of younger people, the result has been to leave rural areas with a declining labor force and an increasing percentage of older people and young children. Given this situation, the speed at which the rural population is aging exceeds the speed at which China is urbanizing. Even as a large number of towns are being "hollowed out," however, some are prospering and drawing in people. The demographic distribution of people in the countryside is therefore marked by concentrations in certain new urban clusters.

These three demographic changes in China's rural population – a decline in the total number of rural people, the rapidly aging population, and the concentrations in certain towns – will have a fundamental impact on the social and economic development of rural areas in the future. They provide the context for the initiative of building a moderately prosperous society in an all-round way in rural areas. This chapter seeks to forecast the future structure and number of China's rural population in the year 2020. Based on its conclusions, it then proposes three specific "pathways" toward dealing with future changes in China's rural population and its labor force.

1. Number, geographic distribution, and structure of China's rural population in the year 2020

It is important to come up with a fairly accurate projection of how many people may indeed be living in rural areas in the year 2020. A variety of existing factors may influence actual changes in rural population. Nevertheless, it is highly significant in practical terms to understand the future situation of rural demographics and to prepare policy contingencies based on the results. Population projections may be based on the historical trajectory as well as current trends. Looking at the big picture, future demographic changes in rural areas will depend on the behavior of rural people as they make decisions about migrating and where to live, but they will also depend on population policies and public policy guidance. Past experience indicates that rural residents will naturally move toward cities when there is an obvious disparity in urban–rural development. However, the scale and pace of this movement will also be influenced by public policies and particularly those policies that relate to the household registration system.

Number of rural residents in 2020

The Sixth National Population Census of China, undertaken in 2010, put the total population of the country at 1.34 billion. Using this figure as a starting point and assuming no change in gender and age structure as well as the total fertility rate of 1.5 at the time of this Report, also assuming no change in the current second-child policy,[1] we estimate that the total population of the country in 2020 will be 1.42 billion. If the second-child policy is extended on a nationwide basis, such that every couple is allowed to have two children, then the total population is expected to reach 1.49 billion by 2020 (CDRF, 2012). According to the report entitled *National Planning for New-type Urbanization, 2014–2020* that was issued in March of 2014 (henceforth referred to as "new-type urbanization planning"), China's degree of urbanization will reach 60 percent by 2020. Rural residents will therefore constitute 40 percent of the population. Given these two possibilities, depending on the second-child policy, China's total rural population in 2020 could be either 570 million in the first instance or 590 million in the second.

At the end of 2013, China's population was 1.36 billion and its rural population was 630 million, or 46.3 percent of the total (NBS, 2014). Between 2008 and 2013, that rural population declined by 76 million, or roughly 15 million every year. If this rate of decline continues, the rural population will go down by 100 million by the year 2020, to 530 million.

No matter which scenario occurs, it is clear that China's rural population will continue to follow a declining trajectory. However, the rural population as estimated from the decline between 2008 and 2013 is a lower figure than the rural population as estimated from results of the sixth census of 2010, as well as from the projections made by the *National Planning for New-type Urbanization,*

2014–2020. This means that it is extremely likely that the rural population may decline at a faster rate than what is planned for in the *National Planning* report. By 2020, the percentage of rural people in the total population may be far lower than the 40 percent rate that is in the plans.[2]

Given current trends in policy changes, future policy adjustments may accelerate the process of urbanization. This will have the effect of encouraging more rural people to migrate to cities. The *National Planning for New-type Urbanization* tends to focus on the process of turning the floating population into permanent urban residents and on such issues as deepening reform of the household registration system. All such policies will undoubtedly reduce the number of children who are "left behind." They will have the effect of enticing ever more rural residents to work and reside in urban areas.

Urbanization policies therefore contribute to the decline in the rural population, but two other demographic factors are also accelerating this process. One is the reduction in the number of children in a family, and the other is the imbalance in China's sex ratio at birth.[3]

One of the results of the long-term application of China's one-child policy has been a swift decline in the number of children in rural households. This situation has made rural families focus ever more intently on their child's education. Added to that is an increase in rural household income in recent years, which has led quite a few families to decide to move into cities for the sake of their child's education. According to surveys undertaken by our research group, once a child enters middle or high school, a growing number of the heads of rural households migrate to urban centers and rent houses near a secondary school in order to look after the living needs of a child who has started school there. This behavior on the part of parents is intensifying the decline in the rural population.

China's gender ratios began to diverge from a normal pattern in the 1980s, given the country's one-child policy and the preference of people for a male child. The gender imbalance is more severe in rural areas, as compared to cities (CDRF, 2012). As a consequence, the number of single males of a marriageable age is vastly greater in rural areas than the number of available women. Moreover, as the migration to cities increases, many rural women of a marriageable age leave local areas, further exacerbating the problem of single men. Given this situation, buying a residence in a neighboring city has become a prerequisite for marriage in many rural areas, so that the young couple can live in town after the wedding. The way in which an imbalanced sex ratio affects marriage is yet another reason for declining numbers of China's rural population.

The distribution of China's rural population in the year 2020

As China's rural population has continued to decline, its geographic distribution has also changed in notable ways. These changes are reflected not only at the provincial level, with increases or decreases depending on the province, but at the village level.

Viewed from a regional perspective, the decade between 2000 and 2010 saw considerable differences in the degree to which rural populations declined in various provinces, while some provinces not only did not lose rural populations but saw them increase. Figure 2.1 illustrates these changes. Among China's thirty-one provinces, municipalities, and autonomous regions, three locations saw increases in a rural population to varying degrees, namely Shanghai, Tibet, and Xinjiang.[4] Some places saw a considerable drop in rural populations, such as the Chongqing municipality (51 percent) and Jiangsu (35 percent). Other places saw only a slight decline, such as Heilongjiang (3.3 percent) and Hainan (2.7 percent). As urbanization proceeds and as the difference in growth rates among different areas increases, the degree to which different provinces gain or lose rural populations will also continue to increase. The current pattern of such changes will serve as the foundation on which rural populations come to be distributed by the year 2020.

Viewed from a more local perspective, within each county, the distribution of population among different townships [*xiangzhen*] and towns [*cun*] is also changing. Starting in the 1980s, the number of townships and towns began to change radically with the implementation of changes in China's administrative systems governing these jurisdictions. Most particularly, the policy known as "withdrawing townships and merging [their administration] with towns" led to a swift decline in the number of townships. Over the past decade and more, the number of towns has basically remained the same while the number of townships has declined

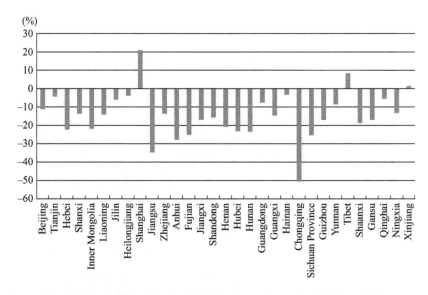

Figure 2.1 Changes in China's rural population by province, from 2000 to 2010

Source: Calculated according to data from the Fifth and Sixth National Population Census of China.

dramatically. It has gone from over 23,000 in 2000 to under 13,000 in 2013. This represents an average decline of nearly 800 townships every year. In terms of population distribution, this lower number of jurisdictions has led to a redistribution of the population among jurisdictions. At the same time, in certain places it has led to greater economies of scale.

Compared to the changes in population distribution brought on by this administrative action, however, the changes within villages [*zhuang*] are an issue that deserves much greater attention. In recent years, the "hollowing out" and even disappearance of villages has become an increasingly prominent problem (see Box 2.1). There is insufficient data to quantify the extent of this issue, but the fact that it is happening is well documented by research reports and media accounts. One example can represent the trend. Among villages in Yucheng, Shandong province, an investigative survey found that between 8.4 percent and 25 percent of all homes in villages had been abandoned. The extent of vacated land occupied by abandoned residences came to an average of 10 percent of all residential land. In the worst case, the extent of abandoned residential land came to 18.7 percent (Liu Yansui et al., 2009). In contrast to the rapid decline in rural populations in many places, however, another survey has found that the amount of land occupied for residential use in villages has actually increased. According to calculations, between 1996 and 2007, the per capita residential-use land area of permanent rural residents increased by 18.3 percent. The per capita residential-use land area of registered rural residents [those not permanently in residence] increased by 4.4 percent. These figures were, respectively, 50 percent and 25 percent higher than the upper limit of the nationally mandated standard, which is 150 square meters per person (Li Yurui et al., 2010).

Box 2.1   How many more villages are going to disappear?

As urbanization accelerates in China, traditional villages are gradually fading away. Both the numbers of villages and the size of their populations are on the decline. By 2011, the number of "administered villages" [those with a governmental administrative structure] had declined to 590,000, with each containing an average of 1,113 people. Although local areas have implemented the policy known as "integrating or combining villages" in an administrative effort to maintain their population figures, the average per-village population continued to fall after 2005. If we had as many administered villages in 2011 as we had in 1985, the per-village population would be a mere 698. As village populations have declined, the natural boundaries of a traditional village have come to be supplanted by borders that are defined in administrative terms.

If we assume that the declining numbers of administered villages can be attributed, to a certain degree, to administrative readjustment of boundaries, this nevertheless signifies that the traditional lifestyle of natural villages and the physical surroundings of rural residents are changing. Since official data has not been maintained on a continuous basis, precise measurement of the extent of these changes is not possible. The second National Agricultural Census, done in 2006, showed that China had 3.3 million "natural villages" at the time. According to a survey undertaken by Feng Jicai, consultant to the State Council, that number had declined by 2011 to 2.7 million. This means that between 80 and 100 villages in China are disappearing every day.

Source: He Yupeng and Chen Sicheng, "Disappearing Villages," *China Construction News*, February 19, 2014.

The structure of China's rural population in 2020

As compared to the decline in the rural population, and demographic changes at the provincial and county level, changes in the structure of China's rural population by the year 2020 deserve much more concerted attention.

"Population structure" incorporates both gender and age structure. Problems relating to the gender structure of China's rural population have already been noted. The imbalance in the sex ratio at birth in rural areas has led to a preponderance of males, and the situation is not expected to improve in the near future. As more boys reach marriageable age, the "marriage problem" of males in the countryside is going to get worse.

While problems caused by gender structure may primarily affect people at the individual and family levels, problems caused by age structure extend across the entire society. Even as the numbers of China's working-age population are declining, the overlapping problems of an aging population and a low fertility rate are leading to a population age structure in rural areas that can be seen in the graph in Figure 2.2. In the decade between 2000 and 2010, the percentage of working-age people in China's rural areas has continued to decline, while that of the nonworking-age population has continued to increase, particularly that of the older generation. Given the momentum of demographic changes, this trend is not going to be reversed anytime soon. It will continue on up to 2020. Population aging has become the outstanding issue in the age structure of China's rural population.

China entered the status of "an aging society" in 2000. By the end of 2013, more than 200 million people in the country were over the age of 60, or 14.9 percent of the entire population. This aging problem is even more acute in the countryside than in cities, given the massive outflow of young people from the countryside. The aging countryside constitutes a major part of the overall aging problem in the country. In the Fifth National Population Census, conducted in 2000, rural people over the age of 60 constituted 65.8 percent of all people over the age of 60. At that time, the rural population constituted 63.8 percent of the total population, so the discrepancy was roughly 2 percent. By the Sixth National Population Census, done

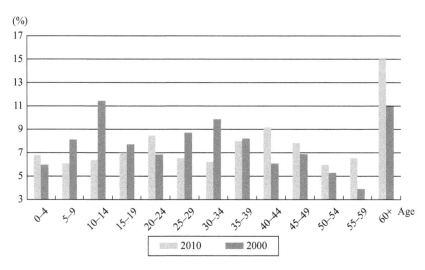

Figure 2.2 Changes in the age structure of China's rural population, from 2000 to 2010
Source: Calculated according to data from the Fifth and Sixth National Population Census of China.

in 2010, rural people over the age of 60 constituted 57.1 percent of all people over the age of 60, but by that time the rural population constituted only 49.7 percent of the total population, so the discrepancy had grown to 7 percent. This ongoing discrepancy cannot be reversed in a short period of time. Prior to 2040, the extent and speed of aging in the countryside will continue to exceed the extent and speed of aging in China's cities (Li Bengong, 2007).

It is worth pointing out, however, that the speed at which the countryside is aging varies from place to place. In areas that began implementing the one-child policy fairly early, or that have a greater exodus of young people, or that have longer than usual life expectancy, the aging problem is more pronounced. In such places, population aging is already posing a serious threat to sustainable development in both economic and social terms. This problem deserves close attention (see Box 2.2).

Box 2.2   The caregiving dilemma in China's "oldest" county

Rudong county in Nantong, Jiangsu province, has been regarded as a model example in implementing China's family planning policies. At the same time, its population is aging at the fastest rate of any county in China, and it has the greatest percentage of older people. Nearly half of its population is elderly.

By the end of 2012, people over 60 constituted 27.57 percent of Rudong's total population of 1.05 million, while people over 65 constituted 20 percent of the total. Both of these indicators far surpass the national average.

Rudong entered the status of "an aging society" back in 1982, when the Third National Population Census was done. Starting in the year 1997, it has experienced a negative population growth every year for seventeen consecutive years.

Why is this county so "old?" Local people sum up the reasons: family planning, education, and longevity. The county began implementing China's family planning policy in the early 1970s and has consistently been a model county in this regard. The steady, low fertility rate has resulted in a negative population growth rate for more than a decade. This is in contrast to the neighboring county of Rugao: since beginning family planning practices, Rudong has brought half a million fewer babies into the world than has Rugao. Meanwhile, the county is known for its focus on education and culture; it sends 3,000 to 4,000 high-quality students out to receive higher education every year, but once these young people are educated, less than 20 percent return. The county is famed for its longevity. Given high standards of living and healthcare, the per capita life expectancy reached 80.12 by the year 2010 and continues to rise. The percentage of elderly people therefore also continues to rise.

"We are fully aware of and concerned about this problem," says Chen Jianhua, chairman of the CPPCC Rudong Committee. "The reason is that the pace of aging is too fast." He has put the issue at the top of the agenda for the Committee. "Who is going to till the fields?" he asks. "As everyone in the family gets old, who is going to care for us?"

Source: Finance of IFENG.COM, http://finance.ifeng.com/news/special/caizhidao/, December 4, 2014.

Based on calculations applied to the Sixth National Population Census (2010), by the year 2020 China will have 242.11 million people who are over the age of 60 (CDRF, 2012). If we use the figures projected by the "new type of urbanization" plans, as mentioned, and estimate the percentage of rural elderly at 52 percent of rural populations (which is 12 percent higher than their percentage in the overall population), then we still come up with a figure of 125.9 million people over the age of 60 in rural areas by the year 2020. In three possible different scenarios, therefore, people over 60 in rural areas will still constitute 22.1 percent, 21.2 percent, or 23.8 percent of the entire rural population.

Yet another factor that exacerbates this aging in rural areas is the reverse flow of middle-aged and elderly migrant workers back to rural areas. This is occurring even as young people continue to flow outward to cities. Large-scale population mobility in China began in the 1980s. Figuring that most of those people who left rural areas at that time were around 20, these people are now over 40 or 50. Despite the fact that household registration policies increasingly allow rural migrant workers to settle permanently in cities, it cannot be denied that some of these people, particularly the first generation, prefer to return to their home towns in their later years. This undoubtedly will accelerate the aging of rural areas.[5]

One further trend that should not be overlooked is the decrease in school-age children in rural areas given lower fertility rates and population mobility. This is happening as the aging of rural populations intensifies. Data from the Fifth and Sixth National Population Censuses indicates that the percentage of people over 60 in rural areas increased by 16 percent between 2000 and 2010 while the absolute number of rural children aged 5 to 14 dropped precipitously, by 46 percent. This kind of volatile change in population segments requires targeted policies. As the numbers of older people increase and those of younger people decrease, the structure of public services in rural areas presents different requirements that require policy adjustments. In the future, as we go further in providing resources for compulsory education, we must also invest in public services and improve caregiving services for the elderly in rural areas.

2.   China's rural labor force in the year 2020

The labor force is a fundamental factor when it comes to supporting social and economic development. As such, China's rural labor force is a core issue in any discussion of the future of China's rural areas. Since the start of reform and opening up, the mobility of that labor force has increased tremendously while reform of the household registration system has, comparatively speaking, been slow to catch up. This has led to a *de facto* distribution of labor that is seriously at odds with household registration data. When talking about the "rural labor force," therefore, one needs to differentiate between two different concepts. One refers to people who hold a rural household registration, whether or not they live in the countryside. The other refers to people who do indeed live and work in rural areas for at least six months of the year and who hold a rural household registration. These two categories are in fact overlapping. The first category [who may or may not live in the countryside] can typically be divided into two components of people, namely those who work in agriculture and those who are rural migrant workers and who do not work in agriculture. The second category [who live in the countryside] theoretically might also include people who do not hold a rural household registration. The majority of this group of people does in fact hold a rural registration, however, and they work in both agricultural and nonagricultural jobs in rural areas. The broad-brush description of the "rural labor force" therefore includes three distinct categories of people: those who are engaged in agriculture in rural areas, those who are engaged in nonagricultural work in rural areas, and those who travel elsewhere to work as rural migrant workers. Each of these is now described in more detail.

The agricultural labor force

According to statistics from China's National Bureau of Statistics, China's agricultural labor force totaled 283 million in 1978 and 242 million in 2013. Within this overall category, people engaged in agriculture declined from 70.5 percent of the total in 1978 to 31.4 percent of the total in 2013. This drop of 39 percentage points meant an average annual decline of 1.11 percentage points. The decline in the percentage of people engaged in agriculture was much faster after the start of reform and opening up than it was prior to that time. The twenty-five years between 1953 and 1978 saw just a 13 percent decline in the percentage of people employed in agriculture, or an average annual decline of 0.52 percentage points. In contrast, between 2004 and 2013, the actual number of people engaged in agricultural labor declined by 120 million in China. This represented an average decrease of 12 million people every year, or a decline of 1.8 percentage points every year. If these rates continue, in the year 2020 China will have a total of 170 million people engaged in agricultural work. Their percentage of the total employed population in the country will have gone down to 20.6 percent.

If, however, one looks at the rate of economic growth in China over these past thirty-five years of reform and opening up, and at the speed with which industrial structures have changed, this rate of decline in the percentage of agricultural labor can be regarded either as rather slow or as a statistical underestimation to start with. Once high-speed economic growth took off after the delays of a twenty-year period of the planned economy, it would be logical for the percentage of agricultural labor to drop at a rate commensurate with that growth. Because of this, it would be worthwhile to revisit the data on labor forces by sector as described in the relevant statistical yearbooks, particularly those that give the figures for agricultural labor and changes in those figures.[6] Given the international experience, it may well be that the figures describing China's agricultural labor force have to some extent been overestimated in the past.[7]

This gives rise to an important question: how should we define "agricultural labor" in our estimates of how many people are actually engaged in agriculture in China? Since some official statistics do not define this very precisely, their reliability has been questioned to varying degrees.[8] As everyone knows, the rural agricultural labor force is simultaneously and universally engaged in second jobs that do not involve agriculture. This presents several options when it comes to defining "agricultural labor." One is to determine roughly whether or not a person actually engages in agricultural production at some point during the year. The second is to decide based on the principal source of income of a given person. If income comes mainly from agriculture, that person is defined as working in the agricultural labor force. The third is to base a definition on the length of time a person spends in agricultural work in a given year. If time spent on farming is greater than time spent on other occupations, then that person is part of the agricultural labor force. China National Bureau of Statistics defines a member of the agricultural labor force as someone who is sixteen years of age or older and who receives "labor compensation" or "operating income" for "social labor." This concept therefore defines anyone who is sixteen or older as a member of the agricultural labor force if that person works at all in farming, forestry, animal husbandry, sideline occupations, or fishing (that is, "agriculture" in the broadest sense).

It is rather important to define this issue carefully in looking at the future of agriculture in China. It is critical that we know who is actually "farming," working the ground, taking on the primary responsibility for agricultural production.

Table 2.1 Average length of time the rural labor force spends on agricultural work: data from 2003 to 2012 (unit: days)

Age group	2003	2004	2005	2006	2007	2008	2009	2010	2011	2012
16–20	53.4	43.4	36.3	30.1	25.6	27.4	33.9	31.1	26.6	23.2
20–30	66.6	56.5	54.8	48.0	42.6	40.0	41.5	36.4	33.1	31.3
30–40	111.2	105.9	101.7	93.3	86.2	80.4	76.0	67.2	61.3	58.3
40–50	128.7	126.2	125.1	117.9	110.3	107.0	103.5	98.3	91.1	87.5
55–60	124.4	123.1	120.1	115.5	108.7	104.4	103.5	97.8	94.4	90.3
Average days	102.2	97.6	94.9	88.7	82.4	79.1	78.5	73.1	68.7	66.3

Source: Research Center for the Rural Economy (RCRE), Ministry of Agriculture.

From this perspective, adopting the third kind of definition as just described is appropriate, that is, defining the "agricultural labor force" in terms of the length of time actually spent farming. Aggregating data from specific observation sites in surveys conducted on a nationwide basis (see Table 2.1), the length of time that the rural labor force spent on farming in China declined from 102.2 days in 2003 to 66.3 days in 2012 (Chen Jianhua and Li Jie, 2013). Given this result, an appropriate way to define the "agricultural labor force" would be "a person over the age of 16 who spends at least sixty-six days of the year engaged in agricultural work."

By this definition, China's agricultural labor force constitutes roughly one-third of the entire rural labor force in the country. Within this component, around 65 percent of people are engaged exclusively in farming. In 2012, the average age of a person engaged in farming in China was 48.9. People over 40 have therefore become the primary force of rural agriculture in the country. On average, these people have received 6.7 years of education. Some 5.8 percent have received training in agricultural technology, while 12.5 percent have received training in agriculture in general. Within the overall "agricultural labor force" category, a mere 0.3 percent of the sixteen to thirty age group has received any training in agricultural technology (RCRE, Ministry of Agriculture, 2013).

What these results show is that the people bearing the responsibility for agricultural production in China are declining in total numbers, are aging, and have a low level of expertise or "human capital." These significant considerations should not be overlooked in evaluating the future of agricultural development in China.

The nonagricultural labor force

The overall term for rural people who are engaged in nonagricultural work in China is "rural migrant workers." This term covers two types of people: those who work in nonagricultural fields in their home base for at least six months of the year and those who travel to work elsewhere for at least six months of the year. At the

Table 2.2 Numbers and types of rural migrant workers

Year	2008	2009	2010	2011	2012	2013
Total number	22,542	22,978	24,223	25,278	26,261	26,894
Migrant rural workers	14,041	14,533	15,335	15,863	16,336	16,610
(1) Those with their family left behind	11,182	11,567	12,264	12,584	12,961	13,085
(2) Those migrating as a whole family	2,859	2,966	3,071	3,279	3,375	3,525
2. Locally employed migrant workers	8,501	8,445	8,888	9,415	9,925	10,284

Source: Research Center for Rural Economy (RCRE), Ministry of Agriculture.

Unit: 10,000 persons

end of 2008, China's National Bureau of Statistics established an official system for surveying and monitoring data on rural migrant workers. This assesses the situation of 68,000 registered households in rural areas and the rural migrant workers in more than 7,100 "administered towns" in thirty-one provinces, municipalities, and autonomous regions across the country. Based on the latest survey results, which came out in 2013, China has a total of 269 million rural migrant workers, including 166 million who work for at least six months of the year in places other than their home base (see Table 2.2).

The appearance of nonagricultural rural workers came about as the result of farming families beginning to take up sideline occupations.[9] This practice began in the 1980s, as households universally started to contract for their own agricultural production [via the household contract responsibility system] and as job opportunities increased with industrialization and urbanization. By now, farming families that are engaged in nonagricultural jobs have gone from being isolated examples to being the rule. In this process, China's rural labor force has not only shifted from traditional farming into other occupations but has managed to realize a diversification of sources of income.

The process can be divided into two stages. The first occurred in the mid-1980s when town-and-village enterprises began to flourish and surplus agricultural labor shifted into nonfarming occupations. Households who diversified their occupations led the way in being households with alternative incomes. The second came in the 1990s when job opportunities in local town-and-village enterprises became saturated, and surplus labor began to move out to other places seeking work. This turned into large-scale labor mobility and brought the "rural migrant worker" phenomenon into being. More and more rural families began to have jobs on the side, whether *in situ* or elsewhere.

Alternate jobs and nonagricultural employment have led to the rapid aging of the remaining agricultural labor force. They also are directly impacting farming activities and long-term rural development. By comparing data from the national

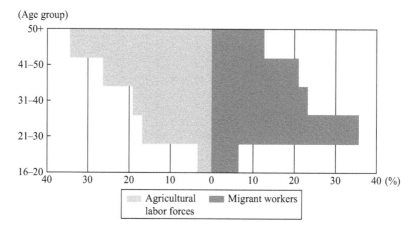

Figure 2.3 Comparison of the age structures of the agricultural labor force and rural
migrant workers

Source: Data from the Sixth National Population Census of China; National Bureau of Statistics, 2012:
National Monitoring and Survey Report on Migrant Workers.

census and the monitoring surveys of rural migrant workers, we have discovered
that the under-30 age group now constitutes less than 20 percent of people engaged
in agriculture. The over-50 age group constitutes 34.6 percent. Meanwhile, the
under-30 age group constitutes 42.4 percent of rural migrant workers, while the
over-50 age group constitutes 12.9 percent (see Figure 2.3).The figures for "rural
migrant workers" include a large component, 38.8 percent, who work in local jobs
and do not travel elsewhere. If comparisons were made with the even younger
people who do leave home to work elsewhere, the contrasts would be even more
striking. For example, a survey undertaken in 2011 by the National Bureau of
Statistics showed that 60.4 percent of locally employed "rural migrant workers"
were over the age of 40, while only 18.2 percent of rural migrant workers who
travelled elsewhere to work were over the age of 40.

The influence of the massive amount of rural labor that is employed in nonfarming jobs goes far beyond rural areas. Among the roughly 270 million rural migrant
workers in China today, 170 million are working away from their original homes.
The situations that these people are currently facing, as well as the futures in store
for them, are something that deserves far more attention.

At the end of 2009, on a nationwide basis, a total of 153 million rural people
were working for more than six months of the year at places other than their native
towns and villages. Some 95.6 percent of these people had migrated to work in
cities and towns. For the purpose of the following exercise, we assume that the
percentage of rural migrant workers who stay home and those who migrate into
cities is the same for the period 2001 to 2011 as it was in the year 2009. Given
that assumption, we can derive a total figure for the numbers of rural migrant

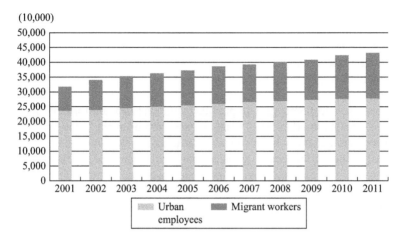

(10,000)

Figure 2.4 Urban employment and structure between 2001 and 2011, as shown by urban residents (light gray) and rural migrant workers who have come into the city (dark gray)

Source: Cai Fang and Lu Yang, "The End of China's Demographic Dividend: The Perspective of Potential GDP Growth," in Cai Fang, Ross Garnaut and Ligang Song (eds.), *China: A New Model for Growth and Development*. Canberra: Australian National University EPress, pp. 55–74.

workers living and working in cities every year, by using the National Bureau of Statistics' annual monitoring reports. We then can see, as shown by Figure 2.4, the extent of the contribution that rural migrant workers make to the labor force of China's cities.

Figure 2.4 indicates that rural migrant workers already account for more than one-third of the total employment in China's towns and cities. Their job performance and their status in job markets to a large extent determine how China's urban job markets now function. Because of this, these rural migrant workers should not be disregarded in any analysis of supply and demand for labor in China or in any analysis of unemployment figures, work conditions, wage payment issues, labor relations, social security conditions, and so on.

Since 2004, the phenomenon of labor shortages has begun to spread throughout China due to inadequate supply of rural migrant workers. In one respect, this reflects the fact that a surplus of rural labor, previously thought to be unlimited, has in fact reached a turning point. One of the most hotly disputed topics in academic circles in China in recent years is the question of how much labor in fact remains to be "shifted" out of agriculture. Does a tremendous amount of surplus labor still exist in the countryside? Opinions are divided on this. Specific calculations differ, but the great majority of research shows by now that China's "transferrable surplus labor supply" is indeed running out. Surveys undertaken in 2013 indicate that the average monthly salary of a rural migrant worker who was working away from his or her home base was RMB 2,609. At the same time, the per capita disposable income of urban residents for that year was RMB 26,955 (NBS, 2014). Meanwhile, the average daily wage of people working in agriculture in rural areas was often RMB 80–100, according to field investigations done by the CDRF project team (CDRF, 2014). Clearly, the way incomes of migrant workers, urban residents, and agricultural laborers are trending toward similar figures corroborates the idea that the supply of surplus labor that can be shifted out of the countryside is coming to an end.

China's fast economic growth provided sufficient demand for labor that rural migrant workers in urban areas gradually saw improvement in the job situation. Such workers generally have education at or below the level of lower middle school. Comparing the jobs-to-applicants ratio (the number of positions compared to the number of people applying for those positions) can therefore reflect the comparative advantage of rural migrant workers with different levels of education. According to records from public employment service agencies, in the second quarter of 2013 that ratio was 1.07 on average. Within this overall figure, the ratio for people with an education no higher than lower middle school was 1.10, while that for people with a college degree was 0.91.

While the wages and job situations of rural migrant workers have gradually improved in recent years, these people still face enormous problems in terms of overall urban living conditions. The great majority are not eligible for social security. As of 2013, a mere 41.3 percent of rural migrant workers had signed any kind of contract with employers. As compared to 2012, a growing number were being asked to work overtime in 2013; people working more than eight hours a day went from 39.6 percent of the total surveyed in 2012 to 39.6 percent in 2013, while the number being asked to work more than forty-four hours a week went from 84.4 percent in 2012 to 84.7 percent in 2013.

The job markets are now presenting a very seductive appeal to rural migrant workers given the labor shortages, rapid increase in wages, and trend toward converging wage structures. As a result, young people from rural areas are entering job markets at a very early age and also jumping quickly from one job to another. This is detrimental to any kind of sustained training in jobs as well as to receiving a basic education. By the end of 2013, only 32.7 percent of rural migrant workers had received any skills training, which means that almost 70 percent had received no occupational training at all. What's more, the dropout rate for children in lower middle school in rural areas in 2011 was 1.6 times what it had been in 2006. This will make these children less competitive in job markets in the future. In 2011, rural migrant workers had received an average of 9.6 years of education, which enabled them to work in labor-intensive secondary-industry jobs (the job requirement in such positions is 9.1 years of education), as well as labor-intensive tertiary-industry jobs where the job requirement is 9.6 years of education. The future trend in China's economy, however, points to slowing growth and a restructuring of industry. Human-resource demands will increase the educational requirement in jobs. Capital-intensive type positions in secondary industries will be requiring 10.4 years of education on average, while technology-intensive type positions in tertiary industries will be requiring 13.3 years of education. It is clear that the educational levels of rural migrant workers will not allow them to shift toward these new types of job positions.

Trends in the rural labor force by the year 2020

Once an economy reaches a Lewisian turning point, it is still possible and indeed necessary to continue to shift surplus labor out of agriculture even though the marginal productivity of labor in agriculture is no longer zero. This must, however, be accompanied by a rise in the productivity of agricultural labor. If the ongoing shift of labor out of agriculture is not compensated for by such things as mechanization, such that the overall level of agricultural productivity rises, the result will be a decline in agricultural output.

The process of economic reform in China has led to improvements in agricultural productivity that are evident in greater productivity of all factors, as well as simply the productivity of labor and the productivity of land. When compared to the experience of other countries at a similar stage in economic development, however, China can be seen to have a huge gap in agricultural productivity, which means there is considerable room for improvement (Figure 2.5).

The shift of the labor force out of agriculture has in fact accelerated the mechanization of agriculture in China in order to conserve labor. Agriculture has been acutely responsive to the scarcity of labor and other production factors as seen by advances in agricultural technology and changes in the mode of production. In the early period of reform and opening up, the emphasis of technological improvement

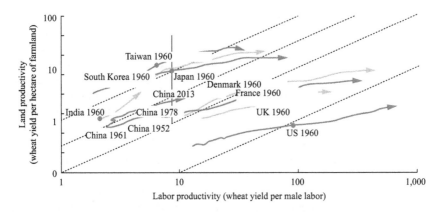

Figure 2.5 Historical comparisons on agricultural productivity

Source: Zhao Wen, *China's Agricultural Development under the New Pattern*. Beijing: Economy & Management Publishing House, 2012.

was not conservation of labor, however, since there was a large reservoir of surplus labor in the countryside. Instead, the focus was on conserving land. This meant that improvements in small-scale agricultural implements came about only slowly. As the shift in surplus agricultural labor has accelerated, the labor shortage has become more apparent and use of larger-scale labor-saving machinery has developed more quickly.

However, the shift in agricultural labor, the process of semiurbanization, and the fact that ownership rights over farmland cannot be transferred smoothly have made it hard to achieve the consolidation of land. This has limited the scale of agriculture and also therefore impacted mechanization and productivity. In reality, "semi" or "halfway" urbanization is incapable of creating a mode of agricultural production that is based on price incentives and economies of scale. Given the uncertainty about their ability to settle permanently in urban settings, rural migrant workers who travel elsewhere to work are reluctant to transfer [i.e., sell] the operating rights to the land over which they have contractual rights back home. Nor are they willing to relinquish rights to land on which their now vacant homes are located. This has led to a serious problem in China's land-use management system, given a certain decline in the usage rates of land for both agricultural production and residential use.

As an example of this problem, in 2012, China had some 263 million rural migrant workers of whom 99.25 million were employed in nonagricultural sectors within their own townships. In terms of their main occupation, these people have already ceased to be "in farming," but they continue to farm as a sideline and they continue to hold contractual rights over their farmland and their residential-use land. Meanwhile, in 2012, China had some 163 million rural migrant workers who had left their home base to work elsewhere and no longer worked at all in agriculture, but their families remained at the home base and still farmed the land. These people too have not let go of the contracts that govern their farmland and residential-use land. In addition to these two categories of people, some 33.75 million others have taken their families to live elsewhere on a permanent basis – they have completely severed ties with rural life and rural production of any kind. They too, nevertheless, continue to hold the usage rights over both their contracted farmland and their residential-use land in most cases. Some people have leased their land-use contractual rights to others who farm the land for them, while still enjoying the grain subsidies provided by the government.

Despite the substantial reduction in the numbers of people engaged in agriculture, therefore, it can be seen that the number of people holding contractual operating rights over farmland has not gone down in any real way, whether those people actually farm the land or not. This has led to an inability to increase economies of scale in Chinese agriculture and has kept the productivity of agricultural labor from improving.

Based on one comparison regarding China's grand goal of economic and social development, it is also necessary that China needs to maintain its speed

Table 2.3 Per capita gross national income in select countries and the percentage of agricultural workers in their labor forces (2011)

Country	Per capita GNI (current dollar)	Employment in agriculture (% of total employment)
Costa Rica	7,660	14.1
Kazakhstan	8,200	26.5
Mauritius	8,230	8.4
Panama	8,610	17.0
South Africa	6,950	4.6
Turkey	10,510	24.2
Uruguay	11,700	10.7
Venezuela	11,760	8.0
Average	9,203	14.2
China	4,940	34.8 (23.5)

Source: China's percentage derives from the *China Statistical Yearbook* of 2011 (http://data.worldbank.
org.cn/). The figure in brackets is an estimate from a background report that contributed to this Report.
Other data comes from the World Development Indicators as put out by the World Bank.

of shifting labor out of agriculture. China's per capita GDP reached USD 6,800
in 2013, which puts the country among the ranks of upper-middle-income countries. The next decade or so will be a critical period for China as it seeks to
move into the ranks of high-income countries. During this period, China still has
tremendous potential for an ongoing shift in agricultural labor as compared to
other middle-income countries with a per capita GDP of between USD 6,000 and
USD 12,000. As an example, in the year 2011, the agricultural-labor component
of other countries at the same stage of development averaged 14.2 percent. This
was 7 percent lower than the figure that Chinese scholars estimate the figure to
be in China, and it was 20 percent lower than the figure given in China's Statistical Yearbook (see Table 2.3). This means that over the next ten to twenty
years, China must reduce its agricultural labor force by millions of people. That
is, it must lower the agricultural labor force by about one percentage point on
average per year.

Meanwhile, the overall demographic profile of China is changing. The working-
age population, 15 to 59, has already begun to decline significantly in numbers.
According to projections of the Sixth National Census of China, this age bracket will
be declining by close to 3 million people on average every year between 2010 and
2020. Labor shortages in China are going to intensify since machinery still cannot
replace human labor on a sufficiently large scale. Since economic growth dictates
an enormous demand for more labor, the ongoing shift of labor from the agricultural
sector must be maintained at a certain speed. For example, between 2007 and 2011,
for every 1 percent increase in the GDP of nonagricultural sectors, there was
a 0.27 percent increase in the demand for labor; that is, the elasticity of demand
was 0.27. Looking at projections for potential economic growth prior to 2020, it is

estimated that 9 million new job positions will be created every year (Du Yang and Lu Yang, 2013). Incremental increases in the labor force cannot meet this massive demand. China's only way out will be to rely on other ways to increase participation in the labor force, including an ongoing shift of labor out of agriculture.

3.   Three pathways for dealing with changes in the rural population and labor force

As already described, major changes are occurring in the geographic distribution of labor in China and in the demographics of rural populations. These form the backdrop to the goal of building a moderately prosperous society in an all-round way in rural areas. Faced with the considerations of an aging rural population and an ongoing decline in the rural labor force, in order to push forward on this goal, China should undertake the following three measures.

Modernize the mode of agricultural production

Advances in science and technology have made massive contributions to the rapid and steady development of China's agriculture. Seen from an overall perspective, however, China's agriculture still relies heavily on manpower. While some regions have undertaken substantial mechanization and are moving to economies of scale, the main mode of agricultural production in China still relies on the household and on small-scale operations. Modernized agriculture is not yet in place: labor-intensive methods still prevail in agricultural production. The ability of such methods to ensure agricultural output is being undermined, however, by the ongoing outflow of labor and the aging of the population that remains in rural areas. Who is going to farm the land and how the land is going to be farmed remain the primary considerations when it comes to future prosperity in rural areas.

Faced with the ongoing decrease in rural labor and the aging of those "left behind," China's mode of agricultural production simply has to change in a fundamental way. The primary pathway to dealing with changes in the patterns of rural demographics, and the rural labor force involves gradually decreasing labor inputs, increasing the support of scientific and technical advances, and utilizing modern agricultural production systems with appropriate economies of scale.

Improve the geographic distribution of the population

The decrease in rural populations inevitably leads to changes in the regional distribution of people in China. At present, such regional demographic changes have two important characteristics. First, the number of actual towns and villages is continuing to decline, and the problem of hollowed-out villages is becoming severe.[10] Second, the population of county seats and "small" cities is continuing to grow.

The issue of hollowed-out villages has drawn attention in recent years since the phenomenon is leading to a waste of rural land resources and to low efficiency in the allocation of public services. From a strategic planning perspective, China's policy of promoting the relocation of hollowed-out towns is significant in the attempt to coordinate urban and rural development. At the appropriate pace, pushing forward such relocation and consolidation of residences and building "core" towns are simply necessary policy decisions. It involves concentrating rural populations, clustering industries, and conserving land by using it more intensively.

Resolving the issue of hollowed-out villages and creating core towns are mutually interdependent processes. First, surveys of land usage in hollowed-out villages are necessary as a reference for policy decisions on how to ensure more rational land use in towns and villages. Second, it will be necessary to reform the current "single-track" system that governs use of residential-use land [an alternative term being used is *homestead land*]. The current system does not allow for compensated land transfers and puts no time limits on use by current holders. This must transition to a "double-track" system that does allow for compensated transfer of residential-use land as well as for ongoing free use by existing holders. Finally, and most importantly, core villages (or communities) must be well planned in advance, with adequate public services in particular that allow them to become long-term residential districts. That is, major efforts must be put into creating viable core towns as a substitute to and resolution of the problem of hollowed-out villages.

Improve the quality of the rural labor force

Given the ongoing decline in rural populations and particularly in the labor force, it is critical to improve the quality of the remaining rural labor force. This depends on education and on training initiatives.

The process should begin with efforts in three specific areas. The first is preschool education. Given that preschool education has the highest social rate of return, having the government pay the bill for this is fully in accord with the principle of overall public benefit and the role of education in society. Preschool education should gradually be incorporated into compulsory education systems. Children from villages and impoverished regions should not miss out on an "even starting line." Enabling them to receive a preschool education will also improve the rate at which such children complete grade school and middle school. Second, we should increase the enrollment rate in high schools to a very large extent and push for universal enrollment. Improving the opportunity to go to college is also an incentive for going on to high school. At present, government spending at the high school level of education is rather low, which puts too heavy a burden on rural families. Meanwhile, the opportunity costs of going to high school are high, and the chances of passing exams to get into college are low. These factors have created a bottleneck in the development of education in the future. In addition to continuing to push for more universal high school education, therefore, the government should move as fast as possible in the direction of free education at the high school level. Third, improve vocational training. China needs a large cadre of highly skilled people. Children who have dropped out of school and joined the labor force at an early age should be given the opportunity to improve their skills in on-the-job training. The upgrading of skills will require vocational education as well as vocational skills training, and it will require stable relationships between employers and employees.

Finally, China must lift the employability of rural migrant workers by a variety of means. These include being more proactive in pushing for equal access to public services, creating social security systems and equal job-opportunity systems that operate across urban and rural areas, improving the stability of labor supply and labor participation rates, alleviating labor shortages, extending the time frame of the "demographic dividend," and so on. The government should be more proactive in building up labor market systems and should implement labor laws and regulations in a far more rigorous way. With respect to labor contracts, it should ensure that coverage is extended to all rural migrant workers, and it should push forward systems that allow for collective bargaining on wages. It should in every way try to improve harmonious labor relations and social stability. Reform of public policies in these many ways can provide incentives for an ongoing shift of surplus rural labor, while also preventing wages from rising too quickly.

Notes

1 The second-child policy allows couples, except those with twins or multiple births, to have two children if either parent is an only child themselves. On November 15, 2013, the Third Plenary Session of the 18th Central Committee of the Communist Party of China adopted the Decision of the CPPCC on some major issues concerning comprehensively deepening the reform. This proposed to "uphold the basic policy of family planning, while implementing the policy allowing parents to have two children if either parent is an only child." Since then, the so-called second-child policy has officially been put into practice.
2 Assuming the rural population is 530 million in 2020, its percentage of the entire population will be 37.3 percent or 35.7 percent, depending on whether the second-child policy remains unchanged or is fully extended.
3 The sex ratio at birth refers to the ratio of newly born males to females within a certain period (such as a year). The normal range of sex ratios at birth is 103 to 107.
4 The increase in Shanghai's rural population resulted from the growing migrant population, while that in Tibet and Xinjiang was attributed to natural growth.
5 First-generation migrant workers and "'next-generation" migrant workers are two relative concepts. According to the definition of the National Bureau of Statistics, *next-generation* refers to those born in and after 1980. First-generation migrant workers are generally regarded as those born before 1980, who started migrating in the early stages of China's massive population flow.
6 Some foreign scholars believe that China's official statistics on agricultural labor forces do not fully reflect the reality of the rapidly changing agricultural production, resulting in a weak data basis for econometrics analysis. As some point out, China's reform has been so fast that the statistical reform has failed to keep pace. See: Martin Ravallion and Chen Shaohua, "When Economic Reform Is Faster Than Statistical Reform: Measuring and Explaining Income Equality in Rural China," *Oxford Bulletin of Economics and Statistics*, 61 (1), 1999, 33–56.
7 Internationally, the percentage of agricultural labor forces in comparable countries has declined rapidly. Japan and South Korea also used to have a dual economy yet they achieved rapid economic growth, and the percentage of their agricultural labor forces

dropped much faster than that in China over similar periods. For example, during the thirty-four years between 1953 and 1987, Japan saw its agricultural labor force decrease 4.5 percent annually. From 1983 to 1997, South Korea saw an annual decline of 5.1 percent, both levels much faster than the decrease in China between 1978 and 2012 (see the background report by Cai Fang and Wang Meiyan).

8 A study estimates the number of China's agricultural labor forces at 187 million, by calculating the per capita and monthly labor inputs of rural labor forces in various economic activities. See Du Yang and Wang Meiyan, "China's Total Employment and Employment Structures: Reevaluation and Discussions," in Cai Fang (ed.), *China Population and Labor Report No. 12: Challenges during the 12th Five-Year Plan Period: Population, Employment, and Income Distribution*, pp. 70–84. Beijing: Social Sciences Academic Press, 2011. According to this study, the official data was overstated by 54 percent. If the number of agricultural labor forces was adjusted to 187 million and the urban and rural total employment was 790 million in 2009, then the percentage of agricultural labor forces in total employment was 24.7 percent instead of 38.1 percent.

9 The practice of taking up sideline occupations is not unique to China. It has existed in the process of industrialization and urbanization of most countries. Japan has conducted intensive study on the classification of sideline occupations, which divides rural households into three categories according to the labor time and income structure: the first are pure rural households whose family members are engaged in nonagricultural work for fewer than thirty days; the second are type-1 rural households whose family members are engaged in nonagricultural work for more than thirty days and at least 50 percent of their income comes from agriculture; the third are type-2 rural households whose family members are engaged in nonagricultural work for more than thirty days and less than 50 percent of their income comes from agriculture (Liao Hongle, 2012).

10 Even in densely populated Hubei province, the number of villages has been shrinking over the past decade. According to a survey, the province had 27,634 village committees in 2003, and the number declined to 25,955 in 2013, a decrease of 1,617 in ten years, or 160 annually. Over the same period, the number of villagers' groups decreased by 7,170, or 710 annually. See Xiong Yibo, Chen Junyi, and Xu Haitao. "Survey Report on the Changes in Villages in Hubei Province," *China Rural Studies* (RCRE, Ministry of Agriculture), Volume 30, Issue 30, 2014.

3 Furthering reform of China's land system and granting greater property rights to rural residents

- The evolution of China's land system, its primary characteristics, and its main problems
- Pushing forward on the reform of the property-rights [ownership] system that governs rural land in China by undertaking the critical step of confirming and certifying ownership rights
- Actively promoting the transferability of contractual operating rights to farmland
- Reforming the management system that governs rural homestead sites [or "residential-use land"]
- Models that explore putting collectively owned construction-use land on the market
- Deepening reform of the system that governs land requisitions [expropriations]
- Being proactive in exploring how to reform the system that governs collectively owned property rights

Land is not only the essential element in farming, but it is the guarantee of a livelihood for rural people and the key element governing social stability and harmony in rural areas. The "land system" is the "basic system" in rural areas in China. It plays a critical role in the process of creating moderate prosperity in the countryside. Up to now, China has employed a system that seeks to preserve arable land as its goal, that imposes controls on the use of land, and that applies overall land-use planning to how land is used. This system is facing increasingly complex challenges, however, with ongoing economic and social development in the country. The appearance of a whole set of new issues is forcing a reconsideration of the existing land system, and requiring us to explore in depth how to reform the system in the future.

This chapter first looks back at how China's existing system evolved. Based on that understanding, it then analyzes the primary characteristics of the system and their major problems. It focuses on five aspects: the confirmation of and certification of property rights, the contractual method of operating land, the way in which "residential-use land" [or the land containing homesteads] is managed, the issue of creating a market for land that is "owned" by rural collectives, and reform of the system by which land is requisitioned [or expropriated] in rural areas. It then puts forth a basic way of thinking about all these issues and proposes countermeasures to deal with the issues. These incorporate more far-reaching reform of the rural land system. Based on all this, it discusses how to advance reform of the system that governs collective property rights in China's rural areas.

1. The evolution of China's land system, its primary characteristics, and its main problems

Evolution of China's land system

In the sixty-five years since the People's Republic of China [New China] was founded, China's land system has gradually come about as an adaptation to the needs of the country's social and economic development.

At the very beginning, China promulgated two documents that were of a constitutional nature in order to address land ownership issues. These were the *Charter of the Chinese People's Political Consultative Conference* [1949] and the *Land Reform Act* [1950]. These enabled the new government to assume ownership of land formerly held by the previous government [Old China,], and they granted permission to confiscate land held by "bureaucrats" and "the comprador class of people with assets." [The term *bourgeoisie* in Chinese is literally "the class of people with assets or capital."] The country then completed land reform within three years, abolished the system of private ownership of land by landlords, and set up a system of ownership of land by *nong min*. [This term was formerly translated into the English word "peasants" but is now either "farmers" or "rural people."]

From 1950 to 1970, China promulgated a series of laws and regulations that established a system of land ownership by rural collectives and a system of land requisition for the purposes of "State construction" [a term that refers to "building up" the State economy]. These laws and regulations included the *Constitution of the People's Republic of China* [1954], the *Exemplary [Model] Charter of Agricultural Producers' Cooperatives (draft)* [1955], the *Exemplary [Model] Charter of Advanced Agricultural Producers' Cooperatives* [1956], the *Regulations on the Work of Rural People's Communes (amended draft)* [1962], and the *Measures for Land Requisitioning [Expropriation] for State Construction* [issued in 1953 and revised in 1958].

After the start of reform and opening up, China began a period of institutionalizing and legalizing land management. A modern system of management was gradually established that "seeks to preserve arable land as its goal, that imposes controls on the use of land, and that applies overall land-use planning to how land is used." During this period, China has revised its constitution three times. In 1986, it issued the country's first *Law on Land Management [Administration]*, after which a series of other laws and regulations were introduced including *Interim Regulations of the People's Republic of China Concerning the Assignment and Transfer of the Right to Use State-owned Land in Urban Areas*, *Law Governing the Management of Urban Property*, the *Property Law*, and the *Law on Land Contracts in Rural Areas*.

The past sixty-five years of experience have resulted in a system that is composed of various laws and regulations that govern land, such as the *Constitution*, the *Property Law*, and the *Law on Land Management*. These are aimed at satisfying the needs of China's "initial stage of socialism," and the needs of a "socialist market-economy system with Chinese characteristics." They constitute the current framework for China's modern land management [administration] system (Liu Shouying, 2014).

Main characteristics of China's land system

The basic framework that governs land management in China is illustrated in Figure 3.1. As this diagram indicates, land is divided into two categories depending on the nature of its "property rights attributes" [i.e., ownership]. Those two categories are "land held under the system of ownership by the people as a whole" [which is mainly in urban areas] and "land held under the system of ownership by collectives," [which is mainly in rural areas]. Land held in rural areas is further divided into two usage categories, one for "agricultural" use and one for "construction" use. Meanwhile, there are six main categories or classifications of land management systems. One applies to protecting and preserving basic farmland, one applies to land contracted out for agricultural production, one applies to construction-use land owned by collectives, one applies to rural homesteads [land under residential areas], one applies to the requisitions and use of collectively owned land, and one applies to allocating rights to use State-owned land.

China's land management system currently has four main characteristics, as follows.

First, the system of rights that governs land in China separates out ownership rights from usage rights. Both are based on a system of socialist public ownership. The land rights system of the country includes four aspects. First, China's land is held under a system of socialist public ownership. No organization or individual

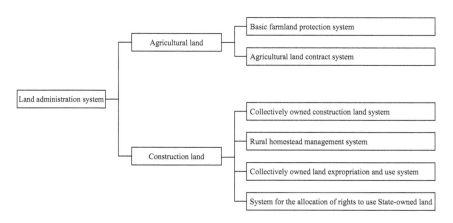

Figure 3.1 Framework of China's land management system

may infringe upon this ownership by buying, selling, or otherwise transferring land through any illegal means. Second, the system of "ownership by the people as a whole" coexists with the system of ownership by collectives. At the end of 2013, the amount of arable land under the ownership of collectives came to 1,413.123 million *mu*. [Since one acre = 0.1647 *mu*, this amount is equivalent to 232.74 million acres.] Of this total, 41.08 percent is held by what are now called *villagers' committees* (these are the equivalent of what were called production brigades ["large teams"] in the time of the former People's Communes). Another 51.55 percent is under the ownership of what are now called *villagers' small groups* (these are the equivalent of what were called production teams ["small teams"] in the time of the former People's Communes) (Ministry of Agriculture, 2013). Third, ownership rights to land are separate from usage rights to land. Fourth, property rights governing land assets are respected and protected. The State protects and regulates land rights via several laws including the *Constitution*, the *Property Law*, the *Land on land management*, and the *Law on Land Contracts in Rural Areas*.

Second, China's mode of administering or managing land is aimed at protecting and preserving arable land and is centered on controlling the use of land. As per the needs of a country that has a large population living on a small amount of land, China's number one priority is food security and the conservation of arable land. When the *Law on Land Management* was revised in 1998, a system of controls over land use was written into the law. The law stipulated that "China's basic national policy is to cherish land, use it rationally, and protect arable land effectively." In order to achieve that, it adopted the strictest possible system for conserving arable land. The country has formulated an overall plan for land use that defines land in terms of specific land-use categories. It places restrictive conditions on land use. It strictly limits the ability to use "agricultural-use land" for other purposes and, in particular, to transfer "tilled or farmed land" to land that is used for construction purposes.

Third, the system of allocating land resources in China is "government led" and "market based." China's land resources can currently be allocated in three ways. First, State-owned land may be supplied by State "grant" or determination, or the State may receive compensation for usage rights. That is, State-owned land is allocated according to a two-track system. The former "track," granting usage rights without compensation via administrative decision, is applied to land used by State organizations, the military, basic infrastructure in cities, public endeavors, and key infrastructure projects that are being nurtured and supported by the State. The latter category includes key projects in the fields of energy, transport and communications, and water conservancy. The second "track" applies to construction-type usage rights for all other State-owned land use, for which there is to be compensation. Compensation is achieved through compensated "transfers," leasing, investments, shareholding arrangements, and other methods. Second, land that is of an "operating nature," that is, to be used for business, is allocated according to a market that operates under the aegis of a government monopoly. Third, holders of usage rights to State-owned land may lease, invest in (via shares), transfer, and also mortgage the rights as according to law.

Fourth, a land administration system has been established that operates primarily on a centralized and unified basis. Prior to 1986, this was not the case – China's land was administered in a dispersed way by a number of departments. In 1986, because of the turf problems caused by this system, China set up a unified management system that applied to urban, rural, and local governments. In 1998, the previous system that allocated quotas for land use to different levels of government was replaced with a land-use control system that was centrally administered. The authority for approving the conversion of agricultural-use land into other uses and for permits to requisition [expropriate] land was pulled back to the State Council and to provincial-level governments. In 2004, China took a further step in "straightening out" the administration of State-owned land resources at the subprovincial level of governments, and in 2006 it took the additional step of setting up a State land inspection and supervisory system. Since then, a relatively centralized system of administering land, with supervisory authority that is top-down, has basically taken shape.

Main issues in China's land system

Up to now, the land system has been able to play a fundamental role in China in terms of promoting agricultural production, ensuring the livelihood of rural people, and holding together the harmony and stability of rural society. In recent years, however, a number of things have changed with the deepening of reform. Rural areas are facing considerable change in the world around them, as well as in their own internal dynamics. As a result, the land system is facing ever more complex challenges. The main problems facing the system can be summarized in the following four aspects.

The first relates to the dualistic system that pertains to property rights and the incompleteness of rights. The *Constitution* of 1982 divided China's land into State-owned [nationally owned] land in urban areas and collectively owned land in rural areas. It made the land in these two areas subject to two different sets of laws. Land in rural areas was governed by the *Law on land contracts in rural area*s. Rural land that was shifted to alternate uses as well as State-owned land in urban areas was governed by the "*Law on management.*" Based on this division, China developed two completely different sets of property rights systems. From the perspective of existing laws and regulations today, land use by rural people confronts tremendous areas in which rights are incompletely defined or not defined at all. An example might be that the operator of contracted farmland is unable to use that land as collateral for loans. Another is that the land under rural residences, or homesteads, is accompanied only by "usage rights" [usufruct] and cannot be sold, transferred, or assigned to others for material gain.

Second, market access for different entities or participants is unequal. As already noted, China's land markets are cordoned off between urban and rural. Different types of rural land are allowed entry to markets according to different types of rules (depending on whether they are contracted farmland, residential land, collectively owned construction-use land, and so on). In addition to this, different types of construction-use land can be assigned [or sold] only in certain prescribed ways depending on whether the land is intended for public purposes, industrial purposes, or business purposes. Land intended for use that contributes to the public good, for example, can be "assigned" [by government officials]. In contrast, land for industrial, commercial, and residential use must be sold on the market through an auction, bidding, or tender process. At the same time, different local [provincial] governments have radically different ways of handling industrial, commercial, and residential land (see Box 3.1).

Box 3.1   Different approaches to using land for industrial, commercial, and residential purposes

Local governments have done their utmost to monopolize authority over the transfer rights to local commercial land and residential-use land. [This prevents the formation of a valid market.] Through limiting supply, local governments then maximize their own income from such land when they employ such market-based methods as auctions, tenders, and price bids to sell it. The way they limit supply is to set up what are called "land reserve centers" that stock up on land by "purchasing" commercial and residential land, by gathering together the "construction-use" land that is already in their jurisdiction, and by gathering in newly available farmland that is converted to nonagricultural use. The central government has repeatedly demanded that local governments use legitimately market-based methods to transfer land-use rights. Nevertheless, the great majority of land transferred for industrial use prior to 2002 was "sold" through prior agreements with buyers [collusion] for very low prices. [That is, local-government officials were in business with, or essentially the same as, those buying the land.]

Source: Wang Hui and Tao Ran, *Reform of China's Land System: Degree of Difficulty, Breakthroughs, and Policy Portfolio*, Beijing: Commercial Press, 2013.

Third, income from any sale of land is unequally distributed among stakeholders. China's current principle with respect to how the increase in the value of land should be distributed is that farmers should receive compensation that is a certain multiple of their annual agricultural earnings from that land.[1] This equation results in inequities, however. When land is converted to new uses, the incremental value derived from a sale goes to the local government for its own use and allocation. The future incremental value of using the land and enjoying its appreciation goes mostly to the new owner, but a portion also goes to the local government. At the same time, only a small percentage of the value received by the local government is spent on rural construction. Between 2008 and 2010, the percentage of income received by local governments that was spent on *urban* construction every year came to an average of 58.76 percent (66.27 percent in

2008, 48.64 percent in 2009, and 61.65 percent in 2010). During the same period, the percentage spent on *rural* construction came to an average of 9.52 percent (10.18 percent, 8.39 percent, and 9.91 percent). The principle by which China currently allows income off land sales to be distributed creates a severely unequal situation among different parties.

Fourth, China's current system of land management enables different parties to have mutually conflicting objectives, and it lacks defined authorities and therefore accountability. After the *Law on Land Management* was amended in 1998, China began to implement a "land-use control system," and it also began to apply an overall planning method for land use. Any use of agricultural land for construction purposes after it was converted to nonagricultural land was subject to the restrictions of the overall plan of the relevant urban area. In reality, however, the overall plan of the relevant urban area was subject only to soft constraints. The provisions of the central government with respect to the permitting process for land quotas at the local level were ineffective. (Such quotas determine the amount of construction-use land that can be allocated every year.) The result has been the unabated appearance of corruption and rent-seeking. Incidents in which local governments broke the law and disregarded regulations proliferated.[2] The conflicts of interest and lack of a responsible party to deal with the problems had the effect of totally undermining the legitimacy and effectiveness of the land system.

In light of these problems, the system needs to be changed. Its complexities and difficulties are growing by the day. This is, of course, an extremely large project, but it concerns the long-term interests of the entire rural population, as well as the social and economic development of the entire country. The starting point for reforming China's land system, as well as the principle to which it must remain anchored, must be "protecting the rights and interests of China's rural people." In the process of implementing reform, the emphasis must be on "ensuring equal rights, opening up market access, and distributing rewards fairly." In reforming the land system, the objective is to establish a system that grants equal rights to land that is held under the two different forms of ownership, that enables a unified market for land, and that enables fairness or equality in the returns from an increased value of land. By so doing, the intent is to transform the way land is utilized and the country's current mode of economic growth.

The most striking problem of the current land system is the lack of adequately defined property rights and functions as related to land and particularly to rural land. Most problems stem from the ambiguity about ownership of rights and interests when it comes to land and from the vagueness of definitions concerning land rights and land functions. These things lead to unequal access to property markets among different players, unfair distribution of the returns from land, conflicts of interest among entities that administer land, and lack of accountability given inadequately defined functions of those entities. The most critical step in reforming the land system in the future, therefore, will be addressing this lack of clarity. Rectifying the ambiguities and lacunae, however, will depend on clearly delineating the entities that hold property rights and accurately defining the full range of what is meant by those property rights.

2. Pushing forward on the reform of the property-rights [ownership] system that governs rural land in China by undertaking the critical step of confirming and certifying ownership rights

The centerpiece of reforming China's land system involves defining property rights to land and protecting property rights to land. This is a necessary precondition as land resources begin to be allocated through market processes as opposed to government determinations. The starting point in delineating property rights over land is a land registration system, that is, a system that confirms and certifies property rights over all different categories of land.

As a basic prerequisite for ensuring that the rights and interests of farmers are protected, the confirmation and certification of rights involve three main types of land, namely agricultural land, land under "homesteads" or residential-use land, and construction-use land owned by collectives. In terms of rights confirmation and certification, the most important of these is agricultural land, that is, the land contracted by farmers.

The evolution of "rights confirmation and certification"

The process of confirming and certifying rights to land began after the rural household contract responsibility system was introduced, after the start of reform and opening up [1978]. Starting from the Third Plenary Session of the 11th CPC Central Committee, China's rural areas began to promote the idea of linking agricultural production to households, using a contractual system. Farming methods that had previously relied on the collective and that was based on the assumption that "the bigger the better and the more public the better" gradually changed and now became based on the individual household. A two-tiered operating system was then put in place that was based on household contracts but supplemented by centralized controls. [In Chinese, this was referred to in shorthand as the combination of centralized and dispersed.] In terms of ownership rights, rural land still belonged to the collective. Under that premise, farmers received contractual operating rights to farm the land.

Problems soon emerged. They involved land distributions, the inefficiency of decentralized operations, and the questionable legality and propriety of having larger and more professional "households." As a result, in 1984, the central government issued a Number One document that reassured farmers by stipulating that their contracts over land had a fifteen-year term. In the early and mid-1990s, when the second round of contracts was under way, the term was extended for another thirty years. In 1998, the Third Plenary Session of the 15th CPC Central Committee adopted a Decision called *Decision of the Central Committee of the Party on Various Important Issues Regarding Agriculture and Rural Work*. This explicitly stated that farmers were being granted "long-term, protected, usage rights to land." This was then later confirmed by the *Law on Land Contracts* of 2002, which stated that "by law, the State safeguards the long-term stability of rural land-contract relationships." In October, 2008, the Central Committee put forth another Decision called *Decision on Various Major Issues to Do with Advancing Rural Reform and Development*. The phrasing having to do with contracted land-use rights was changed from terms that indicated they would not change "for a long time" to terms that said they would not change "in perpetuity" or "permanently." This further stabilized farmers' operating rights to land, therefore also allowing them to transfer those operating rights through a variety of different methods.

As the practice of contracting for land began to be implemented on a widespread basis, the need to define and certify ownership rights over land became obvious. In 1986, Article 9 of the *Law on land management* stipulated that land owned by collectives was to be registered and kept on record by the people's government at the *county* level. Certificates were to be issued certifying the ownership. This law was amended in 1998. On the basis of the existing regulations, the amended law went further in explicitly stating that land under the ownership of farmers' collectives that was, as per the law, being used for nonfarming purposes, was to be registered and put on record by the county-level people's government. Certificates were to be issued that confirmed usage rights for construction purposes.

The actual state of affairs in the process of confirming and certifying rights to land

The main task at the present stage of confirming and certifying rights to land is to take the next step in the second round of contracting land-use rights. That is, on the basis of the second-round contracts and certifications, it is to confirm rights and certificates as based on actual surveys and measurements [mapping] of land area. Certification ensures four different "tallies": the contracted extent of land [physical area], the contract itself, the register that confirms operating rights over the land, and the certificate confirming operating rights over the land. It makes sure that all four conform to one another. In addition, it ensures that four documents are properly executed and "actually reach the household" in terms of confirmed rights. These cover "allocation" of the land, boundary surveys and maps, the land contract itself, and the certificate confirming operating rights to the land. As per law, these four then endow farmers with operating rights to land, and they safeguard those rights with adequate protections, thereby helping to dispel farmers' concerns. Since this initiative safeguards the contracted rights and interests of farmers, is aligned with their common aspirations, and supports their livelihood, its impact should be as far-reaching as the earlier reform regarding rural taxes and fees.

The task of confirming rights and issuing certificates is highly complex, given that it makes adjustments in the rights and interests of rural people [farmers]. In actual implementation, it involves more than just accurate measurement of land areas and locations. It also involves defining the term of contracts, defining the status of people's membership in collective organizations, and defining the extent or boundaries of that collective's authority. All of these things lack crisply definable standards. On top of all this, the rapid exodus of the rural population and slow progress in household registration reform has added to the difficulties of confirming rights and issuing certificates. Although relevant laws and regulations do exist, progress to date has not been satisfactory. Surveys have been conducted on the various policies introduced between 2004 and 2013 on rights confirmation and certification, and the results have been evaluated. Among the ninety-eight counties that were surveyed, pilot programs to "confirm and certify" were carried out in only twenty-nine counties, that is, in 29.6 percent of the total. At the same time, in fifty-two villages that had indeed carried out and completed the process of confirming rights and issuing certificates, close to 40 percent had registered ownership rights in the name of the administered village, and not in the name of the farmers collective. This kind of "overall type of registration" was indeed authorized by the relevant authorities but was not meaningful in addressing the whole point of the process (Liao Hongle and Li Jian, 2014).

There are many practical as well as historical causes for the slow implementation of the process. First, in terms of the practicalities, when land was allocated for the second round of land-use contracts, allocations were based on two considerations, the quality of the land, as defined by "good, medium, or poor," and the distance one had to go to farm the land, as defined by "near, or far away." This new certification requires more specificity. It requires knowing the precise area of each piece of land and its boundaries and location. The work and difficulties involved are enormous. What's more, since taxes and fees were fairly onerous in the early period of the second round of contracting, some farmers simply gave up their contracts and operating rights. Second, the costs of administering the process are high. China currently has 135 million hectares of farmland [1 hectare = 2.471 acres, so 135 million hectares = 333.58 million acres; for comparative purposes, the figure for the U.S. is roughly 938 million acres]. To cover the entire area, China will need to issue an estimated 230 million contracts and survey nearly 1 billion plots of farmland. The numbers and costs involved are staggering. Third, many pilot programs under way in the country are actually taking a wait-and-see attitude. The psychology involves performance on small things but foot-dragging on any serious action. In some pilot program counties, officials evade conflicts by putting aside disputes and waiting for higher levels of authority to figure out what to do. This undermines the whole point of having a pilot program. Meanwhile, costs are an issue. At present, the whole process is being funded by local governments, with subsidies to be provided by the central government as needed. Some local authorities are therefore playing for time, thinking that the early birds may be losers while the late achievers get the subsidies.

After the 18th National Party Congress, China began taking more forceful action to carry out land rights confirmation and certification. The central government issued a Number One document in 2013 that specified that the process was to be completed within five years on a nationwide basis. A Number One document issued in 2014 further accelerated the process and included residential-use land in the surveys that were to be undertaken on land rolls. It also included collectively owned construction-use land in the land rights that were to be confirmed, registered, and certified. In November, 2014, an Opinion was printed and issued called

Opinions on Guidance Measures for the Orderly Transfer of Operating Rights to Land, and for Developing Appropriate Economies of Scale in Farming Operations. This highlighted the importance of the rights confirmation process in stabilizing the situation of land contracts in rural areas. Confirming, registering, recording, and certifying rights over land will be a key part of the "foundation work" in enabling the transfer of operating rights to land. This document also specified that, in principle, the confirmation of and registration of contracted operating rights to land should be at the household level [i.e., not in the name of the village collective, as in the case just cited].

Confirming rights and issuing certificates: methods by which this should be done in the future

From this analysis, it is not hard to see that the process of confirming rights and issuing certificates with respect to land use in China is still at the pilot program stage. Given highly complex reasons, this is true despite forceful action on the part of government policy. Meanwhile, the process of confirming rights over residential-use land is even more delayed. The goal of the process is to safeguard explicitly defined property rights on the basis of an improved land registration system. On the one hand, the process aims to eliminate the way in which the registration and ownership of resources are still being determined by government departments [officials] who may make their own decisions on allocations. This is facilitated by the way ownership of collectively owned land is unclear, rights associated with such land are imperfectly defined, and safeguards are inadequate. On the other hand, the aim is to allow the market to play the decisive role in allocating land resources. This is to be achieved by formulating effective policies, laws, and regulations, improving authorities and functions relating to land, and granting equal protection to those holding contracts to land, according to law.

Circumstances vary enormously over China's rural territory. Ways in which land is used also vary significantly, in terms of contractual farming practices, homestead land use, and land used for construction purposes that is owned by collectives. There cannot be one standardized method by which rights are confirmed, and certificates are issued nationwide. Under the overall guidance of national "opinions," measures should be taken that are appropriate to the specific circumstances. Moreover, as already noted, rural land adjustments affect not only the fundamental rights and interests and long-term well-being of farmers and are not just about land, but they affect the massive changes that are occurring in rural society and rural governance. It is of ultimate importance, therefore, to ensure the fairness, transparency, and equal treatment of the process. All stakeholders must have plenty of opportunity to express themselves in ways that protect the equal right to be heard. On the basis of full and sufficient discussion, all sides should then come to consensus. This too is a necessary part of the process of ensuring that the confirmation of rights and issuing of certificates for land is carried out properly.

3. Actively promoting the transferability of contractual operating rights to farmland

In 2009, results of the second national land survey in China indicated that the country has a total of 135 million hectares of farmland (2,030 million *mu*, or 334 million acres). Per capita, the figure is 0.101 hectares (1.52 *mu*, or roughly one-quarter of one acre). This is less than half of the world's average. The system of contracting rights to operate land has become the basic institutional arrangement by which land is "managed" in the countryside. On the one hand, this system allows the contracting farmer the right to "occupy, use, gain benefit from, and transfer land management rights to" the land. On the other hand, the system allows rural households and also "new-type operating entities" the right to farm the land but also to use the contracted rights as collateral for loans. This makes it more convenient for farmland to be used efficiently and for it to be circulated [bought and sold] within a wider scope. It therefore promotes agricultural development and modernization.

Basic features of the existing system of contracting operating rights to farmland

The system currently in place can be defined by three characteristics.

First, land in rural areas is under collective ownership. This is the most important institutional legacy to come down from the movement that organized rural land into cooperatives in China. After reforms, collective ownership has meant the following: rural households and the collective maintain a contractual relationship with each other; collective organizations hold the right to contract the land and to handle it in general; those using the land may not buy or sell it. Each member of the collective has an equal opportunity to access usage rights to land and also to share in the benefits from converting agricultural land into other purposes.

Second, rural households also have property rights to land. The most important systemic aspect of rural reform is that it bestows land rights on rural household contractors, and, through protecting these property rights, it provides incentives to improve agricultural production and allows for more stable expectations about ongoing systems. Land rights have constantly been firmed up in recent years by clarifying and consolidating the status of rural households and by stabilizing the terms of the contractual relationships (the contract period was extended from fifteen to thirty years, and policies ensured that relationships remain unchanged). Policies have also clarified that the transfer of land-use rights must be based on the household, which makes rural households "own" the land in a more material sense.

Third, household-based operations are the primary mode of agricultural production. This mode of operating has replaced the mode based on production teams in the period of collectivization. It is one of the important achievements of rural institutional reform. This mode of operating is determined by the natural qualities of agriculture and the specific demands of agricultural labor. With support from preferential policies of the government, which benefit agriculture, the area of land farmed under household contracting has steadily increased.

Main issues confronting the current system of contracting operating rights to farmland

The existing system has played a positive role over the past thirty-some years by contributing to such things as increased agricultural production, the release of surplus rural labor from the countryside, and overall social and economic development in rural areas. In recent years, however, the massive outflow of people from the countryside, particularly younger and middle-aged people, has meant that a system based on the household unit is facing increasingly grave challenges. In overall terms, the existing system is facing problems that are clustered in the following three categories.

First, land that is contracted by rural households is small in terms of the size of fields. Land is the most basic production factor for farmers. In the early stage of reform, when it was contracted out to rural households, the process was done mainly on the basis of population, in what was called an "equal field system." This was to guarantee equality and minimize conflicts. The land was divided into different grades by quality, and each level of quality was then divided up equally among villagers, so as to make sure that each member of a given collective organization had some land from each level. This meant that a given area of land might be divided into many small plots, and also that each household might have plots that are located in different places. With ongoing growth of the local population, farmland then became more and more fragmented.

Second, the system that protects rights is applied to a situation in which the right to have a contract over specified land and the right to operate that land are, *de facto*, now two separate things. China's current operative laws say explicitly that the contracted operating rights to the land of rural people are protected. However, this wording unifies the two things into one. In the context of rapid industrialization and urbanization, these two things have in fact divided into two separate aspects of land rights. Laborers who are gone for many years in order to work elsewhere, as well as rural people who own homes in cities, still possess their contractual right to certain plots of land, but they do not operate that land. The conceptual approach of the law, with its inclusive term "contracted operating rights to land," presents difficulties when it comes to the realities of enforcement [that is, upholding a household's "rights" when that household is no longer present in the village and the land is taken for other uses.]

Third, the injection of industrial and commercial capital into the equation has brought on new problems, and the modernization of agriculture may bring more and more of such capital into rural areas. In this process, it is going to be a massive challenge for rural policies to try to meet several objectives at once, namely protecting the rights of individual members of the collective, protecting the right to operate the land, encouraging the transfer of rural land, and achieving agricultural modernization (see Box 3.2).

Box 3.2 Industrial and commercial capital being invested in rural areas

At present, industrial and commercial enterprises are extending their presence into rural areas in two ways. They are engaging in agricultural production directly as well as indirectly. The well-known Sanjiu Enterprise Group [Three Nine] is an example of the first way. It has entered into the agricultural sector through a variety of means, including direct investment, cooperation, mergers and acquisitions, and asset restructuring. It has already purchased or merged with more than twenty listed companies, and it owns control shares of companies with assets that total RMB 1.2 billion. It has built up relationships with 300,000 rural households. Indirect participation is exemplified by the joint establishment of the Dili Group by the foreign investment firms Blackstone Group of America and the Million Summits Holdings Ltd. Company of Hong Kong, among others. Although Blackstone later sold its stake in the Dili Group in 2011, the aim of this had been to rely on wholesale markets such as China's Shouguang Agricultural Products Logistics Park in developing a wholesale and logistical network for vegetables and other agricultural products across China.

Investment of such kinds of capital into China's agricultural sector can lead directly to certain problems. One is that it may cause local governments to force farmers to relinquish their rights over contracted land, since local governments favor land transfers that are on a larger scale. Another is that land may increasingly be put to purposes that are not agricultural and specifically not for grain production. The focus of capital that invests in agriculture is generally on the higher returns that come from secondary and tertiary industries. As agriculture moves into secondary industries, it requires the building of industrial facilities, which then become industrial parks as well as tourist sites for various kinds of "eco" tourism. The problem with this is that land increasingly is put to uses other than agricultural.

Source: Zhang Xiaoshan, *Economic and Social Development in Rural Areas: Outstanding Problems and Solutions* (Background report), 2014.

General principles regarding future reform of the land management system

Laws and policies with respect to land management to date have concentrated on the farmers' right to contract for and operate land. That is, they have emphasized the protection of farmers' "farming" rights and have therefore strengthened their rights to use and benefit from the land. They have not sufficiently focused on other rights, however. One of these is the right to use land as collateral when taking out loans or mortgages. As a right to material property, land contracting rights should encompass a complete set of rights. As already noted, however, the system currently in operation in China combines the two separate rights of contracting for land and operating land. Given that situation, there are major risks inherent in extending the rights to mortgage land and to use it as collateral. Meanwhile, the deficiencies in the current setup of how rights and functions are defined also have delayed China's ability actually to extend such rights. A second kind of property right that has not been addressed is that of inheritance rights, or the ability to pass land to the next generation. Current laws and policies do not address this issue, even though generational shift is occurring in many farming families. In the next stage of reform, improving the handling of these two kinds of rights is an urgent imperative.

In terms of specific ways to start the process, we may want to begin by moving forward the process of "confirming rights and issuing certificates" and pushing forward the ability to transfer contracted land-use rights via a market.

The process of "confirming rights and issuing certificates" must abide by principles that have been noted, which include adopting measures to suit specific circumstances; being equal, fair, and transparent in all dealings; and introducing a process of negotiated settlement by all concerned parties. Concrete steps might begin in the following three areas. First, speed up the process of creating a comprehensive register of land, or what is called a cadastre. [Note: A cadastre, using a cadastral survey, is a comprehensive register of the real property of a country. It is the official register of the ownership, extent, and value of real property in a given area.] This involves clarifying the legitimate ownership, establishing clear boundaries, area, and using every plot of land in rural areas. It involves collating survey results according to a unified way of coding land so as to come up with land-register results that are dependable. It also involves researching and then passing nationwide "guiding policy opinions that will serve as the [political] basis for confirming rights and issuing certificates." Second is the need to integrate two sets of data, the "basic farmland protection" data and surveys and mapping data; to integrate the results of the "second national survey on land and resources" and the "ledger of the second round of penalties" in order to create a digital scale map; and to overlay the pattern and confirm the legitimacy of contractual land-use rights and certificates. Third, with respect to collectively owned land, the level to which "rights" are confirmed (that is, all the way to the members of the collective or just to the collective as a whole) must be evaluated. This should be determined by members of each collective economic organization at the village and group levels. The resolution of issues should be determined by democratic negotiations according to both past considerations and the actual current situation. Ultimately, each member of each collective economic organization should have a clear idea of his lawful rights. This then serves as the basis for exercising those rights according to law.

After the completion of confirming rights and issuing certificates, the effective way to resolve current problems relating to agricultural land will be to push forward a market-based system for transferring land usage rights [that is, allowing the sale of contracted operating rights to land]. Some places have already achieved a measure of success in doing this (see Box 3.3). Moving forward, we can combine the existing experience in various places to develop a network of services and management expertise in marketing land usage rights. This will contribute to the monitoring of prices, land areas, and the usage of land under consideration. It will encourage service providers involved in land-use transfers to improve systems relating to land productivity appraisals, escrow services, information disclosure, and price estimates.

Box 3.3 Developing a market in Shanghai for the transfer of contracted operating rights to land

Shanghai has set up a market for contracted operating rights to rural land that is already functioning in a normal fashion. This has been done on the basis of confirming or renewing the second round of contracts for rural land and stabilizing those relationships. Given that farmers have guaranteed long-term usage rights to land, this process actively explores ways to protect the legitimate rights and interests of those who hold the contracts to rural land.

According to an official with the Shanghai Municipal Agriculture Commission, Shanghai has now completed the work begun in 2009 to stabilize and improve upon work relating to the extension and confirmation of second-round contracting. This work has involved 1,113 villages in the ninety-seven townships that are engaged in agriculture in nine of Shanghai's districts and counties. By the end of November, 2011, 99.68 percent of land-usage contracts had been signed, and 99.44 percent of the associated rights had been certified.

The market-enabling transfer [purchase and sale] of these rights is now in operation through seventy-four "township transfer administration and service centers" set up to handle the business. These centers basically cover all agricultural areas in Shanghai. Each center is staffed with three to five administrative personnel, and each village has designated a person to serve as an information channel. The process is intended to guide and regulate the transfer of land-use rights. The intent is gradually to form market mechanisms and administrative services that allow for the fair, transparent, and equal-access transfer of land-use rights.

According to the official with the Shanghai Municipal Agriculture Commission, Shanghai has also now set up a system for managing documentation on land-use contracts and transfer of those contracts that standardizes the collection and filing of records. This serves to ensure the authenticity, accuracy, and completeness of records so that the entire process of land contracting and transferring of contracts can "stand up to the test of time." Pilot programs on registering land-use rights are under way in eleven villages in nine townships of the Jinshan and Fengxian districts.

Source: "Developing the Market for the Transfer of Contracted Land-Use Rights in Shanghai," January 19, 2012. www.xinhuanet.co.

A secondary market in land-use rights that enables leasing, granting rights to others, and mortgaging is an important part of the overall land market. It will play a key role in realizing the ability to raise funds through using land as collateral and thereby in using land more efficiently and intensively. Nurturing the secondary market in land-use rights will involve three considerations. The first is actually setting up a tangible market [a real market] for land. That means allowing such land-use rights as are appropriate for a market to be transferred, leased, and mortgaged in ways that are open and public. It means providing a variety of services that ensure that the market for land is operated on a consistent basis [unified or standardized], regulated, and carried out properly. The second involves strengthening legislation having to do with a secondary market, clarifying definitions of land-use rights, and regulating the transfer of those rights. At the national level, the State should set up a system of laws that is aimed specifically at a secondary market in land and should provide regulatory and policy support as necessary for the sound functioning of a secondary market in land. The third involves improving rules relating to transactions, including information disclosure and administrative services, so that the secondary market for land can develop in a vigorous way.

4.   Reforming the management system that governs rural homestead sites ["residential-use land"]

The term *homestead site* refers to the land on which rural housing is built. The system governing this specific kind of land is an important component of China's rural land system. In the sixty-five years since the establishment of New China [1949], this system underwent changes that were similar to those affecting the contracted land-use system but that also saw differences in institutional arrangements. Changes now affecting rural social and economic development, including the outflow of population from rural areas, now present challenges to the homestead-site system and dictate the need for reform.

Basic characteristics of the existing system

Since the founding of New China, land under homestead sites in rural China has gone through systemic changes that included a shift from private to collective ownership. The system governing such land as it exists today includes the following three main characteristics.

First, homestead sites [the land under rural residential land] are held under a system of collective ownership. This means that rural households must obtain "usage rights" to that land by going through the rural [village] committee [Party committee]. When the rural household is no longer using such land, the Committee may "take it back." When land under rural residences is being "reorganized" or when quotas for such land are being traded [or transferred], the primary entity involved is also the village committee. Because of this, with respect to ownership rights for land under rural residences and with respect to usage of such land, collective organizations are not merely the primary entities involved in a legal sense, but they possess very real power to dominate and control the allocation of such rights.

Second, rural households hold "ownership rights" over their actual houses. China has kept to this idea that rural houses are owned by rural people for a long time and has protected the right of rural people [farmers] to buy and sell, lease, mortgage, pledge, or otherwise transfer their rights to their actual homes. Neither the government nor collective organizations may infringe upon these rights. This concept of home ownership is firmly embedded in the minds of rural people as well.

Third, rural homestead sites have two more qualities: they may be used for free but only by those who qualify for the status of membership. That is, only members of the collective economic organization are qualified to apply for receiving them; nonmembers are unable to receive such land. If one is a member, one may receive such residential land for no compensation. Since the rights associated with rural residential land only include "occupation rights" and "usage rights," however, non-members are unable to obtain such land via a transaction or transfer process. Under the system currently implemented in China, the practice is "one household one home." Once a farmer gives up his home, therefore, he cannot apply to receive another. Because of this, farmers also cannot transfer the land under their homes to nonmembers of the collective economic organization.

Problems with existing policies regarding rural homestead sites [the land under rural residences]

The principle behind collective ownership of rural residential land is something that arose in China during the period of "people's collectives" in the 1960s. Since the start of reform and opening up, systems governing such land have constantly improved to the extent that a fairly complete structure of "rights" is now in place. However, the very real conflicts between the long-standing household registration system and the mass exodus of people from the countryside brought on by rapid urbanization have meant that the existing homestead-site system is under severe challenges. Those challenges include the following.

First, the transfer of homestead sites is a universal practice despite policies restricting such transfer. In legal terms, nobody has the authority to lease, trade, or transfer residential land; in actual fact, a market in homesteads via hidden transactions is a growing and robust trend. This market is particularly notable in areas surrounding cities and in more developed regions and takes the form of the leasing and straight buying and selling of housing, as well as "cooperative building of housing." Market demand for transfers of homestead land is considerable. To a degree, this process has lowered the costs of urbanization in China and has helped urbanization and industrialization by increasing incomes for former occupants of the housing and providing living places for newcomers in cities. However, this kind of spontaneous market activity is also in direct conflict with China's existing laws (see Box 3.4).

Box 3.4   The controversy over "housing that enjoys limited property rights"

The new conclusions of the Third Plenary Session of the 18th CPC Central Committee on the issue of collectively owned land in rural areas have generated a new wave of controversy. This involves the question of whether or not housing that currently enjoys limited property rights should be legalized.

This term *housing that enjoys limited property rights* refers to newly built housing on land that was sold to people who are not part of a given village. Such land was originally rural residential or vacant land that was collectively owned. It was built upon with the understanding that the needs of legitimate village residents were already being met. Buildings [housing] constructed on such land receive property rights certificates that are issued by the village committee. Nevertheless, unlike buildings constructed on State-owned land, these buildings cannot be used as collateral for mortgages or loans. When sold, the payment must be in one lump sum and cannot be made in installments.

Two different points of view have been presented with respect to this kind of limited-rights housing.

Those opposed to the building of limited-rights housing include the Ministry of Housing and Urban–Rural Development, the Beijing Municipal Bureau of Land and Resources, and such people as Ren Zhiqiang an Hua Sheng. Their opinion is that such housing is illegal and should not be made legal. Moreover, projects currently under way or in planning stages should be stopped. Projects currently built should either be torn down, or the usage rights of the original owners of the household sites should be protected, while supplementary measures should be taken to confirm their rights.

Those in favor of the building of limited-rights housing include professors Zhou Qiren, Sheng Hong, and Hu Xingdou. They believe that relevant laws should be amended and improved upon such that limited-rights housing is accorded legal protection.

The two sides base their opinions on the following evidence.

Those opposing: (1) Limited-rights housing has no standing in existing laws, and the functions of administrative departments handling such housing do not include the issuing of relevant certificates. Such housing therefore does not possess a right to legal protection that is equivalent to protections afforded to normal housing. (2) Such housing is being developed and built solely on the initiative of rural collectives without going through permitting and approval procedures. This will therefore lead to an increasing loss of land and particularly a decrease in arable land. (3) Most buyers of such housing are urban residents. This means that resources are being snatched away from rural people.

Those supporting: (1) Limited-rights housing exists in a gray area of law, an area that operates by the principle that things are allowable if not explicitly forbidden. Limited-rights housing has not actually broken any laws. (2) According to Article 62 of the *Law on Land Administration*, once rural people either sell or rent out their housing, they are not allowed to apply for or receive further homestead-site land. By implication, this means that rural people do indeed have the right to sell their own homes. (3) Developing limited-rights housing has enormously positive consequences when it comes to rural development and economic growth, which also contributes to lifting rural people out of poverty as quickly as possible. (4) From the standpoint of making property rights "equal" among people, limited-rights housing should be accorded the same rights as other housing. (5) Legalizing limited-rights housing has major implications for "power for money transactions" in real estate [that is, officials granting permits in return for personal financial gain] and for curbing corruption. (6) Legitimizing limited-rights housing will play an indispensable role in alleviating the social conflicts being caused by housing shortages and excessive housing prices.

In October, 2014, China's Ministry of Land and Resources completed a pilot program plan for reforming the country's systems governing rural homestead sites. Although the plan allows for transfers of residential land in various ways, including leasing, shareholding structures, and straight sale among others, it places strict limits on the people who can be involved. Transfers of ownership must occur within the membership of a given collective economic organization. This implies that the ability of urban residents to purchase housing, including limited-rights housing, in rural areas is still within "forbidden territory in terms of laws and policies."

Source: Wang Debang, *The Issue of Limited-Rights Housing: A Commentary*. http://www.aisixiang.com/data/76098.html; http://www.js.xinhuanet com/2014–10/26/c_1112979228.

The first challenge facing the homestead system therefore has to do with the universal practice of the transfer of homestead sites, despite policies restricting such transfers. The second has to do with the difficulties of actually administering the policy of allowing each household to receive one home for free. This policy has essentially not been followed since the mid- to late 1990s in coastal parts of China and in areas surrounding major cities. Differentials in land prices have soared with increasing urbanization. Land for urban construction has become more difficult to come by, leading to the capitalization of land assets. Uncompensated allocation of housing in these areas has become a thing of the past. Meanwhile, it has also become more difficult to make sure that each household has only one homestead in urbanizing areas. As land has become more obviously valuable, farmers have used their existing homesteads to the maximum and then also built additional housing outside their originally allocated homestead area. Some have built housing that goes well beyond the per capita living areas mandated by provincial and municipal authorities. What's more, despite the fact that the practice is not conducive to conserving arable land, traditional farming areas are continuing to allocate homestead-site land to people for free. Another problem relates to the building of larger homes back in the home town when rural workers have earned sufficient income in cities to afford such homes. Instead of building merely on their originally allocated homestead site, they are now building on top of contracted agricultural land. This has led to a massive loss of arable land in agricultural regions, particularly in the central China plains area.

Third, "usufruct rights" [the limited legal right to use something that belongs to another] are incompletely defined so that it is difficult for owners of homestead-site property to participate in any increase in the value of their land. According to the *Property Law*, the usage rights of farmers to homestead sites are explicitly defined as usufruct rights. Central-government policies and documents have repeatedly emphasized the safeguarding of these rights, which include the right to possess, the right to use, and the right to benefit from homesteads. The first two are endowed with actual legal protections, but the last is not. Clearly, in legal terms a contradiction exists with respect to usufruct rights that then leads to the frequent practice of "overlooking" and infringing upon farmers' rights in this regard. The problem is particularly severe in areas that are undertaking relocations of people in order to reorganize village designations, concentrate populations, or "swap" homestead sites for apartments. In these instances, farmers generally receive new housing as compensation, but they fail to share in the increased income from their old land. Their old land is now newly designated as "construction-use land" and transferred to others (Zhang Yunhua et al., 2011).

Fourth, the chaotic expansion of homestead sites is not conducive to a sound process of urbanization. Since the actual situation is at such odds with the legality of the situation, the government faces the problem of having nobody who can be held accountable, nobody "in charge." It becomes impossible to implement urban plans and to control actual usage of land. In the absence of government regulations and control, homestead-site sprawl is rampant. In addition, the "villages-within-cities" phenomenon has involved unauthorized construction of buildings in urban areas that lack any kind of planning. These places are characterized by inadequate public facilities, a lack of governing structures, and serious public security issues. They present an entirely different aspect as compared to other parts of a city. They add to the costs of municipalities and will be extremely hard to remove or renovate in the future. In recent years, some rural areas have begun to revoke villages and achieve more intensive use of land by concentrating populations in residential areas. The aim has been to tie together increases of construction-use land in one area with decreases in another so as to use land more effectively. In this regard it has achieved a measure of success, but problems remain (see Box 3.5).

**Box 3.5   The shift of rural homesteads and the policy
of tying together land increases and decreases**

In recent years, local governments have attempted to make it possible to "shift" rural homestead sites by "tying together increases and decreases in land." What this means is that a given area restores what had been defined as "rural construction-use land," including homestead-site land, to farmland, by shifting and consolidating populations and by redefining village boundaries. After doing this, a neighboring municipal or county government can add to its annual allotment of land by requisitioning an equivalent amount of farmland from areas surrounding the city that have been vacated. These areas are then used for urban and industrial construction. The idea is to keep the total amount of construction land from increasing dramatically by reducing the amount previously held within rural areas and reallocating it to urban areas. This helps satisfy the need for land to undertake urban development. It helps achieve the objective of conserving farmland while also ensuring the supply of land for industrialization and urbanization.

In practice, however, it is easy for problems to arise in the course of implementing this policy. This is due to the way deep-seated contradictions in China's existing land management structures and land system remain unresolved. For example, local governments are keenly eager to increase their land allocations, making it hard for them to respect the principle of farmers' self-determination [i.e., local governments engage in forced land requisitions]. The public spending that is involved also leads to high levels of financial risk.

In September of 2014, China's Ministry of Land and Resources issued *Guiding Opinions on promoting land conservation and more intensive use of land*. Through overall top-down planning of reorganized land use, by linking increases and decreases in construction-use land in urban and rural areas and other such policy measures, these *Opinions* aimed at a more dynamic use of rural construction-use land. In any given township, the *Opinions* approved of adjustments in the geographic location of rural construction-use land. They noted, however, that the handling of the process is to be done at the provincial level of the Ministry of Land and Resources. Newly designated areas are to be incorporated in the provincial-level program that governs this linking endeavor.

Source: Liu Shouying, "*The Rural Land System and Building a Moderately Prosperous Society* (Background report); Hu Qifeng, "Promulgation of the Overall Plan for Conserving Land and Using Land More Intensively on a Nationwide Basis, *Guangming Daily*, September 26, 2014.

Measures for further reform of the rural homestead-site system in China in the future

The first measure is to clarify the bottom line in terms of safeguarding the property rights of farmers to usage and benefits from homestead sites, that is, the "real rights to usufruct." This "bottom line of the reform of China's homestead system" involves protecting the rights of rural households to occupy and use homestead sites. Ownership rights of homestead sites belong to the collective, while usage rights belong to rural households, but in reality collectives hold much greater authority and control over allocations, while laws and policies emphasize their rights much more than they emphasize the rights of farmers; in fact, therefore, it is easy for "ownership rights" to infringe upon the rights of usage. Because of this, as China's laws are revised, we recommend that China go further in clarifying and strengthening farmers' usage rights to their homestead sites, in accordance with the principle of usufruct rights to homesteads. At the same time, we should speed up our work on confirming rights and issuing certificates for rural homestead sites. On the basis of overall principles of usufruct, we should improve usufruct rights in legal terms with specific respect to household sites. On the basis of existing rights to possession and use, we should bestow the "right to benefit" and the "right to transfer" on people with homestead rights.

Second, reform the system by which homestead sites are allocated and traded [transferred]. Given a rural population that is increasingly leaving villages, the inadequacies of the existing system are obvious. Receiving homestead sites for free is detrimental to protecting farmland and using land more intensively; the "membership nature" of the requirements for holding homestead sites is not in line with villages and towns that are "breaking through" or changing existing borders or with a population that is increasingly urban mixed with rural; valuing homesteads as a property asset conflicts with the idea of a homestead as a "home." We recommend selecting pilot program sites in different kinds of areas, as experiments in reform of the homestead system. The emphasis should be put on requiring payment for receiving, withdrawing from, recovery of, transactions relating to, and circulation [transfers of] homestead sites. In this process, it will be necessary to break out of the confines of requiring membership in a given area and of defining the village community in terms of certain boundaries. The basic direction is to exchange what was a welfare-allocation form of rights for an asset form of property rights. It is to realize a situation whereby farmers have full usufruct rights with respect to homesteads, so as to promote more efficient use of land.

Third, push forward experiments that enable farmers' homes to be used as collateral for mortgages and that enable them to be transferred. Under the existing system, ownership rights of the land under homesteads belong to the collective, while usage rights belong to the rural household; ownership rights of the buildings on the homestead belong to the household. The system therefore involves three different kinds of rights. Since rights of ownership and those of usage do not enjoy the same degree of protection, it is highly likely that the collective organization will be the primary beneficiary if policies are changed to allow use of the underlying land as collateral and to allow transfers to others. Contrary to the desired results, this will infringe upon farmers' rights. In contrast, the homes of farmers are their own private property. These houses have always enjoyed protection under the law. Clarifying that farmers have the right to mortgage these houses, use them as collateral for loans, and transfer them to others will serve to ensure that farmers benefit from [the appreciation of] their asset. Naturally, implementation of this right can be tried only in certain areas first. The ability to use the underlying land of homesteads as collateral and the ability to transfer it can wait until conditions are suitable.

5. Models that explore putting collectively owned construction-use land on the market

Problems facing the systems that currently apply to collectively owned construction-use land in China

First, the total acreage of land devoted to collectively owned construction-use purposes in China is enormous, but in most cases the land is being used illegally. At present, many cities and their surrounding areas in China have massive amounts of such land that was formerly villages, abandoned plants, and obsolete properties. In Guangdong alone, such land occupies more than 3.6 million *mu* of territory. This is twelve times larger than the amount of land put into new construction in Guangdong every year. Similarly, according to surveys, Shenzhen currently has 917.77 square kilometers of construction-use land. Of this total, 390 square kilometers was formerly owned by rural collective economic organizations. Of the total, only 95 square kilometers is being used legally.

Second, most of the construction-use land owned by collectives is being developed in a chaotic fashion. Without the ability to be used as collateral, it cannot be used in a financing capacity. In contrast to State-owned land that is put to construction uses, collectively-owned construction-use land lacks legal guarantees. The principals carrying out the building are generally farmers who are operating on their own accord. They are developing in ways that are chaotic, fragmented, and dispersed, resulting in highly inefficient use of land. At the same time, China's existing *Law on Land Management* forbids using collectively-owned construction-use land as collateral for any kind of financing. This greatly lowers the value of the land in the market. It limits the ability of such land to be capitalized, and it raises barriers to entry for those wanting to access the market for collectively owned land.

Third, overall efficiencies are limited since collectively owned construction-use land is not incorporated into urban–rural planning. Laws and regulations that currently pertain to land planning and urban planning say that collectively owned land must first be turned into State-owned land via requisitions. Only then can it be incorporated into urban plans. Only then can the basic infrastructure of municipal governments be extended to towns and villages. The result has been that the industrialization of and building on collectively owned construction-use land are processes done without any planning whatsoever. Instead, the universal practice is to build at will, inasmuch as "rural people privately build housing at random." Collectively owned construction-use land is carved up into small parcels, greatly reducing any chances for economies of scale. At the same time, any plans that towns and villages devise themselves are seldom recognized or legitimized by the government. The result is that the costs of basic infrastructure in such places must be borne by the collective organization itself, which increases its fiscal burden.

Explore the possibility of putting collectively owned construction-use land on the market

In order to build a land market that is effective in unifying urban and rural areas and that allows for equal access, it is necessary to ensure that the rights pertaining to the two different kinds of ownership systems applying to land are equal in terms of protections. Both collectively owned land and State-owned land must be able to enter the market on equal terms. What this means is that, after confirming rights and issuing certificates for collectively owned construction-use land, we should explore ways to rationalize the distribution of benefits. In concrete terms, this involves the following two aspects.

First, set up a market for the sale of property rights pertaining to rural collectively owned business-type construction-use land. At the same time, set up a system for distributing the benefits of the gains in value from the land. The existing base of collectively owned construction-use land was derived mostly for free or at a very low cost. The usage rights associated with this land are in fact equivalent to administratively allocated usage rights. They simply retain the form of being collectively owned. Because of this, a comparison can be made to the way urban land, administratively allocated by the State, enters the market. Because of this, any collective construction-use land that is either of a business or a private nature and that is in rural areas and meets conditions for eligibility should be managed in the same way as allocated land in urban areas in terms of how it is handled. After the user of the land or the recipient of the transaction pays a certain standardized amount of the gains in land value, the recipient obtains usage rights to use the land and to lease, mortgage, and use it as equity shares while the collective still maintains collective ownership of the land. As for newly increased collectively-owned construction-use land, a policy-type tax should be levied on it according to standardized rates. The net yields from the transfer of collectively owned land should use the levels of State-owned transfers as reference, and, as collectively owned construction-use land enters the market, governments should collect a portion of the gains in land value according to unified standards. The administration of the gains in land value of collectively owned construction-use land should be handled in the same way as benefits from the paid use of State-owned land. Rural collective economic organizations should be the entities handling the transfer of land used by town-and-village enterprises, public welfare-related endeavors, and vacant land. To ensure fairness, the benefits from such transfers should accrue to the village collective once deductions are made of the gain in land value that go to governments. These funds should be incorporated in the village-level budget and used for designated purposes in a strictly regulated way (Zhang Xiaoshan and Li Zhou, 2008).

Second, set up a unified market for urban and rural construction-use land. Guide rural collectively owned construction-use land in the direction of being accessible to the market. In the process of circulating [buying and selling] collectively owned construction-use land, when the land is used either for public welfare initiatives set up by villagers' groups or is "newly added construction-use land," it should be managed as per land allocations that still retain collective ownership. Any land that was formerly rural residential-use land or that has been vacated through reorganizing villages in order to conserve land should first be restored to farmland. Any that is "adjusted" into construction-use land must comply with land-use regulations. It must be entered into construction-use land plans and must satisfy requirements for being given priority as collectively owned construction-use land.

Reform of China's rural land administration system must be tied into the system that governs the country's urban State-owned construction-use land. Urban and rural construction-use land must undergo coordinated reform, and the market for both types of land must be integrated. Rural land that is used for business purposes, such as for private enterprises in rural areas, should be gradually paid for. The paid-use system should gradually be applied to all new construction-use land in both urban and rural areas. "Newly added construction-use land" that is for public welfare initiatives set up by villagers' groups may be allocated for free, after the conversion of agricultural land into nonagricultural purposes is applied for and approved. It should then be registered in the catalogue of "administratively allocated land" in the same way as State-allocated land, and it should be managed in a centralized way.

Box 3.6   Administrative measures of Guangdong province regarding the circulation of rights to collectively owned construction-use land

In 2005, the provincial government of Guangdong province issued Decree Number 100, titled *Administrative Measures of Guangdong Province for the Transfer of Rights to the Use of Collectively Owned Construction-use Land*. Its purpose was to regulate [standardize] and promote the circulation of such rights via an orderly market in order to use land more rationally. [This Decree included the following stipulations.]

1. When land that is collectively owned by farmers is obtained for the purposes of nonagricultural construction, all relevant State industrial policies must be respected, in addition to local comprehensive land-use plans,

urban plans, village plans, and township plans. Any agricultural land that is being converted to construction use must abide by the annual quotas for land to be used only for agriculture.

2. Collectively owned construction-use land may not be transferred if any of the following conditions applies. (1) Such transfer does not comply with the comprehensive land-use plans of municipalities, towns and villages, and townships. (2) There is any dispute over the ownership rights to the land. (3) Judicial or administrative entities [organs] determine, as per law, that it is necessary to "seal off" or restrict land rights in any way. (4) The usage rights to the land are those for rural peoples' homesteads.

3. Collectively owned construction-use land that has been obtained via assignment, transfer, or leasing may not be used for real estate development of commodity housing or for housing developments [residential construction].

4. If the rights to collectively owned construction-use land are assigned, leased, or mortgaged, any infrastructure on the property and any other physical improvements will also be assigned, leased, or mortgaged at the same time. The collectively owned land-usage rights represented by these things will accompany the transfer of rights.

5. The assignment, leasing, or mortgaging of collectively own construction-use usage rights must be approved by two-thirds or more of the members of the relevant collective economic organization's villagers' committee or by two-thirds or more of the representatives of the village. Land that is collectively owned by the township or town is operated and administered by the collective economic organization of the township or town. In case there is no such collective organization, the people's government of the local jurisdiction will be responsible for operating and managing it.

6. The following construction projects may use collectively owned construction-purpose land: (1) all kinds of industrial and commercial enterprises, including State-owned, collectively owned, and privately owned, sole proprietorships, foreign-invested enterprises [including Sino-foreign joint ventures, Sino-foreign cooperative businesses, wholly foreign-owned entities, "three in one" entities that process raw materials, or assemble parts, or make products according to client's samples], shareholding companies, jointly operated enterprises, and so on; (2) public welfare endeavors including facilities and other public benefit undertakings; (3) entities that build housing for rural residents.

7. If the State requisitions the land in the interests of the public, or if it confiscates the land according to law, the owners of rural collective land and the users of rural construction-use land will comply with State requirements.

8. Any users of land must comply with the purposes to which the land is to be put as stipulated in regulatory documents issued by the relevant municipal and county people's governments on construction-use land. If alterations to land use must be made, they must first be approved by the

owners of the land and the administrative bodies in charge of plans for the area, and they must first be reported to the people's governments of the municipalities and counties in order to receive permission.

9. Income gained from the assignment, lease, or transfer of collectively owned land must be entered into the collective assets of the rural collective and administered in a unified way. At least 50 percent of such income should be deposited in a bank account (rural credit cooperative) that is specifically set up for the purpose and should then be used specifically for social security for members of the collective. These funds must not be diverted for any other purpose. Specific procedures are to be decided upon by the provincial social security department, together with relevant authorities from provincial agriculture, civil affairs, finance, and health departments. These specific measures are to be implemented after approval from the people's government at the provincial level.

10. When rights to the use of any collectively owned construction-use land are assigned, transferred, or leased, prices must be reported to the department in charge of land, and taxes must be paid on the transaction as per law. If the transaction has resulted in an increase in the value of the land, taxes on that increment must be paid to the people's government at the municipal and county levels, as per the same levels of taxation as required by the transfer of State-owned land. Administrative measures governing the collection, payment of, and use of the tax that is so derived shall be formulated by the finance department at the provincial level of government together with other government departments at the provincial level including the land and resources department and the provincial price bureau. Such measures will be implemented after being submitted for approval to the people's government at the provincial level.

Source: Guangdong Provincial People's Government.
http://www.gd.gov.cn/govpub/zfwj/zfxxgk/gz/200810/t20081006_69957.htm.

6. Deepening reform of the system that governs land requisitions [expropriations]

Since reform and opening up began, China has urbanized at an average rate of 1.2 percentage points every year, and this has led to a tremendous demand for land. Once a municipality's own allocation of construction-use land is not enough to meet the needs of urban expansion, the main way cities sustain urbanization has been to requisition neighboring rural land. Procedures for such requisitions have constantly been improved, but as of now the system has not given rural people adequate protections for their rights and interests. Indeed, any mechanisms for protecting such rights are far from being in place. In recent years, conflicts arising from requisitioned land have become the single major issue in rural social governance. In the future reform of China's land system, as we standardize and regulate the procedures for land requisitions, it is imperative that we include adequate legal protections for the rights and interests of rural people.

Main issues relating to China's system of requisitioning land

The first issue is the overly broad way in which the principle of "requisitioning in the interests of the public" is applied. Over the past sixty years, the *Constitution*, *Law on Land Management*, and amendments to those documents have all stipulated that land can be requisitioned only for purposes that serve the public interests. The only exception during this sixty-year period was in 1953, with the document called *Measures for Expropriating Land for Purposes of Building Up the Nation*. To this date, however, no law has clarified what is actually meant by "public interests." Nor has any law explicitly set forth the uses to which requisitioned land should be put or the allowable scope of such requisitions. This vagueness has made it easy for governments and those wanting to make use of land to take over rural collectively owned land via "requisitioning" it. It has created loopholes that enable public authorities to infringe upon private rights via ostensibly legal means. Not only does this violate the underlying rationale of the law, but it also is not in accord with the fundamental principles of a market economy.

The second issue relates to how compensation for requisitioned land is set at rates measured by the original use of that land. Since China lacks a market in land property rights, it also lacks a valid way to determine prices for such rights. When governments requisition land, therefore, they have not been able to compensate farmers by using actual land property values. In response to ongoing increases in demands from farmers, they have generally paid compensation that is based on multiples of the value of agricultural production from the land, and they have also been increasing the rates. Since there is no mechanism in place for compensating according to actual land values, however, the primary "relief" mechanism has been to relocate farmers and provide alternative housing for them together with alternative jobs. This way of providing a certain amount of "labor relief" in return for multiples of the agricultural return from the land is simply not a long-term solution. It does not guarantee the livelihood of farmers. It cannot provide adequate safeguards for people who have lost their land. As a result, social conflicts are intensifying. In response to this, some places are experimenting with ways to grant minimum living allowances to farmers whose land has been requisitioned (Huang Xiaohu, 2011).

Specific ways to deepen reform of the land requisitioning system

First, clarify the term "uses that are in the public interest" and reduce the scope within which land requisitioning can take place. According to the spirit of the *Constitution of the People's Republic of China*, land requisitions can take place only if they are in the public interest. The difficulties of defining "public interest" have meant that no catalogue or listing of land usage that is in the public interests has been set forth. Reform of the land requisitioning system should draw on the experience of a document regarding State-owned land that was put out in 2011, called *Regulations on Compensation for the Requisitioning of Buildings That Are on State-owned Land.* This enumerates each foreseeable public-interest use to which the land can be put. It thereby defines the scope of "public interests." Given that legislative bodies [organs] cannot anticipate everything when setting forth legislation that enumerates all possible uses that are in the public interest, they may leave room for expanding the list in ways that they deem appropriate in the future (Development Research Center of the State Council, and the World Bank, 2014).

In addition, land that is taken for building public infrastructure may still be taken by "requisitioning methods," but mechanisms must be set up to regulate and control these methods. The scope of *compensated* requisitions of State-owned land should be increased, while "administrative allocations" of land for nonpublic purposes should be reduced. The practice of requiring compensation for land usage should start from the types of land use that will be commercially profitable. This includes basic infrastructure projects that are "reform-suitable" and any municipal projects or social endeavors that will be used for business purposes. For example, within municipal planning zones, where the demand for construction-use land is enormous and in areas where the incremental increase in value of land is high, an experimental approach would be to allow the government preferential right to purchase land under a "land reserve system." Requisitioning land for nonpublic purposes would be prohibited. Requisitioned land would be strictly limited to purposes that are in the public interest (Zhang Xiaoshan and Li Zhou, 2008).

Second, put strict limits on the authority of governments to requisition land via compulsory methods, and regulate the procedures for requisitioning land. The purpose of allowing governments to require land requisitions [by eminent domain] again comes back to public interest. Such interest generally relates to social and economic progress, or it can relate to environmental protection. However, forceful expropriation can be a highly destructive blow to those who are losing their land. Therefore, authority to requisition land should be placed under the regulatory framework of laws and regulations that explicitly set forth the circumstances under which land can be requisitioned, the uses to which such land can be put, the procedures that must be followed in the process, and the standards by which compensation must be made. In addition, ongoing explorations should attempt to find ever more reasonable approaches.

In terms of procedures for requisitioning land, first, requisitioning must be done in full compliance with legal procedures, and measures must be fair and equal. The way to do this is to formulate regulations, make sure there is sufficient discussion [negotiation] in advance of any action, engage all parties in planning, make the appeals process easy, and ensure effective constraints over the government's discretionary powers. Second, requisitioning must be done with the existence of adequate regulatory oversight. "Adequate" refers to oversight that is transparent and that has effective checks and balances. Transparency and effective checks and balances are also opportunities for reducing corruption and the abuse of power. Third, compensation must be fair and equal. Explicit and consistent ways of valuing land should be formulated so that those being affected by the land requisition, including land owners, residents, and land users, receive fair and timely compensation whether that is in the form of cash or of resettlement to somewhere else.

Third, the amounts paid for requisitioned land should be increased, and mechanisms should be in place to provide reasonable, standardized, and diversified forms of guarantees for those affected. Efforts to find ways to ensure that the standards of living of rural people who are being displaced do not decline have been carried out in recent years. One way is to increase compensation. Another is to urge local governments to put a social security system in place for these people. However, these two ways have not changed unequal and unfair treatment, given the constant increase in both land values and the amount of money that can be made off land transfers.[3] In order to ensure that a comparable increase in the percentage of incremental land value goes to dispossessed rural people, we recommend that China go further in improving the compensation system. First, set up mechanisms that allow for adjustment of the compensation standards. Gradually increase the compensation standards and also increase the percentage of incremental gains in land value that goes to dispossessed rural people. Second, ensure that a social security system is truly and effectively in place for such people. Places that have not yet established such a social security system should set up systems as fast as possible as per the requirements of the State Council and should ensure that coverage is extended to dispossessed rural people. In places that do have a social security system in place, efforts should continue to improve upon mechanisms that provide reasonable, standardized, and diversified forms of guarantees for those whose land has been requisitioned. In addition, funds required for such social security should be explicitly included in the costs of transferring [assigning] land-use rights.

Fourth, establish a system for distributing the benefits of gains in land values in ways that are fair and equitable and enjoyed by all parties involved. When governments requisition collectively owned rural land, it should be done via legal methods, and the government should increase the percentage of the gains in land value that is distributed to rural people. They should set up distribution systems for such increased value in ways that are fair and accessible to all, and they should ensure that the standard of living of the affected farmers actually increases and that their long-term livelihood has adequate safeguards. This requires accelerating reform of the land requisition system. It means going further in improving the resettlement system as compensation for land, expanding channels by which resettlement can occur, exploring a process of reserving some land specifically for resettlement,[4] having the land held through shareholding systems with former occupants, and so on. The aim is to realize a situation that gives farmers long-term benefits and security whether or not collective ownership is retained. This also means improving the dispute resolution system and ensuring that farmers have an "open and smooth channel" by which they can protect their lawful rights and interests. Next, profits derived from gains in land value should go to the public as opposed to the government – a clear distinction should be made. Gains in land value that go to the local government – in particular those that just go to some government officials within the local government, as "revenues outside the system" – must be avoided. Every effort should be made to ensure that gains in land values do indeed benefit society. Finally, establish a land fund system. Pool a certain percentage of income from land, and use it to mitigate the influence that market volatility has on local government finances. Allocate this pool of funds over time so that there is a reasonable distribution of proceeds every year.

7. Being proactive in exploring how to reform the system that governs collectively owned property rights

Over recent years, many changes have occurred in the amount of assets held by collective economic organizations, as well as the membership of those organizations. This is particularly true in villages in more advanced coastal areas and in the suburbs surrounding major cities. On the one hand, some collective economic organizations have amassed considerable assets from fees for requisitioned land and the accumulation of fixed assets.[5] On the other hand, the composition of the membership of such collectives is becoming ever more complex, as former members transition to becoming urban residents and as the transient rural population increases in wealthier cities and towns. The share of a collective's assets that members themselves own is often unclear, so it is quite easy for the "owner" of property rights pertaining to the collective to be obscured. Decision making can be autocratic, oversight inadequate, and distributions arbitrary. This is detrimental to conserving and increasing the assets of the collective itself. It can easily damage the interests not only of the collective but of the collective's members.

The central government has been active in trying to reform this situation by exploring how to modify the property rights system of collectives. In 2007, the Ministry of Agriculture issued *Guiding Opinions on Steadily Advancing the Pilot Reform of the Property Rights System of Collective Economic Organizations*. After that, reforms were launched in various areas, which mainly took the form of creating shareholding cooperatives [or partnerships]. This involved appraising the collective's assets and coming up with a valuation of those assets, establishing a shareholding entity, defining who owns shares and who manages the shares, and so on. Between 2009 and 2013, on a nationwide basis, the number of villages that had completed this kind of reform of its collective property-rights system went from 10,700 to 28,000. The valuation of qualified assets went from RMB 221.06 billion to RMB 367.12 billion (see Table 3.1). During this same period, the number of shareholders and the volume of dividends paid out to them also increased rapidly. In overall terms, this reform has proceeded more quickly in more economically advanced provinces and municipalities,[6] although there has been a gradual increase in the number of villages that quantify their net ledger assets and turn the results into shares.[7] Volatility in the distribution of dividends has been fairly substantial.[8] Explorations in these areas have laid a foundation for setting up a rural collective property-rights system that has a more defined ownership, explicit duties and

Table 3.1 Progress in the reform of the property-rights system governing China's rural collectives

Item	2009	2010	2011	2012	2013
Villages having completed the reform (10,000)	1.07	1.29	1.66	2.4	2.8
Quantified assets in total (RMB 100 million)	2,210.6	2,528.1	3,295	3,618.6	3,671.2
Shareholders (10,000)	1,063.8	1,718.6	2,315.7	3,710.2	3,830.3
Accumulative dividends paid by villages having completed the reform (RMB 100 million)	365	440.6	548.7	812.8	924.1
Dividend per share (RMB)	662	511	492	346	525

Source: Ministry of Agriculture. *Annual Statistical Reports on Rural Management in China.*

Note: This table is a compilation of data from the annual statistical reports that describe "rural operations and administration" in thirty provinces and municipalities (not including Tibet).

responsibilities, benefits that are enjoyed by all parties, strict protections, regulated transfer of interests, and effective supervision.

Reform of the property-rights system governing rural collectives in China has achieved a certain degree of success and has been able to draw together experience on ways of doing things. However, in actual implementation of reforms, each of the different places has come up against very practical problems that are in urgent need of being addressed. This is due to the institutional constraints of many existing laws and regulations. The problems need to be examined in depth until we come to consensus on the issues, so that relevant policies can then be introduced.

On the scope of collectively owned assets that are quantified in order to be distributed as shares

The quantification of collectively owned assets refers to the process by which such assets are allocated to collective members in the form of shares, according to certain prescribed standards. At present, however, there is no consensus about the scope of assets that should be included in such quantification. The controversy is ongoing (see Box 3.7).

Box 3.7   Different opinions about the quantification of collectively owned assets

Collectively owned assets can be described in a narrow sense as well as in a more inclusive sense. The narrow definition includes operating assets as well as nonoperating assets. The broader definition also includes such resource-type assets as land. The use, handling, and distribution of income from resource-type assets therefore also constitutes an essential part of the management of a collective's assets.

One point of view holds that the quantification of assets should refer to the "net operating assets." This kind of quantification method is easier to handle since it avoids a number of difficult questions such as how to value land and other resource-type assets. It is also easier to adopt modern corporate modes of management with this approach, which means that financial oversight is easier and the process of reform encounters fewer problems.

Another point of view holds that operating assets, nonoperating assets, and resource-type assets should all be entered into the scope of quantification of a collective's assets. Only then can the rural collective ensure that its assets are being fully considered, and only then is any reform of property rights actually addressing the whole question. Only by considering all of its assets will the collective be able to stimulate a more dynamic local economy. If all assets are included, the total amount of assets will have a greater value and play a larger role in the economy and thereby do more to realize and protect the rights and interests of local people [farmers].

Source: Summarized by Song Hongyuan.

Prior to the time the central government issues unified standards on the matter, the quantification of collectives' assets can still go forward. The three types of assets (operating, nonoperating, and land) can be quantified by category and tallied either simultaneously or consecutively. Local governments may first quantify operating assets and later do the nonoperating and resource-type assets. It is also possible not to quantify resource-type assets. However, it would be better to do this as soon as possible. Since the collective derives compensation from land that is requisitioned as well as from the replacement of assets, those benefits should be added to the collective's total revenue so as to ensure that members of the collective share in the returns off their assets (Huang Yanxin et al., 2014).

Defining the qualifications that determine membership in collective economic organizations

Population mobility is increasing by the day in China, given rapid social and economic development. This includes mobility between urban and rural areas and among different parts of the country. The "members" of a given rural collective economic organization are no longer absolutely congruent with the "villagers" in that location. In many cases, there are more "villagers" than there are "members," particularly in the more developed areas. In 2013, a Number One document of the central government proposed efforts to define the qualifications that determine membership in collective economic organizations. At present, however, the relevant departments have not yet put forth specifics on how to do this. In practice, the definition of membership is being handled mostly by the towns and villages themselves. As a result, it is subject to the influence of local factors, such as local customs, traditional concepts, and past precedent. The "native soil" nature of the decision making is pronounced (Huang Yanxin et al., 2014).

The determination of how to define membership in collective economic organizations should, in the final analysis, be done by all members of the collective through a democratic decision-making process. This process should be based on respect for history, the matching up of rights and responsibilities, consistent standards, and transparent procedures. It should take household registration information into account, as well as the situation with respect to the contractual operation of farmland and the contributions that a given person has made to the collective. All of this is in addition to the need to take relevant laws and regulations into account. Methods being adopted by Pingluo county in Ningxia can serve as a good reference (see Box 3.8).

Box 3.8   Pingluo county in Ningxia launches a pilot program to define membership in collective economic organizations

Pingluo county in Ningxia launched an initiative to identify and confirm membership in village collectives in order to strengthen administrative control over the "three resources," namely collectively owned funds, assets, and resources. It then set up a system for managing collectively owned assets that defines property rights [ownership], that explicitly sets forth rights but also responsibilities [accountability], and that manages village collectives' assets in a scientific way.

Urbanization, economic development in cities, and increased mobility of rural populations have led to greater diversity and complexity when it comes to the urban or rural "status" of rural people, household registrations, land circumstances, and so on. For example, some people still have contractual operating rights to land and still live in the village and farm that land, even though their household registration has been transferred elsewhere. People marry into village families or marry out to families in other places but do not transfer their household registration. Some people now are of a "cadre status" yet still hold onto their farming rights and long-term residency in a village as if they were "farmers." Some college graduates work "outside" after graduating, at nonofficial jobs, yet transfer their household registration back to the village. Circumstances like these make it hard for the village committee to determine membership of the local collective with any degree of accuracy.

For this reason, Pingluo county developed a program called *Interim Measures for identifying membership in collective economic organizations*. Based on four identification references, this specified thirteen situations in which membership should be granted and five situations in which it should not. The county then selected thirteen townships to conduct the pilot program. Each was given one month in which to select a village that was to complete the identification of its own members based on the given criteria.

By the end of May 2014, the work of identifying membership in each of the thirteen pilot sites was basically complete. A preliminary count came up with 5,872 households and 20,923 people who had been defined as members of collective economic organizations. In conducting this process, the village committees held villagers' congresses to determine the status of special situations by vote. It also put up public notices twice, so that the status of special situations could be handled properly. The work of identifying collective members then served as the underlying basis for quantifying the "three assets" of each village and issuing shares. This work on the part of Pingluo county amassed considerable experience that can now be extended county-wide. It also provides experience that can be used for reference by other parts of the country.

Source: Office of Rural Land Management System Reform Leading Group of Pingluo County. *Special Report on Reform of the Rural Land Management System in Pingluo County*, Issue 7, 2014.

The three levels of ownership of collectively owned assets

By the end of 2013, 41.08 percent of China's farmland was held under the ownership of "villagers' committees" and 51.55 percent was held by "villagers' groups." To this day, however, the question of the [government] level at which collectively owned property rights should be defined remains unclear. During the period of People's Communes in China, a system was put in place that declared that village land and other collective assets were "owned by three levels of collective ownership, with the brigade [production brigade] serving as the basis." The production brigade was the primary entity holding property rights over village land. After rural areas in China began to implement the system known as the household contracting responsibility system, the question of which level of authority now actually "owned" land was never explicitly defined by law in any unified way. Article 10 of the *Law on Land Management* stipulates, "As per law, land owned by rural collectives belongs to the villagers' collectives and is to be operated by and managed by either the collective economic organization of the village or the *villagers' committee*. Land in villages that has already been divided into two or more levels of rural collective ownership via rural collective economic organizations is to be operated by and managed by either the collective economic organization or the *villagers' group*. Land that already belongs to rural collectives at the township (town) level is to be operated and managed by the collective economic organization of the township (town)."

At present, there are three different forms of rural collective ownership in China: villagers' groups, village collective economic organizations, and township collective economic organizations. In reality, the boundaries of "collective" ownership in the system of collective ownership of rural land have already quietly changed. In some areas, the ultimate owner has transitioned from the level of what used to be production teams to that of what used to be production brigades. That is, the land has transitioned from being owned by villagers' groups to being owned by administered towns. When changes in the ownership of land occur, and when the land is put to new uses, the negative consequences of this quiet shift in ownership become more pronounced. This is most notable when the distribution of benefits is involved.

This problem has not been adequately addressed in theoretical terms in China, nor have any effective solutions been found in actual practice. By now, it is imperative that efforts be made to find solutions as reform proceeds.

Regarding methods of quantifying collectively owned assets and issuing shares

The structure of collectively owned assets is complex, while qualifications defining membership in collectives remain ambiguous. Meanwhile, village-level organizations are quite diverse by now. All of these things mean that there are currently a variety of ways to quantify collectively owned assets and turn them into shares (see Box 3.9).

Box 3.9   Efforts to quantify assets and turn them into shareholdings in the Minhang district of Shanghai

Depending on the type of village within its borders, the Minhang district of Shanghai has adopted different reform methods in handling the quantification of assets.

The first method involves revoking the administrative structure of the village and defining shares on the basis of quantifying all of the assets of the collective. The second involves not revoking the village and quantifying only a portion of the assets. Some villages have quantified operating assets while putting land and nonoperating assets in the ledger but not quantifying them. Instead, they charge usage fees when resources are actually used, and these are shared by all original members of the collective. A third method being carried out in areas that are currently agricultural involves quantifying the contractual operating rights to the land and creating shares based on that value. In five villages within the town of Pujiang, for example, the area of contracted land is divvied up into shares with one share for one *mu* of land area. The income from this land mainly comes from transferring usage rights to the land. Other areas are welcome to explore their own new methods depending on their specific situations. The shareholding rights to collectively owned assets are mainly owned by individuals. The question of whether or not there should also be shares owned by the collective itself depends, ultimately, on the rural people themselves. Their choices must be respected as the decision is made by collective economic organizations through public procedures.

Source: Summarized by Song Hongyuan.

In terms of managing the shares, we should formulate and issue *Administrative measures for managing the shares of new-type rural collective economic organizations* as soon as possible. These measures should address a number of issues through explicitly regulating such things as defining shareholders, structure of shares, capital infusions and expansion in the number of shares, and the quantification of new assets in terms of share values. Through the effective management of shares, the hope is to make the collective sector of the economy a competitive force that develops vigorously and is able to provide good services to its members. In addition, as soon as possible, we should develop and put out *Administrative measures for income distribution from new-type rural collective economic organizations*. These should regulate [standardize] the income distribution of the collectives that have been restructured. They should gradually enable the collective to narrow the scope of welfare benefits that it provides to members. When collective assets are turned into shares for common ownership, the shares held collectively by the entity itself should be distributed out to individual members. When reform of the collective's property rights system results in a "cooperative shareholding system," taxes on dividends from the shares may enjoy reductions, exemptions, or refunds. The intent of this is to reduce the burden on farmers in substantive ways.

Organizational forms that result once reform of rural collective property rights systems is achieved

Reform of the collective property rights system in China should be done in ways that allow for differences in the level of economic development and quantity of assets in different regions. Guidance policies should be developed for different categories of situations and should be pushed forward in an ordered and sequential way. Legal-person [corporate] forms should be explored, depending on the different circumstances that apply to agricultural areas, economically advanced areas, and areas that are being turned into residential districts as opposed to rural land.

Current practices can be divided mainly into the following three types. The first establishes village economic cooperatives. These must be confirmed and certified by the level of people's government that is above the county level. The second registers an entity as a "specialized farmers' cooperative." This is done according to the *Law on specialized farmers' cooperatives*. The third registers as a corporate legal-person entity, in accord with the *Company Law*. In addition, some collective economic organizations undertaking reform still carry on production and conduct business operations under the name of the original entity.

Reasonable, scientific, corporate governance structures are the way to safeguard democratic decision making, democratic management, and democratic regulatory oversight. We must therefore formulate and issue policies that relate to what are called the "three committees" and the "four rights" within corporate governance structures. The three committees are the shareholders' meeting, the board of directors, and the board of supervisors. Mechanisms to ensure rights relate to the property rights of the legal person, the ownership rights of the investors, the rights of investors to carry out supervisory oversight, and the right of the legal person to serve as agent. As these policies are developed, we should also seek to improve the external institutional environment for legal-person corporate governance structures. This includes such things as clarifying and straightening out relationships among three entities: the Party branch at the village level, the village committee, and the new-type collective economic organization. The purpose is to enable rural people to truly become the primary investors and primary decision makers in the collective sector, as well as its primary beneficiaries. They should be the true "owners" of the collective in reality and not just in name.

Adjustments to existing laws, regulations, and policies

In 2014, the central government set forth a Number One document that called for "pushing forward reform of the rural collective property rights system to turn it into a cooperatively owned shareholding system, in order to protect the rights and interests of rural people in collective economic organizations." This was in response to the growing number of problems in recent years that relate to management of collectively owned funds, assets, and resources. It represented an active response to efforts being made at the grassroots level to achieve reform. Existing laws, regulations, and policies with respect to this issue are both contradictory and conflicting. The discrepancies have become an institutional barrier to further reform. Only by resolving inconsistencies in policies, laws, and regulations and by addressing the existing situation in the management of rural funds, assets, and resources can a viable plan go forward smoothly. Only then can it hope to achieve the desired results. We recommend that relevant government departments seize the moment, do the necessary research, and come up with guiding opinions and implementation measures. They should push forward revision of relevant laws and regulations. In an orderly and regulated way, they should advance reform of the system that governs collective property rights in rural areas.

Notes

1 According to the existing law, the compensation for farmers affected by requisitioning [expropriation] shall not exceed thirty times the annual land yields from the land's original use. Calculated on the basis of RMB 2,000 per *mu* per year, one mu of farmland will be compensated with a total of RMB 60,000 (2,000 × 30). Factoring in compensations for young crops, facilities, relocation expenses, and other factors, the maximum amount was RMB 100,000 per *mu* in 2007 (See Zhou Qiren, *Urban and Rural Areas in China*. Beijing: China CITIC Press, 2014).

2 In 2010, 66,000 cases of illegal land use occurred nationwide, involving a total area of 677,000 *mu* and encroaching upon farmland totaling 270,000 *mu*. In 2009, national and provincial key projects accounted for 45 percent and 55 percent of the total area of land and farmland being used illegally. See: Han Jun, *China's rural reform 2002–2012*. Shanghai: Shanghai Far East Publishers, 2012.

3 Although expropriation and demolition fees account for 37 percent of proceeds from the transfer of land-use rights, the increase in this part is mostly due to the rise in

compensation for demolition and relocation in urban–rural interface areas. Most farmers affected by expropriation still get very low compensation, and the level of social security for them, though varying from place to place, is generally low.

4 Reserved resettlement land means that, in addition to cash compensation paid to farmers and villages, local governments also return a certain percentage of the expropriated land to villages for the resettlement of farmers. On the reserved resettlement land, village collectives can conduct commercial or industrial development on their own or in cooperation with developers, and profits from such development will belong to village collectives. The mode of reserved resettlement land was first implemented in Shenzhen in the early 1980s and was adopted by Zhejiang and Shanghai between 2003 and 2005. Practice has shown that such a mode is acceptable to farmers and easy to operate. Its advantage is that the compensation in the form of land can make up for the drawback of cash compensation for expropriation and allow farmers to have steady and long-term returns.

5 By the end of 2013, village-level collective economic organizations registered ledger assets of RMB 2.4 trillion combined, or an average of RMB 4.084 million per village (Ministry of Agriculture, 2013).

6 As of the end of 2013, villages in Beijing, Jiangsu, Zhejiang, Shandong, and Guangdong that had completed the reform of the collective property rights system accounted for 85.5 percent of the national total, up 4.8 percentage points compared with the previous year. Villagers' groups in Jiangsu and Guangdong that had completed the reform accounted for 67.3 percent of the national total (Ministry of Agriculture, 2013).

7 As of the end of 2013, villages that had completed the reform of the collective property rights system registered quantified assets of RMB 367.12 billion, up 1.5 percent from 2012, accounting for 25.3% of the net ledger assets of villages (Ministry of Agriculture, 2013).

8 From 2009 to 2012, the dividend per share declined from RMB 662 to RMB 346 before it surged to RMB 525 in 2013, up 51.3 percent compared with 2012 (Ministry of Agriculture).

4 Achieving a balance in the supply and demand for grain in China and ensuring food safety in terms of the quality of food

- The resource constraints that limit China's grain production
- The supply and demand for grain and trend lines
- Changes in global supply and demand for grain and its impact on China
- The situation with respect to food safety and establishing a regulatory system that addresses the situation
- Implementing the new national food security strategy

Food security is a major strategic issue that affects China's economic and social development in every way. It is a prerequisite to building a moderately prosperous society in an all-round way, and it also safeguards that process. The term *food security* implies not only the quantity of food that is sufficient to meet the needs of the nation, households, and individuals, but it implies safeguarding the safety and nutritional value of food. Since reform and opening up, China has met the objective of "basic self-sufficiency in cereal grains and absolute grain security." This has been achieved despite the country's limited extent of arable land and other resources. In 2014, total grain production reached 607 million tons, double the figure in 1978, which represented an average annual increase of 1.94 percent. This was a remarkable achievement. Nevertheless, constraints on China's grain supply are becoming ever more apparent given shortages of natural resources, an increase in production costs, and a deteriorating ecological environment. In contrast, the demand for grain remains a hard constraint. Not only will the contradiction between supply and demand intensify in the future, but supply will increasingly be subject to the volatility of international markets. In addition, China lacks effective supervisory/regulatory control over food quality. Incidents to do with food quality are proliferating, leading to concern on the part of the public. Against this overall backdrop, ensuring food security for the country and making sure food is safe will be a monumental task as we seek to create a moderately prosperous society.

After taking a look back at the dynamic nature of changes in China's grain and food production, this chapter analyzes the situation in 2020 in terms of both food security and food safety. It bases this analysis on the existing domestic, as well as international situation in supply and demand, and on China's current food safety situation. It presents policy recommendations for long-term food security for the country and for ways to safeguard food safety.

1. The resource constraints that limit China's grain production

Reduction in the quantity as well as quality of arable land

China's demand for "construction-use land" is constantly increasing given the requirements of urbanization and industrialization. Over the short term, it will be very hard to reverse the trend of a decreasing amount of arable land. This weakens the foundations of grain production and supply. Statistical data published by the country's Ministry of Land and Resources in 2013 indicates that construction-use land increased by 41.78 million *mu* over the past thirteen years and that it now occupies the absolute majority of prime farmland in the country. The amount of rice fields in just five provinces – Guangdong, Jiangsu, Shandong, Zhejiang, and Fujian – went down by 17.98 million *mu*. This is roughly equivalent to eliminating territory equal to the entire province of Fujian in terms of the loss of rice-producing land. Policies insist on creating a balance between "increases and decreases" as land is given over to construction purposes, of linking the pluses with the minuses, but in actual practice soils that are badly polluted are put to agriculture while better land goes to construction. The problem of the deteriorating quality of farmland cannot be fundamentally resolved in any short period of time. What's more, during the process of researching this background report, the research team discovered that many fields are now simply being abandoned. This is happening in villages in the eastern, central, and western parts of China and is influenced by the exodus of labor from villages, the aging of people still engaged in agriculture, the increase in agricultural production costs, and so on. When fields are relatively far from a farmer's home or the soils are not as productive, farmers abandon the field. In some places, this problem is so acute that even better land is sometimes abandoned in suburban areas close to cities. This too has substantially reduced the amount of arable land in the country.

The threat of water shortages and intensification of competition among departments [different economic sectors] for the remaining water

China's grain and food production is constrained by a shortage of water resources. The country's per capita endowment of water comes to just one-quarter of the world's average. On a per *mu* basis, water for agriculture is roughly one-half of the global average, and this has already become a major factor limiting China's grain and food production. Given the trends of economic development, population increase, economic and social advances, and environmental restoration efforts, the nonagricultural demand for water is going to increase, and the amount of water going to agriculture is simply going to decrease (see Figure 4.1). According to the projections of China's water simulation model [CWSM], for each additional percentage point of urbanization in China, the percentage of water used for agricultural purposes in the country will go down by 0.47 percent. Given reallocations

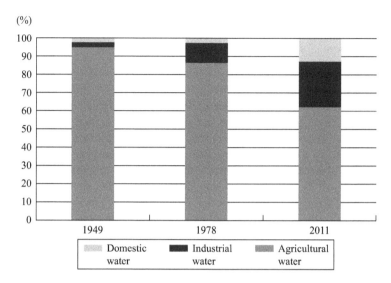

Figure 4.1 Comparison of the amount of water used by different sectors of China's economy –
        household use, industrial use, and agricultural use – in 1949, 1978, and 2011

Source: National Bureau of Statistics and Ministry of Environmental Protection, *China Environmental Statistical Yearbook.*

among sectors of the economy, we predict that the percentage of total water used by agriculture in the year 2020 will have declined to 58 percent. The percentage of water used by rice production will have declined by 4 percentage points compared to the amount used today. By 2020, irrigation of farmland will increase by around 4 percent in the thirteen main grain-producing provinces of the country, which is far less of an increase than the 16 percent recorded over the past ten years. A shortage of water resources, along with competition among departments for that water, means that agricultural departments in the country urgently need to improve the efficiency with which water is used.

Uneven geographic distribution of resources and structural issues as a result of where food is produced in China

China's water resources are unevenly distributed in the country, intensifying shortages in areas that have limited land and also limited water. The per capita amount of water in China overall is 3,487 cubic meters. Arable land in China constitutes 30 percent of the total land area, and the amount of water available per *mu* of arable land, on average nationwide, is 4,317 cubic meters. Areas north of the Yangtze River hold only 16.8 percent of the country's total water resources, however. In per capita terms, these water resources come to only 770 cubic meters per person. Meanwhile, areas north of the Yangtze River hold 70 percent of the country's total volume of arable land. On this land, per *mu* water resources come to just 470 cubic meters. Grain production is gradually leaving areas south of the Yangtze River, so that the territory north of the river has become China's primary food production base (Han Jun et al., 2012). The structural issues of water and land availability therefore present even greater problems for China as it seeks to ensure stable and sustainable food production.

The increase in production costs

The prices at which land is transferred in China continue to increase, which has led to an increase in the production costs of grain. In recent years, as different ways of farming have developed in China, together with greater economies of scale, transfers of arable land have been happening at a greater pace and on a greater scale. Rental rates for land have continued to rise (see Table 4.1).

Wage levels of agricultural labor are also rising and constitute an important part of the increase in production costs of agriculture. Prior to the late 1990s, wage rates for unskilled agricultural labor remained quite stable. Starting in the 21st century, however, nonfarm wages for rural migrant labor began to increase. Between 2008 and 2013, the average monthly income of rural migrant workers who travelled away from their homes to work increased from RMB 1,340 to RMB 2,609. This meant an average yearly increase of 14.2 percent (see Figure 4.2). Between 2000 and 2012, RMB-per-day wages for agricultural labor increased by an average annual rate of 20.1 percent per year. Labor as a percentage of total agricultural production costs went from 35.5 percent to 39.7 percent.

The mechanization of agriculture is confronting technology dissemination problems, as well as pressures from rising costs. On the one hand, geographic considerations limit the application of technology in certain areas, such as the small size of fields, which makes certain equipment inappropriate. Transport issues in mountainous areas also make it hard to use certain agricultural machinery. On the other hand, the application of higher technology in agriculture is slowed down by the costs of both buying and using the equipment. Between

Table 4.1 Area and price of household contracted land in circulation

		2009	2010	2011	2012	2013
Household contracted land	Circulated area (10,000 *mu*)	15,154.1	18,668.3	22,793.3	27,833	34,102.0
Circulated area	Proportion (%)	12.00	14.65	17.84	21.24	25.70
Circulation price	Land lease fee per mu of land (RMB/*mu*)	173.65	381.46	623.69	862.55	879.75

Source: Data on circulated area of contracted land comes from national rural operation and management statistics from 2009 to 2013; data on land lease fees is calculated from the monitoring data obtained at fixed countryside observation points nationwide.

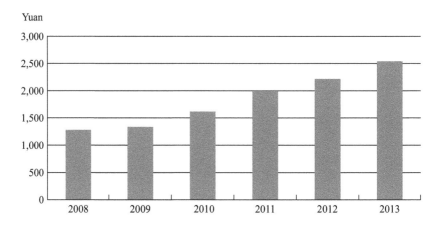

Figure 4.2 Change of monthly income of migrant workers from 2008 to 2013

Source: National Bureau of Statistics, *2013 National Monitoring and Survey Report on Migrant Workers.*

2000 and 2012, costs for agricultural equipment rose dramatically and went from being 14.9 percent of the material costs of agricultural production to being 29.6 percent of those costs.

2. The supply and demand for grain and trend lines

Agricultural production and output of various agricultural goods

Any sustainable increase in food and grain production in China is going to be limited by the impact of a number of factors that include decreases in the quantity of arable land, water shortages, as well as uneven distribution of water resources, rising production costs, and technical issues holding back mechanization. According to the projections of China's Agricultural Policy Simulation and Projection Model (CAPSiM), the total quantity of China's grain and food production in 2020 will decline by 3.63 percent compared to the level in 2012.[1] Changes in different agricultural resources affect the production quantities of different kinds of agricultural commodities in different ways. The situation with respect to plant oils, sugar, vegetables, and fruit, among other things, is shown in Table 4.2.

The increase in demand and changes in the structure of consumption

Since the start of the 21st century, China's total grain consumption has grown at an average annual rate of 2.5 percent. This period represents the fastest rate of increase since the start of reform and opening up. The total demand for grain is

Table 4.2 Impact of change of agricultural resource factors on yield of major farm produce from 2012 to 2020

	Overall impact	*Restriction of water resource use*	*Arable land turned to land for construction*	*Rise of labor cost*
Total food production	−1.3374	−0.4458	−0.4458	−0.5201
Rice	−2.5262	−1.8575	−0.2972	−0.3715
Wheat	−1.2631	−0.6687	−0.2972	−0.2972
Corn	−1.3374	−0.1486	−0.5201	−0.6687
Soybean	9.7333	12.1852	−1.486	−0.9659
Plant oil	−2.6748	−1.4117	−0.743	−0.5201
Sugar	−2.229	−0.9659	−0.6687	−0.5944
Vegetable	−0.743	−0.2229	−0.4458	−0.3715
Fruit	−0.8173	0	−0.4458	−0.2972
Pork	−0.8173	−0.0743	−0.1486	−0.6687
Beef	−0.8173	0	−0.0743	−0.6687
Poultry	−0.8916	−0.0743	−0.2229	−0.6687
Dairy product	−1.0402	−0.0743	−0.1486	−0.8916
Aquatic product	−0.8173	0	−0.0743	−0.743

Source: CAPSiM simulation result.

Note: The result is calculated from the CAPSiM simulation result in the formula: impact value = CAPSiM simulation result × (2020 urbanization rate − 2012 urbanization rate).

expected to continue to rise, given development trends in the country, population growth and structural changes in urban and rural components of the population, increases in the level of and structure of consumption of both urban and rural residents, and relatively fast ongoing increases in the need for grain as animal feed and as an industrial input. Relevant research on this subject predicts that by 2020 China's total grain demand will exceed 670 million tons (Zhao Qiguo and Huang Jikun, 2012).

Looking at the experience of other countries, China is in a period of rapid structural change in terms of its food consumption. First, incomes of both urban and rural people are rising, which leads to gradually changing and upgrading food habits. Second, the rural population is shifting toward cities and industrial occupations, given the impetus of urbanization and industrialization. Both modes of eating and the types of food being consumed are changing. Consumption of animal-type foods, including meat, chicken, eggs, and milk, is continuing a rapid rise. Demand for grain used for animal feed and industrial purposes is therefore also continuing to rise.

Agricultural trade and net imports

The total amount of grain/food that China imports is constantly increasing given the rise in consumption demand as well as the restructuring of consumption.

The type of food being imported also continues to diversify. The country's imports of certain types of grain and grain oils used as animal feed mean that its dependence on foreign markets and foreign resources is fairly high. Analysis conducted by the State Council's Development Research Center and the World Bank indicates that grain/food imports will reach 108.918 million tons by 2020. Exports will reach 3.086 tons, which means that net imports will come to 105.832 tons. China's rate of self-sufficiency in food will have declined to 84.3 percent by 2020 (see Table 4.3).

The gap between supply and demand of agricultural products

The results of multiple research studies on the subject forecast a relatively large gap between supply and demand for agricultural products in China in the future. Results of analysis conducted by the State Council's Development Research Center and the World Bank put that gap at 105.832 million tons: China's total output of grain/food in 2020 will come to 568.122 million tons, while total demand will come to 673.954 million tons. This disparity is close to nine times the gap between supply and demand in 2012 (see Table 4.3). Some research results estimate an even larger disparity – specifically, 170 million tons by 2020 (Yang Jianli and Yue Zhenghua, 2014).[2] Even the more optimistic estimates put the gap at close to 50 million tons by 2020 (Lu Xinye and Hu Feifan, 2012).[3]

Results of these analyses indicate that China's supply and demand situation for grain and foods will show the following characteristics by the year 2020. First,

Table 4.3 Projections of supply and demand for grain in 2020 and actual figures for 2012

		Total food production	Rice	Wheat	Corn	Soybean
2012	Production	589,570	142,965	120,580	208,190	13,600
	Import	86,890	2,369	3,701	5,208	67,530
	Export	2,830	279	0	257	385
	Net import	84,060	2,090	3,701	4,951	67,145
	Total demand	601,477	117,372	112,686	198,278	73,718
	Self-sufficiency rate (%)	87.5	98.6	97	97.7	16.8
2020	Production	568,122	120,449	110,339	224,070	14,966
	Import	108,918	1,244	2,628	19,794	79,536
	Export	3,086	531	0	140	327
	Net import	105,832	712	2,628	19,654	79,209
	Total demand	673,954	121,161	112,967	243,724	94,175
	Self-sufficiency rate (%)	84.3	99.4	97.7	91.9	15.9

Source: Development Research Centre of the State Council and the World Bank, *China: Promoting Efficient, Inclusive and Sustainable Urbanization.* Beijing: China Development Press, 2014.

Units: thousands of tons

Table 4.4 China's supply and demand for pork, beef, mutton, chicken, eggs, milk, and aquatic products in 2012 and a projection for 2020

		Pork	Beef	Mutton	Poultry	Egg	Dairy products	Aquatic products
2012	Production	46,159	5,296	3,409	17,319	19,998	38,680	33,178
	Import	522	49	119	49	0	6,181	2,208
	Export	66	12	0	181	61	105	3,253
	Net import	456	37	119	−131	−61	6,076	−1,045
	Total demand	46,615	5,333	3,528	17,187	19,937	44,756	32,132
	Self-sufficiency rate (%)	99	99.3	96.6	100.8	100.3	86.4	103.3
2020	Production	56,194	7,272	4,384	22,379	23,462	56,906	4,380
	Import	728	165	328	67	0	11,725	2,975
	Export	65	4	0	180	47	51	3,298
	Net import	664	161	328	−113	−47	1,1674	−323
	Total demand	56,858	7,433	4,711	22,266	23,416	68,580	43,485
	Self-sufficiency rate (%)	98.8	97.8	93.1	100.5	100.2	83	100.7

Source: Development Research Centre of the State Council and the World Bank, *China: Promoting Efficient, Inclusive and Sustainable Urbanization*. Beijing: China Development Press, 2014.

Units: thousands of tons

the rate at which demand for grain increases will be notably higher than the rate at which domestic production increases, which means that China's self-sufficiency in grain will continue to decline. Second, with the exception of oil made from soybeans, the production of other edible oils will roughly keep pace with demand, with only a modestly increasing gap. Third, the consumption of animal and aquatic products will continue to increase rapidly, but for most products, supply and demand will be roughly in balance.

3. Changes in global supply and demand for grain and its impact on China

Global supply and demand for grain

Grain output has been increasing at a moderate pace on a global basis since 1990 – the average annual increase in production has been 1.47 percent. In terms of the percentages of the total held by specific types of grain, corn output has been taking a larger share, while the percentage of rice has increased only slightly. Wheat output as a share of total grain output has gone down dramatically (see Table 4.5). Grain production around the world is concentrated in such countries as China, the United States, India, Indonesia, and Brazil. Between 1990 and 2012, these five countries accounted for an average of 54.84 percent of global grain production (see Figure 4.3).

Table 4.5 Comparison of total global production of corn, rice, and wheat between 1990 and 2012 and percentages of the total held by each commodity

Year	Corn		Rice		Wheat		Food
	Production	Share (%)	Production	Share (%)	Production	Share (%)	Total production
1990	4.83	24.77	5.19	26.62	5.92	30.36	19.50
1995	5.17	27.28	5.47	28.86	5.43	28.65	18.95
2000	5.92	28.76	5.99	29.10	5.86	28.47	20.58
2001	6.16	29.22	6.00	28.46	5.90	27.99	21.08
2002	6.05	29.80	5.71	28.12	5.75	28.32	20.31
2003	6.45	30.86	5.87	28.09	5.60	26.79	20.90
2004	7.29	32.00	6.08	26.69	6.33	27.79	22.78
2005	7.14	31.51	6.34	27.98	6.27	27.67	22.66
2006	7.07	31.65	6.41	28.70	6.03	26.99	22.34
2007	7.90	33.57	6.57	27.92	6.13	26.05	23.54
2008	8.27	32.75	6.89	27.29	6.83	27.05	25.25
2009	8.19	32.78	6.85	27.42	6.87	27.50	24.98
2010	8.40	33.92	6.96	28.10	6.54	26.41	24.76
2011	8.86	34.19	6.95	26.82	7.00	27.01	25.92
2012	8.63	33.91	7.00	27.50	6.56	25.78	25.45

Source: Data from 1990 to 2010 comes from statistical database of Food and Agriculture Organization of the United Stations (http://faostat fao.org), and data from 2011 to 2012 comes from database of U.S. Department of Agriculture (http://www.fas.usda.gov/psdonline).

Units: hundred million tons

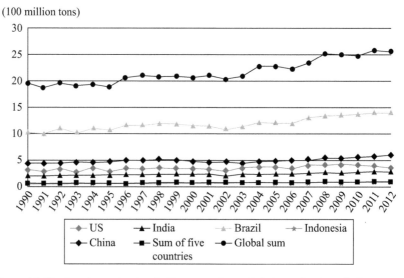

Figure 4.3 Total grain production in five countries and their production relative to total global grain production

Source: Statistical database of Food and Agriculture Organization of the United Stations. http://faostat fao.org.

Table 4.6 Global supply and demand for grain since 2000

Year	Production	Demand	Inventory	Trade	Inventory/ consumption ratio (%)
2000	18.58	18.68	3.23	2.94	17.29
2001	19.05	19.04	3.34	2.91	17.54
2002	18.33	19.19	4.25	3.06	22.15
2003	18.87	19.58	4.98	3.03	25.43
2004	20.71	20.11	4.45	3.03	22.13
2005	20.48	20.31	4.40	3.23	21.66
2006	20.14	20.22	4.60	3.36	22.75
2007	21.49	21.57	4.27	2.73	19.80
2008	22.86	21.82	5.20	2.81	23.83
2009	22.63	22.34	5.34	2.76	23.90
2010	22.59	22.79	5.09	2.85	22.33
2011	23.48	23.27	5.23	3.15	22.48
2012	22.84	23.14	4.97	2.94	21.48

Source: Statistical database of Food and Agriculture Organization of the United Stations. http://faostat fao.org.

Unit: 100 million tons

On the demand side, between 2000 and 2012, global demand for grain increased from 1.868 billion tons to 2.314 billion tons. People in developed countries mainly consume grain indirectly, whereas those in developing countries mainly consume it directly. In terms of trade, volatility in world grain markets has been substantial since 2000. In terms of inventories, global grain inventories have remained stable and have even shown some increase despite the fact that demand has exceeded production.

Projected changes in the global supply and demand for grain

The United Nations Food and Agriculture Organization has predicted (2013) that international supply and demand for grain/food will be as follows by the year 2020. First, the amount of acreage from which cereal grains are harvested will basically remain stable on a global basis, and output will increase at a stable rate. Given a modest increase in cultivated land area and increasing yields per unit of area, by 2020, worldwide production of grain is expected to reach 2.595 billion tons. This is an increase of 12.1 percent over 2011 and represents an average annual increase of 1.3 percent. Second, global consumption of grains will maintain a steady increase. Consumption of grains is influenced by such factors as demographics and economic development but also by the economic policies of a given country, for example, generating energy from biomass. If there are no dramatic changes in the speed of global population growth and in the overall economic situation, by 2020, global consumption of grain is expected to reach 2.588 billion tons. This is an increase of 12 percent over 2011 and represents an average annual increase of

1.3 percent. The increased consumption is lower than that of the previous decade, when it was an average of 2 percent per year. Ongoing increases in the base figure of population mean that required grain rations will continue to increase at a rate of 1.1 percent. Third, the situation with respect to supply and demand of grain will shift in a positive direction on a global basis, and traded supply will basically remain stable. In contrast to times of food crisis and a gap between supply and demand, the projection is that there will be a net surplus in the supply of grain by 2020 that is on the order of 7 million tons. If global supply and demand does indeed shift in a positive direction, the future ability of the world to supply adequate grain can basically be assured. By 2020, the projected trade in grain on a global basis is expected to reach 328 million tons, which represents an increase of 18.8 percent over 2011 and an average annual increase of 1.9 percent. Fourth, grain inventories will increase modestly on a global basis. If weather is normal, the forecast is for an average level of inventories of 548 million tons in 2020. This represents an increase of 11.8 percent over 2011, or an average annual increase of 1.3 percent.

Changes in world grain markets and the impact of these changes on China

After China joined the World Trade Organization, it reduced import taxes on imported grain, and the size of the country's imports began a constant increase. China's grain markets became ever more tied in to international grain markets. The volatility in international production of grain, import and export markets for grain, speculative activity, and exchange rate changes have had an increasing impact on China's own supply and demand for grain and its own market prices. At the same time, China's own supply and demand and changes in market prices have had a fairly major impact on global grain markets. Research conducted by relevant organizations has forecast that, by 2020, China's imports of corn will reach 19.794 million tons, which will contribute to boosting international market prices of corn by 4.5 percent. Imports of soybeans will reach 79.536 million tons, which will contribute to raising international market prices of soybeans by 6.8 percent. (State Council Development Research Center and World Bank, 2014.) This indicates that any volatility in international grain markets and prices will make it harder for China to achieve a balance between its production of grain and its supply and demand for grain. These factors will also have a major impact on the effectiveness of regulatory policy measures and China's ability to regulate its own grain markets and prices.

As global demand for grain continues to increase, China will find it increasingly difficult to increase its own grain imports by a significant amount. The number of countries needing to import grain is constantly increasing as newly emerging economies develop quickly and as developed nations expand the uses to which they put grain. Competition for grain imports is therefore intensifying. Egypt can serve as one example. In 2010, Egypt's grain imports reached 16 million tons, which was an increase of 23.1 percent over the previous year. In 2012, the United States used 63 million tons of grain for ethanol production alone. What's more, the degree to which grain exports are concentrated in a few hands is increasing; it is increasingly possible for the world trade in grain to be controlled by just a few countries. This increases the uncertainty surrounding China's grain imports. The global imbalance in supply and demand for grain is going to exist on a long-term basis, while structural and regional problems are going to become more and more pronounced. China will therefore be facing a fairly grim situation in the future as it seeks to increase grain imports.

4. The situation with respect to food safety and establishing a regulatory system that addresses the situation

The concept of food safety encompasses both quantitative and a qualitative aspects with respect to foods and processed food products. China's current situation does not allow for optimism. This is due to such factors as the worsening ecological environment, the unregulated [chaotic] nature of market operations, and the impotence of regulatory actions. Food safety incidents are increasing in frequency and have become the target of public concern. The seriousness of the situation has galvanized the government into strengthening regulatory systems that address food safety in an all-round way and building institutions that deal with the problem.

China's food safety faces a variety of challenges

Three prominent issues encapsulate the severe challenges that China's food safety is currently confronting.

First, China's agriculture is functioning in a worsening ecological environment, and the overall conditions for agricultural production are deteriorating. These things constitute a major threat to food safety. Addressing latent dangers in the quality aspect of food safety is the priority for policy makers. For a long time, many places in China have applied massive amounts of chemical fertilizers, pesticides, and plastic sheeting in an effort to increase production and increase yields. While this did help grow the industry as a whole, it also polluted agricultural areas in ways that are becoming worse by the day. In addition to those kinds of pollution, the pollutants generated by industry and by sewage are destroying the environments and necessary conditions within which farming has to take place. These conditions are having a huge influence on the quality of agricultural products and on food safety. The overapplication of chemical fertilizers, pesticides, plastic sheeting, and other such inputs is not going to change fundamentally in any short period of time, given that China's agriculture is still "extensive" as opposed to being intensive. The polluting of soil and water resources is therefore hard to turn around in the short term; the ecological environment within which farming operates, and the conditions it has to deal with, are not going to see improvement soon. All of these things constitute monumental threats to food safety and to the quality of agricultural products. They pose a seriously damaging threat to the health of urban and rural residents.

Second, the chaotic nature of the market poses a severe challenge to the quality of agricultural goods and to attempts to regulate food safety. At present, 200 million people in China are engaged in producing agricultural products. They operate on a small scale and are not highly organized. In addition, China has more than 400,000 enterprises making food products and more than 3 million entities operating in food-related outlets, not including the countless numbers of small factories and small stalls dealing in food production and food sales. This alone serves as a major constraint on improving food quality and ensuring food safety in the country. Those engaged in food-related operations are driven by profits. Their rampant use of chemical pesticides directly threatens the physical health of those who eat their foods. Given the low levels of awareness of food quality issues in China, however, producers can disregard external influences in the course of producing, transporting, and preserving [prolonging the shelf life] of food. As a result, the market is flooded with products that are past their expiration date and that have "gone off." Added to the problems is the fact that regulatory systems with mechanisms to deal with food quality and food safety have been slow to be established in China. The ability to investigate conditions and regulate industries is not sufficient to meet the needs of the situation. This presents severe challenges when it comes to effective regulation of food safety and the quality of food products.

Box 4.1   A case of food poisoning and its causes: "lean meat powder"

"Lean meat powder" is an adrenal nerve stimulant. It is the generic name in China for a variety of chemicals that include clenbuterol hydrochloride and ractopamine. Added in appropriate quantities to feedstock for pigs, it increases their growth rate and also increases their lean meat ratio. However, used over a long period of time as an additive in animal feeds, concentrations easily build up in the bodies of the chickens and livestock, particularly in their internal organs. Normal cooking temperatures do not eliminate the harmful toxins. When meat and internal organs with heavy residues of the toxins are eaten by people, they can trigger symptoms of poisoning, and they are particularly dangerous for people with high blood pressure and heart disease. The use of ractopamine is extremely prevalent in the United States and Canada. Thanks to strictly controlled processes and a reasonable withdrawal date, such use does not pose a threat to human health, whereas clenbuterol hydrochloride is extremely harmful. Due to safety considerations, China, the European Union, and Russia have all prohibited lean meat powder [of any kind] as an additive to animal feed stocks.

However, incidents with drastic consequences that have involved illegal additives have repeatedly occurred in China. This places higher and more urgent demands on the country's food regulatory system. In September 2006, a series of cases erupted in Shanghai that involved the poisoning of people who had eaten pork and innards from pigs treated with lean meat powder. More than 300 people were treated in hospitals for the poisoning. In November, 2008, seventy employees of the Zhejiang Jiaxing Zhongmao Plastic Industry Co., Ltd. began to have alarming symptoms after lunch – swelling feet, abnormally fast heart rates, and vomiting. This too was diagnosed as being caused by lean meat powder poisoning. In February, 2009, more incidents of poisoning occurred in Guangzhou with seventy people showing symptoms. Reviewing these incidents, we note that common threads included not just evidence that the poisoning came from pork containing lean meat powder that had been sold in markets and that people were breaking the law in pursuit of their own economic interests by using illegal additives, but there was evidence of negligence on the part of inspection departments and a lack of supervisory regulation over how food is distributed and sold.

In recent years, China has increased the severity with which it deals with such cases. In November 2011, according to a report presented by a senior official from the Ministry of Agriculture at the 9th China Food Safety Convention, nine government departments joined together to carry out a campaign specifically aimed at "rectifying" the lean meat powder problem. By the time of the convention, 125 cases were being investigated, ninety-eight suspects had been arrested, and the underground network running production and sales had basically been destroyed.

Source: News materials culled from xinhuanet.com.

Third, poverty exposes the more vulnerable populations in society to greater food safety concerns. Poverty limits accessibility to food safety guarantees. Despite China's fast growing economy and a universal rise in people's standard of living, poverty is still a prominent problem in the country. At the end of 2013, rural areas still had more than 80 million impoverished people, while another 20 million in urban areas were living at the level of minimum living standards. These people survive at extremely low standards of living. When you cannot get enough food, your goal is to stay alive; it is hard to think about food security and pay any attention to the problem. The health and interests of women and children in particular are therefore often compromised.

Food safety regulatory systems and policies in China

Over time, China has developed a system of regulating food safety that combines coordinated efforts with a division of responsibility. The State Council's Food Safety Committee is responsible for overall planning and guidance. The State Council's Office of Food Safety is the implementing body on behalf of the Committee, responsible for comprehensive coordination and regulatory oversight on a nationwide basis. Each province, autonomous region, and directly administered jurisdiction has set up Food Safety Committees led by senior people in their governments [i.e., government principals]. Regulatory agencies responsible for agriculture, food, pharmaceuticals, and so on have all set up organizations targeted at food safety regulation. Other relevant government bodies also have their own specific food safety regulatory organizations, including the National Health and Family Planning Commission, the Ministry of Commerce, the State Administration for Industry and Commerce, and the State Administration of Quality Supervision, Inspections, and Quarantines. Each level of government below the national level has corresponding organizations.

With ongoing improvements in the system of food safety regulation, China has also strengthened its relevant legislation in recent years and the work of

Table 4.7 National institutions responsible for food safety regulation in China and the responsibilities of each

Name of institution	Responsibility
State Food and Drug Administration	Understanding food safety situation in production, circulation, and consumption; urging lower-level administrative organs to strictly implement administrative permit policy and fulfill responsibilities of supervision and management; undertaking work of food safety statistics collection; analyzing and predicting the general status of food safety and conducting risk warning and exchanges on relevant risks; participating in formulation of food safety risk monitoring plans and conducting risk monitoring.
National Health and Family Planning Commission	Organizing efforts to formulate food safety standards and launch related work on food risk monitoring, evaluation, and exchange; evaluating safety of new food ingredients, new varieties of food additives and new varieties of food-related products; playing a role in drawing up conditions for accreditation of food safety inspection institutions and inspection specifications.
Ministry of Agriculture	Regulating quality and safety of domestic primary farm produce in production; implementing quality supervision and authentication of various agricultural products and green food and protection of new varieties of agricultural plants.
General Administration of Quality Supervision, Inspections, and Quarantine	Managing quality, measurement, entry, and exit goods inspection, entry/exit health quarantine, entry/exit animal and plant quarantine, import/export food safety and certification and accreditation, standardization and related work nationwide and enforcing administrative laws.
State Administration for Industry and Commerce	Drawing up specific measures and methods for safety supervision and management of food in circulation; organizing efforts to practice supervisory inspection and quality monitoring and to implement related market access systems upon food in circulation; investigating and punishing major food safety emergencies and cases related to food in circulation.

implementing the legislation. At present, two specific laws and their implementing articles have now been announced and are being put into effect, the *Law on the Quality and Safety of Agricultural Products* and the *Law on Food Safety*. Together with already existing laws, China has formed a system that incorporates a fairly complete set of laws and regulations. Existing laws include the *Law on Food Hygiene, Law on the Protection of Consumer Rights and Interests, Standardization Law, Environmental Protection Law, Animal Epidemic Prevention Law, Law on Import and Export Commodity Inspections,* and *Law on the Quarantines That Apply to Animals and Plants That Enter or Exit China's National Borders*. A National Committee on the assessment of food safety standards was set up that then formulated standards for a system of reviewing and permitting products. It implements a whole series of standards that have to do with food safety and the quality of agricultural products. China has also participated actively in formulating and adopting internationally recommended technical standards and has taken the initial steps in setting up a system of technical standards relating to food safety.

Table 4.8 Policy documents that have been issued in China since the start of the 21st century on food safety management

Time of issuance	Policies and rules
July 2003	*Notice of the General Office of the State Council on the Implementation of Food and Drug Quality Assured Project*
May 2004	*Notice of the General Office of the State Council on Printing and Distributing the Special Rectification Plan on Food Safety*
September 2004	*Decision of the State Council on Further Strengthening Food Safety Work*
March 2005	*Notice of the General Office of the State Council on Printing and Distributing the National Special Rectification Plan on Food and Drug in 2005*
March 2006	*Notice of the General Office of the State Council on Printing and Distributing the National Special Rectification Action Plan on Food Safety in 2006*
Adopted in April 2006, implemented in November 2006	*Law of the People's Republic of China on Quality and Safety of Agricultural Products*
April 2007	*Notice of the General Office of the State Council on Printing and Distributing the National 11th "Five-Year" Plan on Food and Drug Safety*
April 2007	*Notice of the General Office of the State Council on Printing and Distributing the National Special Rectification Plan on Food Safety in 2007*
July 2007	*Special Rules of the State Council on Enhancing Quality Safety Supervision and Management of Food and Other Products*
August 2007	*Notice of the General Office of the State Council on Printing and Distributing the National Special Rectification Action Plan on Product Quality and Food Safety*

(*Continued*)

Table 4.8 (Continued)

Time of issuance	Policies and rules
August 2007	*Notice of the State Council on Strengthening the Work on Product Quality and Food Safety*
September 2008	*Notice of the General Office of the State Council on Printing and Distributing the Notice on Abolishing the Food Safety Inspection Exemption System*
November 2008	*Notice of the General Office of the State Council on Issues Concerning Adjustment of the Food and Drug Supervision and Management System below the Provincial Level*
February 2009	*Notice of the General Office of the State Council on Printing and Distributing the Rectification Plan on Food Safety*
Adopted in February 2009, implemented in June 2009	*Law on Food Safety of the People's Republic of China*
March 2009	*Notice of the General Office of the State Council on Earnestly Implementing the Law on Food Safety*
July 2009	*Regulation on the Implementation of the Law on Food Safety of the People's Republic of China*
February 2010	*Notice of the State Council on Setting up the State Council Food Safety Committee*
March 2010	*Notice of the General Office of the State Council on Printing and Distributing the Food Rectification Arrangement in 2010*
March 2011	*Notice of the General Office of the State Council on Printing and Distributing the Major Work Arrangement on Food Safety in 2011*
June 2012	*Decision of the State Council on Strengthening Food Safety Work*

5.   Implementing the new national food security strategy

China has consistently placed a high degree of importance on both food safety and food security. In terms of the goal of establishing a moderately prosperous society in an all-round way, the subject of food security incorporates the following aspects. The first is security in quantitative terms. This means ensuring a balance in supply and demand, and ensuring that food production is given adequate policy weight to ensure availability of supply. The second is security in qualitative terms. Food and grain production must concentrate on both of these considerations to ensure that people in the country not only eat well but eat safely. The third consideration is environmental protection, or "ecosystem safety." Production of grain and food must be done in ways that allow for long-term sustainable use of the resources provided by the ecosystem. Production methods must promote the sustainable development of agriculture.

The core contents of the new national strategy for food security and its requirements

International experience shows that a country's food security policies and the focus of those policies shift over time. They are constantly being adjusted to stay in line with that country's economic development and with the international environment. Developed countries generally emphasize nutrition and stable prices. Countries with abundant per capita agricultural production generally do not put undue emphasis on overall quantities of grain or the security of supply lines. The focus of their food security is mainly on price stability and ensuring food security for impoverished people in the country. In contrast, countries with scarce agricultural resources focus on protecting the main food consumption items that they themselves produce (for example, rice or potatoes). This is done in order to maintain a fairly high degree of self-sufficiency, but such countries also focus on providing an adequate supply of food for their people through international trade. In December 2013, China held a central government rural work conference on this issue. This conference took a lesson from the international experience already noted. To meet the new situation and new requirements of China's domestic resource situation, its pattern of supply and demand for food, and changes in the international trade environment, the conference set forth a national food security strategy. This strategy can be described as "implementing a situation that is mainly self-reliant, that is based upon domestic supply as supplemented by the appropriate level of imports, and that ensures production capacities by focusing on greater reliance on science and technology." The aim is to achieve "basic self-sufficiency in cereal grains, and absolute security in grain rations [a specified amount per person]."

In order to craft this national food security strategy and implement it under the new circumstances, two important relationships must be handled properly. First, food quantity must receive adequate attention, but, at the same time, food quality and food safety should receive much more attention. The improvement in people's standard of living in both urban and rural areas places new and higher demands on the quality of food. Ensuring that food is safe requires that government policies put greater weight on food quality and food safety. Second, while guaranteeing adequate supply of food at the current time, we must also focus on the sustainability of agriculture in the future. For a long time now, we have been paying a very high price for raising output and increasing yields. Ensuring food security now means that we must accelerate a switch to more advanced and more sustainable agricultural methods.

Building and implementing the national food security strategy under the new circumstances will mean we need to seize hold of five major tasks. First, we must keep to the "red line" of 1.8 billion *mu* of arable land – that is, make sure the country does not go below that figure. To do that, we must improve upon our policies of maintaining a balance in land that is "occupied" for construction purposes and land that is supplied for agriculture elsewhere in return. The total amount of farmland must not decrease, the uses to which it is put must not change, and its quality must not be allowed to deteriorate. Second, we must mobilize the enthusiasm of farmers to plant grain in the country's main production areas, as well as the enthusiasm of governments in those areas. Maintaining a stable growth in grain production will require greater government protection and support. This means allowing the market to play the decisive role in allocating resources and enabling farmers to see greater benefits from the grain they grow. It means granting real benefits to grain-producing areas. Third, we must explicitly define the responsibilities and accountability of the central government and local governments. The central government bears the responsibility for maintaining an overall balance in the supply and demand of grain on a nationwide basis; local governments bear the responsibility for ensuring a balance in supply and demand at the local level. Fourth, we must give adequate attention to the financial inputs required for upgrading agricultural practices, and we must ensure that we promote the results of scientific innovations and technological improvements on a more widespread basis. Fifth, we must put a high priority on conserving grain. China allows for a prodigious amount of waste as it produces, circulates, processes, and consumes food. Even the waste at dinner tables is shocking, which is where conservation must start, but it must then focus on waste in the processes of harvesting and storing, selling, and processing. The entire society must inculcate an attitude toward not wasting food.

In today's global economy, food security for a given country does not mean relying exclusively on that country's own production. International markets should be made use of as well, to a reasonable degree, in order to maximize the efficient allocation of production factors. As China's role in the global economy becomes more important, its domestic grain markets will unavoidably be impacted by supply and demand fluctuations in international markets. It becomes even more important, therefore, to keep adjusting the balance of supply and demand within China even as we use international markets to the proper degree. China's enormous trade surplus gives it the capacity to import grain from the rest of the world. Under the condition that we maintain overall food security, China may import as appropriate. It also may set up strategic cooperative relationships with major grain-exporting countries; it may indeed become the driver influencing world grain markets. The country may also provide favorable trade opportunities to those developing countries engaged mainly in agriculture. In practical terms, using international imports will be important as a way to moderate China's current wasteful method of grain production – wasteful due to its "extensive" type of agricultural production. Even though China's total grain production increases every year, we have not fundamentally changed the way in which extensive production methods require ever greater reliance on factor inputs in our traditional mode of agriculture. This traditional mode uses production factors [inputs] in highly inefficient ways. In addition, China's extensive mode of grain production does not employ environmental protection technologies, and the lack of such technologies is destroying the ecological environment for farming. Again, imported grain can serve as a major supplement to our domestic grain production. This not only allows us to use better rotation methods in order to make sure we are restoring soil fertility, but it can also help in reducing short-sighted behavior that is willing to sacrifice the ecological environment in order to gain better yields. In sum, the use of international markets can improve China's domestic supply and demand equation. It can improve the efficiency with which all production factors are allocated, and it can lead to a more harmonious relationship between China's grain production and China's natural environment.

Main ways in which China should guarantee its food security

With respect to strengthening China's overall ability to produce grain and how that can be done in a sustainable way, the country must integrate its production capacity with measures that protect the environment within which agriculture operates.

The first thing is to improve the comprehensive productive capacity for grain in the country. The productivity of China's agricultural labor and the productivity of its land have enormous room for improvement. The main way to realize that potential is to use greater economies of scale in various ways. Appropriate and orderly methods should be used to achieve labor productivity and land productivity that move forward together. The second thing is to change the way in which the environment is disregarded as farmers use detrimental methods to increase yields. We must protect the agricultural eco-environment in ways that are effective. That involves surveys for heavy metal pollution in areas being used for agriculture. Through environmental risk assessments, it means determining which areas are most in need of remediation. It requires dividing the worst areas into functional sections and applying remediation treatments according to the degree of pollution, in addition to adjusting crops as necessary. In areas in which pollution is so severe that it is truly necessary to stop farming, we should set up effective subsidy mechanisms to ensure that farmers still have an income and some kind of job. We should pull together the results of existing efforts to convert polluted agricultural fields into wooded areas. We must prevent any attempt to cut down the trees and return the polluted land to farming; instead, we should expand the area and scope of tree planting in land that has been withdrawn from agriculture. We must implement a special system of subsidies to protect land quality, and provide incentives and subsidies for farmers who are willing to let land lie fallow in order to restore fertility and who are willing to restructure or reduce the amount of fertilizers and pesticides that they use.

A number of steps should be taken to improve water conservancy, improve farmland quality, and strengthen the basic infrastructure for water conservancy projects as well as mechanisms for controlling and protecting such facilities. First, improve the quality of farmland. Expand the scope of pilot projects that are testing soil and formulating ways to improve fertility and improve organic matter. Put a major effort into promoting farming technologies that protect soil. Implement reasonable rotation schedules and intercropping; in every way possible, reduce the damage done to the soil by farming. Encourage and guide farmers in the direction of returning stalks to the soil and using "green" manure and more organic fertilizers to increase organic matter in the soil. Second, coordinate remediation measures in grain-growing areas in terms of addressing issues having to do with water, soil, fields, woods, and roads, so that more effort is put into improving middle- to low-productivity land and into farming a higher percentage of high-productivity land. In addition, strengthen the building of infrastructure for greater water conservancy. Accelerate the renovation of facilities in large and medium-size irrigated areas, and upgrade irrigation and drainage pumping stations and the treatment of small and medium-sized streams. Expand the coverage of water conservancy facilities to small farms in key counties. Build more small-scale reservoirs, reinforce existing reservoirs, and develop highly efficient water-saving types of irrigation. Increase the use of rain catchment, and put more effort into creating small ponds for storing water, both for flood control and for drought mitigation. Third, improve the control and protection mechanisms that govern farmland water conservancy projects. Further reform the management system that handles such projects and speed up the effort to provide subsidies for operating and maintaining irrigation and drainage projects. Launch the reform of the property rights system that governs both fields and water conservancy facilities. Clarify the ownership of such facilities, including who is responsible for management and control and who is responsible for costs. Through a process of giving rewards instead of subsidies, or of first requiring completion of a project and then paying the subsidy, explore setting up new mechanisms for achieving better basic infrastructure for water conservancy. Implement a policy that funds water conservancy measures out of income from land transfers. Increase the rates that must be paid for the use of water, and increase efforts to actually levy water-use bills and get payment. Initiate a nationwide plan for drought mitigation that includes improving the ability of farming to handle floods and deal with drought. Implement a nationwide plan to build up high-quality farmland; explore projects within that plan and mechanisms to fund and oversee it.

In terms of the vital need to "storm the pass" and apply scientific techniques to farming, we must promote agricultural technology that uses modern seed advances, push forward mechanization, and improve the service systems that provide agricultural technologies. These are the key priorities. Within these priorities, first, step up efforts to overcome key science and technology problems. Increase funding for basic research and R&D in biotech fields. Improve the quality of fertilizers and promote the use of organic fertilizers. Build "informatization" into the entire process of agriculture, as well as systems for mechanizing and using higher technologies – including a focus on an agricultural Internet of Things and the use of precision equipment. With a focus on more refined processing of agricultural goods, promote technologies that have emerged from New Age R&D. Second, develop a modernized seed industry and push forward the mechanization of agriculture. This includes protecting and further developing a diversity of agricultural products. It includes cultivating high-quality varieties through importing, processing, selling, and promoting such varieties so as to move toward new-generation upgrading of agricultural resources. Through corporations, set up systems that can create new hybrids, and ensure that high-caliber human resources, as well as financial and technical resources, flow toward those corporations. Accelerate the process of mechanizing the entire process of agricultural production. The focus here should be on the lack of mechanized planting and harvesting. Ensure that mechanization is coordinated across the spectrum of using the right seeds and hybrids with the right cultivation technologies and the right equipment. Actively support the development of service industries that can handle all aspects of farm equipment, including repair and leasing of equipment. This includes supporting the development of cooperatives and other entities that can provide such services to farming operations. Third, improve the servicing systems that can promote greater use of agricultural technology. This means strengthening the institutional basis for providing services that are in the public interest at the grassroots level. It means improving the conditions of organizations that promote agricultural technologies and upgrading the service capacities of organizations at the town and village or regional level. This includes support for farmers' cooperatives, specialized service companies, specialized technology associations, farm agents, businesses engaged in agriculture, and other organizations that can provide services. In their role of providing operating assistance, these for-profit [business-type] service organizations should provide all-round services that are low cost and convenient for farmers engaged in food production. We should encourage for-profit businesses to participate in public-interest services through such means as government procurement, targeted commissioning, incentives and subsidies, and invitations for tenders. We should encourage them to develop such initiatives as irrigation and drainage projects and comprehensive pest management systems. We should integrate resources in order to build rural service centers and cooperatives that provide a full range of services. The aim is to create regional "platforms" that provide commercialized services for agriculture, so as to push forward more advanced operations in agricultural production and to ensure that the technologies and advances reach every field and every farmer.

Box 4.2   Accomplishments in developing rice hybrids

The base population that already exists in China is enormous, which has triggered concern both inside and outside the country about how to feed this population. Some foreign observers have even wondered if the total sum of the world's grain exports will be enough to feed China alone. A series of accomplishments in developing rice hybrids is serving as a powerful response to these concerns.

A man named Yuan Longping is, for many people, the very symbol of China's effort to achieve food security. In 1973, the hybridization of rice was formally declared a success in China as yields went from 300 to 500 kilograms per *mu*. In the decade between 1976 and 1987, the increase in rice production due to hybrids totaled 100 billion kilograms. In 1996, the Ministry of Agriculture launched an initiative called the "China Super-Rice hybridization program." A number of high-yield varieties were developed that allowed for increases in yield on the order of 100 kilograms per *mu*, enabling the field to enter a new stage of development every five years. In October of 2014, the Ministry of Agriculture announced the results of Stage Four of the initiative when production in Xupu county, Hunan province, reached a new record of 1,026.7 kilograms per *mu*.

The bottom-line economic results of the rice hybrids initiative are promising. In 2013, the area on which super-rice is planted in demonstration plots yielded more than 131 million *mu*. This exceeded the requirements of the Plan by more than 1 million *mu*. The area constitutes 29.1 percent of China's total land area planted to rice. Within this area, Hunan consistently achieves world records for rice production over a fairly large area. According to rough estimates, farmers who are planting super-rice hybrids are earning an extra RMB 150 per *mu*.

At the same time, China's rice hybrids are now being used in more than thirty countries and regions around the world. The United Nations Food and Agriculture Organization promotes the planting of hybrid rice as a strategic initiative as it seeks to resolve world hunger problems.

Source: Culled from material from people.cn, china.org.cn, and cctv.com. L. R. Brown, *Who Will Feed China? Wake-Up Call for a Small Planet.* New York: W. W. Norton & Company, 1995.

Measures to improve price-formation mechanisms for grain and to enable systems that are regulated by a market include the following: (a) instituting mechanisms for price formation, (b) creating sound market-regulating systems, and (c) allowing the reasonable use of international grain markets. First, on *price-formation mechanisms*, the State determines a target grain price that is based on the equation, production costs plus basic earnings. When the market price is too high, the government provides subsidies to low-income consumers. When the market price is lower than the target price, the government provides subsidies for the price differential to producers. The aim is to have grain price formation be accomplished completely in accord with market supply and demand. Second, on *systems that are regulated by a market*, the overall aim is to guarantee that the domestic supply of grain via the market is basically stable. To do this, we should use such measures as an overall approach to the grain reserve and the amount of grain taken in and sent out from that reserve, together with adjustments that use imports and exports. We should continue to put in place responsibility/accountability systems known as the "rice bag system" for provincial governors and the "vegetable basket system" for municipal mayors. We should launch an initiative that conducts direct surveys of counties that are major grain producers, so as to compile and publish a national grain price index. We should determine the reasonable extent to which prices should fluctuate among different kinds of grain. We must use scientific methods to determine the actual functions of the grain reserve and the optimum size of that reserve, and we should increase the responsibilities and accountability of local [provincial] governments with respect to that reserve, especially in major grain selling areas. The aim here is to optimize the geographic distribution of reserves and the composition of different grain types. Meanwhile, we must improve upon the administrative systems that govern the grain reserve at the central-government level, and we should encourage businesses involved in the grain markets that are eligible by meeting certain criteria to participate in "policy-type" purchasing and storing of grain. Third, on *the reasonable use of international resources and grain markets*, we should conduct research and then formulate an international markets strategy. This includes increasing guidance on import plans, optimizing the sourcing and geographic distribution of grain imports, and setting up stable and reliable grain trade relationships [partners]. We must adjust and improve upon the import structure of major agricultural products and, as appropriate, increase imports of soybeans, vegetable oils, and milk products, among others. We must strengthen the inspection and quarantine system that governs vegetable products coming into and leaving the country, and we must attack and end the practice of private smuggling of grain. This is to ensure quality control of imported grain, as well as the safety of domestic industries. We should accelerate the strategy of encouraging agricultural companies to "stride forth into the world" by cultivating the development of large-scale enterprises that can be internationally competitive and that deal in grain, edible oils, and other agricultural businesses. We should support these enterprises in efforts to develop cooperation in importing and exporting, as well as in the production of grain and various kinds of food. We should encourage financial institutions to be proactive in this effort. By creating innovative ways to finance these efforts, they should support international trade in grain and the initiative of having Chinese agriculture "stride out into the world." Financial institutions should explore the possibility of setting up a fund for international trade in agricultural commodities, and a fund to support overseas agricultural development.

As for ways to improve grain production and policies to support this effort, we should (a) improve our agricultural subsidy policies, (b) set up benefit compensation mechanisms, and (c) provide greater insurance coverage. First, on *improving agricultural subsidy policies*, we should actively expand the pilot programs and improve upon those already under way that have to do with methods of providing subsidies for agricultural products. The aim here is to stabilize the grain reserve, increase the total amount produced, improve upon methods, and make gradual adjustments as needed. We should continue to make direct subsidies to farmers who grow grain. We should provide comprehensive general subsidies for improved seed varieties, farming equipment, and financing. New subsidies should give preference to key agricultural products, new types of agricultural operators, and key production areas. We should launch pilot programs that provide subsidies to producers depending on the actual acreage of land put into grain or the actual amount produced. We should increase the accuracy of subsidies with respect to orientation and results. Subsidies for farm equipment should be increased, and we should continue to promote pilot programs that encourage depreciating old equipment and upgrading to new equipment. We should provide key technical assistance in crisis prevention and drought prevention to enable stable production. Second, on *setting up benefit compensation mechanisms*, we should strengthen State treasury transfer payments to major grain-producing areas, and we should increase incentives and subsidies to the major provinces and counties that grow "commercial" grain [grain sold for a profit on the market]. We should encourage the main parts of the country that actually sell grain to invest in producing parts of the country via various methods. We should have them take on a part of the responsibility for achieving the national grain reserve goal. We should support the development of processing industries in major grain-producing regions, and we should at the same time reduce the amount of auxiliary funding that goes to major grain-producing counties that is directly used on construction projects including grain production. We should launch pilot programs that set aside land for rehabilitation and pilot programs that experiment with ways to remediate agricultural soils that are polluted with heavy metals. We should launch pilot programs that attempt comprehensive treatment methods for places in which underground water exceeds the channeling capacity of drainage systems. We should increase the strength of our efforts to prevent area-wide pollution of agricultural land. We should improve the mechanisms that provide benefits and subsidies to major grain-producing areas by supporting conservation subsidies that protect arable land. Third, on *providing greater insurance coverage*, we must increase the percentage of any subsidy that goes to insurance premiums for major grain crops, with such subsidies coming from both the central government and provincial-level governments. At the same time, we should gradually reduce or eliminate the premium insurance that comes from county-level governments in major grain-producing counties. We should increase the coverage rate as well as levels of insurance on food grains such as paddy rice, wheat, and corn, and we should increase risk levels of insurance.

We should encourage insurance companies to launch special preferential insurance for agricultural commodities and to provide subsidies for premiums, with the understanding that the central government will support this effort through such methods as replacing subsidies with rewards. We should encourage diverse forms of mutual cooperative insurance. We should standardize government administrative handling of the reserve funds that are intended to be put aside for major agricultural disasters. We should accelerate the establishment of decentralized, nongovernment-controlled mechanisms that use government public finance support for agricultural insurance that insures against major catastrophe.

Key policies and measures for safeguarding food safety

First, we need to improve the laws, regulations, and technical standards that relate to food safety. To do that, we must push forward the process of reviewing these and then accelerate the formulation and revision of auxiliary legislation, regulations, and normative documents that support the *Law on Food Safety* and the *Law on the Quality and Safety of Agricultural Products*. We must speed up the work of compiling and revising our standards having to do with food safety. This includes reviewing and integrating the existing laws and regulations that relate to the safety quality of food-related agricultural products, food hygiene, food quality standards, and food industry standards. We must accelerate the formulation and revision of standards that relate to a host of different areas, including standards related to food additives, standards related to the material used in food packaging, the regulation of operating methods in food production, control standards for food safety in restaurant and food service environments, standards for pesticide residues in foods as well as the residue of chemicals used in animal production, standards for pathogenic microorganisms, standards for pollution residues in foods, standards for testing, and standards on the major food products in general. The aim is to improve the national system of standards as a whole as it relates to food safety.

Second, we need to improve the regulatory institutions and oversight systems that relate to food safety. We must establish sound regulatory institutions that handle food safety and operating mechanisms to implement regulations. In gradually improving the institutional framework, we must clarify the functions and responsibilities of relevant departments and eliminate overlapping areas while filling in regulatory gaps. We must establish sound comprehensive cooperative mechanisms in the handling of food safety. This means strengthening capacity building in overall coordination and improving the effectiveness of regulatory oversight. We must improve the systems by which we conduct performance evaluations and improve the degree of regulatory scrutiny over local governments and the departments that work in the area of food safety. We must formulate ways to bring to account those who violate food safety laws and regulations and ensure that those who were responsible for regulatory oversight in such cases are indeed held responsible. We must strengthen the leadership, organizational ability, and cooperative aspects of food safety regulation work, and we must incorporate performance targets in the work performance evaluations of local government officials. We must push forward capacity building in the organizations that deal with agricultural food quality and with food safety at the municipal and county levels of government. We should set up and ensure the sound functioning of regulatory public service institutions that deal with agricultural product quality at the town and county levels.

Third, we need to strengthen management over agricultural production processes and step up treating [cleaning up] the environment where food is grown. This involves setting up and ensuring the sound functioning of regulatory systems that cover the entire process of ensuring food safety: improving industrial policies, constantly modernizing the food industry, standardizing processes, and raising the level of standards. We should strengthen administrative controls over the inputs that go into agriculture. This means implementing beneficial agricultural practices and using fertilizers, pesticides, veterinary drugs, and feedstock additives only to the appropriate and reasonable degree. It means launching remediation projects to clean up soil and water sources, cleaning up the environment around areas where agricultural products are made. It means strengthening regulatory controls over such production sites and making structural adjustments when farmland is in polluted regions. It means increasing the force of environmental remediation efforts in polluted areas that are still producing agricultural products.

Fourth, we must increase efforts to build an information platform and, in that regard, assist the regulatory systems that govern the food safety of imports and exports. In meeting the information demands of managing agricultural product safety and food safety, we should set up a national food safety information platform with complete functions, unified standards, shared information, and internet connectivity. This food safety information platform will be composed of one primary system at four government levels, namely central, provincial, municipal, and county) and of subsystems that operate within each regulatory department handling food safety (see Figure 4.4). The primary and subsidiary systems will

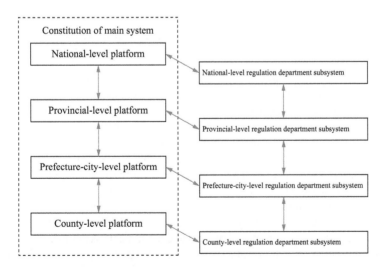

Figure 4.4 National food safety information platform

be connected via horizontal links to form a network. Through this national food safety information platform, the aim is to promote the informatization of the work of monitoring and testing for food safety, regulating and enforcing regulatory laws, and creating food safety regulations and standards.

Fifth, we need to improve the nutrition of certain targeted groups of people. In this regard, the State Council of China issued an opinion called *Opinion of the General Office of the State Council Concerning Implementation of the Nutrition Improvement Program for Rural Students at the Age of Compulsory Education.* This states the principles behind the nutrition program: it is government led, it first conducts pilot programs, it is targeted to specific needs, and it focuses on key priorities. The most direct way to improve the food quality of impoverished populations is to increase their income levels and their purchasing power. By increasing income levels, we increase the ability of households and individuals to actually get food. Tying together education policies and poverty-reduction policies in an effective way is another direct way to improve student nutrition. Providing adequate nutrition during childhood is the fundamental way to ensure the caliber of a country's future labor force. As such, it is a classic kind of "quasi public good." We must therefore improve the sustainability of the program to improve student-age childhood nutrition by improving relevant legislation. We should take full advantage of lessons learned both at home and abroad and should promote nutrition intervention policies and specific programs in a stable way and as suited to China's circumstances. In order to provide policy-formulating bodies with adequate data, we must strengthen our research into the costs and effectiveness of providing meals and of strengthening food quality and improving the nutritional value of food. We should also conduct comprehensive analysis of the results of policy implementation, so as to support ongoing policy formulation.

Box 4.3   The plan to improve the nutrition of rural children at the age of compulsory education

The rate of malnutrition among children is far higher in impoverished rural areas than it is in cities in China. In 2006, the China Development Research Foundation and the Center for Disease Control and Prevention in China set up a joint survey team to investigate the nutritional status of students in two impoverished counties in the Guangxi Zhuang Autonomous Region. The results were shocking. In Du'an and other counties in Guangxi, students ate nothing but salted soybeans and white rice all year and therefore were severely malnourished. Starting in 2007, the Foundation began cooperating with local governments in a program to improve nutrition in Du'an county as well as in Chongli county of Hebei province. They set up canteens and provided subsidies so that students could eat hot meals. After three years of a pilot program, the results of evaluations proved that the provision of meals in school canteens was not only clearly effective in improving nutrition, but

. it raised children's interest in studying as well as their grades. It sparked greater social equality and served as an important way to prevent poverty from being passed from one generation to the next.

This experiment provided a reference point and sufficient evidence for the formulation of relevant policy at the national level. In October 2008, the Third Plenary Session of the 17th CPC Central Committee passed the *Decision on several major issues to do with promoting reform of rural development.* This noted that "improvement in the malnourished condition of rural students should go forward in tandem with promotion of compulsory urban and rural education." Following on this, the State greatly increased funding for the program of providing living allowances for students who attend schools in impoverished areas, with the aim of ensuring that student nutrition is improved by financial support.

In 2010 and 2011, the China Development Research Foundation launched a program to evaluate the results of this policy. The second report in particular found that, despite increased spending by the government for living allowances, improvement in student nutrition was not in fact ideal. After this report was published, the media began to report widely on the issue and undertook its own social surveys. The problem of malnourishment in impoverished areas and the provision of children with meals received tremendous attention as well as a high degree of government concern. The *National Reform and Development Program for Improving Education over the Mid- to Long Term, from 2010 to 2020* noted the need to "improve student nutrition and raise the level of nutrition of students in impoverished regions." The government then also launched nutrition improvement programs for rural primary school students in ethnic minority regions and impoverished areas.

In November 2011, the State Council officially launched the Nutrition Improvement Program for compulsory education students in rural areas, for the purpose of decreasing student malnutrition, enhancing the physical constitution of children, and improving educational quality. The Program covered 23 million middle-school and primary-school students at the stage of compulsory education, in 680 contiguous impoverished areas. Costs were completely covered by public finance at the central government level. The subsidies came to RMB 3 per student per day, or RMB 600 for the year. The total cost of the program was RMB 16 billion. The overall planning of the program was conducted at the provincial government level, with implementation carried out at the levels of municipal and county people's governments. The program was intimately connected to child development and antipoverty initiatives. Implementing it was an important strategic measure in the process of realizing sustainable development in China and building a strong nation through developing human resources.

In 2012, as commissioned by the National Student-Nutrition Office, the Foundation launched a project to evaluate the nutritional improvement program of rural compulsory education students. The evaluation report concluded that this program had basically realized its intended goals. Among the various ways of providing meals, the most effective had been the provision of meals in school canteens. This had basically met the daily nutritional needs of students.

In 2013, governments at various levels continued the effort and increased public spending on the program. Between 2011, when the program was launched, to the end of 2013, central finance allocated a total of RMB 30.03 billion in subsidies for nutritional improvement in this area. It allocated another RMB 30 billion for the building of the canteens. This was in support not only of the nutritional improvement program in the first group of neighboring impoverished areas but also for the launch of local pilot program initiatives in other areas. In 2014, central finance allocated RMB 17.14 billion for a Nutrition Improvement Program. Since November 2014, subsidy allocation standards for areas covered by the pilot programs have increased from RMB 3 to RMB 4 per student per day and have reached RMB 800 per student per year. The nutritional status and physical well-being of students at the age of compulsory education in neighboring impoverished areas have continued to improve.

Source of data: China Development Research Foundation.

Notes

1 China's Agricultural Policy Simulation and Projection Model (CAPSiM), developed by the Center for Chinese Agricultural Policy, can be used to analyze the impact of Chinese urbanization on domestic food production and demand. It can also predict the supply and demand balance of major farm produce in the coming years until 2030. CAPSiM involves fourteen varieties of farm produce including rice, wheat, corn, sweet potatoes, potatoes, whole grains, soybeans, cotton, oil crops, sugar crops, vegetables, fruits and melons, and nine varieties of animal by-products such as pork, beef, mutton, poultry, eggs, dairy products, fish, and shrimp.
2 Yang Jianli and Yue Zhenghua (2014) estimate that by 2020, China's total food demand will reach 860 million tons, while supply will be 690 million tons, leaving a gap of nearly 170 million tons.
3 Lu Xinye and Hu Feifan (2012) estimate that by 2020, China's food consumption will reach 693 million tons while food production reaches 644 million tons, leaving a gap of nearly 50 million tons.

5 Changing the operating systems that apply to Chinese agriculture and speeding up agricultural modernization

- Overall framework of the "new-style agricultural operating system"
- The necessity and the urgency of setting up a new-style agricultural operating system
- The current status of new-style agricultural operating systems, and problems
- Overall rationale for developing the new-style agricultural operating system and basic requirements
- Priorities in developing the new-style agricultural operating system and policy measures

Against the backdrop of industrialization, urbanization, and an aging population in China, modernizing the country's agricultural industry is imperative if we intend to ensure food security. Modernizing agriculture will in turn require the support of the "new-style agricultural operating system" that is described in this chapter. This so-called new-style agricultural operating system is based on the household contracting system, its core operators are "new-style" operators, and it is supported by "socialized" [nongovernmental] services and financial services. These components form a modern agricultural operating system that could be called a three-dimensional compound system. This chapter first looks back at the evolution of the systems governing agriculture in China. Then, aimed at the most outstanding issues facing rural operating systems, it suggests specific policy recommendations with regard to how to change systems and speed up the process of modernizing agriculture.

1. Overall framework of the "new-style agricultural operating system"

The evolution of the systems governing agriculture in China since the start of reform and opening up

Between 1978 and the 18th National Party Congress in 2012, the evolution of institutional arrangements governing China's agricultural operating system can be divided into four main stages. All relate to the household contracting system and the extension of that system to rural industry. The first stage began with the convening of the Third Plenary Session of the 11th CPC Central Committee in 1978. This pushed forward reform of the country's rural economic institutions by encouraging the implementation of a household contracting responsibility system that linked households to agricultural production. People's Communes were abolished in this process. By the end of 1983, 98 percent of all rural households were engaged in the contracted form of production. The second stage began in 1991 with the Decision called *Decision of the CPC Central Committee on Going Further in Strengthening Agriculture and Rural Work.* This called for a two-tiered operating system that combined both centralized and decentralized operations management on the basis of confirming that the household contracting system, as a fundamental system within rural collective economic organizations, must be stabilized over the long run and constantly enriched. The third stage began in 1998 with the Decision of the Third Plenary Session of the 15th CPC Central Committee called *Decision on Various Major Issues to Do with Agriculture and Rural Work.* This confirmed the long-term stability of the system based on household contracting. It noted that China must keep the two-tiered operating system that combines centralized and decentralized operations [management] with the household contracting system and that the household contracting system serves as the basis for this system. It confirmed that the household operating system serves as an operating layer within the overall structure of collective economic organizations. Given that household operations are highly adaptable and full of vitality, it confirmed that they must be adhered to on a long-term basis. The fourth stage began in 2008 with the Decision set forth by the Third Plenary Session of the 17th CPC Central Committee. This called for innovations in agricultural operating systems and speeding up a transformation of farming methods. Household operations should shift in the direction of using advanced technology and production methods, and efforts should be made to farm on a more intensive basis. Unified operations should develop greater cooperation and alliances among households and should move in the direction of establishing diversified, multilevel forms of services that contribute to agricultural operations. The emphasis now was put on organizing farming operations into various kinds of structures.

The various components of new-style agricultural operations and their interconnections

The Decisions set forth by the 18th National Party Congress in 2012 and the 18th National Party Congress in 2013 noted that China should adhere to and improve upon the basic operating system in rural areas as it moves toward a "new-style operating system" that integrates several features. These include more intensive agriculture, more professional agriculture, more institutionalized agriculture [i.e., formed into organizations], and more socialized agriculture [funded by and organized by society at large as opposed to the government]. While adhering to the fundamental standing of the household in agriculture, these Decisions also pushed for innovations that involve the concurrent development of several alternative forms of operations including collective operations, cooperative operations, and corporate operations.

First, the household contracting system remains fundamental in the process of developing new-style entities in agriculture and creating new ways to improve farming. As rural productivity constantly rises, moreover, this system will be the wellspring for increased economies of scale of other operating entities. It will also gradually diversify with ongoing industrialization and urbanization. Professionally oriented larger households engaged in specialized aspects of agriculture, as well as larger household farms, will become the main entities of the new agriculture that develops on the basis of household operations. They will be the backbone of the new-style agricultural operating system. They will become the major suppliers of agricultural goods that are sold on the market and particularly of commodities produced on larger tracts of land. They will become the core strength of cooperative operations. Second, farmers' cooperatives, also based on household operations, will be both the lynchpin and the mainstay linking diverse entities engaged in farming operations. As a form of organization, these cooperatives result from alliances and cooperative relationships among farming households. They are the core of new-style agricultural operating systems, the key force that will be leading household operating entities in the process of competing in both domestic and international markets. Third, agricultural enterprises as an operating [management] method have arisen out of the need to handle such things as transport and the marketing, storage, and processing of grain. They are the forward-looking part of the new-style agricultural operating system and are a key platform that allows decentralized operations to deal effectively with major nongovernmental markets. They are a core force in distributing the value-added benefits to different parts of the industrial chain. Fourth, socialized [or nongovernmental] services for agriculture and rural financial services provide production services and financial services for agricultural operating entities. They constitute a major support for the new-style agricultural operating system. They tie together the indispensable services that the system relies on and are a fundamental safeguard in the process of pushing forward the modernization of agriculture in China (see Figure 5.1).

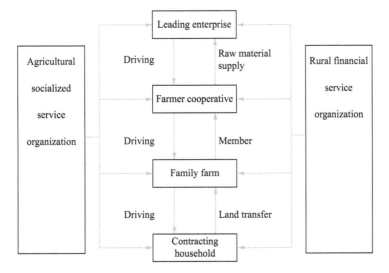

Figure 5.1 Overall structure of the new-style agricultural operating system

2.   The necessity and the urgency of setting up a new-style agricultural operating system

Since the beginning of the 21st century, the processes of urbanization, informatization, and marketization, as well as China's degree of internationalization, have occurred in the context of two major developments. One is the ongoing nonelastic growth in demand for agricultural products within China. The other is the huge shift of the rural labor force and growing constraints on agricultural resources, leading to ever greater market competition. These changes pose challenges to the overly small scale of Chinese farming, as well as its overly dispersed nature, both of which are fundamental characteristics of the country's traditional mode of farming. These things all contribute to several urgent imperatives. China must quickly develop "new-style agricultural farming entities." In changing the systems that govern farming operations and transforming the ways in which agriculture develops, the country must lay a firm foundation for the industry in the future.

Challenges facing the existing ways in which agriculture is developing

In 2013, China's urbanization rate had already reached 53.7, and more than 260 million people had already transitioned out of being part of the farming labor force. Since farming produces fairly low returns and the status of rural society is not considered to be very high, the new generation of "farmers" is not as willing to actually engage in farming. This has led to strong young men leaving the rural workforce, to a decline in the quality of the rural workforce, and to seasonal and regional shortages of farm workers. Traditional farming families are by now dispersed enough that old people, women, and children constitute the main force in agricultural production. The aging of rural areas and the taking on of part-time and second jobs are making it quite clear that China's fragmented small-scale mode of farming cannot continue. The problems are encapsulated in the constant refrain, "Who is going to till the fields and feed the pigs?" The situation presents intense

Table 5.1 Size of arable land managed by farming households

Management area	Number of households (10,000)	Proportion (%)
Less than 10 *mu*	22,659.3	86.0
10–30 *mu*	2,819.3	10.7
30–50 *mu*	611.4	2.3
50–100 *mu*	197.1	0.7
100–200 *mu*	53.2	0.2
More than 200 *mu*	25.7	0.1

Source: Rural Economy Research Department Taskforce of Development Research Centre of the State Council, *Study on Stabilizing and Improving the Rural Basic Management System*. Beijing: China Development Press, 2013, 47.

challenges to the future of China's agriculture. By now, it is simply imperative that we develop what is being called a "new-style agricultural operating system," as characterized by the cultivation of specialized larger farming entities, larger family farms, the formation of rural cooperatives and key [dragon-head] enterprises. These will constitute the diversified entities and operations of the new system.

As domestic and international markets become ever more integrated, market risk and international competition intensify by the day. On the one hand, the international supply and demand for agricultural commodities and the volatility of international prices continue to impact China's domestic markets. This started after China's entry into the World Trade Organization and continues, given the rapid pace at which China is opening up its agricultural markets to the outside world. On the other hand, conditions within China are also having a great effect on agricultural markets, including gradual improvement in the systems that govern domestic markets, rapid development of the futures market, the state of the overall economy, and changes in the capital markets. International and domestic supply and demand, energy, capital, and other factors are by now all interconnected and overlapping. Under their influence, total volatility in the markets for China's agricultural products has increased, and the frequency of fluctuations has also increased. Meanwhile, the overall scale of China's imports and exports of agricultural commodities continues to grow. The dramatic increase in imports of soybeans, cotton, corn, and edible oils in recent years has put obvious pressure on China's domestic production. Traditional farming households are still the mainstay of production within China. The main force in buying and selling continues to be the large number of farmer-brokers who operate through the agricultural operating system. They are simply not up to the dramatic changes in agricultural markets and the massive amount of agricultural imports.

The contradiction between limited agricultural resources within China and the inelastic nature of increased demand is becoming more apparent. It will be impossible to maintain the country's former practice of achieving agricultural growth by relying on greater labor inputs and existing resources. Not only is there the problem of a huge population living on limited land area with inadequate water, but urbanization, industrialization, and fast economic development have taken up even more land and water, intensifying the constraints on resources needed for farming. In addition, rapid urbanization has changed the structure of people's eating habits, meaning that the demand for industrial use of agricultural products is increasing. Overall increases in demand indicate a trend line that is inelastic. Meanwhile, although the past ten years have seen consecutive increases in domestic production and abundant harvests, in aggregate terms, supply and demand are roughly balanced. Unlike the 1990s, when there was "more than enough [a surplus] in abundant years," we now have a "basic balance, with structural shortages and even somewhat tight supply over the long term." These things have notably increased the difficulty of ensuring food security in China and adequate supply of key agricultural goods.

Meanwhile, with economic progress and higher incomes, the demands of urban residents with respect to food *safety* have notably increased. Since the start of the

21st century, not only are people able to consume more, but access to the internet has led to a much greater awareness of food safety issues on the part of urban consumers. Demands for greater food quality and food safety are constantly increasing. In contrast, the food supply system is composed of traditional small-scale farmers and small-time farmer merchants. Not only does this make inspections and regulation difficult, but it is hard to set up standardized regulatory systems that encompass the entire process, both in terms of standardizing administrative procedures and in terms of tracing the source of problems when issues arise.

The importance of establishing a new-style agricultural operating system

The first thing is to improve the returns on farming as relative to other industries and to safeguard farmers' incomes. The massive shift of the labor force out of rural areas and the degree to which the rural population is aging may indeed have lowered the total number of farm hands in the countryside, but these changes have also relieved what had for a long time been a difficult ratio of too many people relative to farmland. As appropriate economies of scale begin to be used in farming, larger-scale operations are also upgrading their systems. By raising the efficiency of farming and the incomes of farmers, the new-style agricultural operating system will resolve the problems of nobody to take over farming and letting land go fallow.

The second thing is to improve the ability of farmers and agricultural operations to handle risk and to be competitive in markets. Necessary policy approaches include speeding up the development of agricultural enterprises, farmers' cooperatives, and other new-style agricultural operating entities. They include integrating production, processing, and sales. They include extending the industrial chain and promoting the integration of preproduction, production, and postproduction links in that chain, increasing the degree to which agriculture forms institutions and organizations, increasing the value-added component of agricultural products, and, finally, developing financial service entities in rural areas and ensuring that they play their intended role.

The third is safeguarding adequate supply to meet the demand for grain by breaking through the constraints posed by input factors. China is faced with a double-barreled problem: resources are limited while the demand for grain keeps growing. The country must move faster in transforming how it "grows" its agricultural industry. This means using more advanced science and technology and better production methods, increasing investment in terms of both technology and capital, putting greater effort into improving yields, and improving the utilization rate of resources and the productivity of agricultural labor. It means increasing the comprehensive productive capacity of agriculture and its capacity for sustainable development. In comparison with traditional, small farming households, specialized large households and family farms are better able to adapt to new conditions by making use of new varieties and new technologies. They have a much greater demand for modern production factors. Specialized large cooperatives and so-called dragon-head, or key enterprises, will be the vehicle for integrating agricultural factors in the most effective way. They will be providing farming households with technical advice and services. Because of this, pushing to develop new-style agricultural operating entities is highly significant in the process of consolidating agricultural operations in China and expediting a change in how farming is done in the country.

The fourth element in establishing a new-style agricultural operating system involves developing a system that safeguards food quality. Developing new-style agriculture operating entities will mean that China is able to draw together dispersed farming households into organizations that can carry on production, that can unify the supply of production materials and technical standards, and that can provide administrative oversight of quality in the entire process of farming and the entire production chain of food production. It means that we will be able to set up tracking systems that go "from the table back to the field where the crop was grown," in ensuring both agricultural food quality and food safety. Through such organizational forms as "specialized large households," "specialized cooperatives," and key enterprises, the aim is to satisfy the requirements of urban and rural consumers with respect to food safety.

3. The current status of new-style agricultural operating systems and problems

The core issue in establishing new-style agricultural operating systems is that of developing the primary operating entities that are and will be involved. Meanwhile, nongovernmental organizations that service agriculture and rural financial organizations that provide financing services to agriculture are necessary as auxiliary support. As China's rural economy becomes more market-oriented and more specialized, new-style agricultural operating systems are already forming in an embryonic way. The main evidence of this is that new-style operating entities are more dynamic, and service systems are clearly already more capable at handling the needs. Rural financing systems are handling needs better as well. However, in terms of really modernizing agriculture in China, the current situation still has quite obvious "short staves in the bucket," limiting factors that hold back progress. These require further action to reform institutional mechanisms and to support the sound development of all kinds of operating entities, nongovernmental service entities, and rural financing organizations, so as to provide the necessary support for modern agricultural development.

The primary types of new-style agricultural operating systems and the status of their development

In this volume, the term *new-style agricultural operating systems* is used to distinguish new-style entities from China's traditional form of household-based operating entities that operate on a completely independent [autonomous] basis. It refers to commercialized agricultural organizations that deal directly in either grain or nonstaple agricultural production and sales. Generally such entities have fairly large economies of scale, extensive equipment, and high levels of managerial expertise. They are efficient in that they use resources efficiently per unit of output. At present, such entities include "specialized large households," "family farms," "rural specialized cooperatives," "shareholding cooperatives, and "industrialized agricultural key [dragon-head] enterprises."

Specialized large households have developed in the context of rural economies that increasingly use a division of labor for separate industries. As a result, "agricultural operating organizations" have gradually coalesced to meet market competition. Family members do most of the work, but production is specialized and standardized. These entities mainly do not work through agents. They are market-oriented and sell through contracts, and they have little overhead costs when it comes to meeting any regulatory requirements. According to relevant statistics from the Ministry of Agriculture, by the end of 2012, there were 682,000 such specialized large households dealing in grain production in China. They farmed a total of 134 million *mu* of land, which is roughly 7.3 percent of China's total arable land.

At the same time, there are a total of 877,000 *family farms*, as defined by specific criteria. These farm a total of 176 million *mu* of land, roughly 13.4 percent of China's total area of "contracted arable land" [that is, land under *cheng-bao* contracts]. Within this figure of 877,000 family farms, 861,000 also raise animals, or essentially 98.2 percent of the total.

Box 5.1 Experimenting with family farms in the Songjiang district of Shanghai

The Songjiang district of Shanghai is located to the southwest of the city and is one of its main suppliers of agricultural products. A portion of the district is located in the Huangpu River watershed protection area where industry is not allowed. Given the shift of agricultural labor into nonagricultural, jobs as well as the aging of the population, this area faces a relatively intense problem of, "Who will farm the land?" Explorations into developing a so-called family farm system in Songjiang therefore began in the second half of 2007. By the end of 2012, a total of 1,206 family farms were raising grain and various kinds of food on 136,600 *mu* of land [about 22,500 acres]. This acreage represented 80 percent of the farmland of the district, and the practice of family farming in the Songjiang district was able to develop quite rapidly.

The government of the Songjiang district provided certain guarantees to family farms with respect to the ability to transfer land, decide about who should operate it, and what socialized services to use. Promoting land transfers in the direction of family farms has had several advantages. It has standardized the way in which transfers were made, it has encouraged older farmers to transfer out of their contracts to the land since they were able to get retirement subsidies on reaching retirement age, and it has strengthened policy support for people who are themselves directly engaged in raising grain. With respect to selecting managers [or operators], it has standardized the procedures for determining who farms the land by clarifying market-entry requirements and -exit mechanisms. It thereby has stabilized the team of operators and helped develop the necessary professionals to carry on family farming. In terms of socialized [nongovernmental] services, Songjiang set up professional servicing systems and promoted the development of better equipped farms and higher standards of field maintenance. It constantly improved the models for providing socialized [nongovernmental] services.

Family farms in Songjiang have some unique features. One is that the family unit is the primary organizational form of agricultural production. Production relies on family members, and family income derives mainly from farming. A second is that the operators of family farms are mainly local people. After a period of professional training, they have sufficient expertise in farming and operations, as well as the technical skills to handle crop growing and animal breeding, to be eligible for the status of "professional farmer." Third, the scale of the resulting farms is kept at levels that allow for economies of scale but that are not too large that they keep more farmers from enjoying the opportunity to increase their own incomes.

Source: Sun Lei, *Explorations and Practices in Family Farms in Shanghai.* Hong Kong: Shanghai University of Finance & Economics Press, 2013.

Farmers' cooperatives are a form of organization for agricultural production and processing operations that provide a number of benefits to farmers. Through alliances and cooperation, they enable farming households to negotiate more successfully in the market, they lower production costs and transaction costs, they increase the ability to get financing and to mitigate risk, and they increase the benefits that go to farmers from the added value of farm goods. Professional [or specialized] cooperatives are a mutually beneficial, business type of organization. They are based on the system of family-contracted operation of the land. They are composed of producers and operators who produce the same kind of product or provide the same kind of services and the people who use those products or services. The joining together of people is voluntary, and the management of the resulting organization is democratic. Shareholding cooperatives are a type of cooperative business organization in which farmers get shares by investing land or other assets. Basic features of farmers' cooperatives include the following: their members are mainly farmers, decision making is carried out by a one-person/one-vote system, income is mainly distributed according to patronage amount, and expansion is via horizontal alliances. According to data from the State Administration for Industry and Commerce, by the end of June 2013, there were 828,000 such registered farmers' professional cooperatives in China on a nationwide basis. Actual membership in terms of households came to 65.4 million. This number represents 25.2 percent of all farming households in China. Within the total number of cooperatives, 45.9 percent are engaged in crop farming, while 27.7 percent are engaged in raising animals.

Table 5.2 Development overview of specialized farmer cooperatives from 2008 to 2013

Year	Number (10,000)	Total input (RMB 1 trillion)	Year	Number (10,000)	Total input (RMB 1 trillion)
2008	11.09	0.09	2011	52.17	0.72
2009	24.64	0.25	2012	68.90	1.10
2010	37.91	0.45	2013	98.24	1.89

Source: State Administration for Industry and Commerce.

Box 5.2   Land shareholding cooperatives in Sichuan's Zhanqi village, which is in Tangchang town, Pi county

Zhanqi village is located 30 kilometers away from Chengdu. At the end of 2011, it was composed of 1,704 farming households who possessed 2,158.5 *mu* of farmland, which came to a per capita area of 1.27 *mu*. The number of people of an age to still farm came to 980, 80 percent of whom lived and worked locally. Zhanqi village has joined with the local collectively owned enterprise in the village, which is called the Chengdu Jifeng Industrial Corporation. In 2007, through land rearrangements, Zhanqi village was able to obtain another 400 *mu* of land, and it also took in invested capital of RMB 98 million from the Chengdu Small Village Investment Co., Ltd. The villagers then began to concentrate in communities, while the industries began to concentrate in industrial parks, and farming could operate with larger economies of scale on larger tracts of land. This provided greater opportunities for the land shareholding company to develop.

The Zhanqi village collective and farming households contributed RMB 500,000 in cash (from the collective) and 1,760 mu (from the households) as shareholding capital, while abiding by the principles of voluntary participation, compensation for contributions, and actions as defined by law. They then jointly established the Zhanqi Village Land Shareholding Company, Ltd. Income to the cooperative came from renting the land, as well as from operations carried on by the collective itself. The cooperative undertook three different kinds of operations once the land was transferred. The first involved building a modern agricultural industrial park. The second involved leasing land to large crop-farming households. The third involved leasing land to key [dragon-head] enterprises for other operations. As a result, the Zhanqi village cooperative was able to serve the following functions. It enabled the consolidation of land resources and raised the efficiency with which land was being used. It allowed for financing from a variety of sources, helping the village to develop. It allowed farmers to become "citified" and raised their standard of living *in situ*, as opposed to having to move elsewhere. And it created a platform by which the benefits of development were shared, allowing the cooperative to serve a public welfare function.

Source: Sichuan Academy of Social Sciences Taskforce. Practice and Exploration on Rural Land Share-Holding Cooperatives, *Western Economic Management Forum*, March 2013.

The industrialization of agriculture is occurring through what are called *dragon-head enterprises* [leading or key enterprises]. These are mainly engaged in the production, processing, and distribution [sale] of agricultural products. In addition, these enterprises link the interests of farming households in ways that enable the integration of production, processing, and sale of the products. This kind of corporatized method of operations represents a fairly high degree of market orientation and is therefore an "organizational form" suited to more modern agriculture. Enterprises that are "corporatized" have sound corporate governance structures and property rights that have been clearly defined. They are efficiently managed, have advanced facilities and technology, and have a fairly strong ability to raise funds and mitigate risk. The value-added component of their products is higher, and they can exert a fairly strong "radial influence" in terms of economic development. All these features argue in favor of opting for the dragon-head form of organization. According to statistics from the Ministry of Agriculture, by the end of 2013, there were close to 120,000 such dragon-head enterprises in China. Among them, 56.9 percent were engaged in growing and processing crops, 27.4 percent were engaged in animal husbandry, and 6.6 percent were producing aquatic products. Industrialized operating organizations, as represented primarily by dragon-head enterprises, are now exerting a radial influence on more than 40 percent of all farming households in China and more than 60 percent of all production bases [land]. Dragon-head enterprises are by now the primary vehicle by which industrial and commercial capital is coming into the countryside and investing in farming in China (see Table 5.3 and Box 5.3).

Table 5.3 Development overview of agricultural industrialized leading enterprises in recent years

Year	Number (10,000)	Sales income (RMB 1 trillion)	Year	Number (10,000)	Sales income (RMB 1 trillion)
2010	9.92	5.02	2012	11.8	6.88
2011	11	5.7	2013	12.33	7.86

Source: Agricultural Industrialization Office, Ministry of Agriculture.

Box 5.3   The Wens model for industrializing agriculture: the Guangdong Wens Food Group Co., Ltd.

The Guangdong Wens Food Group Co., Ltd., is a large, modern, IT-enabled enterprise dealing in agricultural and animal food products. Its activities include the raising of livestock, food processing, equipment for agriculture and animal husbandry, as well as real estate development and industrial investments. It initially began as a chicken farm in 1983, in Xinxing county, Guangdong. The so-called Lezhu chicken farm experimented with the equation company + farming household, and the Wens model went on to be highly successful. In 2013, the company supplied 848 million chickens to the market, as well as 10.13 million pigs, and 14.72 million ducks, all for consumption of the meat. Total income from sales revenue of these products came to RMB 35.2 billion.

The most notable feature of the Wens model is that it ties together dispersed farming households in a form of cooperative production, as described by the equation company + farming household. First, households voluntarily apply to join the system. The company sends representatives to guide the household on the construction of chicken coops. Both sides sign a contract. The company sets up a dedicated account for the household in addition to IT-enabled, digital documentation. The household pays a cooperation security deposit at a standard rate that ranges from RMB 3 to 5 per chicken. For this sum, it receives chicks, chicken feed, and various veterinary medicines for the chickens at specified times. As stipulated in the contracts, the company also provides technical assistance to households at specified times. In a timely manner, it takes in and pays for chickens that have been raised to a specified number of days. After deducting the costs of chicks, feed, and medicines, it splits income with the households on a fifty-fifty basis.

The enormous success of the Wen model can provide lessons in the following respects. First, it builds up a community of shared interests among a diverse group of entities. It ties together farming households and the company in a way that shares both risk and benefits. It divvies out the sums spent on fixed asset investment and production costs, through agreements that guarantee a certain price and that formulate a minimum purchasing price policy. It provides mechanisms for secondary distribution. It enables the absorption of an enormous amount of "people-based" [private] capital, while sharing both risk and benefits with the providers of that capital. Through a shareholding plan for employees, it ties the interests of employees into the future growth prospects of the company. By maintaining a sound relationship between the company and its customers and between the company and its competitors, it has been able to maintain beneficial order in the market. This creates a positive external environment within which the company can grow. Second, the model has built the framework for a scientific approach to organizational structure. On top of the basic equation of company + farming household, it constantly experiments with new organizational forms. While carrying out management within the company that integrates all aspects, it also promotes a flatter organizational structure. This has led to regional integration in addition to improving the company's own competitiveness. Third, the company has focused on the unification of agricultural operations. It has applied industrial operating concepts and planning methods to agriculture. The strategic positioning of the Wens Group involves applying "integrated industrial-chain operations" to agriculture. The group is constantly consolidating and strengthening its competitiveness by focusing on the raising of livestock as its primary business and by sticking to the objective of growth through developing agriculture as an industry.

Source: Hu Xiaoyun and Huang Liangui, *Winning by Following a Model: The Industrialization of Chinese Agriculture – Group Analysis of Dragon-Head Enterprises.* Hangzhou: Zhejiang University Press, 2013.

The current status of socialized service organizations in agriculture

Organizations described as "agricultural socialized service organizations" can be divided into two main categories. The first category is that containing public interest, or public-welfare-type service organizations; these mainly include entities set up by the national government at grassroots levels to provide such services. The second consists of operating-type service organizations, that is, for-profit business organizations, which include all those types that are not public-welfare oriented. In fact, many economic cooperative organizations include both characteristics. According to statistics from the Ministry of Agriculture, by the end of 2013 there were 152,000 public-welfare-type service organizations in China of all kinds, and more than 1 million for-profit operating-type service organizations. (The latter do not include farmers' specialized cooperatives or industrialized agricultural dragon-head enterprises.) These service organizations are playing an increasingly important role in mechanizing agriculture, in preventing and controlling plant diseases and pests in crops, and in preventing and controlling animal diseases and epidemics among livestock.

Table 5.4 Status of institutions promoting agricultural skills in China at all levels of government, on a nationwide basis, in 2012

	Number	*Proportion in total (%)*	*2012 compared with 2011*	
			Change in number	*Change in ratio (%)*
Nationwide	79,011	100.0	−19,501	−19.80
Provincial-level	260	0.33	−88	−25.30
Prefecture-level	2,416	3.06	−786	−24.50
County-level	19,573	24.77	−2935	−13.04
Township-level	56,762	71.84	−15,692	−21.66

Source: Scientific and Technological Education Office, Ministry of Agriculture, Analysis Report on Development Status of Grass-roots Agricultural Skill Promotion System Nationwide in 2012.

Box 5.4   The Hunan Anbang New-agricultural Technology Co., Ltd.

This company originally sold only inputs for agricultural production. In the process of trying to grow, it discovered that its sales of such inputs were shrinking since farmers were abandoning farmland due to losing money on it. In order to protect its own markets, the company then began to provide services for the entire agricultural process, and it entered this field by participating in the process of land transfers. It started experimenting with specialized and standardized services as a way to achieve greater economies of scale.

By now the service model of the Anbang Company employs a complicated form of systems engineering. It requires different tiers of management and specialized division of labor and responsibilities. At the county level, the Anbang Company sets up subsidiaries that are responsible for their own profits and losses and keep independent accounts. Depending on the size of its base area, each county subsidiary has between ten and twenty "comprehensive agricultural service centers." The Anbang Company owns integrated seedling cultivation factories, "smart" [IT-equipped] fertilizer stations, grain drying centers, and so on. It is mainly responsible for formulating standardized technical plans for production and for providing either individual services or a full range of services having to do with seed selection, seedling cultivation, mechanized transplanting, formula-based fertilizing, field cultivation, professional pest prevention, mechanical harvesting, and grain drying. In addition, the company also will plant seedlings, apply pesticides, do soil testing and apply appropriate fertilizers, dry grain, and serve as guarantor of loans, among other things. The county-level subsidiaries are responsible for providing guidance on integrated services to townships. They are responsible for collecting the production plans of large households, among other information. They assemble reports on production plans and the demand for various agricultural inputs. They also sign service agreements with the "three kinds of specialized agricultural cooperatives," namely those dealing in agricultural equipment, in improved varieties of rice, and in pest control and prevention. They charge depending on services rendered. The township "comprehensive agricultural service centers" serve as the main link with the final customers, farming households. They gather together production plans from dispersed farming households, as well as information on the purchasing needs and service needs of these customers. Such things include what crops are being planted and demand for seedlings, pesticides, fertilizers, and so on. Customers also provide them with feedback on the quality of products supplied. Via videos created by agricultural experts, the centers may also provide farmers with the necessary technical training on various aspects of agriculture. The cooperatives engaged in agricultural equipment and in pest control are composed of operators working in these two areas. They provide services according to written contracts and perform field cultivation, seedling transplanting, and other key production processes on contiguous fields. The cooperatives engaged in high-yield rice varieties are composed of large-household producers. They are responsible for land "circulation," for formulating specific plans for each parcel of land that is farmed, and for dealing with both the enterprises on the one hand and the farming households on the other in settling accounts. Large-household producers are responsible for basic farmland management, except for those services outsourced to others. They keep independent accounts of their income. Each usually farms an area of around 200 *mu* [33 acres].This mode of farming, using specialized service companies, leverages the technical strengths of public service institutions in soil testing, fertilizer recommendations, and the monitoring of destructive pests. It also allows specialized cooperatives to provide labor-intensive services. From the bottom up, townships report on farm input needs and service requirements to county subsidiaries, which report them on up to the company. They also provide feedback on the quality of inputs. Farming inputs and services then flow from the top down, so that demand is efficiently linked with supply.

The Anbang Company has gradually extended this model for farming in ways that allow the farming household and the company to achieve a win-win situation. Due to the specialization and division of labor, the entire process is mechanized. This lowers the amount of labor required in farming and allows farmers to go from handling 10 *mu* to handling between 200 and 500 *mu*. Large producers can earn around RMB 150,000 a year in farming income. By using advanced technologies for soil testing, by applying only the appropriate kinds and quantities of fertilizer, and by using specialized and consistent, unified methods of pest control, the quantities of fertilizer and pesticides have been reduced – fertilizer usage rates have gone down by 8–10 percent. Not only does this save on the production costs of farming, but it increases crop yields. Bottom-line results have gone up by some RMB 300 per *mu*. The company earns its income primarily from marketing the crops that are produced, as well as the inputs that are used for production, from organizing the outsourcing of services and from value-added processing of grains, as well as other links in the overall process. A full range of services per *mu* of land earns the company around RMB 100 per *mu*; specific services earn between RMB 20 and RMB 50 per *mu*. The larger the scale of operations, the more the income the company generates.

Source: Xi Yanqing, Zhao Liang, Jiang Yugui, "Comparison and Control Analysis regarding productive social service models" , Rural Management, April 2013.

The current status of rural financial services organizations

Systems that can provide financial services in rural areas are an indispensable part of the new-style agricultural operating system. A system with all necessary functions should be able to handle diversified financial services, including savings deposits, loans, insurance, futures, and securities. Under the dual urban–rural system as it developed in China, however, development of cities and industry took precedence over any development of the countryside and agriculture. A very substantial amount of rural savings were therefore taken in by such banking channels as the postal-bank system, rural credit cooperatives, and State-owned banks, and these funds were then drawn out of the countryside. As a result, rural financial markets remained undeveloped. Prior to the 21st century, there was essentially no insurance or securities business in the countryside at all, while credit was severely limited (Liu Minquan et al., 2006).

Since 2003, China's agricultural development policies have been adjusted, and rural financial markets are beginning to welcome new opportunities. They are now facing rapid development as indicated by the new round of reform of rural credit cooperatives. The situation today is that three different kinds of credit markets are developing in tandem, namely commercial-type credit, policy-type credit, and cooperative credit. New types of banking entities, such as village banks and micro-finance companies, are now constantly emerging, and the ability to finance farmers, farming, and the rural economy is notably stronger than it was before. By the end of 2012, the aggregate rural loan portfolio in both local and foreign currencies of all financial institutions at the county level and below in China came to RMB 14.5 trillion. This represented 21.6 percent of the total balance of loans in the country. This rural loan balance had increased by 188.6 percent over the total at the end of 2007. Loans to farming households at the end of 2012 came to RMB 3.6 trillion, a sum that represented 5.4 percent of all loans. This figure represented an increase of 170.1 percent over the balance at the end of 2007. Meanwhile, the number of towns that lacked any financial institutions whatsoever went from 2,945 in October of 2009 down to 1,686 by end-2012. By end-2012, more than 84.4 percent of loans being made by the "new-style rural financial institutions" were going to farmers, farming, and the rural economy, as well as to small enterprises (Xie Ping and Xu Zhong, 2013).

In addition to "proper" financial institutions that have registered with authorities in industry and commerce departments, the countryside also has a variety of other unofficial financing methods that serve rural financial markets. These include private lending, mutual aid societies, loan agents, and business credit. These unofficial methods take advantage of the low cost of transactions and excellent information channels that have developed over time among neighbors and relatives in rural areas. They supplement the financing of agriculture and small businesses in the countryside in ways that go outside normal financial channels. Since they also lie outside of normal financial regulatory processes, however, at times they can lead to credit crises and all kinds of disputes. This can adversely affect normal business operations in the countryside, as well as social stability (Liu Minquan et al., 2003).

In the area of insurance, pilot programs to extend policy-type insurance for farming are constantly being expanded, while pilot programs offering commercial-type insurance and major catastrophe insurance are also being pushed forward (China Development Research Foundation, 2014). Statistics indicate that between 2007 and 2011, premium income from Chinese agricultural insurance exceeded RMB 60 billion in cumulative terms. The average annual increase in income from premiums came to 85 percent. In 2012, total nationwide premium payments for agricultural insurance in China reached RMB 24.06 billion. By now, China's agricultural insurance markets are second only to those of the United States in size.

Characteristics of the new-style agricultural operating system and its problems

First, the "status" of the new-style agricultural operating system has not been clarified. The State has still not issued any methods for registering such new-style agricultural operating entities as "large households" and "family farms," nor has it implemented any procedures in this regard. This places severe constraints on the ability of such entities to grow, as well as on the development of rural cooperatives and rural shareholding companies. Registration still faces both legal and policy hurdles, which puts operations and management at considerable risk.

Second, the internal operations of many new-style operating entities are quite irregular. This lack of standardized operating procedures in rural cooperatives can be characterized in the following summary: bylaws are incomplete, governance structures are unsound, democratic management does not really take place, the distribution of benefits is not in accord with rules, and so on. Some rural cooperatives still have the problem of insider control by the core people involved. Some operating entities have not in fact set up mechanisms to ensure that the interests of farming households are tied in to results. This has led to the inability of farming households to actually increase their income from production. Many farming households are not yet able to enjoy their fair share of the increase in value of industrialized farming operations.

Third, agricultural socialized services are not keeping pace with what is needed. The ability of new-style agricultural operating entities to develop specialized production is tied in to the provision of professional services by modernized service organizations. At present, however, agricultural socialized service systems are not yet sufficiently developed, so their ability to deliver public-welfare-type services is quite weak. Meanwhile the for-profit business-type service organizations are still relatively incompetent when it comes to providing services. Methods of providing services are backward, services are limited in variety, and overall standards of service are low.

Fourth, in overall terms, the system of financial services in rural areas is out of date and inadequate. Even though progress has been impressive in the past ten years, rural financial markets are still rife with problems in terms of both supply and demand. On the supply side, such financial institutions as postal savings banks and rural credit cooperatives have massive problems when it comes to internal governance structures. In addition, they are unable to innovate, and there are substantial barriers to entry for other more innovative approaches in the financial arena, while exit mechanisms are not yet developed. The types of financial services being provided are limited, and it is hard to generate any synergies among different services. All of these things limit capacities on the supply side. On the demand side, there has been no fundamental change in the way in which farming households operate on a small scale and face tremendous risk. The level of financial expertise among rural people remains low and also prevents small and medium-sized businesses from entering financial markets and using financial services. In addition to all this, regulatory capacities are limited in rural finance. This includes regulatory control over the systems that levy credit, and those that govern deposits and insurance. There are limited regulatory controls on pricing and limited infrastructure when it comes to regulating issuance of credit and the systems that govern deposits and insurance. All of these things hold back the development of rural financial markets.

Fifth, government policy support for new-style agricultural operating systems is not in place. At the level of formulating policy, objectives have not yet been clarified as to why we need policy support. Supporting measures are not specific enough, and some are not forceful enough in their degree of support. In terms of enforcement, only a fraction of enforcement measures are actually implemented; many measures have not been put into effect at all. Meanwhile, the lack of oversight and evaluation of policy enforcement procedures leads to some measures being out of date while others cannot be adjusted and improved in time to be effective.

4. The overall rationale for developing a new-style agricultural operating system and basic requirements

In the course of building a moderately prosperous society in an all-round way, our basic objectives should be to promote ongoing increases in the income of farmers and to safeguard food security and food safety. Our main tasks should be to promote agricultural modernization, to develop new-style agricultural economic entities and to improve the new-style agricultural operating system.

Choosing different organizational forms and operating methods depending on type of agricultural production

In creating new ways of handling agriculture, we must stick firmly to the fundamental status of family operations, while pushing forward the joint development of all kinds of operating entities and service systems. Given the premise of maintaining the "basic operating system" in rural areas, constructing a new-style agricultural operating system is in fact an improvement and advance upon the system that uses household contracting for production and that employs a two-tiered administrative system combining both centralized and decentralized operations. The tier that is described as "decentralized" [or independent] mainly means developing specialized large households and family farms in order to increase the degree to which farming is intensive, to increase the size of family operations, and to raise levels of specialization. The tier that is "centralized" [or unified] mainly means cultivating farmers' cooperatives, dragon-head [leading] enterprises, socialized service organizations, and rural financial services organizations. It means improving the degree to which agricultural production is carried out through organizations, is industrialized, and is "socialized" [carried out by society at large as opposed to government]. The vast numbers of contracting households will still be the important base of agricultural operations.

The raising of crops and animals are production activities suited to family operations, and the emphasis should be on developing large specialized households and family farms. The crop-raising and livestock-raising industries are a process that intertwines economic reproduction and natural reproduction. With families as the basic unit for production, the interests of all members are highly aligned while the motivation to produce and the sense of responsibility for the results of labor are high. This matches the characteristics and requirements of the industries. The experience both inside China and abroad is that family operations continue to be the dominant mode of agricultural production. The benefits of using family operations are even more apparent when raising field crops on large tracts of land, given the vagaries of nature and the uncertainties of when people have to go out and work. In the case of livestock and poultry breeding, specialized large households and family farms require the assistance of other forms of operating entities and services. Different operating methods should be adopted depending on the specific agricultural industry and product being produced. In places in which labor has transitioned out of agriculture to a greater degree and in which secondary and tertiary industries are more developed, the main orientation should be in the direction of family farms. In large-scale crop-raising and livestock-raising industries that require more capital and higher technology, from actual experience we can see that corporate operations are more appropriate. This applies when agriculture requires facilities that meet high standards or when improved traits are being developed. In places that have fairly prosperous rural collectives and high management capacities, it will also be appropriate to develop large-tract crop-farming operations through the use of land shareholding cooperation.

For the purchase of farming inputs and for the marketing of farming products, as well as for production-type services, it is appropriate to use a cooperative form of operations. The emphasis here should be on developing farmers' cooperatives and agricultural socialized service organizations. The cost of purchasing inputs and marketing products is fairly high in terms of all agricultural production costs, while provision of services is quite specialized. Because of this, we can consider gradually separating out such things from family operations and making them independent. Individual farming households are in a weak position relative to merchants who supply inputs and market products, while going through intermediary organizations raises transaction costs. The experience of other countries shows that operating on a cooperative basis can improve the negotiating ability of individual farmers. In developing such farmers' cooperatives, the emphasis should be on production-type services such as purchase of inputs, marketing of products, use of farm equipment, and protection of crops. To enable cooperation among a diverse membership, it will be necessary to foster internal credit arrangements and alliances among cooperatives and to expand the methods and areas in which cooperatives operate.

For the processing of farm products and logistical links, it is appropriate to think of enterprises or corporate structures. The priority here is to create key [dragon-head] enterprises that can be powerful drivers of the agricultural industry. The capital requirements of processing and logistics are substantial while the need for standard-ization is high. These things mean that operating entities must have deep-seated funding and management capabilities, as well as the ability to respond to markets. At present, it is hard for either households or the great majority of cooperative entities to meet these demands. Experience has shown that corporate-type operations have clear advantages in these areas. The State should encourage and guide investment capital into areas in agriculture that are appropriate to corporatized operations. It should encourage commercial and industrial capital to invest in modern production factors and operating methods, and to provide preproduction, production, and postproduc-tion services to specialized farming households and farmers' cooperatives. The aim is to develop integrated agricultural operations. In developing the processing and logistical sectors of agriculture, the priority is to cultivate dragon-head enterprises but also to strengthen their radial influence. They should set up effective links with farming households, specialized large households, family farms, farmers' coopera-tives, and other entities through such means as order-based procurement, secondary refunds, and shareholding cooperatives in order to combine interests in ways that share the risks and the profits through win-win cooperation.

In order to construct a new-style agricultural operating system, we must focus on the proper handling of several important relationships

There are major disparities in economic and social development in different parts of China, while different business entities also operate under vastly different conditions and develop at different speeds. Methods used by different entities also vary greatly.

In developing a new-style agricultural operating system and creating new operating models for the practice of agriculture, we must therefore proceed on the basis of China's overall basic realities while taking into consideration regional differences. This means focusing on the proper handling of the following important relationships.

The first relationship is between the new-style agricultural operating entities and the household contractual operating system [*cheng-bao*]. It involves developing the former while maintaining the stability of the latter. The new-style agricultural operating system is to be built on the foundation of this *cheng-bao* system. It is highly important to handle this relationship properly and to preserve the stability of the household contractual operating system. Farmers' cooperatives, dragon-head enterprises, and other forms of new-style operating entities can provide household operations with a variety of production services. They can help generate higher incomes for farming families. Meanwhile, household operations can provide new-style operating entities with stable sources of processed materials and can realize increased efficiencies and value-added through extending the production chain and expanding the value chain. In our handling of policies and systems, we must provide support to both household contractual operations and new-style operating entities.

The second relationship is that between new-style operating entities and agricultural socialized services. Consolidating farming, that is, farming more intensively through the use of new-style operating entities, will require a whole series of professional services relating to market supply and demand of agricultural products, price changes for agricultural products, production technologies, financing, and insurance. Many of these things are already beyond the ability of operating entities to handle on their own, while the costs of doing it alone are too high. They require "socialized service organizations" that operate on a larger scale to provide the services for them. In developing new-style agricultural operating entities, therefore, we must put even greater priority on developing socialized agricultural services.

The third relationship is that between appropriate economies of scale and raising the yields or productivity of the land. Through expanding economies of scale and using modern inputs and operating methods, new-style agricultural operating entities can improve the productivity of labor as well as the productivity of the land. If scale becomes too large, however, and exceeds operating capacities and levels of management, so-called economies of scale become counterproductive. New-style entities should therefore suit their operations to the needs of local land resources and market conditions. They should be aware of the limits of their managerial capacities, and they should develop appropriate economies of scale in their agricultural operations.

The fourth relationship is that between new-style agricultural operating entities and the rate at which rural labor is transitioning off the land. On the one hand, the development of new-style entities is conducive to shifting surplus rural agricultural labor off the land. New-style entities often are both willing and able to use mechanization to replace hard physical labor, which is also beneficial to raising the productivity of agricultural labor. When mechanized methods cannot substitute for labor in some places or for some processes, new-style entities may hire people who are somewhat older but more experienced to do the work. They thereby enable some of the surplus labor [younger people] to shift toward nonagricultural occupations while still using those who cannot shift to other occupations in productive ways. On the other hand, new-style entities must ensure that there is mutual benefit in shifting labor into other occupations. The process must be done according to the needs of the people themselves who are being defined as surplus rural labor. Rural land transfers must be done in ways that are both positive and stable, and agriculture must be developed using appropriate-size operations.

The fifth relationship is that between government guidance and market forces. The government should play the dominant role in some instances; some things must not be pushed casually in the direction of the market, such as organizations that deal with public-welfare-type services. Things that involve key aspects of agricultural operations, such as disseminating new technologies, ensuring adequate financial support, and so on, should receive reasonable government guidance. Scholars have pointed out that government can be effective in certain interventions, including policies regarding technical innovations having to do with agriculture, allocating research funds, and the disseminating the results of research (Lin Yifu, 2005). On the other hand, the role of the market must be respected as well, including its price-regulating functions and its ability to allocate resources. Both government and market will play key roles in furthering the modernization of agriculture in China. Neither can be disregarded; both must support one another.

5. Key tasks and policy measures in developing the new-style agricultural operating system

Key tasks

The first key task is to encourage people to circulate [shift, transfer] their contractual operating rights over land in the direction of specialized large households and family farms and to develop larger-scale operations of various kinds. We must improve how we administer rural land transfers as we encourage this process. This involves creating a sound market for transfers of operating rights over contracted land. It involves building a platform to enable such transfers and setting up service systems at the three levels of county, township, and village governments. It means creating channels for the free flow of information on supply and demand and providing services that give guidance on contracts, price negotiations, and dispute resolution. The aim is to guide land transfers in the direction of being voluntary, conducted as per laws, and carried out in a stable fashion. Under the premise that the wishes of farmers must be respected, we should actively promote different methods of transferring rights: transfer to assigned agents [authorizations], transfer to shareholding cooperatives, and transfers on a seasonal basis. We should promote transfers of an entire village, organization, and swath of land, so as to increase the size of farming operations. We should promote profit distributions that can be made in kind as well as in cash and ability to adjust rental rates in a dynamic way. If land is entered into shareholding arrangements, there should be a minimum distribution every year, and so on. We must stabilize land-transfer processes and relationships and ensure that the rights and interests of both sides are respected according to law. The second thing is to set up effective mechanisms that enable specialized large households and family farms to have priority in receiving land transfers. Through public-finance support, we should establish different categories and levels of subsidies, so as to encourage households that are granting land-use rights to set up long-term leasing contracts with large households and family farms. The aim is to develop stable and appropriate economies of scale. The third thing is to set up mechanisms for certifying and cultivating "model family farms." Family farms may apply for this on a voluntary basis. We should set up certification, administrative, and training systems for such family-farm certification. On a targeted basis, we should establish supportive policies that use public finance, taxes, and preferential financing terms to encourage the right results.

The second key task is to guide farmers in strengthening alliances and different forms of cooperation so as to have a variety of new-style farmers' cooperatives. We should put major effort into these farmers' cooperatives, as per the principle of "advancing with vigor, gradually standardizing [regulating], strengthening support, and raising the caliber of results." First, this involves developing specialized cooperatives that meet consistent requirements, which means concerted application of the *Law on Farmers' Specialized Cooperatives*. It means guiding cooperatives to formulate bylaws that are consistent with their actual circumstances, to set up internal governance systems that operate properly and actually achieve a situation in which decision making and management are democratic. Second, this involves developing land cooperatives in a stable and consistent way. Adhering to the principle of voluntary participation by farming households means that such cooperatives should be promoted in a stable and secure way. Administrative procedures for registering the establishment of both rural land-shareholding cooperatives and rural collective-shareholding cooperatives should ensure that false registration, under the pretext of being a cooperative, does not in fact infringe upon the land-contract rights of farmers. Third, this involves encouraging the establishment of allied farmers' cooperatives. On top of specialized cooperatives, we should support the allied operations of cooperatives that deal with the same industry or the same kind of product. We should put in place preferential tax policies that help promote this, that support farmers' cooperatives as they develop and circulate [sell] value-added agricultural products. We should put major effort into the ability to store, market, and process agricultural commodities. The aim is to increase competitiveness in the market and to build higher capacity among farming households. Fourth, this involves guiding cooperatives in the direction of launching internal credit cooperation, that is, self-funding via the pooling of funds. This must operate according to established principles: "restricted to use by members of the cooperative, used only for development of the cooperative's business, allowing share participation but not allowing erosion of savings, and distributions of dividends but not of [bank] interest." On the condition that those principles are met, we should guide cooperatives that have a strong business foundation, are fairly large in scale, have a good ability to mobilize resources, and have a good credit record in order to begin to use internally generated funds as credit to finance further business development. We must set up appropriate regulations to govern this process, to ensure that it is done on a "regular" [as opposed to irregular] basis, and to ensure that it proceeds in a sound way.

The third key task is to cultivate large, powerful, dragon-head companies that engage in industrialized agriculture. We should then link their interests with other entities via sound mechanisms. We should go further in cultivating such companies given the rationale for "optimizing resource allocations, concentrating operations, developing greater economies of scale, and pushing forward entire systems." This involves three key aspects: creating larger and stronger companies, linking their interests to those of farm households, and guiding industrial and commercial capital to invest in rural development in ways that will foster the growth of large companies. First, we should nurture a group of companies to lead the charge in advancing the agricultural industry by supporting their formation through mergers, reorganizations, acquisitions, and controlling shares in other companies. We should set up "model bases" to serve as examples of the industrialization of agriculture, and we should build public-service platforms that help strengthen technological innovation, methods of inspecting and ensuring quality, logistical information, and brand promotion. We should constantly upgrade the ability of model bases to take the lead in modernizing agriculture. Second, in ensuring that the interests of these companies are aligned with those of farmers, we should expand the practice of "order-based agriculture," standardize the terms of contracts and procedures for signing contracts, and explicitly define rights and responsibilities. We should encourage farming households, family farms, and cooperatives to invest in such dragon-head enterprises by using capital, technology, or other factors. The aim is to form entities that have interests in common through linking up property rights. Third, in guiding investment capital, we should integrate the building of all kinds of modern industrial parks for agriculture, with the investment of industrial and commercial capital in agriculture. We should guide such capital to help modernize agriculture through the vehicle of such parks, so as to optimize the geographic distribution of the industry and consolidate its foundation. In terms of development plans, we should link the investment of capital into agriculture with the development of agricultural industries by encouraging investment in such things as developing improved varieties of seeds and animals, high-standard agricultural facilities, the diffusion of scientific and technical results, and other fields that are appropriate to corporatized operations. In addition, we should encourage industrial and commercial capital to invest in unproductive mountainous areas and other places where the land is not easily farmed due to topography. We should encourage investment in the pre- and postproduction of services related to processing, marketing, and technology. We should constantly seek to expand the radial influence of these large companies.

The fourth key task is to construct new mechanisms for "socialized services" and to cultivate a diversity of service entities. Given our policy orientation of "diversifying entities, making services more professional, and operations more market-driven," we should accelerate the integration of public-welfare types of services and business-type [for-profit] services and the coordination between single-purpose services and comprehensive services, as we create a new-style agricultural socialized services system. In doing this, we first should continue to strengthen the systems that govern public-welfare services in agriculture. We should institute systems for hiring people for public-service organizations and should standardize the criteria for putting people in such jobs. The "work responsibility system" in which these people engage must focus on public-welfare activities that cover all villages and reach all households [as well as cooperatives, enterprises, and base areas]. This must be their primary mode of operations. We will gradually develop new mechanisms that can deliver public-welfare services via having these service personnel focus on demonstration ["model"] households while they in turn mobilize the extension of public-good services to other households. In this way, we should constantly strengthen our capacity to deliver public services to rural areas via public-service institutions. Second, we must speed up the process of developing for-profit service organizations in agriculture. Via the use of government procurement, targeted commissioning, incentives and subsidy programs, and invitations to tender bids, these for-profit business-type entities can be guided to participate in the provision of public-good services. Production services that might serve as examples are the prevention and control of plant diseases and harmful pests, the prevention and control of animal diseases and epidemics, the building of irrigation and drainage systems on farmland, and the use of and also removal of plastic sheeting when used in agriculture. We must also cultivate intermediary service organizations that relate to agriculture, including accounting and auditing, asset appraising, consulting on laws and policies, and so on. Third, we must constantly seek to find innovative ways to provide socialized services. We should combine our existing "platform" as it relates to agricultural services with other services to create an integrated services platform that, at the county level, covers such things as technical guidance, the marketing of commodities, the supply of inputs, land transfers, the servicing of farm machinery, prevention and control of epidemics, and so on. We must ensure that the supply of such services is effectively linked to demand. We should promote certain models for delivering services, which include specialized services company + cooperative + farming household, rural collective economic organization + specialized services team + farming household, and agriculture-related enterprise + experts + farming household. By summing up the experience of the best examples, we should make full use of the demonstration effect. Fourth, we should launch the establishment of so-called model counties with respect to agricultural socialized services. On a nationwide basis, we can select a group that leading officials feel are worthy based on their ability to serve as models for other counties and municipalities. based on their good foundation. We can use them as models in how to cultivate service entities, broaden the field of services, innovate in methods of providing services, build a better climate for development, and so on. In doing this, we should explore the most effective mechanisms by which we push forward the work of agricultural socialized services.

The fifth key task is to make full use of innovations in agricultural sciences and technologies. In this regard, we should make use of a combination of both traditional and newly emerging technical methods. We must raise the overall level of technologies employed across the entire spectrum of agricultural processes, from farm production to business operations. We must begin to optimize agricultural operations in general. First, this means guiding scientific resources to invest in agriculture, integrating market forces in order to spur greater dissemination of scientific results, and ensuring that research results are transformed into actual production. Second, it means emphasizing the convenience of e-commerce and internet technology in dealing with agricultural commodities that are of a commercial nature. Through timely information exchange, business entities dealing in agriculture can understand the supply and demand status of the market, as well as more detailed information on market conditions. They can avoid losses caused by not having access to information and can improve operating efficiencies.

The sixth key task is to step up efforts to expand financial support for farmers, farming, and the rural economy and to improve actual results via developing a rural financial services system. Through further reform of rural financial markets, we should alleviate the existing "financial repression" experienced by rural financial markets. We should loosen interest-rate restrictions on rural financial markets in an orderly way so that credit and loan markets can reflect the actual conditions of the supply and demand for capital. We must build greater infrastructure for rural financial markets, with an emphasis on building credit evaluation systems for farmers and small and medium-sized companies. We should also make such systems more unified and consistent over a larger area. We should use the full potential of modern information technology in this regard in order to create rural financial services that meet the needs of a diversified body of rural people. We should increase the severity of investigations into irregular types of financing, and we should increase our "guidance" over economic sectors [departments] that engage in irregular types of financing. Irregular practices should be regulated so that they can properly supplement regular finance.

Measures to resolve problems in developing the new-style agricultural operating system

Reform the rural land management system. First, we must improve the policies that relate to the contracting of rural land. We should launch a full-scale effort to confirm rights and certify registration with respect to rural land. We should explore the possibility of separating out "contracting rights" from "operating rights" and ways to do that. On the basis of confirming and putting in place ownership rights of collectives, we must stabilize contractual rights and invigorate operating rights [i.e., allow them to be transferred]. The essential nature of a certificate describing "land *ownership* rights" is that it confirms property rights over land that are held by the collective. The essential nature of a certificate describing "land *operating* rights" is that it describes the membership rights of a collective economic organization. The "land *operating* rights certificate" is what is used to transfer rights and what should be able to be used as collateral for a loan. Second, we must improve mechanisms that allow for the orderly transfer of land. Relevant authorities should issue the necessary "guiding opinion" as soon as possible. This should encourage and support local governments in setting up a dedicated fund that is to be used on achieving economies of scale in farming operations. It should encourage farms to transfer contracted operating rights to large households, family farms, farmers' cooperatives, and other such new-style agricultural operating entities. Relevant authorities should formulate specific ways to do this. They should establish a regulatory system that allows market access to industrial and commercial enterprises that can lease farmers' contracted land. The focus of the system should be on due diligence and corroboration of the extent of a company's financial resources, the businesses in which it is engaged, the actual transfer contracts, uses to which the land is to be put, and so on. Relevant authorities should strengthen supervisory oversight over the progress being made with respect to project investments, payment of rents [to farmers], protection of resources in the farmed area, and so on. Third, we must improve the basic situation that applies to land. That means trying to address the issue of highly fragmented contractual arrangements through such things as land swaps in order to consolidate farm ground. We recommend that central finance set up a special fund to facilitate this. Counties (as well as cities and districts) that have made clear improvement in swapping land parcels in order to achieve consolidation would be rewarded financially [as opposed to receiving subsidies in advance to achieve the process]. In addition, the various initiatives [as already described] should be integrated, that is, those involving "confirming rights and issuing certificates," "swapping land-use rights to consolidate farm ground," and "building basic infrastructure on farm ground." Project funds that apply to these should be combined, that is, those relating to "bases for growing commercial grain crops," "the development of high-quality fields," "comprehensive development of agriculture," "reorganization of fields," "water conservancy projects on farmland," and so on. Major effort should be put into creating larger swathes of contiguous high-quality farmland that produce good yields despite adverse weather conditions.

Explore innovative ways to develop rural financial and insurance systems.
First, this means improving the financial system in rural areas, developing a variety of "new-style rural financial institutions," creating new ways to deliver financial services and products, and allowing farmers' cooperatives to deal in cooperative credit arrangements. It means providing financial support for the entities engaged in new-style agricultural operations. It involves expanding the scope of what can be used as collateral for rural loans, as well as improving the mechanisms that disperse risk in financial institutions in rural areas. It involves incorporating the following into the range of things that can serve as collateral for loans: the land operating rights of new-style agricultural operating entities, property rights to housing, auxiliary facilities on farm ground, large-scale farming equipment, and so on. In this process, we must set up credit evaluation systems for new-style agricultural operating entities. This includes establishing a rating system that grades credit and extending the amount of credit that can be made available to entities. We must explore new mechanisms for guaranteeing loans, which might include having public finance set up loan-guarantee companies that provide such services to new-style agricultural operating entities. We also could set up mutual-assistance loan-guarantee funds at the village level that provide guarantees for new-style agricultural operating entities, and we could have dragon-head companies provide such loan guarantees to cooperatives and family farms. Second, this means improving agricultural insurance systems. This can be done by increasing the variety of policy-type insurance products available to farming, especially for such agricultural products as vegetables and fruit, which have a fairly high risk coefficient. We should set up a fund for subsidizing insurance that covers major

agricultural disasters, with public finance support. We should increase the amount of subsidies for premiums for such insurance, in order to reduce natural risks that hinder our development of new-style agricultural operating entities. For large grain-producing households and grain-producing cooperatives, we should launch pilot programs that provide subsidies for types of insurance that are indexed to weather, grain yields, and grain prices. We should explore pilot insurance-subsidy programs for new-style agricultural operating entities that trigger insurance depending on the income derived from grain production.

Box 5.5   The mutual aid cooperative of the Moslem population [*hui-min*] in Mayu town, Rui'an city, Zhejiang province

Founded in March 2011, the Huimin mutual-aid cooperative is the first of its kind in Wenzhou city. It is one of seven pilot projects in Zhejiang province that are exploring the feasibility of rural financial mutual-aid systems. The cooperative has 698 members and registered capital of RMB 5 million. It is composed of three different cooperatives that came together for this purpose, one specializing in vegetables, one in "silvery beans," and one in noodles.

The mutual-aid cooperative employs corporate governance structures, assumes risk on its own, and takes responsibility for both profits and losses. Each member invests a minimum of RMB 100 into the pot, but no member can hold more than 10 percent of registered capital. That is, nobody can invest more than RMB 500,000. The equivalent of a shareholders' meeting is the highest organizational structure of the entity, called in this case a "meeting of cooperative members." Routine issues are decided upon by a board of directors. The interest rate that applies to the savings of the cooperative is determined by State regulations; there is no limit on the total sum of savings. The interest rate charged on loans is equivalent to that of credit unions, but it is lower than that of commercial banks. It is divided into six different categories with the highest rate being a rate that is over 1 percent per month. Individual loans [or credit lines] are limited to a total of RMB 750,000. All businesses in the cooperative rely on it for their financing. Every year, 50 percent of operating profits are distributed in dividends.

By March 2013, after being in operation for just one year, the cooperative was able to realize its objective of conserving its principle and showing a small profit. Total assets were RMB 28.26, deposits were RMB 17.8, the outstanding loan portfolio was RMB 24.3, the cumulative amount of loans had come to RMB 56.15 million, and interest income was RMB 2.09 million. There had not been a single instance of a nonperforming loan or a loan that was overdue.

Three primary lessons can be learned from this pilot program. First, scale is of the essence. It is not possible to reach profitability without operating at a certain size; even without nonperforming loans, it will be impossible to keep operating. Moreover, only at a certain scale of operations is it possible to deal with risk. Second, controlling risk is the main safeguard of the system. The cooperative limits its businesses to those of members of the cooperative, which lowers its risk. Relying on three separate cooperatives also limits risk since loans are not overly concentrated in one business line, and production is spread out over off-seasons and peak seasons of different products. Third, cooperative arrangements with regular financial institutions increased the service capacities of the cooperative. The Rui'an Rural Cooperative Bank provided it with assistance in the form of both capital and a network, which enabled the businesses within the cooperative to carry on business in an orderly way.

Source: Rural Economic Research Center of the Ministry of Agriculture, *Observations and Thoughts: Rural Economic Research of Ministry of Agriculture in 2012*. Beijing: China Agriculture Press, 2012.

Box 5.6   On micro-loans: the Ri Sheng Long Micro-Credit Companies, Ltd.

This company was established in December 2005, as one of the first group of seven micro-loan companies to which China's central bank extended operating permits. Jointly funded by three "natural persons" [as opposed to "legal persons," or corporations], it started with RMB 22 million in registered capital. The company is run by three leadership positions that operate under the authority of a shareholders' meeting, namely an executive director, a supervisor, and a general manager. The "responsibility/accountability system" of the company requires that the general manager take responsibility, under the leadership of the shareholders' meeting. The company is staffed by eleven people; the general manager presides over three departments: Accounting, Loans [credit], and General Affairs.

According to central bank regulations, the target customers of the company are to be mainly involved in the "three agricultures"; namely they must relate to farmers, farming, or the rural economy. Once rural households submit applications to the company for loans, the company first conducts due diligence, then submits loans as approved by a five-person committee that meets every other day. This meeting is attended by the general manager, a deputy general manager, the chief accountant, the manager of the Loan/Credit Department, and a loan officer, who make decisions via a democratic process. If the need is extremely urgent, communications can be done by telephone. In terms of interest rates on loans, as per central bank regulations, loan rates may be no higher than four times the benchmark lending rate of banks. The company extends four different types of loans, depending on what kind of collateral is used as a guarantee. These are called pledge loans, mortgage loans, guarantee loans, and credit loans. The monthly interest rates for loan terms that range from one month to three months vary from 12.9 percent to 15.6 percent.

In its first year of operations, the company extended a total sum of RMB 45.439 million in loans. Of this, it was paid back RMB 19.465 million, leaving an outstanding loan balance of RMB 25.974 million. It generated interest income of RMB 2.51 million. The company's rate of success in having the principal on loans paid off on time was 100 percent, and its rate of success in getting paid the interest on these loans was also 100 percent. The profit from the business came to RMB 1.81 million. Loan terms mainly ranged from three to six months. The products being funded were mainly fruit and nut trees, crop farming and livestock breeding, transport undertaken by farming households, and micro-businesses in rural areas.

After several years of experimentation and growth, the company has learned some lessons. It deals with the problem of information asymmetry by hiring local people with years of experience in banking, which has increased the rate at which loans are approved. It has developed various ways of guaranteeing loans. It also faces certain problems, however, which include its unclearly defined status on the part of the government and its inadequate amount of capital.

Source: Ri Sheng Long Micro-Credit Companies. http://www.njrsl.com/.

Increase financial support from public finance. We should target new-style agricultural operating entities as we allocate the increased funding for subsidies, in order to enable them to reach adequate size. This means giving priority to family farms, rural cooperatives, and dragon-head companies in terms of both subsidies and rewards. To a certain extent, we should subsidize the transfer [circulation] of land to new-style agricultural operating entities, given the fairly high rates that apply to such transfers right now. We should provide incentives for new-style agricultural operating entities that produce organic products, green-type food products, and pollution-free farm products in order to standardize production of such things and increase their levels of production. We should increase training programs for the principals engaged in family farms, rural cooperatives, and dragon-head companies, as well as for technical personnel, so as to improve managerial levels and technical expertise.

Improve policies on the use of land for agricultural facilities, that is, policies having to do with agricultural-type construction-use land. We should continue to create and implement policies regarding the use of and protection of land for agricultural facilities, particularly in terms of giving priority to new-style agricultural operating entities as they use land for production facilities and auxiliary facilities. We should make more effective use of land that is lying idle in rural communities, as well as land designated as construction-use land and land designated for reclamation and rehabilitation. We should lend support to new-style agricultural operating entities as they use such land for greenhouses, livestock pens, aquaculture ponds, animal-breeding and seedling-cultivation centers, disposal stations for the organic matter generated by livestock and poultry breeding, farm-machinery storage facilities, as well as facilities for drying, preserving, warehousing, and processing agricultural products and facilities for biomass fertilizer production. Water surfaces and their adjoining beaches should be governed by rules that apply to "agricultural facilities-use land" if they serve the purposes of new-style agricultural operating entities either directly or indirectly. Such entities should be given long-term operating rights over such areas. When comprehensive land-use plans are being revised, the practical need of such entities for agricultural facilities-use land should be taken into full account.

Build sound mechanisms for developing human resources. In order to cultivate the human resources necessary for professional farming, at the national level, long-term and medium-term training programs should be set up that focus particularly on training the key people in large households, family farms, cooperatives, and farm agencies, including those who operate equipment and those who spray fields to protect crops. We need to build up a large body of people who are professionals in the technical aspects of modern farming. We must therefore expand the scope of training for farmers and increase subsidies for programs. We should look into setting up systems that deliver vocational education training to farm operators. We should establish a human resources data bank of the heads of cooperatives and on-site "base areas" for training programs. The aim is to create high-caliber teams that serve as the leaders of and advisors to cooperatives. In addition, we must speed up the training of those responsible for dragon-head enterprises – there is an urgent need for highly professional managers in the field of industrialized agriculture. We should formulate policies and measures that enable graduates of educational institutions at the college as well as high-school levels to work in agricultural fields in rural areas; we should encourage such graduates to start up family farms and rural cooperatives.

Explore innovative ways to conduct operations and to manage organizations. First, ensure that agricultural production becomes more systemic and organized. High priority should be placed on the proper development of farmers' specialized cooperatives; we should accelerate their growth and nurture them to become entities that serve farmers, have free and easy and entry and exit procedures, have equal rights, and are democratically managed. They should become modern agricultural operating organizations that lead farmers into participating in market competition both domestically and internationally. Second, establish linkage mechanisms that tie in the interests of new-style agricultural operating entities. Promote the in-depth fusing of dragon-head enterprises and cooperatives. Promote the galvanizing organization model described by the equation: dragon-head enterprise + specialized cooperative (specialized association, collective economic organization) + family farm (specialized large household). Encourage farmers to place their contracting rights to land in these organizations in return for shares, and encourage dragon-head enterprises to launch the practice of profit rebates and dividend distributions, as a way to increase farmers' income. Encourage dragon-head enterprises that have a mixed form of ownership to engage in the industrialization of agriculture. Push forward the development of "Groups" and ensure that their interests are intimately tied to farming households and farmers' cooperatives.

6 Increasing the income of farmers and ensuring fair distribution of income

- The current situation of farmers' income with respect to the objective of setting up a moderately prosperous society in an all-round way
- On promoting a further shift of the rural population toward cities and speeding up the growth of wage-type income among farmers
- Improving agricultural productivity and laying a firm foundation for increases in operating income from agriculture
- Increasing the strength of preferential policies for farmers and increasing transfer-type income for farmers
- Increasing the forcefulness of poverty-alleviation policies and eliminating absolute poverty

The process of creating a moderately prosperous society in an all-round way must maintain the ongoing rapid rise in rural incomes. It must eradicate absolute poverty and at the same time lead to stabilizing and somewhat decreasing the gaps in incomes between urban and rural and within rural areas. In the thirty-some years since reform and opening up began, the ongoing rapid rise in rural incomes has lifted several hundred million rural people out of poverty and resulted in tremendous all-round improvement in their lives. Nevertheless, the average level of incomes in the countryside is low, and the number of impoverished people remains enormous. Not only is there still a huge disparity between rural and urban incomes, but the disparity within rural incomes is growing and remains an unresolved issue. Right now, China is in the midst of transforming its mode of economic growth and is facing a stage shift in the speed at which the economy is expanding. This may create the conditions for addressing these problems, but it also brings with it new challenges. This chapter describes the characteristics of farmers' incomes in China, then presents specific ways to improve rural incomes and equalize fairness in income distribution through wage-type income, agricultural income, and transfer payment income. It also explores how to increase the force of poverty alleviation efforts and eradicate absolute poverty in a fundamental way.

1. The current situation of farmers' income with respect to the objective of setting up a moderately prosperous society in an all-round way

Changes in rural incomes in China since the start of reform and opening up have displayed the following characteristics. First, incomes have risen rapidly. In 1978, the net per capita income in rural China was just RMB 133.6, whereas by 2013 it had reached RMB 8,895.9 (see Figure 6.1). After allowing for rural inflation factors, incomes rose by an actual 11.8 times, which meant an average rate of increase of 7.6 percent per year.[1]

Second, average income levels are still relatively low. As calculated by international purchasing power parity in 2011, per capita rural incomes in 2013 were roughly USD 2,450. If you look upon China's rural areas as a separate economic entity, this level of incomes would rank it 180th in the more than 210 countries and regions on the globe, roughly equivalent to Papua New Guinea and Bhutan.

Third, the accomplishments of poverty alleviation have been enormous, but the impoverished population is still huge. By the World Bank standard, which puts the international comparable poverty line at USD 1.25 in consumption per day, in 1981 China's overall incidence of poverty was as high as 84 percent. By 2009, the rate had fallen to 11.8 percent. This accomplishment was mainly due to improvements in rural incomes.[2] Nevertheless, given the massive size of China's population, the total number of its rural impoverished is still staggering. According to China's own nationally determined poverty line of RMB 2,300 per capita income, as proposed in 2011, rural China still contained 82.49 million impoverished people in 2013. After more than thirty years of economic development, the remaining poverty is mostly concentrated in remote parts of China, where resources are depleted, both material resources and human capital are scarce, and poverty alleviation is harder to accomplish.

(RMB)

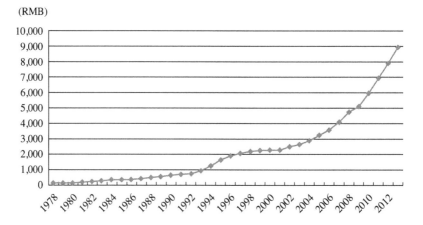

Figure 6.1 Growth of per capita net income of farmers (1978–2013)

Source: *China Statistical Yearbook 2014.*

Fourth, the disparity between urban and rural incomes is pronounced. The situation can be seen just from the relative growth rates of the two areas. Between 1978 and 2013, per capita rural net incomes rose faster than urban incomes in sixteen of the thirty-five years, yet the disparity between urban and rural still widened (see Figure 6.2). The ratio between per capita urban disposable income and per capita rural net income went from 2.57 times [urban to rural] in 1978 to 3.33 times in 2009. After that, it gradually dropped back a bit to 3.03 times in 2013 (see Figure 6.3).

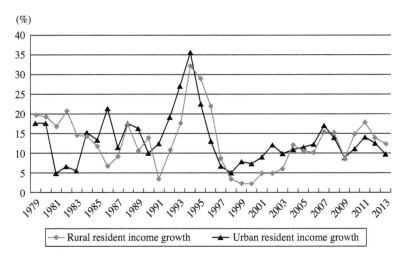

Figure 6.2 Urban and rural income growth
Source: *China Statistical Yearbook 2014.*

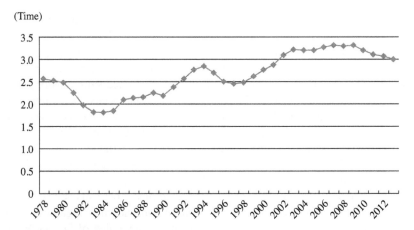

Figure 6.3 Change of urban/rural income ratio
Source: *China Statistical Yearbook 2014.*

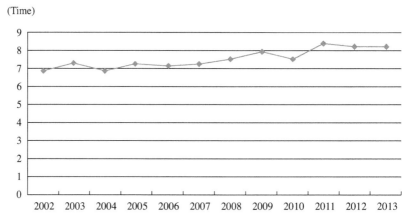

(Time)

Figure 6.4 Income ratio between top and bottom 20 percent households in income ladder in rural areas

Source: *China Statistical Yearbook 2014.*

Fifth, the disparity in incomes within rural areas generally shows a widening tendency overall. Since reform and opening up, this gap has widened every year with just a few exceptions. After 2000, the gap within rural areas moderated somewhat, and the Gini coefficient in rural incomes went only from 0.35 in 2000 to 0.39 in 2010 (Li Shi, 2012). In terms of the comparison between the top fifth and the bottom fifth of rural household incomes, the disparity within rural areas is also widening somewhat, but the gap has moderated in recent years (see Figure 6.4). The ratio went from 6.88 in 2002 to 8.24 in 2013 [top fifth as compared to bottom fifth].

Each of the inherent requirements of creating an all-round moderately prosperous society – raising income levels, promoting more equality in income distribution, and completely eradicating absolute poverty – carries its own weighting, and they are all interrelated. They are the very substance of creating a moderately prosperous society. However, a multitude of challenges confront the process of trying to transform these three cardinal requirements into concrete policy goals. One of them is that China is currently in the midst of a "stage-shift transformation" in its rate of economic growth. Over the past thirty-some years, the country grew at an average annual rate that approached 10 percent. Given the past experience of different types of industrialized countries with respect to economic growth rates and the laws they have followed, China entered a window of time between the end of its 12th Five-Year Plan and the beginning of its 13th Five-Year Plan in which economic growth started slowing down. The country's potential growth rate may drop another level until it reaches a rate of around 7 percent (State Council's Development Research Center Task Force, 2013). This judgment regarding a stage shift has already been confirmed by the evidence of a number of factors. What's more, policy makers and the public at large have already come to accept it as reality, such that it has become "the new normal."[3]

The 18th National Congress of the Chinese Communist Party explicitly set forth the new goal of establishing a moderately prosperous society in China in an all-round way by the year 2020. There are three specific ways in which the Report of the 18th Party Congress relates to the income of farmers. First, the net per capita income of rural people is to be doubled by 2020 over the year 2010, which means that incomes will have to maintain a 7 percent rate of growth every year to achieve this. Second, the disparity in income distribution is to be reduced. This means that to achieve a modest decline and not allow the gap to increase, the speed at which rural incomes increase cannot be less than the speed at which urban incomes increase. At the same time, the disparity in incomes within rural areas is to be stabilized and then decline, which means that the rate at which the lowest incomes rise every year on average cannot be less than the rate at which the highest incomes rise. Third, levels of social security are to be increased, and the country is to achieve a major reduction in the number of people that are the focus of poverty alleviation efforts due to having improved their status. If we achieve both a decrease in the number of impoverished people receiving welfare and we raise standards of social security, China will be able to achieve the elimination of absolute poverty. That is, through such means as economic growth, targeted poverty-alleviation campaigns, and improvement in social security, the income levels of the entire body of the rural population should be above the absolute poverty line.

Having said this, it will be quite hard to achieve the targets of the 18th National Party Congress with respect to lifting incomes. It is going to take enormous effort, and the reasons are as follows.

First, in order to ensure that an increase of rural incomes keeps pace with economic growth, the goals as presented in the 12th Five-Year Plan are essentially on target. However, since the 1990s, the personal incomes of Chinese have been declining as a percentage of the national income; from a level of around 50 percent, they fell to 39 percent by the end of the 11th Five-Year Plan period. Turning this trend around is not going to be easy; it will require putting a great deal more force behind the intent to transform the country's mode of economic growth, as well as its mode of income distribution.

Second, with respect to reducing the disparity between urban and rural incomes, between 2010 and 2013, the average per capita net income of rural people rose at a faster pace than the disposable income of urban residents, but it is unclear whether or not this is a sustainable trend. The things propelling this change have included factors that play a long-term role, including structural changes in supply and demand for labor and increases in labor productivity. They include the increase in the demand for labor brought about by stimulus-type investment in basic infrastructure after the financial crisis. They also include the cyclical and short-term role played by a rapid rise in agricultural commodity prices (Li Shi, 2012). If we intend to keep rural incomes rising at a faster rate than urban incomes, we will need to consolidate the sources of income increases in rural areas. That means creating conditions under which farmers can earn more income.

Third, with respect to stabilizing the growing disparity among rural incomes and reducing that disparity somewhat, the income of low-income groups in rural areas starts from a very low base so that a modest increase brings with it a fairly large rate of increase. However, since low-income farmers are mainly living in areas where productivity of the land is poor, and since they have few reserves in terms of human and financial capital, there is little possibility of using market mechanisms to achieve a fast rise in incomes. It will be necessary to rely more on transfer payments to raise income levels. The precondition for doing this is to set up a universal social security system in these rural areas.

Fourth, with respect to eliminating absolute poverty, the first three objectives as just described might be categorized as "pushing for greater increases," while the goal of eliminating absolute poverty is more along the lines of "holding to a bottom line that is acceptable." In eliminating absolute poverty, we must make use of the various roles played by "development-oriented poverty alleviation," "human capital-oriented poverty alleviation," and "security- [insurance]-oriented poverty alleviation." After close to thirty years of trying development-style poverty reduction, those people who are still impoverished in the countryside are facing even worse conditions than before. This holds for their ability to produce and make a living as well as to their reserves of human and material resources. Therefore, it is going to be even more important to use "security-oriented poverty alleviation," via social security systems, to lift them out of poverty.

In order to realize the objectives as set forth by the 18th National Party Congress, it is imperative that we formulate reform policies and measures that will propel an increase in farmers' incomes. We should aim in particular at increasing wage-type income among farmers and at new incentive mechanisms that stimulate increased incomes. Meanwhile, we must hold fast to our existing policies that give preferential treatment to farmers/agriculture in order to maintain stable increases in "transitional-type" income during the process. At the same time, we must go further in accelerating reform of the "rural land management system." We must unleash the potential of income increases from the assets already in the hands of rural people, that is, "asset-type income." Since Chapter 3 of this volume already addressed the subject of reform of the rural land system and issues to do with clarifying property rights, this chapter will not go into that again. Finally we must establish a sound social security system, to serve as a support for the process of eliminating absolute poverty and reducing income disparities within rural regions.

2.   On promoting a further shift of the rural population toward cities and speeding up the growth of wage-type income among farmers

International experience has shown that when a country advances from the stage of being a low-income country to that of being a high-income country, urbanization must necessarily take place and the rural labor force must shift to becoming "urbanized." This is also necessary if there is to be balanced development between urban and rural areas. Experience over the past thirty-some years in China has also indicated that one important path toward lifting rural incomes and developing rural economies involves having the rural labor force "go out" to work and shift their place of employment to cities.

A number of factors will determine exactly how many people remain to be "shifted" out of agriculture and into nonagricultural jobs in the next few years and how much of a labor force will indeed be "flowing" [migrating] into cities for jobs. The first factor depends on the situation of the labor force that remains in the countryside. If there is indeed a certain amount of labor left in rural areas, then the shift of agricultural labor to other jobs will continue. Second, it depends on the compensation levels of agricultural jobs relative to nonagricultural jobs. One of the most decisive factors in labor migration toward cities is relative income levels (Harris and Todaro, 1970). Another factor relates to whether or not the "floating labor force" (rural migrant workers) can get social security benefits and public services and at what level. That is, if cities can indeed provide better social security provisions and public services, then cities can attract greater numbers of workers to take up urban jobs. The phenomenon called "education migrants" has cropped up in recent years. To a certain degree, this shows that higher-quality education at the middle-school and high-school level in cities attracts rural labor and is a major influence on the decision of rural labor to move into cities. Finally, the extent of an ongoing shift of rural labor into cities will depend on the expectations of people and their evaluation of how urban and rural areas will develop in the future. The behavior of the labor force and the motivation to "migrate" does not depend solely on conditions at the present time. Behavior also depends on expectations about the future. In this sense, if the disparity between urban and rural in terms of economic prospects continues to grow, then more of the rural labor force will continue to flow into cities. If not, then that flow may not occur.

From China's current conditions, it looks as though the trend of rural labor flowing into cities will continue and that this will continue to have a huge impact on the increase in farmers' incomes. Therefore, in order to increase the speed at which farmers' incomes increase and to realize the income goals associated with establishing a moderately prosperous society, China's entire society, as well as the government, must push for the ability of rural people already living in cities to become true "city people," as well as the ability of those still coming in from outside to be real city people. This must happen in order to attract a greater labor force from rural areas into cities, as well as a greater population in general into cities, to take up jobs and settle down.

Naturally, the exodus of the rural labor force cannot go on forever. It has limits. Moreover, in light of the food security constraints that China is facing, keeping a certain amount of labor in the countryside for agricultural production is an absolute necessity. This is also an issue that the government must face and deal with. As we approach the year 2020, this issue will become ever more pronounced and difficult to handle.

3. Improving agricultural productivity and laying a firm foundation for increases in operating income from agriculture

In the past ten or more years, increases in the operating income of farming households have been less than increases in income from other sources. If you divide the twelve years of the start of the 21st century into two periods, the first six years were a period of medium-paced growth, while the second six years were a period

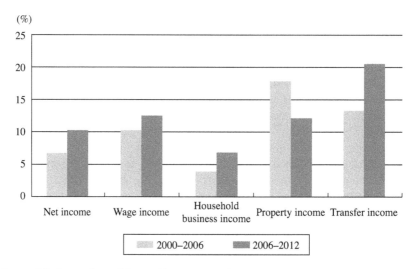

Figure 6.5 Comparison of farmers' income growth at two stages in the 21st century (annual
     average growth)

Source: Calculation and drawing based on figures about rural income structure in *China Statistical
Yearbook* for related years.

of high-speed growth. From Figure 6.5, it can be seen that these farmers' incomes
increased at markedly different rates in these two periods. Increases in income of
different kinds also showed large differences. Farm operating income for farming
households increased more slowly than any other kind of income.

Seen from the perspective of development economics, it should be possible to
lift farmers' income from farming fairly rapidly by increasing reforms having to do
with agricultural practices and by supplementing that with policies that assist agricultural development. On top of this, maintaining a stable increase in the prices of
agricultural commodities should play a positive role in increasing farmers' incomes.
As indicated by Figure 6.6, between 1994 and 2013, farmers' average operating
income from farming increased in years in which prices of agricultural commodities
rose more than the prices of consumer goods in rural areas. The opposite also held
true. When costs of agricultural production held steady while prices of agricultural
commodities rose, this was particularly beneficial to increases in farmers' income,
particularly to net income. From this, it can be seen that modest increases in agricultural prices are helpful in increasing farmers' incomes. More specifically, it is
necessary to keep increased prices at levels no less than increases of the overall
price level if we are to see a positive impact on farmers' incomes. This should be
taken into consideration as the government considers policy options.

China's past experience proved that the huge amount of surplus labor in rural
areas was a key deterrent to the growth of farmers' incomes. Another way of putting this is that one major route to increasing farmers' incomes will be to have
agricultural labor shift into nonagricultural jobs. The shift of agricultural labor

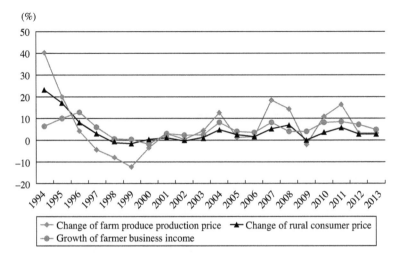

Figure 6.6 Correlation between price change of farm produce and agricultural business income growth of farmers

Source: Calculation and drawing based on data in *China Statistical Yearbook* for related years.

into nonagricultural jobs within the countryside, as well as the shift of that labor into cities, has a double-barreled effect. First, it diversifies sources of income as well as increasing the nonagricultural component of income. Second, the decrease in the agricultural labor force actually increases the productivity of the remaining agricultural work force, which then increases agricultural income. When there is surplus labor in agriculture and nonagricultural jobs are bringing in much more compensation than agricultural jobs (unit wage rate), the "income-increase effect" gained by migrating elsewhere for a job will be far more obvious.

Since the time that economic reforms were launched in the countryside, nonagricultural industries in rural areas have developed at an extremely fast pace. The percentage of the rural labor force that is engaged in nonagricultural jobs continues to grow, and the nonagricultural-type income that "farmers" earn continues to rise, in absolute terms as well as a percentage of net income. By 2011, nonagricultural income was 52 percent of all net income (see Figure 6.7). We can foresee that in the next few years the percentage of nonagricultural jobs both in rural areas and in cities will continue to rise, and nonagricultural income will also continue to rise as a percentage of total income. In order to support momentum for this trend, all levels of government should work on nonagricultural job creation for the rural labor force.

In this regard, one thing we should recognize is that the slow development of service industries in rural areas is a "short stave in the bucket," that is, it is holding back social and economic development. Major effort must be put into changing this in the next few years. Opportunities for nonagricultural jobs in rural areas will be closely tied to the development of service industries. As the government increases its spending on public services in rural areas, these may well grow

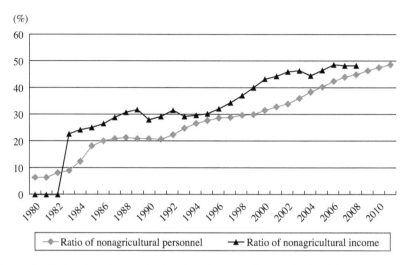

Figure 6.7 Ratio of rural nonagricultural employees and nonagricultural income
Source: Calculation and drawing based on data in *China Statistical Yearbook* for related years.

quickly. For example, upgrading capacities and levels of early-period education for children in rural areas means that the government must support the development of kindergartens, which will attract more of the rural labor force toward children's education. Another example: in order to improve levels and the quality of social services for the elderly in rural areas, the government must support the growth of caregiving industries. This will create job opportunities outside of agriculture. In addition, rural tourism is currently growing at a fast pace and absorbing more rural labor. Rural tourism must be well planned and orchestrated, which means that the government must support it with public spending and supportive financial policies. This may well become an important industry in rural areas in the future, with the ability to absorb a certain amount of rural labor.

4. Increasing the strength of preferential policies for farmers and increasing transfer-type income for farmers

In the past ten years, preferential policies for farmers of various kinds have played an enormous role in ongoing fast-paced growth of farmers' incomes. This has been particularly the case since 2004, when government policies with respect to rural areas changed in fundamental ways. In 2004, the government adopted preferential farm policies that were categorized as "granting more, taking less, and invigorating by relaxing controls." The "granting more" policies mainly involved farming subsidies for rural families, a social security system with coverage for all, and increased public investment in rural areas. The farming subsidies included grain subsidies, comprehensive subsidies for inputs, subsidies for better varieties, subsidies for purchase of farm equipment, and subsidies aimed at specific crops and specific parts of the country (Li Shi et al., 2013). In a certain sense, removing farmland from crops and returning it to woodlands has also been a kind of agricultural subsidy policy. In addition, other policies over the past few years have been an expression of "granting more to farmers" on the part of the government. This includes such things as the minimum living allowance, the medical insurance program known as "new countryside cooperative health insurance," and the social pensions within the new countryside policy. The "taking less" part of the policy mainly involves reform of the system governing rural taxes and fees and the "exemptions and reductions" on farming taxes, as well as the "two exemptions and one subsidy" policy with respect to grade schools and middle schools.

Under the influence of these beneficial policies for agriculture and for rural people in general, quality of life as well as levels of income have seen a notable increase. The transferable-type income of farmers has risen rapidly. As Figure 6.5 shows, according to surveys of rural households, transferable real income of rural households on average rose by 13 percent between 2000 and 2006 and by more than 20 percent between the years 2006 and 2012.

It should be said that the effect of the "granting more" and "taking less" policies has gone beyond just improving farmers' transferable-type income. For example, subsidies on the part of the government for the new countryside cooperative health program, via the two exemptions and one subsidy, have had an impact on students of grade schools and middle schools. This is not reflected in increased transferable income. The "hidden subsidy" part of these farm benefit policies have therefore led to real benefits that are not incorporated in income statistics. Table 6.1 lists the amount of public spending in certain farm benefit policies. These inputs have in fact reduced the spending needs of families, which is equivalent to increasing their net income. A conservative estimate of public spending on just six items in

Table 6.1 Fiscal spending on certain policies intended to benefit farmers

Policy name	Total fiscal input	Per capita level of beneficiaries
Two exemptions and one subsidy	Financial input from 2006 to 2010 was made to reduce an expenditure of RMB230 billion by farmers nationwide.	Financial burden was reduced by RMB250 annually for each family with primary school student(s) and by RMB390 for each family with junior middle school student(s).
Nutrition Improvement Program for Rural Compulsory Education Students	The central government allocated RMB 16 billion every year for nutrition improvement of children in contiguous poverty-stricken areas, benefiting over 26 million students.	Subsidy for each student per day was RMB 3. The standard was increased to RMB 4 since November 2014.

(Continued)

Table 6.1 (Continued)

Policy name	Total fiscal input	Per capita level of beneficiaries
Vocational education	From 2006 to 2013, the central government allocated RMB 47.2 billion in grants for secondary vocational students. From 2009 to 2013, the central government earmarked a RMB 28.9 billion tuition subsidy for secondary vocational students.	Tuition was exempted for all rural (including county and town) students, urban students majoring in agriculture-related disciplines, and students with financial difficulties in secondary vocational schools. Beneficiary students accounted for 91.5% of the total in these schools.
New-type rural cooperative medical system	In 2013, the new-type rural cooperative medical system raised a total of RMB 297.25 billion. Calculated based on the ratio of government payment and individual payment, central and local government input around RMB 224.5 billion.	In 2014, per capita subsidy standard for new-type rural cooperative medical system and resident medical insurance was increased by RMB 40 on the basis of 2013, reaching RMB 320.
Rural medical assistance	In 2011, government input at various levels for rural medical assistance reached RMB 12.17 billion.	Per capita hospitalization assistance was RMB 1,687.
Renovation of rural dilapidated buildings	In 2014, central government earmarked RMB 23 billion to subsidize renovation of rural dilapidated buildings.	The central government's subsidy standard was RMB 7,500 per household on average. On this basis, another RMB 1,000 was offered to each household in poverty-stricken areas, and another RMB2500 was offered to the most impoverished households living in landlocked areas along the national border and to each model household for building energy conservation.

Source: Related reports and news coverage released to the public.

Notes: a. "Fund Guarantee Mechanism for Rural Compulsory Education," *China Financial and Economic News*. www.cfen.com.cn (http://www.efen.com.enweb./meyw/2014–07/15/eontent_1105063. html). b. National Health and Family Planning Commission, 2013 Statistic Bulletin on Development of Health and Family Planning in China. http://www.moh. gov.cn/guihuaxxs/s10742/201405/886f82drfa344c3097 f1d16581a1bea2.shtml. c. Notice on Increasing Fund-Raising Standards of New-Type Rural Cooperative Medical System and Urban Residents' Basic Medical Insurance in 2014 jointly released on April 25 by Ministry of Finance, National Health and Family Planning Commission and Ministry of Human Resources and Social Security. d. Social Assistance Department of Ministry of Civil Affairs, Review on Progress in National Urban and Rural Medical Assistance Work in 2011. http://dbs.mca.gov.cn/article/csyljz/llyj/201306/20130600474603.shtml. e. Document No. 76 of Ministry of Finance in 2014: Notice on Doing Well in Renovation of Rural Dilapidated Buildings in 2014. http://www.mof.gov.cn/zhengwuxinxi/zhengcefabu/201406/t20140620_1101977.html.

the list of farm benefit policies comes to between RMB 350 billion and RMB 400 billion per year. This is equivalent to raising the per capita income of farmers by RMB 450 to RMB 500.

Nevertheless, we also must be clear about the fact that while social welfare benefits and social security have gone from nothing to something, these programs are still highly limited in the extent of security they provide. Not only are levels of security on the low side, but there is still a pronounced disparity between the rural and the urban situations. The minimum living standard can serve as one example. Starting in 2011, the government adjusted the standard per-person payment of poverty alleviation upward, so that the nationwide average per person per year under the poverty alleviation program came to RMB 2,300. With inflation, this was again raised in 2013 to RMB 2,736. However, no corresponding adjustment was made in the minimum living standard applied to rural areas. Figure 6.8 shows the geographic distribution of minimum living standards in each county and region of the country. More than 3,000 of a total of over 3,200 counties had minimum living standards that did not come up to RMB 2,736. Minimum living standards were therefore lower than the rural poverty alleviation standard. Among these counties, more than 1,000 had minimum living standards of less than RMB 1,200. The minimum living standard in these places was around 44 percent of the average poverty-alleviation standard for 2013. This means that the role played by establishing a "bottom line" in the "rural minimum living allowance" program is highly limited.

Another thing to note is the variability in the minimum living allowance among different regions. As shown by Figure 6.8, the lowest 10 percent of the "minimum

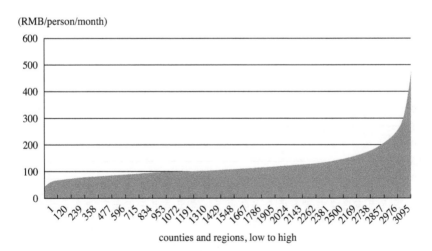

counties and regions, low to high

Figure 6.8 Rural subsistence security standards in different counties/regions in 2013

Source: Calculated based on data provided by the website of Ministry of Civil Affairs.

Note: The horizontal axis is number of counties and regions ranked low to high according to subsistence security standard, and the vertical axis is subsistence security standard (RMB/person/month).

living allowance" standards are not even getting RMB 70 per person per month. Meanwhile, counties and districts with the highest standards are getting more than RMB 200 per person per month. The highest is making almost three times the lowest. Those counties and districts with low minimum allowance standards are often those that are the furthest back in terms of economic development, which also means that the budgetary capacities of their local governments are weak. The most basic requirements of living are of an inflexible nature, however. There is therefore a glaring gap between the ability of the system to ensure a certain level of living and the very real needs of impoverished groups. This makes it difficult for the minimum allowance system to serve its function in reducing income disparities within rural regions, as well as those among different regions.

There is still a fairly large gap between the *minimum living allowance standards* for people in rural areas and those for residents in cities. Nevertheless, the gap is less than that between the income of rural people and the income of urban residents. To an initial degree, this shows that the minimum allowance does indeed play a role in reducing the urban–rural income differentials. Figure 6.9 shows the gap in minimum living allowances for residents of both urban and rural areas in all provinces in the country in the year 2013. The indicator of difference here is the ratio between minimum living security standards of urban residents and those of rural residents. The higher the value, the wider the gap is. It is not hard to see from Figure 6.9 that the minimum living allowances in cities of all provinces are higher than in rural areas, and the gap widens the more economically undeveloped a region is. In China's thirty-one provinces, autonomous regions, and direct-jurisdiction municipalities, there are twelve places in which the disparity in minimum living allowances between cities and countryside is more than double.

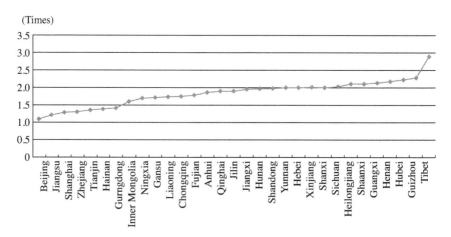

Figure 6.9 Rate in minimum living allowances for residents of both urban and rural areas in all provinces in the country in the year 2013

Source: Calculated based on data provided by the website of Ministry of Civil Affairs. http://files2.mca. gov.cn/cws/201310/20131023092658128.htm.

These places are basically clustered in China's central and western regions. This disparity in part reflects the difference in living costs between urban and rural areas, but it also reflects the lack of financial wherewithal that is necessary to reduce the distance between minimum standards in urban and rural areas. Since China's middle and western parts of the country are the main areas in which low-income people and also impoverished people are most concentrated, this means that it is imperative that we raise the rural minimum allowance. Central finance has to take on more responsibility in this regard. In both spending and in policy support, it should "lean further" in the direction of the middle and western parts of the country. This must be done so as to alleviate poverty as well as to increase farmers' incomes.

In addition to these measures, we should expand social benefits systems to incorporate new types of programs. The government should define the country's more vulnerable groups in terms of different categories and then apply transfer payments accordingly. The unemployable are one example. We must extend the definition of minimum living standards so that it covers not only low-income groups of people but also handicapped people, orphans, people who have AIDS, and the children and elderly in low-income families, as well as single-parent families. Transfer payments should be made accordingly. For example, the issue of child nutrition in rural areas has always been something that deserves greater effort on the part of the government. The problem of child malnutrition is still severe, particularly in certain backward areas and impoverished households. To a great degree, this then impacts a child's ability to study and other developmental factors. Right now, the program in which the entire country is engaged is a significant measure, but it should still be expanded in scope and given greater funding.

5. Increasing the forcefulness of poverty-alleviation policies and eliminating absolute poverty

In creating a moderately prosperous society in an all-round way, it will be necessary to deal with the whole set of problems posed specifically by poverty. In China's economic development over the past thirty-some years, one of the accomplishments most applauded by the international community has been the fact that the great majority of rural impoverished people have been lifted out of poverty (see Figure 6.10). In theoretical terms, three factors can account for this kind of improvement. The first is economic development: economic growth and improvement in incomes help alleviate poverty. The second is the effect of income distribution: lowered income disparity also helps relieve poverty. The third is the effect of poverty-alleviation policies. Since China's government policies in this regard are targeted at impoverished areas and are "developmental" in nature, it is hard to separate out the effect of poverty-alleviation policies and the role of economic growth. More accurately, it should be said that the tremendous decline in the numbers of impoverished people in rural areas can be attributed to a combination of economic growth and poverty alleviation policies.

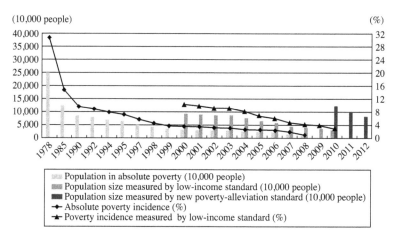

(10,000 people)   (%)

Figure 6.10 Downward trend of rural poverty-stricken population and poverty incidence in China

Source: Yang Sui, *Study on Chinese Household Income Liquidity*, doctoral dissertation, 2013.

Nevertheless, we absolutely cannot treat the situation of rural poverty lightly. Only if we put more effort into alleviating poverty will we reach the goal of fundamentally eliminating absolute poverty by the year 2020. In terms of the geographic distribution of China's impoverished population, there has been no fundamental change in where poor people are located in the more economically backward parts of China. According to data from the National Bureau of Statistics on poverty, in 2012, more than one-half of impoverished people lived in 592 counties that are formally defined as "impoverished." The rest lived in other rural areas. In order to improve the accuracy with which we target poverty alleviation policies and the effectiveness of results, it will be necessary to coordinate poverty alleviation policies with development programs over a broader area and to take a more overall, coordinated, approach to planning. In recent years, the State Council has designated fourteen clusters of contiguous areas that are particularly impoverished. In 2012, according to the national poverty-alleviation metric that uses the figure of a farmer's net per capita income of RMB 2,300 (in constant 2010 prices), the population of these fourteen areas had an impoverished population of 50.67 million people. The incidence of poverty overall was 24.4 percent. The impoverished population within these fourteen defined areas constituted 51.2 percent of China's entire impoverished population. The fourteen designated areas are as follows: (1) the six-basins mountainous area [Liupan], (2) the Qin-ba [Tsinling] mountainous area, (3) the Wuling mountainous area, (4) the Wumeng mountainous area, (5) the Yunnan-Guizhou-Guangxi rocky desertification area, (6) the western-Yunnan border area, (7) the southern ranges of the Da Hinggan mountainous area, (8) the Yanshan-Taihang mountainous area, (9) the Luliang mountainous area, (10) the Dabie mountainous area, (11) the Luoxiao mountainous area, (12) Tibet,

(13) the "Tibetan area within four contiguous provinces," which includes parts of Sichuan, Yunnan, Gansu, and Qinghai, and (14) the three prefectures of southern Xinjiang, which are Kashi, Hotan, and the Kizilsu Kergez Autonomous Area.

The Chinese government has adopted two modes of poverty alleviation over the past thirty years in recognition of the way development in the country has been uneven and impoverished populations have tended to be concentrated in less developed areas. The first has been development-oriented poverty alleviation. The second has been direct assistance to impoverished people. Actual practice has shown that the first mode has been more appropriate for poverty-stricken areas with concentrations of poor people, while the second has been more appropriate to economically developed areas that have only scattered pockets of poverty. Both are necessary, however, and the first is absolutely indispensable.

Impoverished regions tend to have worse conditions than normal rural areas in several respects, namely levels of income and consumption, basic living facilities, and the provision of medical services. In order to change these conditions, the government has strengthened its poverty alleviation efforts since 2000, and specific policies have improved the income of farming households, as well as the status of economic development in impoverished areas. In the past decade, the speed at which farming households' income has risen has exceeded the rise in rural incomes overall, under the impact of targeted poverty-alleviation development work. When a farming household receives financial assistance under one of these projects, the income of that household increases at a markedly greater pace than the income of households not included under the project. Poverty-alleviation projects in which farming households themselves reported that they had participated also achieved a certain percentage rise in incomes. Quantified estimates of the income effect of poverty-alleviation funds also show the effectiveness of poverty alleviation funds and policies, and poverty-alleviation policies have had a positive effect on improving the production capacities of impoverished regions. However, poverty alleviation policies and projects tend to benefit the region more than they do the actual impoverished household. While poverty-alleviation projects do increase overall average incomes of households in impoverished regions, they are not as successful at increasing the incomes of impoverished households in impoverished regions. In this sense, the programs have actually exacerbated certain unfortunate patterns of income distribution in such regions. Data in the *Report on China's rural poverty monitoring survey, 2010* reveals that although average farmers' incomes in key poverty-alleviation counties rose at a faster pace than the national average in the period between 2002 and 2009, the disparity between the highest 20 percent of household incomes and the lowest 20 percent of household incomes also increased. The income of the highest one-fifth of households was 4.63 times the lowest in 2002; it went to being 5.53 times the lowest in 2009.

At present, the government's poverty-alleviation policies are facing challenges at three different levels. On the macro level, income disparities overall are increasing in China's society, and economic growth is providing fewer benefits to poor people. That makes it harder for impoverished people to share in the benefits of both the economy and the market. At the middle level, it is harder for poverty-alleviation policies to target specific groups, given reductions in the total number of impoverished people and their greater diffusion throughout different regions. The question of where to focus energies is becoming more complex. At the micro level, structural changes in the incomes of impoverished people are making it harder for poverty-alleviation funds and poverty-alleviation programs to meet the technical demands of higher specificity.

In the overall context of setting up a moderately prosperous society in an all-round way, the general objective of China's policy framework for poverty alleviation should be to ensure that impoverished regions and impoverished farming households develop at a faster pace than regular regions and regular farming households. This means not only increasing their incomes and standard of consumption but also improving levels of social security and public services, and it also means bettering poor people's own development capabilities. Only if these things are achieved will China's impoverished regions and impoverished groups of people truly enter a moderately prosperous society, and only then will China's rural areas achieve an "all-round" moderately prosperous society. In order to achieve these things, we offer the following recommendations.

First, improve the incentive mechanisms within poverty-alleviation policies. Poverty-alleviation policies and regulatory oversight of programs should be given stronger weighting in the performance ratings of government officials. Meanwhile, we must strengthen regulatory oversight over the funds earmarked for poverty alleviation and ensure that the disbursal of earmarked funds, allocated for specific programs, is tied closely to results. At the same time, in areas in which poverty-alleviation results are outstanding, we must allocate more auxiliary-program-type funds as an incentive. These may relate to assisting particularly vulnerable groups, reducing the possibility of their falling back into poverty due to illness, lack of education, or natural disaster. By making sure that the growth in funding is kept to a modest increase through both increases but also decreases in allocations, we should provide greater funding support for poverty alleviation while also avoiding detrimental forms of incentives.

Second, increase the strength of spending on poverty alleviation policies that address impoverished regions and impoverished households. Research has proven that if impoverished households can obtain project funding, they can increase the speed at which their incomes increase. It is imperative that we increase poverty-alleviation budgets and the amount of funding put into poverty-alleviation projects so as to enable more impoverished farmers to receive funding from poverty-alleviation projects and thereby begin to improve their incomes. At the same time, the effort must be on finding effective mechanisms that deliver the results to the actual household. On the one hand, this means increasing the amount of funds currently being put into poverty alleviation efforts that go to the actual household, as well as subsidies that go to the household. It means reducing restrictions on auxiliary funds for impoverished households. On the other hand, this means introducing experimenting with more direct ways of delivering policies and projects "to the household." These could, for example, include village-based mutual-aid funds, conditional transfer of cash to impoverished households, and training of and job placement for impoverished workers.

Third, set up targeting mechanisms and project-selection models that are community based and that improve structures and mechanisms for poverty alleviation aimed at results with greater precision. Projects that require impoverished families also to put in inputs have become a bar to actual participation into these projects. Instead, poverty-alleviation projects that are community based can effectively integrate the needs of impoverished people within the community. Using this as the criterion for selecting projects can ensure that greater benefits actually accrue to impoverished groups. Another effective way to limit obstacles to accessing programs of impoverished people is to grant greater decision-making powers to the people themselves, so that they decide on how programs are carried out. In other words, we should set up models that are based on having the community and impoverished people themselves decide on projects, so that the performance of projects is more accurately focused on the right target.

Fourth, the government, the market, and society at large should combine forces to play a better role in furthering poverty-alleviation policies and projects. This means not only increasing public spending on poverty alleviation but, more importantly, creating an organic union between poverty-alleviation policies and poverty-alleviation projects. We should concentrate social forces, use the resources of the government and market means to combine one-off programs, industry- [sector]-related programs, and social programs in an organic way. This not only will ensure an adequate number of projects, but it will target impoverished farming households and increase farmers' incomes.

Fifth, we should set up mechanisms to enable development in a coordinated way across jurisdictions. Often a given region will involve several local government jurisdictions, while the overall difference in farmers' incomes across the region is not so apparent. We need to set up coordinating and linking mechanisms among different governments and use a top-down planning perspective in how we apply funds of local governments, so that poverty-alleviation development efforts have greater force. In some particularly poor parts of contiguous impoverished areas, the lack of basic infrastructure is a major factor holding back development of the region. We recommend that the National Development and Reform Commission, the Poverty-Alleviation Office, the Ministry of Finance, and others lead the way in organizing and setting up a working group that meets jointly to focus specifically on this issue. It should increase spending on the building of basic infrastructure in such areas.

Sixth, we should integrate poverty alleviation programs and the minimum living allowance system and combine the two "bottom lines" that are now defined as a "minimum living allowance" and a "poverty-alleviation minimum standard." According to the poverty-alleviation sensitivity to economic growth as described in this book and using the currently defined metric for "poverty" in China, if China's economy grows at an average annual rate of 7 percent until 2020, and if we continue with existing policies, a conservative estimate shows that the impoverished population in the country will decline by 30 to 40 million people. If the remaining impoverished population is no more than one-third below the minimum poverty line, the remaining gap, in constant 2013 dollars will be an average of RMB 900. If we incorporate this entire group of people within the minimum living allowance program, the amount of additional funding required will come to between RMB 27 billion and RMB 36 billion. [None of these calculations include administrative and management costs.] If the remaining impoverished population is more than one-half below the minimum poverty line, the additional funding required will come to between RMB 43 billion and RMB 56 billion. In 2013, fiscal revenues for the country as a whole came to RMB 12.9 trillion. By a conservative estimate that assumes that fiscal revenues will grow at the same pace as GDP, in 2020, fiscal revenues will exceed RMB 20 trillion. Even if we take the "one-half below the minimum poverty line" figure for the remaining number of impoverished in the country and incorporate that entire population within the minimum living allowance program in terms of costs, this sum will come to between 0.2 percent and 0.3 percent of total fiscal revenues. It is completely within the possibility of our finances to shoulder this burden.

Box 6.1   Targeting poverty with mutual-aid funds and the results of this kind of poverty alleviation

Mutual-aid funds in impoverished villages are a kind of unconventional, policy-related, rural micro-financing organization. They have enormous potential to reduce poverty and to increase farmers' incomes. These are growing rapidly throughout the country since they increase the efficiency with which government funds for poverty alleviation are used, and they mitigate the way in which farming households in impoverished areas are excluded from normal financial channels. By the end of 2012, such entities had taken root in 17,000 impoverished villages throughout the country. Their aggregate amount of capital came to RMB 4.4 billion.

Mutual aid funds refer to micro-credit organizations that are self-managed by communities and that are set up on the basis of public-finance poverty-alleviation funds. The main characteristics of these mutual-aid funds in impoverished villages include the following: the funds allocated from public finance for poverty alleviation are used at no cost, they are self-managed by communities, they operate by making small-sum credit loans, and they are aimed at alleviating poverty.

At the various links of participating in such programs, making use of them, and profiting from them, these mutual-aid funds have successfully avoided a problem of previous poverty-alleviation programs, namely that other programs "benefit the rich but not the poor." These instead target impoverished groups of people, and the participation rates of such people are higher. Loan rates are higher (see Table 6.2), reflecting the fact that mutual-aid funds are an effective way for poverty-alleviation projects to target actual poverty.

Table 6.2 Benefit for different income groups from the mutual-aid funds

	House- holds that participate	House- holds that use	House- holds that make profit	Ratio of participation (%)	Ratio of use (%)	Ratio of earnings (%)	Ratio of benefit (%)
Group of lowest income	94	57	32	34.1	60.6	71.1	34.0
Group of low income	103	52	30	37.9	50.5	68.2	29.1
Group of medium income	89	42	21	34.0	47.2	58.3	23.6
Group of high income	82	32	21	30.3	39.0	77.8	25.6
Group of highest income	91	39	18	33.7	42.9	62.1	19.8

Source: Zhang Weibin, Research on Mutual Aid Funds Poverty Targeting and Reducing Impacts, Doctoral Dissertation of Renmin University of China, 2013.

A task force at the Renmin University of China that was studying this subject established a random-sample data-gathering process that used "propensity score matching" to estimate the effectiveness of mutual-aid funds in increasing incomes. The results of the evaluations showed that, between 2009 and 2011, households borrowing such funds had incomes that were on average RMB 875 to RMB 1,696 more than households that had not yet borrowed such funds. The lowest-income group that borrowed funds had increased their incomes by an average of RMB 1,865 over those not borrowing funds, within the space of just these two years. For the low-income group, this figure was RMB 2,328: overall, the effect of borrowing from mutual-aid funds was dramatic for the low-income group. The effect was far higher than on other income groups. This result shows that mutual-aid funds have an even more notable effect on increasing incomes when farming households are at a mid- to lower level of income.

Notes

1 The Rural Consumer Price Index was not systematically released until 1985. In order to make income in 1978 statistically comparable with that in 2013, a report released by the National Bureau of Statistics on October 31, 2008, is used as the basis for approximately estimating the price deflator from 1978 to 2007, and then the Rural Consumer Price Index from 2007 to 2013 is used to calculate the rural price deflator from 1978 to 2013. With this method, the annual average growth rate of rural actual income from 1978 to 2013 is calculated to be 7.55%.
2 Data comes from World Development Indicators (WDI) released at the website of the World Bank [http://data.worldbank.org.cn/data-catalog/world-development-indicators].
3 Downward growth is not the exclusive feature of the new normal. New normal also includes the value orientation of development, development method, and substantial adjustment of economic structure.

7 Improving China's social security system and its systems for providing public services

- Optimize the allocation of educational resources, and improve the quality of education in rural areas
- Improve the rural old-age security system, and speed up the building of systems that provide services to the elderly in rural areas
- Improve the rural healthcare system, and raise levels of health among rural residents
- Improve the housing conditions of rural residents and ensure that vulnerable populations have a place to live
- Push forward the building of public service facilities in rural areas, and improve the living conditions of people in rural areas

The Third Plenary Session of the 17th CPC Central Committee set forth basic targets as part of the intent to create a moderately prosperous society in an all-round way by the year 2020. One of these was to make the provision of public services far more equal in urban and rural parts of China. The level of public services in rural areas is a measure of any country's economic and social development, as well as of rural social and economic development. It is an important indicator of how well coordinated urban and rural development is in the country, and it is the key issue when it comes to creating the "all-round" part of a moderately prosperous society. Since reform and opening up but particularly since the start of the 21st century, the Central Committee of the Communist Party of China and the State Council have both put a high priority on furthering endeavors relating to the so-called three agricultures: farmers, farming, and the rural economy. They have put forth the development strategy of "a new socialist countryside" and have effectively raised levels of policy funding in support of public services in rural areas. Notable accomplishments have been made in building up public services systems in rural areas as a result. However, the long-existing dichotomy between urban and rural in China involved putting the priority on developing cities and building up rural public systems and communities so as to support the cities. The amount of public spending on building public facilities, improving compulsory education, providing for public cultural services, social security, and so on has been dramatically lower in rural areas than it has been in urban areas. This has led to a tremendous gap between public-service resources "possessed by" rural as opposed to urban areas and therefore to a gap in levels of existing public services, as well as the ability to supply public services. In terms of public services, rural areas are the short stave in the bucket. Indeed, this overly large disparity in basic public services represents the biggest constraint to building a moderately prosperous society in an all-round way (Hui Liangyu, 2012). Improving rural social security and public services systems has vital policy implications. First, social security and public services are the single most important long-term factor affecting people's lives. We can lay a firm and enduring foundation for moderate prosperity in the countryside only by grasping hold of this key endeavor in a meaningful way. Second, increasing public spending on rural manpower, improving rural productivity, and increasing nonagricultural jobs in rural areas will create the engine for driving a unification of urban and rural areas. These things will create enduring support for that process, and they will also safeguard the sound development of urbanization in China. They embody highly significant strategic implications.

1. Optimize the allocation of educational resources, and improve the quality of education in rural areas

Education is the very foundation of social and economic progress in rural areas. It is also critical to the urbanization of the country and the modernization of its agriculture. As urbanization continues at a fast pace in China, the rate of 1 percent per year of the population becoming "urbanized" means that a large amount of surplus rural labor is entering cities every year. Raising the educational levels of this surplus labor is an effective way to ensure an orderly shift and a manageable process. As research of the American economist Micha Gisser [Professor Emeritus, Economics, University of New Mexico] has shown, for each 10 percent improvement in standards of education, you induce 6 percent to 7 percent more farmers to move out of the agricultural sector (Drankakis-Smith, 2000). At present, every level of government in China regards the development of education as a strategic priority. Some western provinces are implementing development policies that call for education to "overtake and surpass" other areas. Guizhou, for example, has established the grand goal of achieving universal fifteen-year basic education throughout the province within a time frame of three to five years (Zhao Kezhi, 2014). Since 2000, China has made tremendous progress in compulsory education overall. Governments have increased spending on rural compulsory education, reducing the burden formerly held by rural families to pay the fees themselves. This has played an important role in increasing enrollment rates in primary school, as well as in improving the quality of education. In order to reach the goal of putting 4 percent of gross domestic product into education, governments have increased investment in this area tremendously in the past ten years. More of the incremental additions to government spending are put to education in rural areas. The policy that the central government began implementing in 2001 called the "two exemptions and one subsidy policy" is of particular note. This played a very positive role in driving the development of compulsory education in rural areas.

At the same time, we must be aware of the fact that developing rural compulsory education is a long-term and monumental task. First, levels of rural compulsory education and the quality of that education are still far below the levels in urban areas. The trend shows that enrollment rates at the compulsory-education level are coming closer together in urban and rural areas, and indeed in some areas the gap is becoming negligible. However, we cannot overlook the ongoing disparity in the quality of education. Issues are still being debated as to how to measure educational quality, in terms of which indicators can be considered objective and comprehensive, but limited measures of educational quality show that the differential between the quality of urban and rural compulsory education is not notably diminishing. The quality of education in some remote areas is simply appalling. Second, primary and middle-school students are going to cities in droves in search of better education. Urban schools cannot accommodate them due to budget constraints. They simply cannot adjust "supply" fast enough to meet the need. Many are already operating at overcapacity, which has affected the quality of their teaching. Finally, many teachers in rural schools are underqualified and poorly educated. Teachers are also poorly paid and have few social security benefits. This means that it is hard for an urban teacher to think of teaching in the countryside, and indeed this kind of movement is unreasonably constrained.

Preschool education in rural areas is yet another short stave in the bucket in rural education. A wealth of research, as well as actual experimentation in other countries, has shown conclusively that early childhood education contributes to upgrading human capital and breaking the cycle of poverty from one generation to the next. It also helps improve social equality. Statistics in China indicate that the percentage of children who receive any formal preschool education is less than 50 percent; in more backward areas, the figure is less than 20 percent. After a plan called *Action plan to achieve three years of preschool education* was launched in China, the gross enrollment rate went from 56.6 percent in 2010 to 64.5 percent in 2013 in those areas administering the plan. The results were very gratifying. However, the initial three years of this endeavor were conducted mainly in county seats and townships and did not actually reach into villages. Children in impoverished areas were therefore deprived of the opportunity to participate. The 680 counties in China that represent clusters of contiguous poverty-stricken areas are mainly located in either mountainous areas or steppe zones. Some 70 percent of China's impoverished population lives in these areas. They contain roughly 9 million children between the ages of 4 and 6. Faced with the towering costs of living in a city in order to put a child in a proper school, all these people can do is "gaze at the prospects of an education and utter a sigh" (Lu Mai et al., 2014).

Mid-level vocational education can play a fundamental role in a modern vocational education system. First, such education is an important career path for students who have finished nine years of compulsory education. Studies conducted in the past have shown that more than 60 percent of rural students either go back to working on the farm after basic education, or they "go out," becoming rural migrant workers.[1] This group is the most vulnerable to leaving school. Mid-level vocational education provides them with the opportunity to have a twelve-year level of education. Second, such education is also a vehicle for providing lifelong learning and continuing education for adults. It can play a key role in improving the skills of farmers and increasing their income levels. It can help shift China's massive population burden in the direction of becoming a human resource advantage. It can spur the processes of economic restructuring and industrial upgrading, and it can accelerate the process of urbanization. In recent years, the central government has allocated funds specially earmarked for promoting vocational education in rural areas. These have supported the building of county-level vocational centers throughout the country. Given that the absolute majority of people receiving such education comes from disadvantaged families and rural areas [survey results indicate that 89.9 percent of mid-level vocational students are from rural families, while 5.1 percent come from impoverished families within cities],[2] a policy was initiated in 2006 that provides financial support for such students. Its aim is to attract more impoverished students into the vocational-education system, to facilitate their ability to receive such education, and thereby to further educational equality. In 2009, this went further in exempting school fees for students studying agriculture-related subjects in vocational education, as well as for students from economically distressed rural families. In 2012, the State took further steps to improve the system of subsidies and exempted school fees for mid-level vocational education. It expanded the coverage of the exemptions policy. These supportive policies have enabled more and more rural students to receive mid-level vocational education. Data from a survey undertaken by the China Development Research Foundation showed that 56.9 percent of mid-level vocational schools had increased enrollments in 2013 over 2012, and the average increase came to 28.1 percent of the total number of students. Meanwhile, 47.7 percent of the schools have exceeded their goals for enrolling students (see Figures 7.1 and 7.2). In 2014, the Central Ministry of Finance allocated a sum of RMB 4 billion that was specifically designated for improving the quality of modern mid-level vocational education. It was targeted at improving the overall conditions for setting up schools to conduct mid-level vocational education, at upgrading basic capacities in mid-level vocational education, and at shifting it in the direction of rural areas that had higher population densities and the need for it in terms of industrial development, as well as shifting it in the direction of ethnic-minority and impoverished regions. In addition, through reform measures to enable greater Sino-foreign cooperation in setting up schools, and to link up mid-level and higher-level vocational training, the quality of vocational education teaching has improved. More resources are now available to improve quality. However, rural vocational education must still be regarded as a weak link in the entire chain of education. First, China's rural communities still have the traditional idea that one has to have a higher education to be regarded as having achieved something in life. This puts vocational education at a disadvantage, since it holds lower prestige value in the minds of rural people. Second, the ongoing basic weakness of vocational education in rural areas means that local administrative officials dealing with education do not put as much priority on it as they do on normal middle schools, so they provide it with less funding. Equipment and facilities are outdated, resources for professional teachers are tight, and the quality of the education is low.

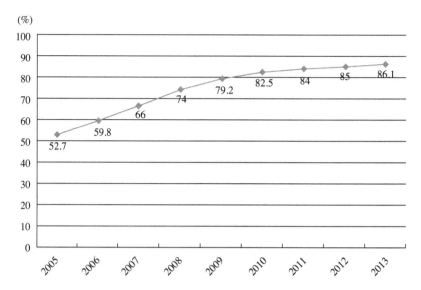

Figure 7.1 Gross enrollment rate of senior high schools (2005–2013)

Source: *Statistical Bulletin of Educational Development in China* (2005–2013).

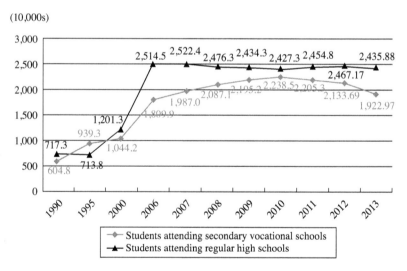

Figure 7.2 Number of students attending secondary vocational schools and regular high schools (1990–2013)

Source: *Statistical Bulletin of Educational Development in China* (1990–2013).

Box 7.1 The poverty-alleviation effects of the government's policies in support of mid-level vocational education

Policies that provide financial support for China's mid-level vocational education mainly refer to national-level exemption of fees and subsidies for tuition. Other things, however, include the system of on-the-job training, a kind of internship, the scholarship system, the system that exempts and reduces school fees in schools, student loan programs and the system that allows for deferred payment of tuition, as well as the social financial assistance system.

Surveys indicate that 89.9 percent of mid-level vocational education students come from rural families and that 5.1 percent are from impoverished families within cities. Many of these students were formerly those "left behind to be cared for by others." Moreover, 84.8 percent of them are not the sole child in the family; 31.5 percent of the fathers of mid-level vocational-education students do not have a stable job. Some students come from single-parent homes, some are living on their own, some are from divorced families or families with a disabled member. Surveys discovered that such people comprise as many as 42 percent of students in some schools. Such family conditions hurt the prospects of these students in terms of both getting a degree and moving ahead in life.

The policy that exempts tuition has a very clear effect on poverty reduction. Surveys have discovered that these policies cover close to 90 percent of students in mid-level vocational education. All such students who come from rural areas are qualified under the policies. Using the average figure of RMB 2,000 per year per student for calculations, this came to roughly 22.5 percent of the average rural resident's net income in 2013. The standard for a national tuition grant is roughly RMB 1,500 per student year, which represents 30 percent of the living costs of an impoverished student who is required to live at school. This amount was roughly equivalent to 16.9 percent of a rural resident's net per capita income in 2013. The national financial-assistance policy has had the effect of lowering the costs of attending school for mid-level vocational students, and it has lowered the rate at which rural families, especially those in western villages, go into poverty as a result of paying school fees. Of the responses from the head of the family in surveys that were conducted, 31.1 percent said that they would take exemption of school fees into account in making decisions about mid-level vocational education; 37.1 percent of the heads of households felt that such exemption of fees was a major contribution to the finances of the family; 86.2 percent of students who received financial assistance felt that the national policy of providing financial assistance for school fees reduced the economic burden on their families and helped guarantee that they could complete their education.

Source: Research Group of China Development Research Foundation. *Evaluation Report – Effects of State Funding Polices for Secondary Vocational Education*, November 2014.

Faced with new problems that have emerged in the sphere of rural education, we now must contemplate new countermeasures. First, we must improve the mechanisms that safeguard spending on compulsory-level education by increasing the force of transfer payments from central-government coffers as well as from provincial-level government finance. Based on progress made in integrating villages, we should create a group of high-caliber primary schools and middle schools in township seats in order to satisfy the demand for high-quality education of rural students. We should provide these schools with high-quality educational resources from cities, at no cost. Resources should be provided to rural areas in step with how they are provided to urban areas.

Second, we should clearly define the responsibilities and accountabilities of governments at all levels with respect to developing rural education. We should experiment with new methods of administering preschool education. We must adopt conscientious and effective mechanisms to ensure that the children of the floating population of rural migrant workers, as well as the population of children left behind to be cared for by others, do indeed get a preschool education. "Delivering the education to the village" [by having teachers carry out education activities in villages] is a fairly inexpensive and feasible way to do this for impoverished rural children and we should put a major effort into setting up pilot programs at the village level. We should seek to meet the goal of having a gross enrollment rate of 85 percent in three years of preschool by the year 2020.

Finally, we should redefine our goals regarding rural vocational education and training, using a scientific approach. In seeking to develop a "new-style of farmer" who is versed in the use of technology and management skills, we should use vocational education and training as the tool. Through the use of vocational education and training, we should enable professional farmers to receive professional-type certifications and employment qualifications, so that they have the capacity to handle modern farming operations. With respect to those farmers who remain behind on the farm, we should launch targeted training programs that provide highly practical forms of education and training so as to improve the quality of life of farmers, how they live as well as how they engage in production. We must increase coverage of programs providing basic vocational training in cities in order to step up the percentage of rural laborers who have taken up residence in those cities. We should aim for training programs that provide full coverage of such people by the year 2020.

2.   Improve the rural old-age security system, and speed up the building of systems that provide services to the elderly in rural areas

China's rural areas are entering the demographic stage of "an aging society" earlier than urban areas due to the longstanding migration of younger people out of the countryside. Aging is also happening at a faster pace than the speed of aging in urban areas. At the same time, the ability of rural families to take care of elderly people has deteriorated rapidly given family planning policies in China and the shrinking of family size. Given this overall background, the task of improving social pension systems [old-age security systems] in rural areas and creating systems that can provide services for the elderly have become highly significant.

In the past few years, China's "new-style system for safeguarding the care of older people in rural areas" has made good progress. A system that provides coverage for all rural people has basically been set up. When the Chinese government began promoting the "new-style social [old-age] insurance system" in 2009, it proposed to have complete coverage of the system by the year 2020 and basic coverage of the entire population of rural townships by the end of 2012. By the end of 2013, the number of people being insured under the new-style social insurance system came to 474 million (Ministry of Human Resources and Social Security, 2014). This represented 120 percent of the employed population in rural areas.[3] Another important component of the new-style rural social insurance system is that it provides a stipend for people aged 60 and above. Although the rates are not yet very high, the vast majority of the older people in the countryside do get a stipend. This undoubtedly does play a good role in improving the quality of life among elderly people in the countryside, but the role it plays in ameliorating poverty is even more apparent.

For China to have set up a basic pension system in the countryside for rural people in the short space of five years is a major accomplishment and a major social advance. Since this effort is still in its early stages, however, it unavoidably has problems and room for improvement. These can mainly be summed up in the following three areas.

The first problem concerns the levels of insurance coverage that one can choose. The great majority of rural residents choose the lowest-cost option.[4] Even though choosing a higher option allows a person to enjoy more government subsidies, the great majority still choose to pay out the lowest amount in premiums. There are many reasons for this, but it cannot be denied that the uncertainties inherent in the system at this time are one of them. According to relevant regulations, those who want to pay the minimum premiums must pay for fifteen years before receiving benefits. Younger people may be able to draw on pension funds for a longer time, but exactly how much they will be drawing by the time they start receiving payments is hard to tell. Even if the premium paid by the individual and the government-subsidy portion paid by the government both go into a personal account, many factors can influence whether that sum goes up or down in value. Since there is indeed a risk of the funds in individual accounts declining in value, paying out more in premiums means you are increasing that risk. Purely out of desire to avoid risk, therefore, participants in the insurance program will choose the lowest level of premium payment as the least risky option.

The second problem is that payments paid out to recipients of the program are too low. Ever since the start of rural pensions [insurance for older people], the sums paid out to older people over the age of 60 have not fundamentally changed. In the past, the main way in which older people were cared for was via "homecare at home," but this is now changing given the one-child policy as well as reproductive behavior. Children are gradually taking on less responsibility for caring for parents, and older people are now relying more and more on society for support.

Because of this, the low pension payments currently being received by many older people in the countryside are simply not enough to pay for basic living requirements. They are not enough to keep them from living in poverty.[5] What's more, the overly low payments have the effect of weakening the incentives for participating in the entire system, which is detrimental to the long-term sustainability of social pension insurance in the countryside.

The third problem is that there are no distinctions in age levels in the system, which universally grants the same amount irrespective of how many years a person has worked. The retirement situation in China's cities is different from that in the countryside, however. In cities, once people "retire," they generally do not keep working, and they then rely on pensions to live out their days. In the countryside, there is no such thing as "retirement." Older people, especially those between the ages of 60 and 64, continue to do farmwork and are still fairly self-reliant. After 65, however, their ability to work begins to decline. The basic social pension does not make any distinction in the amount they take in, however; it does not provide more financial support to those over 65. As a result, it is hard to prevent a decline in people's standard of living (Zhang Hongbo, 2009).

In setting up the rural system of providing for older people, we not only need to improve upon the old-age security/pension system through a more scientific approach, in order to resolve the issue of the sources of funds to care for people, but we need to improve upon the services that are available for older people. As younger people in their prime have migrated toward cities to take up jobs and live their lives, the process of "an aging society" in the countryside has accelerated, and issues relating to caregiving for older people who still live there have become much more pronounced.

First, services for older people have not yet become a primary focus of policy makers. At the policy-making level, models that have already been shown to be effective in the urban setting, such as a model that is "dominated by government spending but also contributed to by private capital," are not being implemented in the rural setting due in part to the way in which rural inhabitants are dispersed, and it is harder to apply such models. For a long time now, the focus of government services for elderly people in the countryside has been on what are called the "five types of households that need special guarantees" and on other such especially vulnerable groups. Government is also gradually beginning to place a priority on "empty-nester" households and older people who are incapacitated or partially incapacitated, but that is a drop in the bucket compared to the needs of the great majority of older people (Chen Ganquan, 2013).

Second, there is a structural problem in the demand for services for the elderly and the supply of such services. As the problem of "an aging society" has speeded up, the demand for intensive care services for the elderly in the countryside has not only grown, but levels of demand have been rising. According to random-sample surveys, at present, the percentage of the total number of older people who are willing to choose centralized old-age services is 4 percent (Li Feng et al., 2012). Meanwhile, according to relevant data, the total number of nursing home beds available for older people in China comes to just 1.59 percent of the total number of elderly in the country. Data from the Sixth National Census indicates that at present the total number of older people in the *countryside* in China comes to around 108.8 million people. There is a gap between the demand for intensive care services for these older people and the supply of such services. The gap is on the order of 2.43 million people. Moreover, the great majority of nursing homes in townships and villages are small, and their equipment is outdated. The rural healthcare services system for older people is simply inadequate to meet even the basic demands of people who need such services in rural areas.

Box 7.2   The living conditions of elderly people in Laoying village, Hubei province

1.   Low levels of income

The main sources of income for people in this village are agricultural production and assistance from children. The survey showed that the financial assistance that children might provide in a year is, however, no more than RMB 500 in the majority of cases. What's more, only a tiny percentage of children provide any money at all. This village is in a hilly region, so that only some of the land can be farmed, and farmed plots are irregularly shaped in addition to being tiny and dispersed. It is fundamentally impossible to farm them with mechanized equipment. In some areas, there is no irrigation at all, so people just rely on rainwater. Older people generally farm between 1 and 3 *mu* of land [roughly between one-fifth and two-fifths of one acre]. After deducting the costs of seed and fertilizer, the net income from 1 *mu* of land comes to only around RMB 400. When you add in any assistance from children and government transfer payments, older people in this village have a household annual income of roughly RMB 1,000.

2.   High risk of getting sick

According to the data from our investigation, the incidence of heart disease and arterial sclerosis is rising since local older people suffer from high blood pressure. Over the past decade, the number of people whose cause of death was "illness" [as opposed to old age] has come to over 50 percent of all deaths. To some extent, the "new-style rural cooperative healthcare insurance" has resolved the problem of people sliding into poverty as a result of major illness, but people are generally reimbursed for costs only if they go into a hospital, and the percentage of costs that are reimbursed, as well as the scope of reimbursed payments, is limited. Any medicines to treat more chronic diseases and the more commonly seen types of illness are paid for out of the pockets of people themselves. "We pay ourselves" is what older people told us, but this is actually another way of saying that older people have trouble getting any treatment at all. Given limited incomes, older people are fundamentally unable to handle medical costs when they get sick.

3. Imbalance in the relationship between generations

A growing imbalance in what used to be the rights and duties [obligations] between generations has exacerbated the difficulties of older people. A saying in the area vividly expresses the relationship between parents and the next generation, which is that "sons are kings, daughters-in-law are queens, and grandchildren are leeches." In our investigation, we learned that conflicts between generations in the village accounted for 60 percent of all disputes and that "unfilial behavior" was common. Deterioration of relationships between generations has severe consequences. According to our findings, in the past ten years, thirty-five people over the age of 60 had died in the past ten years in this village, and of those, eight had died of unnatural causes, or 22.85 percent. The causes given were mostly intergenerational conflict, nobody looking after the person, or painful illness.

4. Poor mental health and impoverished lifestyle

Given the limited amount of land to farm and the schedule of actual farm work, which requires just two to three months, older people have a great deal of free time on their hands. Our investigation discovered that older people in this village mainly spend their time watching television. Some get together to play mahjong. People commented that they are bored watching television, but they also cannot play mahjong all the time – and mahjong means they sit in one place without moving their bodies, plus they also get into arguments over the game, which only makes them more unhappy. In short, the life that older people face is one of great tedium, and the social intercourse of older people is highly circumscribed.

Source: Li Yuanxing, *Rural Social Problems* (Background Report).

To deal with the actual circumstances of older people in China's countryside, we must increase the strength as well as diversity of reforms in order to resolve problems with the old-age pension system and the systems that provide services in general to older people.

First, we should increase incentives with respect to the rural old-age pension/ insurance system so that more people participate. Whenever economic circumstances allow, we should get people to opt for higher levels of coverage, and we should increase the fund-raising capacity of insurance funds. Not only does this mean that the government must put more financial support into the rural old-age pension system, but government must lessen the uncertainties that people have about their future ability to benefit from the system. We should be able to provide a figure for each person that indicates the amount he or she will be drawing in the future at a certain age, depending on the time that person stops working.

Second, we should explore ways to create different levels of old-age insurance coverage benefits. That is, different payment amounts could be given to different age groups of elderly people in the countryside. There could be a lower age group, between 60 and 64, and a higher age group, over 65. With respect to the former, the current payment for "basic old-age pensions" on a uniform nationwide basis is RMB 55 per month. In the future, this should be indexed to inflation and should increase accordingly (Gong Weicai and Xue Xingli, 2012). With respect to the latter, we should gradually raise the standard so that the standard rural payment to people is the same as the urban standard by the year 2020. That is, the per capita basic pension would reach between RMB 200 and 250 per month for people over the age of 65. According to projections of this report, by the year 2020, there will be a total of 120 million older people in rural areas of China. Some 40 million of these will be between the ages of 60 and 64, while 80 million will be over the age of 65. By to the plan just described, China will need to put roughly RMB 260 billion into a "basic old-age pension plan." This amount is well within the financial capacity of the government.

Finally, we should investigate setting up a more diverse model of providing services to older people that is based on having people live at home but is supported by community [centralized] living. On the one hand, the government can integrate the two issues of vacant housing in villages and the need for healthcare services in those villages in which older people live in fairly concentrated numbers. We should aim to have old-age service "stations" for people who are still living at home that provide a range of services such as daily caregiving, emotional support, healthcare, and cultural activities. On the other hand, publicly supported elder care institutions should provide a minimum of services for free or low cost, aimed particularly at low-income older people and people who are economically incapacitated or semi-incapacitated. This would include caregiving and nursing. The government should integrate various rural elder care service organizations into fully functional nursing homes. These should be of reasonable size and capable of providing a full range of services.

3.   Improve the rural healthcare system, and raise levels of health among rural residents

Creating a better rural healthcare system is a critical part of the process of setting up a moderately prosperous society in an all-round way.

China's "new-style rural cooperative healthcare system" has made major progress over the past ten years. Nearly all rural residents are now participating in this system (see Table 7.1). In 2012, the entire country achieved the objective of having all of China's thirty-on provinces, municipalities, and autonomous regions covered under the system. The rate of participation has reached high levels. Starting in 2013, the level of assistance provided per person per year by all levels of

Table 7.1 Development of the New Rural Cooperative Medical Scheme (NCMS)

Year	Number of counties (cities and districts) implementing the NCMS	Number of participants (100 million people)	Rate of participation (%)	Per capita funding (RMB)	Fund expenditures of the year (RMB 100 million)	Number of beneficiaries (100 million people)
2005	678	1.79	75.66	42.10	61.75	1.22
2008	2,729	8.15	91.53	96.30	662.31	5.85
2009	2,716	8.33	94.19	113.36	922.92	7.59
2010	2,678	8.36	96.00	156.57	1,187.84	10.87
2011	2,637	8.32	97.48	246.21	1,710.19	13.15
2012	2,566	8.05	98.26	308.50	2,408.00	17.45

Source: *China Health Statistics Yearbook 2013.*

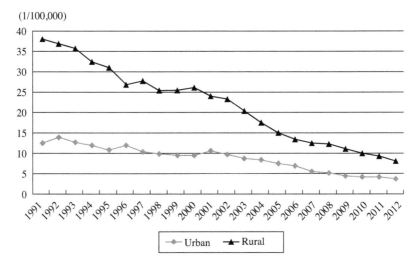

Figure 7.3 Maternal mortality rate in China from 1991 to 2012 (1/100,000)
Source: Prepared based on data from *China Health Statistics Yearbook 2013.*

government combined went up from RMB 240 to RMB 280. The percent of hospital payments that are reimbursable went up to around 75 percent. The work to provide safeguards against major illness within the new-style cooperative healthcare system has also been pushed forward. Due to the protections provided by this system, the dual problems rural people have had – "not being able to get in to see a doctor and not being able to pay" – are now being addressed and relieved to a certain extent. Overall, health in rural areas has greatly improved.

Various healthcare indicators show considerable improvement in the levels of health of rural people over this past decade or more. As shown by Figure 7.3, the rate of maternal mortality has consistently declined between 1991 and 2012, going from 38 per hundred thousand to 8 per hundred thousand. Over a twenty-year period, this rate has dropped by close to 79 percent. At the same time, the rate at which children under the age of 5 die, as well as the infant mortality rate, have also gone down dramatically. The former went from 59 percent in 1991 to 12 percent in 2012 (see Figure 7.4), and the latter went from 71 percent in 1991 to 17 percent in 2012 (see Figure 7.5).

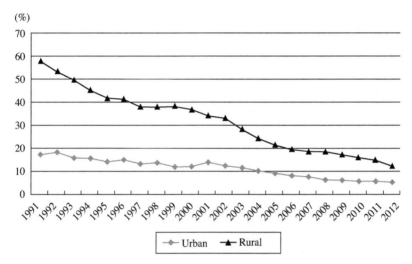

Figure 7.4   The mortality rate of children under 5 in China from 1991 to 2012
Source: Prepared based on data from *China Health Statistics Yearbook 2013.*

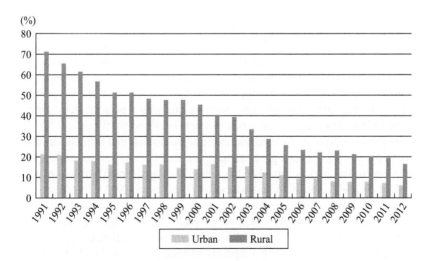

Figure 7.5 Infant mortality rate from 1991 to 2012
Source: Prepared based on data from *China Health Statistics Yearbook 2013.*

Nevertheless, China's rural areas still lack a healthcare system that is comprehensive, reasonable, and sustainable. The funding of rural healthcare insurance systems is inadequate, there is a dearth of professional healthcare providers, medical facilities and equipment are backward, and the problem of "sliding into poverty as a result of illness, or sliding back into poverty as a result of illness" is still unresolved. The problems are even more severe in some of China's more backward rural areas. There is still a considerable disparity in the health and well-being of rural people as opposed to urban people in the country. As Figures 7.3, 7.4, and 7.5 indicate, the indicators for maternal mortality, mortality of children under five, and infant mortality are still double the rates in cities. Looking at development trends, it will take another eight to ten years before these indicators for the countryside reach levels of what they currently are in cities. Many things cause these disparities. One important aspect relates to the difference in ability to get public healthcare services. For a long time, the allocation of healthcare resources was unequally distributed between China's cities and rural areas. High-level, high-quality medical institutions were concentrated in cities, and healthcare professionals also migrated in the direction of cities. Rural people received low levels of healthcare services, and the gap between services in cities and those in the countryside was very considerable. According to research conducted by the Academy of Macroeconomic Research, National Development and Reform Commission, using the indicator of basic healthcare facilities as an example, in 2010, there were 1.16 hospital beds for every thousand people in the "farming population" in China, which was 3.81 beds less than the comprehensive indicator in cities; there were 1.32 healthcare clinic personnel for every thousand people in the farming population, which was 1.82 less than the same indicator in cities. There is also a great disparity in the availability of healthcare resources within large more highly developed municipalities that include the rural districts on their outskirts (Zeng Hongying, 2013). For example, a survey of the conditions of health-resource allocations in the Beijing municipality showed that high-quality care was mainly concentrated in the center of the city, while the availability of hospital beds differed greatly among different districts. The average availability for the city as a whole was 5.09 beds per 1,000 people. In the core part of the city, the figure went up to 10.98, however, while all other districts had figures that were lower than the average. In terms of quality considerations, the disparity is even greater. At present, greater Beijing has fifty-one hospitals that are described as "Triple-A" hospitals, but forty-five of these are located within the eight districts that form the downtown area. In terms of healthcare professionals, the technical personnel staffing facilities in the "town districts" attached to greater Beijing are mainly young or elderly people with low levels of formal education (Liu Jinwei, 2011). In addition to all this, poor hygienic conditions are a major problem in rural China, including the availability of clean drinking water, the problem of toilets, garbage disposal, and environmental pollution – all of which endanger public health. Drinking water is just one example. According to a report published in June of 2012, *Report of the State Council on the Status Of [Government] Work to Ensure Safe Drinking Water*, at the end of 2010, China still had 298 million rural people who were living with "unsafe drinking water problems," and the country still had 114,000 rural schools that could not provide safe drinking water. Not only is there extreme inequality in the availability of healthcare and public health services between China's country-side and its cities and among different regions, but there is also extreme inequality in the allocation of such resources at the grassroots level, that is, between county seats and smaller towns.[6]

Another reason for relatively lower levels of health among rural residents relates to the environmental conditions surrounding these people, which are unfavorable compared to conditions in cities. In terms of hygienic facilities, "hygienic" toilets were available to only slightly over 70 percent of people in rural areas in 2012. The better so-called "sanitary" toilets were available to less than 50 percent (see Figure 7.6). This means that around 200 million rural residents do not use toilets that come up to the most basic hygienic standards, while more than 300 million use toilets that are not up to slightly higher standards.

Overall provision for major illness is one of the component parts of the new-style rural cooperative healthcare system. It has been one of the main measures within the healthcare subsidies and relief program. The great majority of "local" healthcare insurance is planned for and organized at the municipal and county level, that is, funds are pooled and managed at that level. Pooling at a more com-prehensive level is infrequent. There is no comprehensive [shared] healthcare insurance information system. Applications for assistance in the event of major illness are long and complicated. It is hard to get medical care in places outside one's own area and hard to get compensation when medical care has occurred outside the insurance area. Right now, people who live in rural areas can basically get enough to eat, and they have a place to live, and they can clothe themselves. Medical attention is something else and is a major problem. The relief system is

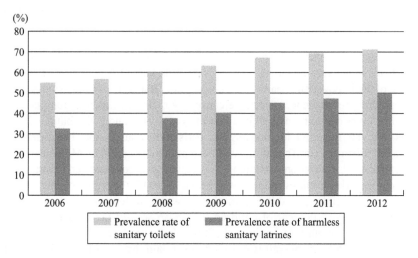

Figure 7.6 Prevalence rate of sanitary toilets

Source: Prepared based on data from *China Health Statistics Yearbook 2013.*

inadequate. For many vulnerable groups, the approach is to "put off worrying about minor illness, endure major illness, and just wait to meet old *Yanwang* [your creator] in the event of severe illness." The procedure right now for vulnerable groups with respect to medical treatment is to pay first for medical fees, then fill out the applications for compensation and "relief" [subsidies]. For Five-Guarantee Households, however, and such vulnerable groups as those on a minimum living allowance, just paying for daily living expenses is hard. Handing over any sum of money at all for medical expenses is impossible. What these people do therefore is give up on any treatment. In July 2011, a World Bank report, *Creating Healthy and Harmonious Lives: Controlling the Prevalence of Chronic Disease in China*, pointed out that the rate of giving up on any treatment was more than twice as high in the countryside as it is in China's cities. As can be seen in Table 7.2, chronic illness is the major cause of death among rural residents in China. Not only is the incidence of such disease rising and adding to the burden on distressed rural families, but this is putting considerable pressure on the sustainable development of rural healthcare insurance.

In addition to setting up improved systems for insuring people and for providing healthcare services in rural areas, we also should focus on the factors that are caus-ing farmers to get sick. These include both smoking and poor childhood nutrition. China is a major producer of tobacco, and its people are major smokers of tobacco; it is also one of the countries that are most hurt by tobacco. According to various reports, in 2008, there were 360 million tobacco smokers in China, or 26 percent of the total population. The number of smokers constituted one-third of the global total (Liu Wanqiang, 2008). Relevant materials indicate that the percentage of smokers in the countryside is even higher. It is worth noting that not only do rural smokers constitute a high percentage of all smokers in China but that the trend is increasing. This undeniably is a major factor leading to the incidence of major illness in rural areas. Moreover, relevant surveys are also now indicating that rural smokers are beginning to have shorter life spans, and this situation is particularly severe in relatively backward parts of the country.

On a nationwide level, the problem of child malnutrition that then leads to health problems is not very apparent, but this is an issue that must not be overlooked in some of the impoverished parts of the countryside. Random sampling surveys have shown that the incidence of disease caused by malnourishment among children aged 0–5 was declining overall between the years 1990 and 2007, but the decline was only very moderate in impoverished parts of the countryside. The differential between urban and rural situations was becoming more apparent. Malnourishment that leads to disease among children 0–5 years in age is concentrated in rural areas, but particularly in impoverished rural areas. In 2007, the status of malnourish-ment among children aged 0–5 in rural areas was as follows: stunted growth was recorded in 14.17 percent of children, low birth weight in 10.17 percent, and anemia in 32 percent (Ma Lexin et al., 2009). In 2010, the rate of stunted growth among rural children overall was 20.3 percent, and the rate of low birth weight was 8.0 percent (Ministry of Health, 2012). In April, 2012, the China Research Development Foundation did a random sampling survey together with the China

Table 7.2 The mortality rate of rural residents and diseases as major causes of death in 2012

Name of Disease	Mortality Rate (1/100,000)			Composition (%)			Rank		
	Total	Male	Female	Total	Male	Female	Total	Male	Female
Malignant tumors	151.47	198.65	102.78	22.96	25.91	18.71	1	1	3
Cerebrovascular diseases	135.95	150.62	120.80	20.61	19.65	21.99	2	2	1
Heart diseases	119.50	123.51	115.36	18.11	16.11	21.00	3	3	2
Respiratory diseases	103.90	114.53	92.93	15.75	14.94	16.91	4	4	4
External causes of injury and poisoning	58.86	78.92	38.17	8.92	10.29	6.95	5	5	5
Other diseases	29.34	29.91	28.75	4.45	3.90	5.23	6	6	6
Digestive diseases	16.79	21.95	11.46	2.54	2.86	2.09	7	7	7
Endocrine, nutritional, and metabolic diseases	10.66	9.92	11.42	1.62	1.29	2.08	8	8	8
Disorders of the genitourinary system	6.62	7.72	5.48	1.00	1.01	1.00	9	10	10
Nervous system diseases	6.26	6.60	5.90	0.95	0.86	1.07	10	11	9
Infectious diseases (excluding respiratory tuberculosis)	5.69	7.78	3.53	0.86	1.01	0.64	11	9	11
Mental disorders	3.10	3.14	3.05	0.47	0.41	0.55	12	13	12
Perinatal diseases	2.72	3.29	2.14	0.41	0.43	0.39	13	12	13
Congenital malformations, deformations, and chromosomal abnormalities	2.11	2.35	1.86	0.32	0.31	0.34	14	15	14
Diagnosis unknown	2.09	2.33	1.83	0.32	0.30	0.33	15	16	15
Respiratory tuberculosis	2.08	3.12	1.01	0.32	0.41	0.18	16	14	1'
Musculoskeletal and connective tissue disorders	1.40	1.19	1.61	0.21	0.16	0.29	1	17	16
Disorders of the blood and blood-forming organs and certain disorders involving the immune mechanism	0.99	1.03	0.96	0.15	0.13	0.17	18	18	18
Complication of pregnancy, childbirth, and the puerperium	0.15		0.30	0.02		0.06	19	20	19
Parasitic diseases	0.05	0.05	0.05	0.01	0.01	0.01	20	19	20

Source: *Yearbook of Statistics China 2013.*

Disease Prevention and Control Center in impoverished areas of Songtao county of Guizhou province. They surveyed the status of nutrition among children aged 3–6. The results showed that 29 percent of children aged between the ages of 3 and 4 had anemia and 19.7 percent of children between the ages of 4 and 5. This was between two and three times the rate seen in urban areas (Wang Mengkui, editor-in-chief, 2013). One group that needs special attention is composed of the "children left behind" in the countryside. Their nutrition and overall health indicators are lower than those of children not left behind.

Given the actual situation in rural areas, improving the health standards of rural people will require concerted attempts to push forward the following items.

First, raise the level of medical insurance [security] among farmers. The existing new-style rural cooperative healthcare treatment system is an excellent program that brings benefits to some hundred million farmers. It has achieved results that are recognized and approved of by society at large, and the system should be maintained and carried forward with ongoing improvements. On the one hand, the government must continue to increase its level of spending on this system. It should increase per capita funding so that the funding level in 2020 is twice what it was in 2013; that is, it should reach a per capita annual amount of RMB 700. At the same time, the government should gradually increase the percentage of medical payments made by farmers that can be reimbursed. By 2020, the aim is to have the percentage of all medical fees be reimbursed at a rate of more than 80 percent. This should help ameliorate the problem of farmers being unable to pay the high costs of seeing a doctor. More importantly, rural basic healthcare services should give priority to finding ways to treat vulnerable groups of people. As the labor force in villages migrates elsewhere for work, the percentage of people defined as vulnerable, those who remain in villages, increases. These people are increasingly at risk as a result of their own health, or specific handicaps, or family reasons. A family with a normal income is able to pay for basic medical services. Low-income groups cannot, however. Paying for normal medical treatment is a heavy burden for them, and seeing the doctor becomes too expensive. We should design specific policies that support medical insurance for these people, such as differentiated handling in medical insurance or raising the amount of medical fees that this group can claim for reimbursement. Some medical services should be offered for free so that when people use basic medical services, they are not, at the same time, being forced to lower their standard of living. As for people with such specific problems as mental illness, neurological problems, physical handicaps, and so on, we should use methods that are different from the normal basic medical services. As the government formulates unified provisions for medical service, therefore, it should also take these specific circumstances into account. It should design the provision of special services for groups of people who are out of the ordinary (Liu Jinwei, 2011). We should make special effort to strengthen medical security and services for children in backward areas of the countryside. This Report recommends that the government institute policies that enable children under the age of 5 to receive free medical care in certain impoverished regions.

Second, set up an integrated medical insurance system that covers both countryside and cities. We should tie together the systems that deal with each, that is, the new-style rural cooperative healthcare system and the urban residents' medical insurance system, as well as the urban workers' medical insurance system [in this case, workers employed in State-Owned Enterprises]. We must make it possible for those who leave their hometown to work elsewhere to have their insurance system automatically shift to the new system. That is, there should be no gaps in the medical insurance of the floating population and rural migrant workers.

Third, raise levels of medical services in rural areas, and make it more convenient to access those services. We should continue to put more spending into all levels of rural medical service organizations, so that they become a fairly complete medical services system and so that medical facilities are constantly being upgraded. This also means also means having systems to attract outstanding medical personnel to move to cities to provide medical care. While raising levels of pay for medical professionals and hospital workers in the countryside on an overall basis, we should provide incentives for the higher-level talent in these institutions. Each clinic should have between three and five positions that are dedicated to professional doctors and that are well compensated, and the hiring should be done via job postings that are nationwide.

Fourth, raise the percentage of medical fees that vulnerable groups can claim for reimbursement. For people on minimum living allowances, implement low-cost treatment for major illness in order to address the post-illness concerns of these people and in order to resolve the basic medical needs of rural impoverished groups and low-income groups. When people are faced with serious illnesses and need to go to the hospital, we should implement a policy of zero-payment up-front. That is, for those impoverished populations who are unable to pay for major illnesses, we should provide a certain amount of financial support as a way to prevent them or their families from carrying major risk. To the greatest extent possible, we should reduce the burden of medical fees for these people.

Fifth, increase efforts to prevent and control chronic disease in rural areas. We must go further in consolidating and improving upon the chronic prevention network that is currently composed of three types of organizations: grassroots clinics, hospitals, and specialized disease prevention institutions. We should strengthen the subsidies for services relating to preventative health care and health maintenance of rural people. We should set up a new system of community health services and set up a network of monitoring stations to monitor the health of rural residents. We should put major effort into promoting public-welfare-type health education, and popularize advice on how to maintain health and prevent chronic disease. We should guide farmers in how to live a healthy lifestyle.

Sixth, set up mechanisms in rural areas that enable people to be self-governing with respect to the conditions surrounding them. A clean, hygienic, environment in towns is an important way to safeguard the physical health of farmers. However, due to the lack of any mechanisms that safeguard this kind of environment, the overall conditions in which people live in townships has been greatly impacted by decreased standards of living and levels of consumption. Hygienic conditions are deteriorating in some townships and towns. Villages have garbage that is not being disposed of properly, and a stench now pervades the air. There is no time to waste in setting up mechanisms by which local people can address the situation themselves. These mechanisms will need a certain degree of financial support. We could adopt procedures by which the government contributes a portion of subsidies, while villagers fund-raise the rest among themselves. Towns in which the labor force capacity is provided by older people and women should have priority in getting such funding, while the work of cleaning should be done by low-income older people and women who are compensated. This ties together improvements in public hygiene with the problem of employment for distressed households, as well as poverty-reduction efforts. Meanwhile, upgrading toilets in rural areas has an impact on the community's public-health environment, as well as on the physical health of farmers. The government should therefore formulate regulations regarding such upgrading, which should be quite practical. The government should also fund the effort with public funds, with the aim of having more than 90 percent of the countryside equipped with hygienic toilets by 2020.

Seventh, realize the goal of having safe drinking water throughout the countryside. In 2005, China launched a drinking water safety project in rural areas that made major improvements. According to the statistics, the program resolved drinking water needs of 410 million rural residents in the space of eight years, as well as 32 million students and teachers in schools. The percentage of the population that benefited from intensive drinking water supply projects in the countryside went from 40 percent to 73 percent (Gao Wen, 2014). The Chinese government's intent is to increase that percentage to 80 percent by the end of 2015, and, by 2020, the intent is to have basically completed the building of a system that protects drinking water "from the source to the tap" in the entire countryside.

Eighth, raise levels of nutrition among rural children. In recent years, the Chinese government has put a major effort into promoting free lunches in rural grade schools and middle schools, and the results are becoming apparent. According to statistics, at the end of 2012, the great majority of rural areas implemented a free-lunch program in compulsory-level schools, which benefited 26 million students. This undoubtedly will play a positive role in raising the physical well-being of students and their overall health. In November 2014, the Standing Committee of the State Council passed *State regulations on child development in impoverished regions*. This provided children of vulnerable families in contiguous impoverished areas of the country with safeguards that start at birth and continue until they have finished compulsory education. Improving the nourishment of children is a complex form of systems engineering that requires nourishment interventions at all ages. It extends the process back toward the beginning, that is, from school-age children back to the prenatal stage. We must accelerate the process of weaving together a kind of "safety net" that contributes to the development of children in impoverished areas overall. By the year 2020, the aim is to have newborn children emerge into the world in a healthy condition, with normal nourishment, then to have them participate in three years of preschool basic education before going on to primary schools and middle schools that also have nourishment safeguards in place (see Box 7.3).

Box 7.3   Nutrition packets: making a good start on lifelong health

1.   Theory-based programs

Starting in 1990, the research team in which Chen Chunming, senior advisor to China's Disease Prevention and Control Center, was working began developing a kind of "nutrition package" that was in keeping with China's traditional ways of feeding babies. It was also easily used, inexpensive, and easy to get. In addition to the normal nutrition that a baby might be getting, this was a supplement intended to provide babies with all necessary nutrition. Although low cost, it was dense in nutritious elements. It used soy powder as a base, and contained nine kinds of micro elements intended to resolve protein deficiencies and ensure calorie intake. The cost of producing each packet was RMB 0.7 to 0.9.

In 2001, the Nutrition Packet program was launched. Researchers selected five impoverished counties in Gansu province for the initial trials, providing the packets for free for 1,500 infants. Each day, a 10-gram packet could satisfy the daily requirements for iron, calcium, zinc, vitamin A, vitamin D, and so on. After six months, the rate of anemia in the infants went down from 34.9 percent to 18.5 percent. By the age of 24 months, children who had been fed with nutrition packets were 1.3 centimeters taller on average than those who had not. The IQ of those with packets was between 1.3 and 4.7 points higher. After tracking these children to the age of 6, the team found that the intelligence IQ of beneficiaries maintained a clear advantage.

2.   Trial implementation and policy advocacy

Starting in September of 2009, the China Development and Research Foundation launched pilot programs in Qinghai's Ledu county and then in Yunnan's Xundian county relating to early childhood development. The research project was called *Project on Early Childhood Development in Impoverished Regions.* Nutrition packets were supplied to 6- to 24-month-old infants for free. This project, which was conducted jointly by the Foundation and the China Disease Prevention and Control Center, among others, showed the following results. In comparison with baseline figures, the rate of stunted growth of 6- to 24-month-old infants declined by between 13 percent and 35 percent. In comparison with non-pilot-program groups, the rate of stunted growth among children in pilot-program areas who were over 1 year old declined dramatically. The rate of stunted growth for children aged 1.5 to 2 years (18 to 24 months) was under the national average for rural areas. The rate at which all ages of children had fevers and diarrhea declined significantly. Based on early-childhood development experiments in the field, as well as actual policy experience, in early 2013, the

Foundation presented a Recommendation to the Central Committee. This was called *Recommendation on setting up a national childhood development program in impoverished rural regions.* This included a recommendation to distribute nutrition packets to babies in impoverished rural regions. President Xi Jinping confirmed the importance of this Recommendation by recommending that the government support it.

3.   Incorporating the *Recommendation* into national policy

Given the high priority that the Central leaders placed on this effort, starting in October 2012, the National Health and Family Planning Commission and the National Women's Federation jointly implemented the child nutrition improvement project in contiguous areas of impoverished rural regions. The project provided infants aged 6 to 24 months with nutrition packets as a way to prevent inadequate nutrition and anemia and to raise overall health levels of infants in impoverished regions. By the end of 2013, the program had already benefited 400,000 infants. In 2014, the central treasury continued to support the project by allocating RMB 300 million, and the scope of the project was expanded from the 100 counties in the contiguous impoverished area to 300 counties. As of 2016, the nation has spent a total of RMB 400 million on the project and has issued nutrition packets to 820,000 impoverished children. In November, 2014, the Standing Committee of the State Council passed the *National Plan on Child Development in Impoverished Regions.* This included provisions to go further in expanding the pilot sites for improving infant and child nutrition among distressed families in impoverished regions.

Source: Compiled by the research team of China Development Research Foundation, November 2014.

4.   Improve the housing conditions of rural residents and ensure that vulnerable populations have a place to live

Housing conditions for people living in rural parts of China have improved notably since the start of the 21st century, and the quality of housing has gone up. According to data from the National Bureau of Statistics, the average per capita amount of space that a rural person lives in went from 26 square meters in 2001 to 37 square meters in 2012. This reflected an increase in the quantity of rural housing, while the increase in quality could be seen in the number of buildings built out of rebar-reinforced concrete. It can be seen from Figure 7.7 that housing built of rebar-reinforced concrete increased by 143 percent, from a per capita 7 cubic meters to a per capita 17 cubic meters. At the same time, the percentage of rural people living in such housing went from 27 percent to 36 percent. The Sixth National Population Census shows that, in 2010, roughly 30 percent of rural households were living in buildings that had been built after the year 2000.

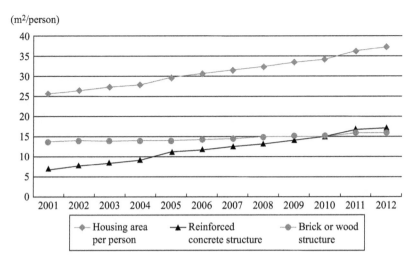

Figure 7.7 Change in housing area and quality for rural residents (2001–2012)
Source: *Yearbook of Statistics China 2013.*

Nevertheless, the requirements of building a moderately prosperous society in an all-round way mean that much more work has to be done if we are to resolve the housing needs and housing quality needs of farmers. One of the key issues in the housing security of farmers relates to quality. The Second National Agricultural Census provided the following data. At the end of 2006, 21.24 million households in rural areas were living in houses made of earthen bricks with bamboo or grass roofs, or 9.6 percent of the total. There were 22.65 million houses that did not have potable drinking water, or 10.3 percent, while 3.16 million households used rainwater for their source of drinking water, or 1.4 percent. For fuel as a source of energy, most rural residents used wood or grasses, including 133.18 million households, or 60.2 percent. For toilets, 94.74 million had either primitive toilets or no toilets at all, or 42.9 percent. In addition, only 24.5 percent of villages had water that had been processed through centralized facilities; only 15.8 percent had centralized collection points for garbage disposal, 30.2 percent had kindergartens or nurseries, and 10.7 percent had playgrounds.

Secondly, the safety of farmers' housing is appalling. In August of 2014, the Ministry of Housing and Urban–Rural Development began an investigation into the extent of "dangerous housing" in rural areas on a nationwide basis. Prior to publication of data resulting from this effort, information on the instability of rural housing was scattered and not highly accurate. From the work carried out by all levels of government in recent years on this issue, however, we can surmise that dangerous housing in rural areas is a problem we urgently need to address. According to various reports, at the end of 2013, Yunnan had 2.2 million households living in dangerous housing (Zhan Jingjing, 2014), as one example. Data from the Sixth

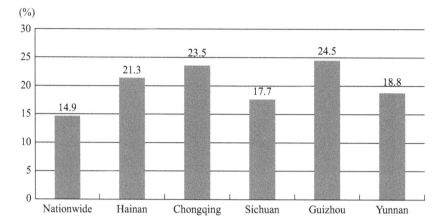

(%)

Figure 7.8 The proportion of rural families living in houses built in or before the 1970s in 2010

Source: National Bureau of Statistics, Tabulation on the 2010 Population Census of the People's Republic of China.

National Population Census shows that 14 percent of rural households still live in buildings built in the 1970s or earlier, while the percentage is higher in western parts of the country. In Guizhou province, the percentage exceeds 24 percent (see Figure 7.8). Older buildings such as these are dangerous to one degree or another. For this reason, each level of government must regard the renovation of dangerous housing as a key task if we are to achieve a moderately prosperous society in an all-round way. Each should seek to realize completely safe housing for farmers by the year 2020.

The issue of dangerous buildings in the countryside does not involve simply dilapidated homes in need of repair. It also includes homes that cannot withstand natural disasters. Since China is subject to frequent natural disasters, housing safety requires that buildings come up to a certain standard of quality in order to withstand shocks. In the past few years, earthquakes of relatively large magnitude in the western part of the country have led to enormous loss of life, and one of the major reasons has been that housing in earthquake-prone regions has not been built to adequate standards. In the next few years, each level of government must put major effort into changing this. Farmers' housing that is in earthquake zones should be examined and evaluated. Once the situation is clarified, policies should be formulated that address the problems, including adequate earthquake-resistant standards for building construction. Funds should then be made available and responsible entities appointed to carry through. By the year 2020, every effort should be made to ensure that rural housing is earthquake resistant and that farmers live in safe housing, housing in which they can feel secure.

The improvement of housing is an important indicator of moderate prosperity, and "moderately prosperous housing" is an important component of a moderately prosperous life. We must gradually set up mechanisms that ensure that vulnerable parts of society have secure housing and that dangerous housing in rural areas is renovated well enough to last a long time – mechanisms that guide and safeguard the technology of housing construction. We should demarcate the authorities of the central government as opposed to local governments over these things, as well as responsibilities for expenditures. We should increase the amount of financial support that the central government provides for renovating dangerous housing and for improving the overall environment of residential areas. We must make maximum use of public finance to address this endeavor by using the leveraging effect of both "incentives" and "subsidies." Public-interest endeavors in rural areas include the building of all kinds of basic infrastructure related to water, electricity, roads, gas, and communications. They include facilities for public services, including cultural aspects. All of these must be improved in tandem with the building of rural housing in order to improve the residential environment of rural areas (see Box 7.4).

Box 7.4   The actions taken by Guizhou province in 2014 to improve living conditions in rural areas

1.   Implementing social security

Target goal: ensure that all of the various policies developed by the Communist Party of China to benefit and strengthen farmers and farming are carried out without distortions or shortcuts. This includes the following: policies to benefit farmers including medical insurance, minimum living allowance, new-type insurance, reforestation (or planting of grasses) on what was farmland, subsidies for grain farming, and so on. It means holding fast to goals and ensuring their completion, holding fast to openness in decision making, and publicizing results. It means strengthening promotion efforts and raising the participation rate in the cooperative medical insurance for the public and the new-style rural old-age social security.

2.   Implementing the water safety program

Target goal: ensure that water supply issues are addressed and resolved, including drinking water for both people and livestock, water for irrigation of farmland, and water for industrial uses. This means grasping hold of opportunities to further the "beautiful countryside" initiative that furthers rural development. It means ensuring that [government] departments that have to do with water provide support and assistance. It means ensuring that those impoverished towns and households with the requisite conditions are able to get running water, and it means that all households have a source of drinking water or a place they can go to get water. It means concentrating water resource projects in grain-growing districts and ensuring that fields have adequate irrigation.

3.   Implementing the electricity program

Target goal: grasp hold of opportunities to further the "beautiful country-side" initiative that furthers rural development. This includes revamping [upgrading] the rural electric power grid. It means increasing promotion of electric power safety, coordinating the departments involved in electric power so that they will support the work of getting power to each household, eliminating hidden safety risks, ensuring that each and every home and each and every village not only has electricity but uses it safely.

4.   Implementing the roads program

Target goal: grasp hold of opportunities to further the "beautiful country-side" initiative that furthers rural development. This means improving roads in rural areas by making sure of support from relevant departments for repairing and building industrial roads and connecting otherwise dead-end roads, "hardening" [blacktopping] roads to homes, and in general resolving any difficulties in transporting goods and people. Make every effort to have every household connected to the road system with "hardened" roads, in villages where that is possible, and make every effort to have every village connected via asphalt roads.

5.   Implementing the housing improvement program

Target goal: grasp hold of opportunities to further the "beautiful country-side" initiative that furthers rural development. This means ensuring that all relevant departments lend their support to rebuilding dangerous housing, to constructing kitchens and toilets, and to beautifying surroundings. It means improving the quality of residential areas by improving their external appearance and their internal livability and safety. This also includes promoting the use of power-conserving equipment and clean energy sources, and it means protecting the ecological environment.

6.   Implementing the communications infrastructure program

Target goal: grasp hold of opportunities to further the "beautiful country-side" initiative that furthers rural development. This means ensuring that all relevant departments lend their support to improving the coverage of telecommunications systems. It means ensuring that each village-level organization in villages has office equipment such as a computer and that activity centers can connect to the internet. In villages where this is feasible, it means deploying broadband equipment, as well as enabling cable television. In households where this is feasible, it means enabling broadband internet connections.

7. Building well-off villages

Target goal: grasp hold of opportunities to further the "beautiful country-side" initiative that furthers rural development. This means picking up the pace of rural construction. Given the prerequisite that the local characteristics and ethnic diversity of a place are to be preserved, this means beautifying villages in scientific ways, making villages into places that are livable, have beautiful surroundings, and are well equipped.

8. Increase assistance for impoverished "ecological migrants," that is, people who have been moved for environmental reasons

Target goal: persist in the work of moving impoverished people for ecological reasons, always with the underlying principle that such movement must be voluntary and must focus on doing the "easy things first and the harder things later." Take steps in ways that focus on key priorities, and encourage experimental ways of handling things. In places that have people living under very poor, remote conditions, when it is economically feasible, cost-effective, and in compliance with the people's wishes, ensure that those who want to move may move and that, once they have moved, they can stay put, have jobs, and are secure in those jobs.

9. Express concern for particularly vulnerable [distressed] groups of people

Target goal: on a regular basis, pay calls on impoverished households, "left-behind children," older people who are living alone, empty nesters, older Party members, families living in poverty who have followed family-planning practices, and so on in order to understand their situations and help them resolve practical problems relating to production, living, studying, keeping accounts, and so on. On key holidays, give emotional support to such people, as well as material support in appropriate quantities.

Source: *The Notice of the Party Building Leadership Term of Guizhou Provincial Committee of the CPC on Issuing the Six Actions and 50 Important Tasks Program of Guizhou Province for Building Well-off Villages*, April 16, 2014.

5. Push forward the building of public service facilities in rural areas, and improve the living conditions of people in rural areas

"Public service facilities" refers to those public goods that are mainly provided by government departments. They are not exclusively for one group or another and are not provided on a competitive basis. This includes administrative management, education, medical care, cultural and physical facilities, and social services facilities (Luo Zhendong et al., 2010). "Rural public service facilities" is a term used in contrast to "urban public service facilities." It refers to things that satisfy the public needs of rural communities and is an overall term used in a broad sense for public goods, labor, and services that are not-for-profit and that are provided for people in such communities (Li Liqing, 2005). Public services and facilities are a prerequisite for social and economic development. To realize moderate prosperity in China's rural areas, we must put a major effort into picking up the pace of providing rural public services and facilities. Despite their extreme importance to rural economic and social development, it is very hard for rural people to provide these things on their own. For one thing, China's agricultural production is done by individual households who are widely dispersed. That, plus the nature of agriculture itself means that farmers must rely heavily on public service facilities. Moreover, this reliance continues to increase as marketization of the economy grows in rural areas (Chen Xiaoan, 2005). For another thing, rural public services and facilities have a spillover effect, which means that consumers can take advantage of them for free. If these things had to be provided completely by a market, they simply would not be available; this in turn means that the government must participate in providing them.

For a long time, the center of gravity of economic growth in China was in the cities. This led to the relative neglect of public facilities in rural areas to the extent that there was an acute disparity between levels of services in cities and levels in the countryside. The emphasis of the new-countryside initiative is on raising levels of public services in rural areas. It is also a primary component of the socialist new-countryside plan (Li Jiange, 2006). At present, quite a few problems remain in how we manage this "building of rural public services and facilities" in the country, however. These problems are in urgent need of being resolved.

First, the administration [management] of public resources in rural areas has been chaotic. In recent years, different departments at the national level have supported the building of certain public service facilities. Since responsibility for the management and actual work of building such facilities belongs to different departments and sectors, however, in actual implementation some things have been given priority, and some have not. This has led to a situation in which there is no overall planning or coordination of resources, and the lack of coordination has occurred both within departments and among different departments.

Second, at the village level, the building and operations of public service facilities are controlled by just one entity. Rural public service facilities are basically built with funding from the county and township levels of governments and departments. The collective economic organization of a village rarely contributes funds. When it does, such cases are mainly in more economically developed areas. Village-run enterprises too rarely lend support. The primary entity that manages and operates grassroots public service facilities is the town government or village committee.

Third, the level of public services and facilities provided by town-level governments cannot satisfy the needs of rural people [farmers]. Since the amount of funding is woefully inadequate, town-level public service facilities cannot meet basic needs. The current situation is that public facilities are inadequate in all ways, including scope, content, and quality. Meanwhile, farmers who have become more prosperous place ever higher demands on what they want from public services, while the actual situation right now is far below this level.

Fourth, since there is no motivation on the part of the public to participate in the endeavor, supply and demand for community services are not in balance – there is a disconnect. In the course of operating rural community services centers, "management" is often weighted heavily in terms of resources, while provision of actual services is slighted. The institutional arrangements of available services are strongly "mandatory" in nature, instead of being flexible and suited to meet the demands of rural people's actual needs. There are no dynamic response mechanisms, so that the situation does not truly reflect the internal demand of rural communities. This has led to a surfeit of things that villagers do not actually need and a lack of services that villagers do need. This wastes the already limited public-service resources of the village.

Looking at the actual situation in rural communities, we must push forward the following efforts if we are going to improve our public services and facilities in rural areas.

First, unify planning from an overall perspective, define standards, coordinate and integrate resources. At the national and provincial levels of government, formulate a development plan as soon as possible that looks at the entire situation. As per the principles of "being conservation-oriented, highly efficient, and good for the people," we should carry out reorganizations of the departments with functions that relate to the funding of rural facilities. We should merge those institutions that have similar functions. We should set up long-lasting and effective mechanisms for monitoring and regulating those projects for which specific funding has been allocated. We should achieve "dynamic" managerial oversight and make sure that performance evaluations are properly conducted and take these projects into account (see Table 7.3).

Second, make use of private–public partnerships [PPP] in both operations and management. Public service facilities need to have greater funding sources for operations and management, as well as ways to cut costs. We should adopt competitive market mechanisms in order to save on costs. Private contractors should be hired to provide such services as cleaning and maintenance in order to reduce expenses. For some types of facilities, such as long-distance learning facilities, equipment for water conservancy projects and farming, and so on, government may increase revenues by making operations more market-based.

Third, change our current method of financial support for specific projects. The method used in the past called for meeting objectives within a certain planned period of time (around five years) for specifically designated projects. The main purpose of this kind of thing was to support the building of service facilities. Once

Table 7.3 Funds invested by different departments in the new-countryside construction project of a village in western China

Name of department	Main construction
Development and Reform Bureau	Residential street construction
Bureau of Water Affairs	Water improvement, reservoir and channel reinforcement, small-scale rural water conservancy projects, and so on
Department of Transportation	Road construction in villages
Office of Poverty Alleviation	The Whole Village Advancement poverty-alleviation project
Bureau of Ethnic and Religious Affairs	Special Development Fund for Ethnic Minorities
Housing Construction Bureau	Rural sanitation projects, renovation of dangerous buildings, and village planning
Land and Resources Bureau	Land consolidation and village renovation
Bureau of Finance	Fund-raising matters on a case-by-case basis, etc.
Bureau of Education	Construction of rural schools, fitness centers, equipment, etc.
Organization Department	Construction of workplaces for village-based institutions, construction of local level institutions, etc.

Source: Zhou Feizhou et al., *Report on China's Rural Public Finance and Public Service Development* (Background Report).

Table 7.4 List of main public facilities in villages and townships of Hebei province ranked by the administrative level

Type		Item	Key township	Rural township	Key village	Grassroots village
Administration C1	C11	Party and government organs and social organizations	●	●	●	●
	C12	Police, courts, and public security management	●	●	/	/
	C13	Construction, market, land, and other management institutions	●	○	/	/
	C14	Economic and intermediary institutions	●	○	○	/
Educational institutions C2	C21	Kindergartens and nurseries	●	●	●	●
	C22	Primary schools	●	●	●	○
	C23	Middle schools	●	○	/	/
	C24	Senior high schools or complete secondary schools	○	/	/	/

Type		Item	Key township	Rural township	Key village	Grassroots village
	C25	Vocational education, adult education and training institutes, and junior colleges	○	/	/	/
Culture, sports, and technology C3	C31	Cultural and recreational facilities	●	●	●	○
	C32	Sport facilities	●	●	○	○
	C33	Libraries and technology-related facilities	●	○	○	○
	C34	Heritage, memorial, and religious facilities	○	○	○	○
Healthcare C4	C41	Healthcare facilities	●	●	●	●
	C42	Disease prevention and family planning facilities	●	●	/	/
	C43	Wellness facilities	●	○	○	○
Business and finance C5	C51	Hotels, restaurants, and tourist facilities	●	○	○	/
	C52	Shops, pharmacies, and supermarkets	●	●	○	○
	C53	Banks, credit unions, and insurance institutions	●	●	/	/
	C54	Haircut, laundry, labor, and other services	●	●	○	/
	C55	Comprehensive repair, processing, and collection points	●	●	○	○
Trade facilities C6	C61	General merchandise markets and vegetable markets	●	●	/	/
	C62	Fuel, building materials, and capital goods markets	○	○	/	/
	C63	Livestock, poultry, and aquatic product markets	○	○	/	/
Social security C7	C71	Rehabilitation facilities for people with disabilities	●	○	/	/
	C72	Nursing homes and welfare centers for children	●	●	●	/
	C73	Old-age service stations	●	●	●	/

● Facilities that should be constructed
○ Facilities that can be constructed
/ Facilities that are usually not been constructed.

Source: *Notice of the Housing and Construction Department of Hebei Province on the Issuance of Guidance for Planning Public Facilities in Villages and Townships of Hebei Province (Trial)*, March 15, 2011.

funding was provided, in a one-time subsidy, however, no further consideration was given to maintenance or upgrading. This method of handling specifically designated projects led to the practice of "focusing on the initial construction but then putting little effort into ongoing management." As a result, maintenance was not done well, leading to insufficient actual use. We recommend looking at the comprehensive grassroots situation in terms of the actual building of and operating of public services and facilities. Policies should be integrated with the actual circumstances of a given area. If an area is developing well and operating conditions are good, and there is room to develop further projects, then financial support should be provided for upgrading and improvements on a two- to three-year time cycle.

Fourth, cultivate funding sources from the private sector, and encourage farmers to participate. In pushing forward the building of moderate prosperity in the countryside, the government cannot handle everything. It cannot be the substitute for everything else. Through group [collective] decision making, among other methods, it should encourage farmers to participate in both the building of and management of public facilities. It should facilitate the formation of "social capital" [private-sector capital], so as to encourage participation by farmers in the full scope of social networks, and so as to build mutual trust, mutual benefit, and cooperative win-win trajectories.

Notes

1 Data from surveys conducted by China Youth Development Foundation in 2005.
2 Research Group of China Development Research Foundation, "Evaluation Report – Effects of State Funding Policies for Secondary Vocational Education," November 2014.
3 Participants of the new-style rural social [old-age] insurance program include not only employees in rural areas but also some employees in urban areas, and therefore the number of insured is greater than the number of employees in rural areas.
4 According to provisions of the State Council on social [old-age] insurance premiums, the program currently has five levels of premiums: RMB 100 per year, RMB 200 per year, RMB 300 per year, RMB 400 per year, and RMB 500 per year. Local governments may set additional levels based on local situations. In practice, some local governments add the level of RMB 1,000 per year.
5 After a substantial adjustment of the rural poverty reduction threshold in 2011, the new threshold was RMB 2,300 per person per year, which was later further adjusted in accordance with the level of consumer prices in rural areas. The threshold was RMB 2500 per person per year in 2013. According to calculations on this basis, the level of old-age insurance benefits for rural residents is 26.4 percent of the rural poverty reduction threshold.
6 Take a county in Tianjin, for example: 75 percent of the medical resources of the country are concentrated in hospitals in the county seat (despite the fact that the population of the county seat accounts for only 23.6 percent of the total population of the county). Although the county seat has only four hospitals, health workers mainly concentrate in the county seat. The county seat has 8.4 doctors per 1,000 people, while rural townships have 2.89 doctors per 1,000 people. The county has achieved the goal of "one village, one hospital," as proposed by the new healthcare reform, and health workers per 1,000 people in rural areas and rural townships are 2.17 and 2.89 respectively, much higher than the national level of 1.46 and 1.30, reflecting the advantages of rural areas within

the jurisdiction of a municipality. However, with one health center in one rural township (40 to 60 persons per hospital on average) and with less than one clinic in a village, it is still difficult to meet the demand of farmers for public health care. The level of medical services in these townships still lags far behind, especially compared to the county seat. Because the population covered by one rural clinic is 1,307 people, some clinics cover a 50-kilometer radius area, and some villagers within the area live a long way from the village clinics.

8 Promoting innovative ways to involve rural communities in self-governance

- The current pattern of governance in rural communities
- Rural communities and their changing dynamics in the current era
- Problems in rural governance at the present time
- Policy recommendations for creative ways to enable governance by rural communities

A "moderately prosperous society" does not refer just to adequate food and clothing. As a way to describe how people live together, it also signifies a society that is peaceful and at ease with itself. Realizing the goal of moderate prosperity in China's rural areas, especially realizing sound democratic systems and social harmony, poses much greater demands on rural social governance. In overall terms, China's farmers have moved forward and benefited since the start of reform and opening up. Rural society has remained stable, which has lent vital support to the government as it pushed forward reform and tried to achieve development objectives. However, as structural changes in the countryside have become ever more acute, as population mobility between city and countryside has grown, and as social values in rural societies have changed, rural social governance is facing new, monumental, challenges. If we are to consolidate the foundation of national political power at the grassroots level and create a social environment that is orderly and peaceful, if we are to provide conditions for two-way flows of resources and population between urban and rural – to the extent that urban and rural are indeed integrated – then we must create new ways to govern rural society. This should be done according to the document called *National governance systems and the modernization of governance capacities*. We must integrate traditional rural-government resources with modern social-governance mechanisms. This chapter first gives a simplified outline of the current patterns by which rural communities are governed in China. It then combines the changes currently underway in rural societies with an analysis of the social-governance issues facing rural areas. On that basis, it makes recommendations on how to strengthen rural social governance by applying innovative methods.

1.   The current pattern of governance in rural communities

The countryside of China is the foundation in which the nation's political power is rooted. In the course of the Chinese revolution as well as the process of reform, farmers have played a critical role. Faced with absolute chaos in Chinese society in the mid-20th century, the Communist Party of China successfully organized farmers and mobilized social forces in the countryside to garner support and participation in revolution and, later, reform. This was a fundamental lesson as China succeeded first in establishing the country [PRC] and then in building it up through the process of reform. At present, China's countryside has taken the initial steps in transforming its traditional mode of governance into a modern mode of governance. It has begun to construct the "basic framework for governance by government" combined with "governance by society at large."

The transformation in the mode of rural social governance in the modern era

In traditional China, the State's political power and the governing of its bureaucratic system could be regarded as a kind of indirect rule over rural society. Traditional China's rural society remained stable on a long-term basis in how people produced things and lived, as well as how they formed their values and ideology. The upper levels of central government authority, as well as the bureaucratic system that went from top down, did not get embroiled in local governance. Instead, at the lower levels, the heads of family-based clans and the local elite were what constituted local authority. They in fact assumed the functions of "governing" rural society (Fei Xiaotong, 1998; Wang Xianming, 1997; Zhang Jing, 2000). Some scholars have gone further in elucidating this system. In traditional Chinese society, two different kinds of "order" and "force" in fact coexisted. One was social order as governed by officials, or "*guan*," which involved the power of "the nation." The other was social or civil order as governed by the locality itself, which involved the power of "the people." The former centered on imperial authority, with a stair-stepped structure going from top to bottom via clearly defined levels of authority. The latter centered on family clans. Clusters of clans formed a beehive structure in self-governed communities. Tying these two orders and forces together were a class of elite "country gentlemen" [*xiang shen*] (Vivienne Shue, 1998). It was precisely because "imperial authority stopped at the county, and self-governance was the rule below the county," that China was able to maintain its stable structure for so long. Political changes might happen at the top, but even as dynasties were changing time and again, the dual structure preserved stability at the grassroots political and social level (Xu Yong, 1992).

This kind of indirect rule relied upon a standardized form of ethics and ideology. As pointed out by one scholar, "State authority did not extend to the county; below the county came ancestral clans; ancestral clans were self-governed, the self-governing relied upon ethics, and the ethics created the gentry" (Qin Hui, 2003). In more recent times, however, as China encountered epic change unlike anything that had come before, governance of rural society also began to loosen up and be modified. This was true particularly after the elimination of the imperial examination system at the start of the 20th century (the *ke-jeu* system). The gentry class then lost the basis on which national structures and bureaucratic ideologies had relied. As an elite group, "country gentlemen" would now cease to exist. The relationship between the State [nation] and farmers [rural people] began to weaken, fragment, and finally come apart altogether (Xiao Tangbiao, 2002). In the context of massive social changes in the early 20th century, intellectuals launched the Movement to Build Up the Countryside, and the Nationalist government [Kuomintang, KMT] launched the Movement to Revitalize the Countryside. Both of these attempted to address the most prominent problems in the countryside through addressing cultural, production, and economic aspects and thereby to "reawaken the countryside" (Xiang Jiquan, 2009). Aimed at improving the situation, these movements failed to succeed, however, for one important reason.

> Each movement focused on some specific actual task or other, but they all shared one common feature. They all accepted the existing social and political organizations as an established fact. They placed absolutely no blame on the things that kept the Chinese countryside from advancing, indeed that kept all of China from advancing, namely the exploitation of imperialism and governance by the vestiges of feudal power (Sun Yefang, 1936).

During the war period, the Communist Party of China launched a series of reforms in the countryside that had to do with land. The Party's organization and mobilization of rural society provided broad support for the Chinese revolution. After New China was founded [the PRC] in 1949, grassroots political structures were set up in the countryside as political authority at the national level was gradually established. Traditional mechanisms for rural self-governance were replaced by "an omnipotent State" [a State that assumes all functions] as "State power completely infiltrated and controlled society." As the collectivization of agriculture was then pushed forward, the management entities governing grassroots political institutions and collective economic organizations were combined into one entity. They formed what became known as the system of People's Communes in which "government and society were unified," in which political and economic functions were combined.

In the midst of reforms that began in 1978, the People's Commune system gradually began to be eliminated. The system was based on the idea of the bigger the better and the more public the better, as in the phrase, "first, big, second, public." This kept it from motivating farmers to produce more, which seriously impacted the efficiency of agricultural production. As a result, the country then began implementing a *cheng-bao*, or contracting system, by which responsibility for agricultural operations was linked to contracts on plots of land operated by individual households. This was known as "operations that are based on the household." In the context of this fundamental reform, the original form of col-lectivized production and the monolithic form of management over that unified production came to an end. The State then reestablished an organizational system of political authority in the countryside, and it implemented policies that were described as "the separation of government from society." The Constitution of the People's Republic of China was passed in 1982. It stipulated that the State was reestablishing the "township" [the administrative unit called a *xiang*]. The People's Government of people's townships now became the grassroots unit ["unit at the fundamental level"] of governmental authority. At the same time, at the vil-lage level, the Constitution set up "farmers' self-governing organizations," namely the "village people's committees." Under the village people's committees, it set up "village people's small groups." The committee managed social affairs at the village level, and the group managed social affairs within the scope of a "group."

Since reform and opening up, the overall framework for rural governance has remained stable, in terms of the government itself. Some scholars describe this structure as "township governed and village ruled." That is to say, townships rep-resent the lowest grassroots-level of government authority, but below that, self-governing mechanisms "rule" at the village level of government. At the same time, as the party holding political power, the Communist Party of China has an organizational network that covers not just the township level but also the village level. The actual functioning of this governance structure has provided the institu-tional foundation for achieving goals of social stability in rural areas. It has helped the Communist Party of China and the government gain resources and support in rural areas and has helped implement the reform and development objectives of the central government and higher-level governments.

Governmental structures that manage/administer rural areas at the grassroots level

The overall structure of China's government goes from the central government to provinces [including autonomous regions and direct-jurisdiction municipalities], to municipalities to counties to townships. In the context of relative stability of this structure, the township has become the primary entity of grassroots social manage-ment or "administration" in rural areas. In 1983, the central government issued a Notification called *Notification on Separating out "Government" from "Society" [Economic Functions], and Setting Up Township Governments*. This said, "In line with reform of the economic structures in rural areas, it is apparent that the cur-rent integrated form of "government-society" is inappropriate. The Constitution has already explicitly ruled that township governments should be established in rural areas and that "government/society should be separate from one another." By 1984, township governments had been established throughout China, replacing the former People's Communes. In 1978, there had been 52,781 People's Communes in the country, while by 1985, there were 91,138 administrative jurisdictions called *xiang zhen*, townships. Because of the large size of many of the previous People's Communes, some were divided into smaller administrative units.

In going from People's Communes to *xiang zhen*, the functions of grassroots-level governments also changed. People's Communes had been institutions that organized agricultural production and governed local society under the planned-economy structure. They served the nation as it started to industrialize by extracting resources from an agricultural countryside. In contrast, the functions of township governments set up after reform began had to be adjusted to suit the needs of "separating out government and society." According to the stipulations of *The Law on the People's Congresses at Each Level of Government of the People's Republic of China, and on the Governmental Organizations at Each Level*, township governments were to serve seven specific functions. (1) They were to carry out resolutions made by the people's congresses at that level, as well as Decisions and Orders made by administrative institutions at the level immediately above them, and to issue such Decisions and Orders. (2) They were to carry out the Plans and the Budget for social and economic development within their level of jurisdiction, and they were to manage such administrative work within their jurisdictions as related to the economy, education, science, culture, public health, and physical culture, in terms of public finance, civil affairs, public security, judicial administration, and family planning. (3) They were to protect assets held under the socialist system of "ownership by all the people" and assets held under ownership by "collectives of the laborers and the masses," as well as legitimate assets held by private citizens. They were to preserve social order and safeguard the personal rights of citizens, as well as democratic rights and other rights. (4) They were to protect the legitimate rights and interests of all kinds of economic organizations. (5) They were to safeguard the rights of ethnic minorities and to respect the customs and traditions of ethnic minorities. (6) They were to safeguard the equal rights of women in the gender equality bestowed upon women by the Constitution and by law. (7) They were to carry out all other affairs that they were asked to do by the level of people's government directly above them.

The seventh function was ambiguous. It was the most sweeping, but it was in fact the most influential in terms of the actual operations of township governments. Each township government confronted a level of government directly above it that had considerable power and resources when it came to personnel decisions and finances. After reform, township governments assumed responsibility for social management and social services, such as carrying out policies of the central government on education and family planning, but they also assumed the previous responsibilities of extracting resources from the local populace, such as taking in the agricultural tax and requisitioning grain. As duties of the township governments were expanded, "stations' and "offices" proliferated in the mid-1980s in order to deal with agricultural and financial affairs. These included the "seven types of stations" and "eight types of bureaus." Additional institutions and personnel led to increasing financial pressures on local-government operations.

Revenues of local governments remained limited, however. Under increasing pressure of spending requirements, township governments often used "outside-the-budget" income to supplement official or "proper" income. This kind of "outside-the-budget" income had two main sources. One was income derived from the business expansion of township collective enterprises. Township governments in areas where the economy was prospering did all they could to grow these enterprises. The second was income taken directly from the hands of farmers within their jurisdiction. This method was used by more of the township governments than the first, and it resulted in an increasing burden on farmers. Given this situation, in order to reduce the number of townships [and lower the administrative burden], the State carried out a number of reductions in administrative jurisdictions by eliminating some and merging them with others. Between 1985 and 1986, the number of townships went down by 19,618. By 1988, the number left was a mere 56,002 – this was 35,136 less than there had been in 1985. In 1993, the State again carried out institutional reform, and "refined and reduced" the number of township administrations, as well as personnel. In 1996 alone, the number of townships went from 48,179 to 45,484. In 1998, the State Council began a fourth round of institutional reform, and it also tied the reductions and mergers of township institutions to the reform of township taxes and fees. By 2001, the number of townships throughout the country had been reduced to 40,161. In 2004, Central issued a Number One document called *Opinion on Various Policies Having to Do with Increasing the Income of Farmers*. This called for further "refinement and reduction" of township institutions and the number of personnel that were supported by public finance. In 2005, the number of townships was reduced to 35,509. By the end of 2011, there were 33,270 townships nationwide, of which 19,683 were *xiang* [villages], and 13,587 were *zhen* [towns.][1]

In September 1986, a Notification was issued by the central government called *Notification on strengthening [our] work on building up grassroots-level governmental authority in rural areas*. The emphasis of this was on the issue of defining the functions of township governments and strengthening those functions. "Townships" as a jurisdiction had been born out of administrative structures in which "government" and "society" were united, that is, People's Commune structures, which combined functions relating to governmental authority and economic production in one entity. Because of this, the process of reform had not instantly eliminated the myriad of threads that connected them to the collective economy. After township governments were set up, they still regarded economic [business] income as their own major consideration. This was part of what enabled the takeoff of China's rural economy in the mid- to late 1980s (Jean C. Oi, 1999), but it also led to the problem of the "corporatization" of grassroots governments. Enterprises were "separated out" as the 1990s progressed, and the glory days of township enterprises were over. A portion of these enterprises went bankrupt and closed their doors, and a portion transitioned to becoming "people-operated" enterprises [*min-ying*], but township governments maintained their ability to earn income from them via such methods as controlling the ability to use land for development. In the process of allocating resources such as land, grassroots governments were very strongly inclined in the direction of self-interest. One result of this was that they were now "in competition with the people" for profits. Another was that local governments put no effort into managing and providing services for things from which they would not profit. This exacerbated the conflicts already inherent in grassroots governance. Transforming government functions became the chief issue in multiple rounds of reform aimed at township institutions. Despite this, such transformation of functions has not happened. Since the start of the 21st century, the State has implemented policies intended to "strengthen farmers, benefit farmers, and enrich farmers." These have involved such things as "having industry support agriculture, and having cities pay back the debt they owe to the countryside." In 2006, the State completely eliminated the agricultural tax. This signified a major change in the way townships had formerly served the function of "extracting resources" from farmers. In 2009, Central issued further documents that deepened reform of township institutions. These stipulated that the task of reforming township institutions was "basically to be completed" by 2012. In actuality, however, although township governments were asked to provide more public services and social management, to this day, the role that these governments play and the functions they perform have not completely changed.

Meanwhile, as China shifted to a new type of economic structure and as marketization and urbanization continued, township governments found they were facing internal contradictions and problems with respect to their own operations.

The first of these can be seen in their hierarchical relationships. Township governments are controlled by the incentives and performance appraisals of the government directly above them. They mainly are responsible to that higher level of government and are not responsible for anything below them. The selection of people serving in township governments is by direct democratic election, that is, the People's Congress of a village or town is formed through direct election of local citizens. This is unlike the People's Congresses of anything above the municipal level of government, where People's Congresses are formed by indirect election conducted by the People's Congress at the level of government just below it. However, township governments do not show any apparent sense of responsibility to the People's Congresses that have elected them. Although the main leaders of the township governments are elected by township People's Congresses, under the system that currently governs how cadres are managed, decisive power is actually held by departments at the government level above townships. In addition, and even more importantly, after China undertook major reform of its tax system in the mid-1990s, more financial resources flowed toward higher levels of government. The operations of grassroots governments were funded mainly by transfer payments that came from "above." This meant that the behavior of township-level governments could be manipulated by incentive mechanisms that the government level above controlled. It also meant that township governments felt little sense of responsibility to their local community.

The costs of supervising township governments on a daily basis are fairly high for the next higher level of government. Township governments deal with this, and the performance evaluations and supervision they have to undergo, via work mechanisms that are driven by short-term window dressing, or "campaigns." This kind of governance mechanism uses irregular procedures to deal with the demands of regular procedures. Township governments can mobilize large quantities of resources in a short period of time using such means and in the process can circumvent existing conventional administrative requirements. By launching so-called campaigns, they are able to complete the task or command that comes down from the government directly above. Through these means, not only do they sidestep any demands made on them by rural society, their local communities, but they dodge the requirements of higher authorities. This makes it hard for the system overall to form institutionalized governance mechanisms.

A second expression of the internal contradictions that township governments are facing has to do with their relationship with grassroots society. First, township governments lack much sense of responsibility. Higher-level governments place priority on responding to local community demands, since garnering grassroots-level support is vital for the political power system. Nevertheless, this is a kind of soft constraint that grassroots-level governments can simply overlook. Instead, they put much more emphasis on "hard constraints," which relate to the quantified quota targets that they are supposed to meet. Second, since the start of the 21st century, the country completely revamped its policies with respect to the "three agri-cultures," but the relationship between township governments and rural societies did not "improve" in a synchronized way. The State began to implement policies that were supportive and protective of farmers, farming, and the rural economy, in ways that "gave more, took less, and relaxed controls." These eliminated the agricultural tax and reduced the amount of resources that were extracted from rural society. These also therefore had the effect of cutting out revenues to town-ship governments; they were no longer required to levy direct taxes and fees on farmers. This reduced the burden on farmers and also reduced some opportunities for conflict between farmers and township governments, but at the same time it led to a situation in which the two became ever more distanced from one another.

In fact, even though reform of the agricultural tax changed the mode by which township governments extract resources directly from local communities [rural society], conflicts between township governments and farmers were not com-pletely eliminated. Against a backdrop of increasing openness between urban and rural society, farmers have constantly become more aware of their own rights and interests, and the main sources of conflict now relate to requisitioning, or taking, of land. Once the agricultural tax was eliminated, the primary source of income for township governments became transfer payments from the government level just above. However, the margin between what local governments need to support themselves is inadequate from these payments, whether they are standard transfer payments or project-related transfer payments. As the costs of urban development rise, local governments have therefore relied more and more on using land as a financial asset. What's more, the current methods of requisitioning land provide a margin of profit for local governments as well, since they themselves can allocate the income from the amount that land had appreciated. This, then, has become the main source of conflict with local people.

Given these kinds of incentives, and lack of constraints, transforming the func-tions of grassroots government is something that simply did not get done. Asking township governments to change from being entities that directly participate in business to being entities that provide public goods and services has not worked.

Governing functions relating to many aspects are simply not happening; things that are not being dealt with include environmental remediation, regulatory oversight over polluting enterprises, regulatory oversight with respect to food safety, protection of arable land, and management of land and water resources. The failure of governments in this regard reflects structural issues in the responsibilities and accountabilities of government, but it also makes it clear that China's system of performance evaluations and incentive mechanisms needs to be changed.

Grassroots democratic self-governance

Outside the structures of government management, self-governance by grassroots societies in rural areas is also an important component of how rural China is governed. Towns and villages are the community structures in which life proceeds in rural areas and also the platform that provides for organized production activities. They are the fundamental unit of rural governance. After the system of People's Communes ended, the State set up grassroots, democratic, self-governing systems at the town and village levels in rural China in order to preserve social stability and also in order to organize group activities so as to manage public affairs and provide public services. The authorities that the State conferred on these self-governing entities included having villagers' organizations and villagers' committees carry out self-management and self-servicing. At the same time, the State clarified that self-governance in towns and villages is democratic governance. It is different from the traditional form of self-governance in China that authorized clans and the gentry to govern the people. Instead, villagers' committees are to implement democratic elections, democratic decision making, democratic management, and democratic regulatory oversight.

Since being established, democratic self-governing systems have played an important role in rural social governance. They have become an effective supplement to the "governmental" management structure. Their functions can be summed up in the following four main categories. First, they fill the vacuum in grassroots management. Once operations were distributed out to households in rural areas, these self-governing systems meant that there was indeed somebody "minding the store." These systems assumed the function of managing collective affairs. Second, they created an effective way for grassroots government to connect with rural society. Through such collective organizations as the villagers' committees, farmers are "organized," and these organizations serve as a conduit for transmitting information up and down. This improves the relationship between political authority and society in rural areas. Third, they expand participation in rural society. Villagers' committees are the vehicle for carrying on democratic elections in village communities, as well as democratic management, democratic decision making, and democratic regulatory oversight. Through democratic self-governance, the rights of farmers to participate in public affairs are realized. Fourth, they create the conditions for furthering – expanding and deepening – democracy. Through the exercise of grassroots democracy, rural communities are constantly improving their ability to participate in government.

This has also created new demands for improved government and has meant that democratic governance constantly deepens the interplay and mutual responses of State power and society.

However, rural society has also been going through dramatic changes since the time the State formally issued the *Law on Villagers' Committee Organizations* in 1988, the law that explicitly set up the democratic self-governing system of people in towns and villages. Urbanization and industrialization have proceeded at an extremely fast pace, swiftly changing the aspect of rural China and the spatial layout of towns and villages. A massive amount of rural labor has moved into cities to work in nonagricultural jobs, while the traditional form of "village" is passing. Both the rural population and the number of towns and villages are dwindling (see Table 8.1).

Against this backdrop, governance at the level of towns and villages must unavoidably cope with a new situation. On the one hand, given the depopulation in some rural areas, villages are being merged in order to maintain relative stability in overall population. At the same time, the traditional natural boundaries that once defined "towns" and "villages" are being replaced by administrative jurisdictions (He Yupeng and Chen Sicheng, 2013). This means that the traditional social relationships that rural communities once relied upon in self-governance are changing, which brings uncertainties into play in terms of "follow-up" management. On the other hand, given the two-way flow of factors between urban and rural areas, rural labor, capital, and land is either flowing into cities or being incorporated in cities. This means that the rural communities that rural governance relies upon are constantly being eroded and weakened. As the younger and stronger members of communities move to cities for jobs, and those that remain are aging, communities find it ever more difficult to deal with affairs, increasing the demands on and need for public services.

Meanwhile, grassroots democracy is also facing pressures from the way the hierarchical system works, as well as internal structural issues.

First, the relationship between governance by "government" and by "rural self-governance" has never functioned smoothly. The universal problem has been

Table 8.1 Changes in the number and population of administrative villages

Year	Number of administrative villages (10,000)	Rural population (10,000 persons)	Population per village (persons)
1985	94.1	80,757	858
1990	74.3	84,138	1,132
1995	73.7	85,947	1,166
2000	73.5	80,837	1,100
2005	62.9	74,544	1,185
2010	59.5	67,113	1,128
2011	59.0	65,656	1,113

Source: *Yearbook of Statistics China* and *China Agricultural Statistical Yearbook* over the years. See also: He Yupeng and Chen Sicheng, *How Many Villages Are Going to Disappear?*, China Economic Report, 2nd Issue, 2014.

how to enable governance organizations to become bodies that actually administer services. Township governments are the final layer of the entire government structure. When a great amount of authority over affairs, as well as responsibility for handling things, was shifted down to townships, township governments became tasked with making things happen. However, township governments have generally regarded villagers' committees as being their own agents, an extension of themselves as an organ of state power. The "guidance" function of township governments has turned into one of direct control; township governments have simply used villagers' committees to carry out their needs. In terms of personnel, some township governments directly interfere in town and village elections in order to make things easier for themselves. Once village cadres have been elected, township governments generally do their performance evaluations and decide on their salaries. In terms of finances, the universal practice has been to have "village finances managed by the township" as a way to standardize public-finance management in towns and villages. In the majority of places, control over the collective assets of villages is within the purview of the agriculture and economic departments of township governments. This effectively guts the self-governance of the town or village. In terms of managing actual affairs, village committees are asked to do a great deal of the work of townships. By "planting other people's fields, they neglect the planting of their own." Grassroots governments [townships] regard self-governance organizations as institutions that are under the internal control of government itself, and they therefore order them to fulfill mandated targets. They divvy up and assign tasks, which influences the ability of self-governance organizations to carry out service-oriented tasks that would benefit the community.

Second, the internal institutions of grassroots governance have also not been organized so as to function smoothly. In terms of power structures, the villagers' committee is formed through democratic elections of villagers. Its authority is bestowed upon it by villagers. Party branches of towns and villages are the grassroots organization of the ruling Party in the country, the Communist Party of China. They play a core leadership role in rural areas. However, despite the explicit regulations set forth in the *Law on Villagers' Committee Organizations* and the *Regulations on the Work of Grassroots Party Organizations*, which specify what each organization is to do, the actual relationship between Party cadres in towns and villages and the villagers' committee can easily become quite tense. Conflicts between the Secretary of the Party branch and the chairman of the villagers' committee are caused in particular by differences of opinion on work issues, or by competition over who is to be in charge of a given project. The conflict between the "leadership authority" of the Party branch and the "self-governance authority" of the villagers' committee has become a major issue affecting the smooth functioning of grassroots self-governance. In order to get away from this structural contradiction, many places have explored a solution of encouraging the members of the Party branch to participate in the elections for the villagers' committee. This often results in both Party secretary and committee chair being one and the same person and in membership in the two committees that is overlapping. This is known as "shouldering the pole with just one shoulder." On July 14, 2002, the Office of the Central Committee of the Communist Party of China and the General Office of the State Council issued a Notification called *Notification on Improving Work with Regard to the Election System of Villagers' Committees.* This set forth four clear recommendations.

> First, [we recommend that] the members of the leadership team of the Party branch be encouraged to run as candidates for villagers' committees and abide by an election process that follows specified procedures, and that they concurrently then serve as members of villagers' committees if elected. Second, [we recommend that] Party members be encouraged to participate in the process of legal elections for heads of villagers' small groups and as villager's representatives. Third, [we recommend that] anyone put forth to serve as Secretary of the Party branch in the village must first participate in elections for villagers' committees and be accepted by the people of the village and only then may that [the person] be recommended for Secretary of the Party branch. If the person is not able to be elected as Chairman of the villagers' committee, then he cannot be put forward as being considered for Secretary of the Party branch. Finally, [we recommend that] Party members who are on the villagers' committee serve concurrently as members of the Party branch committee after an internal election within the Party.

Although this reduced the number of cadre positions in villages and temporarily relieved conflicts of authority, it has also affected the democratic voting rights of villagers. It has affected the system by which the Party is organized, and it has impacted the ability to achieve a separation of Party and government (see Box 8.1).

Box 8.1   Main efforts to find a way to resolve conflicts between the "two committees" governing towns and villages

In addition to the "one-shoulder" method, several other methods of resolving the structural conflicts between Party branches and villagers' committees have been explored in different places. These include the double-voting system, the two-committee system, the one mechanism/three transformations idea, and the Qing-county model.

1.   Double-voting system

This system introduces a competitive process and democracy into the determination of who will be the "responsible person" in the local Party branch. That is, in electing the team in the village Party branch, all the people in the village are asked to participate in a kind of opinion poll and asked to cast a vote in favor or "a vote of confidence." On the basis of that affirmation, the formal Party members' convention may then undertake the formal election of the leadership team. This two-vote process addresses the problem of whether or not the selection of village Party cadres is done on a legal basis. The two-vote system can gradually develop into an institutionalized system that calls for "two recommendations and one vote," which means that the people of the village recommend, the Party recommends from within, and then the Party members vote.

2. Two-committee system

The double-voting system is mainly an improvement on the process of grassroots democratic elections. In contrast, the two-committee system is based on reforming the procedures of grassroots democratic decision making. The "two-committee system" refers to having important decisions at the village level be decided upon according to the principle of "first within the Party, then outside the Party, first among Party members, then among the public at large." A given issue is first discussed at the Party members' convention in order to form a preliminary proposal. This is then given to the villagers' representative assembly to take a vote on and form a proper proposal. Finally, the implementation is supervised by the villagers' affairs supervisory team. Some places have recommended that a procedure known in shorthand as "4+2" be adopted, that calls for four kinds of discussions, two of which are public. This requires that proper democratic decision-making procedures be followed on any major issue. The procedures are the village Party branch proposes, the two committees discuss, the Party members' convention evaluates and deliberates, the villagers' representative committee or the villagers' committee approves or reaches a resolution. The results are made public.

3. The "one system that incorporates three
transformations" idea

The "one-system" part of this concept refers to having self-governed operating mechanisms of villagers placed under the leadership of the Party branch. The "three changes" part refers to standardizing the work of the Party branch in the village, making village self-governance operate under the rule of law and creating a system by which democracy provides regulatory oversight. On the one hand, this emphasizes the leadership status of the Party branch. On the other hand, it attempts to create concrete procedures and operating techniques that standardize the relationship between the two committees. It seeks to set up a cooperative mechanism that allows for a division of labor [and checks and balances] between the two committees.

4. Qing-county model

The Qing-county model refers to a way of doing things that has been implemented in Qing county of Hebei province. This seeks to "improve one organization and adjust three kinds of relationships." This turns the villagers' representative assembly into a permanent village-level organization that is authorized and empowered by villagers' committees. It acts on behalf of the villagers' committee in exercising functions and powers. The model also asks the secretary of the village Party branch to serve concurrently as chair of the villagers' representative assembly. "Adjusting three kinds of relationships" refers to relationships among the village Party branch, the villagers' representative assembly, and the village [Party] commission. The Party branch is no longer a body that previously handled village work and affairs directly. Instead, its core function is to strengthen political leadership. It carries out the "leadership" of villagers' self-governance within the scope of laws and regulations and through democratic methods. Meanwhile, instead of being convened by the village [Party] commission, the villagers' representative assembly is convened by the chairman of the villagers' representative assembly who jointly serves as Party secretary of the Party branch of the village. It is responsible for electing members to the village commission. It is responsible for decision making on major issues regarding village politics and village affairs, as well as for strengthening regulatory oversight over the village commission.

Source: Yang Xinsheng, Evaluation of Conflicts between the Villagers' Committee and the Committee of the Village Party Branch, *Culture and History Vision*, 11th Issue, 2012.

The problems that are being expressed in self-governance at the grassroots level relate to the relationship between "grassroots-level organizations of the Party" and "self-governing organizations of the people." Problems are also occurring in the relationship between "administered villages" [which have a governing structure] and "natural villages." These issues come up in the democratic oversight within villagers' [Party] commissions and democratic management. Democratic elections are often the focus of attention in the "democratic systems" of villages, but in fact democratic management and democratic oversight fail to have any real hard constraints on behavior. This unavoidably leads to "village democracy" that is no more than superficial. Tremendous numbers of "contradictions" arise from this fact (see Box 8.2).

Box 8.2   The Wukan Incident

On September 21, 2011, more than 400 villagers came to the Lufeng Municipal government to present petitions expressing discontent with the Party cadres of their village. Their village is within the Lufeng municipality, in Shanwei, Guangdong province. The grievances related to land, finances, and reelections. After the villagers presented their case, a portion of the overall group gathered to smash and destroy some public property. The incident lasted until September 23, when order was restored. However, ongoing reverberations of the incident lasted for another three months and epitomized the various contradictions and problems that currently affect governance issues of grassroots organizations in China's rural areas in general.

The spark that ignited the incident was the way in which the village commission sold a parcel of collectively owned land to developers. In recent years, some 3,200 *mu* of land had been sold over time by the government, under terms that were kept from local residents. The local residents felt that a large portion of the money gained from these sales had gone into the pockets of local officials. They petitioned the government at the next level up several times, to no avail. More recently, the last remaining parcel of land was also sold to developers, which is what sparked the incident of September 21. To present their demands, the entire village of Wukan held a meeting and elected thirteen representatives to present three demands to the government. One was to investigate the circumstances surrounding land transfers from the time of the start of reform and opening up. The second was to investigate the issue of holding elections at the end of the terms of village commission members. The third was to make village affairs and village finances publicly available. The municipal government then responded that it had formed a work group to investigate the situation. It said that this group would come to Wukan village on September 26. It specified that villagers' representatives could participate in the investigation. However, during the incident of September 21, members of the village commission and responsible people within the Party branch left town. The township government therefore asked the villagers to form a "villagers' representative group." On September 29, villagers of Wukan carried out an election according to traditional methods: each lineage of the village as represented by a different surname proposed between one and five village representatives, which came to a total of 117 people. Among these 117 village representatives, each lineage could choose one candidate for the village council. Finally, thirteen people would be elected from among the thirty-eight candidates who would serve as "temporary villagers' representatives at the council." The responsibilities of this group were to undertake supervisory oversight of the investigation being conducted by the Lufeng municipal government, then to convene a villagers' assembly to evaluate the results. On October 22, some of the women in the women's organization of Wukan village also organized a "meeting of female representatives of the women's union of Wukan village." This took a further step in petitioning the local government and presenting demands. In addition to investigating such business matters as land sales, village affairs, and village finances, they asked for an investigation into the reelection of the slate for the village commission that had occurred in February of 2011. They presented the political demand that villagers be allowed to determine the results of this election by direct elections under a one-man/one-vote system.

On November 19, the leaders of the Lufeng municipal government responded to the request of the villagers, but they did not respond in full to the most important issue, that of land. On November 21, the people of Wukan presented another petition to the municipal government, and around 4,000 villagers gathered to protest against the municipal government. The government leaders received the written demands of the villagers and promised that within fifteen working days they would resolve the land and also reelection issues. However, events took another turn. On December 3, a backbone member of the protest movement was arrested by police and taken away. December 9 was the day that the government had promised to come forth with a response. On this day, however, the Shanwei municipal government notified media that "the incident was intentionally manipulated by certain people both inside and outside the village. It was made use of and fanned up," "outside forces [foreigners] were behind the momentum to create a bigger event," and "this changed the nature of the incident." The media also announced that the temporary representatives' council was being dissolved and that "the women's union" was "an illegal organization." Public security authorities arrested four villagers (among whom was Xue Jinbo, the deputy chairman of the council), on charges of "intentional destruction of property" and "obstruction of official business." On the afternoon of December 11, the family of Xue Jinbo received a notification saying that Xue was in mortal danger and was being treated for an emergency at the hospital. That evening, villagers learned the news that Xue Jinbo had died and that Xue's family members was raising questions about the cause of death. After this, thousands of villagers gathered daily at the center part of town. The local government increased measures to keep Wukan sealed off and to prevent anyone from the media from entering. On December 18, the villagers' assembly decided to hold a protest march on December 21 in order to demand the release of the four villagers.

On December 20, a Party work committee organized by the provincial government of Guangdong came into Shanwei and promised to get to the bottom of the corruption issues surrounding village cadres. It also promised to investigate the death of Xue Jinbo and to release the imprisoned villagers as soon as possible. The work committee told the primary people involved in the Wukan incident that they need not be concerned that actions would be taken against them. On the 21st, the work committee of the province took up residence in Wukan and announced that the corpse of Xue Jinbo was being handed over and that they were asking four representatives of international media organizations to examine it in person; the committee also confirmed the "status" or proper standing of the temporary representatives' council. Not long after, Wukan village held a villagers' meeting and declared that they were cancelling the protest march called for the afternoon of the 21st and that they were also taking down the banners that they had hung in protest around the village. That evening, at 8 p.m., the barriers into Wukan were taken down by both police and the people of Wukan.

After the work committee of the provincial Party commission took up residence, they set up five "small groups." These were to look into the "village collective land," "village financial affairs," "village cadres' violation of laws and Party discipline," "village commission reelection procedures," and "overall coordination." On December 22, one of the villagers who had been detained, Zhang Jiancheng, was released. Another two were also released the next afternoon, Zhuang Liehong and Hong Ruichao. By March 2013, Wukan had reelected a new villagers' committee. In April, two cadres of the "two committees in the original village structure" were sentenced for violation of laws and Party discipline according to law. The Wukan incident then gradually settled down.

Source: Huang Weiping, Feng Xiucheng, and Chen Wen, Investigation Report on the Wukan Incident, *Review on Governance of China*, 2nd Issue, 2013; Peng Tianyu, "Inspiration of the Wukan Incident, Background and Analysis," *World and China Institute*, 299th Issue, 2012.

Third, given the situation of grassroots self-governance as it currently stands in the countryside, villagers' committees, as self-governing organizations of farmers, do not have the capacity to provide public goods and services via "organized mechanisms." This insufficient capacity reflects the inability of self-governing organizations to carry out organized collective activity due to their limited authority in grassroots society. An American scholar has pointed out that when formal organizations lack authority and are unable to govern effectively, this is often related to a lack of cohesiveness or connectedness with the local people. If there are nonformal kinds of organizations in the community, such as temples, clan halls, and so on, more official organizations such as villagers' committees may be able to cooperate with them in order to carry out their functions more effectively (Cai Xiaoli and Liu Li, 2006). From this perspective, in order to achieve better organized collective action to satisfy the community's needs for public goods and services, not only does a self-governing organization need better vertical-type support from the government organization above, but it also needs horizontal cooperation from other social and economic organizations in the rural community.

Explorations in recent years

The lack of adequate governance in rural areas by either the government system or the self-governance system has limited the provision of public administration and services. It has led to insufficient supply of public goods in rural areas. At the same time, it has affected the ability of the State to put national policies into effect at the grassroots level. In a certain sense, one consequence has been to drive a wedge between State power and rural communities. Because of this, in recent years the State has carried out various explorations into how to address this problem in townships and at the lower grassroots level by emphasizing "consolidation of authority" at those levels.

One such exploration has involved consolidating authority at the township level of management. In the management structure that isolates "lines" and "patches" [vertical jurisdictions and geographic jurisdictions], the authority of vertical stove-pipes has become ever greater. Authority over such things as land, industry, and commerce has been taken over by departments at the level of jurisdiction above the township. Meanwhile, because of the policy that determined that counties should handle township finances, the budgets of townships are now also incorporated into the budgets of the level of government directly above. This makes it hard for townships to exercise any authority. The policy has indeed resulted in a gradual "standardization" [regulation] of government management, but it has also lowered the ability of township governments to conduct overall planning and coordination.

Another exploration has involved inserting managerial talent into the management of towns and villages. Through institutionalized channels, the State has assigned cadres to take up residence in towns and serve as town officials. This practice has been carried out in recent years to a considerable degree in areas that have fairly complex situations, including Hebei province, where the number of petitions being submitted to higher authorities is large, and the Xinjiang Uygur autonomous region, where the unstable situation is fairly intense. The practice involves assigning cadres as well as civil servants who are working at the provincial, municipal, and county levels of government institutions to towns and villages to work. The purpose is to resolve grassroots contradictions by "treating problems at the source," to be on site and deal with problems immediately. The State has also implemented the practice of stationing cadres in all impoverished towns in order to provide assistance and speed up rural development. Through yet another method of "sending college students to serve as county officials," it has injected new forces into grassroots communities, but it also has reined in the existing organizations in rural areas by putting more stringent constraints on existing grassroots organizations (see Box 8.3). The policy of having "townships handle village finances" has already become the universal system in rural areas, and management over collective assets in rural areas has now become the responsibility of so-called Township Agricultural and Economic Stations. Meanwhile, the compensation that the State pays village cadres has been put on a sliding scale, with pay related to performance. The performance evaluations are conducted by the level of government above towns and villages, at the township level of Party and government.

Box 8.3 College students serve as town officials

Starting in 1995, Jiangsu province began exploring a method of local management that they called the "eaglet project." They selected certain college students for internship-type jobs in towns and villages. By 2004, some ten other provinces, regions, and municipalities in China had launched similar projects. Following this, the Office of the Central Committee and the General Office of the State Council issued an Opinion called *Opinion on encouraging college students to take up employment at grassroots levels*. This encouraged more places to launch efforts to hire college students as local [village] officials. By early 2008, seventeen places in China had launched similar programs. In March 2008, the Central Organization Department of the Central Committee of the Communist Party of China, together with the Ministry of Education, Ministry of Finance, and Ministry of Human Resources and Social Security, jointly issued *Opinion [draft] on Selecting and Hiring Higher-education Graduates to Take Up Jobs in Villages*. The program was then initiated in thirty-one provinces, regions, and municipalities across China, including the Xinjiang Production and Construction Corps.

By the end of 2013, a total of 410,000 college students had been selected and hired to serve as village officials nationwide. At present, there are 221,000 college students actually in place in jobs as village officials. These cover more than one-third of all "administered villages." Of these college student officials, 33,000 are from ethnic minorities, or 15 percent, 122,000 are women, or 55.3 percent. Of the 221,000 college students serving as village officials, 19 hold PhDs; 7,857 hold master's degrees, or 3.6 percent; 160,743 hold bachelor of arts degrees, or 72.8 percent. Of the total, 136,350 are Party members, or 61.7 percent, and 25,422 graduated from institutions under the jurisdiction of Central-government departments, or 11.5 percent.

By the end of 2013, 29,000 college student village officials had launched more than 20,000 projects to help villages "get rich," as well as 5,200 professional cooperatives, that is, businesses to provide employment and income. These had created 260,000 jobs for rural people. Meanwhile, 74,000 college student village officials had joined the teams of the "two committees." [Of these, 5,802 people were serving as secretaries of the Party organization, and 2,025 were serving as chairs of the villagers' committee.] A total of 4,325 were serving in leadership positions at the Section level of the township. Four of the college student officials were elected to the 18th National Party Congress. Eleven were elected to the 12th National People's Congress.

The Central Organization Department and State Commission Office of Public Sectors Reform, in concert with the Publicity Department of the Central Committee of the Communist Party of China, the Ministry of Education, Ministry of Finance, and other relevant departments, jointly formulated and issued an Opinion called *Opinion on going further in strengthening the work of putting college-students in the countryside as village officials*. This, together with a series of other policy documents, is gradually setting up long-term mechanisms aimed at enduring results. The effort integrates the realities of each specific area with proactive efforts to develop supporting policies relating to such things as how to select and hire the students, how to manage the effort, how to evaluate performance, promote people, enable mobility, and so on. The aim is to create a system that enables college students to "go down" to the countryside, stay there and be effective, and yet retain mobility.

The goal is to cultivate a "backbone force" that will engage in "building a socialist new countryside" in China, as well as a backup force of outstanding talent in the Party and the government that can participate in all lines of endeavor. To do this, some five career paths have been charted that enable a clear development route for college student village officials. These include such things as staying on in the village as an occupation, moving up in the ranks of civil service, launching one's own business, choosing other occupations altogether, and continuing with higher education. By the end of 2013, some 190,000 college student village officials had served out their term in villages. Among these, 69,000 then joined the ranks of civil servants, 54,000 were employed in public institutions, 13,000 started their own companies, 52,000 joined corporations, and more than 1,900 passed exams to go on in higher education.

Source: The official website for college graduate village officials. http://www.dxscg.com.cn/.

These efforts have improved the ability of higher levels of government to place restraints on grassroots-level governments and also to incentivize them in certain ways. To a degree, this has strengthened the capacity of government to exert top-down control over the situation. Nevertheless, it is also hard for these efforts to be really effective. Changing the internal structures of authority within the political power system in China is not enough to really alter the power relationships between the State and society at large. Internal rearranging is not an effective way to expand community participation in order to achieve more harmonious governance. It is not enough to improve the relationship between grassroots political authority and grassroots communities.

2. Rural communities and their changing dynamics in the current era

In the massive waves of change that have washed over China's political, social, and economic situation in modern times, rural areas have also been experiencing an intense transformation. On the one hand, the outside world has constantly battered against traditional rural society, changing social structures and systems of values. On the other hand, rural societies have themselves taken the initiative in the process of reform and indeed have been a primary force behind promoting reform. Given this interaction between the outside world and rural society, if there is any possibility of establishing effective governance mechanisms, it is imperative that we have a clear understanding of the basic characteristics of rural society and the changes affecting it today.

Characteristics of rural society

Rural society has certain modern-society aspects in common with urban society in China, but it also has obvious and unique differences.

One of these is reflected in the system that governs property rights over assets. The most fundamental "factor of production" in agriculture and rural areas is land. In rural areas, the land is managed via the system of collective ownership. China's *Law on land management* stipulates that all land in farmers' collectives belongs to [i.e., is owned by] rural farmers' collectives as per law, while it is operated and managed by "rural collective economic organizations" or by villagers' committees. After reform and opening up began, the "operational responsibility system that linked households to production via contracts" became the basic method by which rural farming operations were carried out. Nevertheless, the system of collective ownership of the land did not change. Because of this, property rights over assets in urban areas have a different basis from property rights in rural areas. Rural collective organizations "own" the property rights in rural areas, whereas urban collective organizations do not.

Another unique difference is that of the structure of society. As Fei Xiaotong wrote in his book *Earthbound China*, having multiple generations stay in one place is the norm for people who engage in farming, while moving elsewhere is the exception. Mobility of people at the grassroots level has always been minimal. "The population in rural parts of China is seemingly fixed to the land, that is, earthbound. In China, this scarcely changed across many generations." This lack of mobility has meant that the rule has been "born here and brought up here." This has also led to a particular kind of relationship among people, one in which children grow up under the gaze of the same neighbors, and those neighbors are familiar to the child. Society is made up of people who "understand" one another, who are not strangers to one another. When overlaid on the pattern of the traditional form of clans and ancestral family groups in China, the result is a social structure of "familiarity" that is totally different from the "society of strangers" that developed in urban areas. This society of familiarity necessarily has an impact on social governance and the creation of governance mechanisms in China, particularly because of the way it defines relationships of authority.

A third characteristic of rural society relates to the density of the population. In administering modern societies, it should be recognized that population density is not just a reflection of the spatial arrangement of people. The density of a population can also reveal elements of social pressure, contradictions, ways by which groups are organized. In contrast to the increasing density of populations via urbanization, the density of populations in rural areas is fairly low. In spatial terms, people generally are concentrated in towns, so the fundamental "unit" of rural communities is the town. Given lower population densities, the way in which groups of people are organized must take practical considerations into account, which means that the mechanisms by which rural and urban societies are organized are bound to be different.

A fourth unique difference relates to how social management and public services are organized. Given low population densities in rural areas, the costs of top-down administration are fairly high. Given higher costs, the number of people who will benefit from a given quantity of investment is lower. The efficiency of public spending on public services in rural areas is therefore lower than it is in high-density urban areas. Although the State has put more priority on equalizing the provision of public services in urban and rural areas in recent years, there is still a dramatic disparity in levels of public services in the two areas. Meanwhile, the lessons learned from administering urban areas, including such things as network effects, are harder to apply to or to reproduce in rural areas.

A fifth consideration relates to the nature of self-governance. Since it is hard for a top-down form of administrative management to reach all the way down to rural areas and cover rural production and lives in a complete way, rural communities have historically had a fairly strong set of self-governing mechanisms. Internally generated adjustments have been key to preserving the stability of rural societies. Although both urban and rural communities have launched grassroots self-governing initiatives, those of rural areas are quite distinct from those of urban areas. The depth and breadth of self-governance in rural society has exceeded that of urban communities, based as it is on collective ownership of land, the "familiarity" aspect of social structures, and the way clan groups serve as the nexus for social networks.

In the past, our understanding of the three agricultures [farmers, farming, and the rural economy] has often meant that we broadly categorized the issues as being "a weak agricultural sector," "impoverished farmers," and "a hardship economy." We defined the issues in terms of agriculture, rural economics, and the income of farmers, all of which essentially relate to the economic side of the equation. Now, we have begun to understand that the three agricultures actually incorporate political and social issues, not just economic ones. Rural development and rural reform therefore need to resolve more than just production and income issues. They need to look at social and political aspects as well. Will it be possible to reconstruct a whole set of social systems and social networks in China's rural areas? Will it be possible to harmonize social relationships, address contradictions, set up mutual self-help entities and launch mechanisms that provide for effective collective action? Can the nation expect "publicly based political authority" [government based on public support] to cover all rural areas as well, so that the country can provide full public services to rural areas and make them subject to full equality and justice? Answering these questions will require much more exploration into social governance in rural areas.

Ongoing changes and reforms in rural society

The first change involves the market environment. China's economic reforms have meant that resource allocation is gradually shifting from a planned-economy mode to a market-economy structure. Rural society has also been rolled up in this massive wave of marketization. As a more unified market is gradually set up that ties together urban and rural economies, such factors as the rural labor force and land are also being incorporated in unified markets. One result is that a large amount of rural labor is leaving the countryside and leaving farming in order to take up jobs in urban occupations that pay more.

In this process of unifying markets, rural communities are also benefiting from the higher efficiencies with which resources are allocated. Their overall level of income has risen dramatically, and lives have improved. At the same time, the loss of large numbers of able-bodied youth is having a direct impact on social structures in the countryside. For a certain period of time, it will be even harder to realize a combined urban–rural integration due to the way in which resources are flowing to nonagricultural sectors of the economy that produce higher results. This also means that disparities between rural development and urban development will continue to grow. Meanwhile, the very concepts that underlie a market economy, such as profit, free competition, equal exchange, and so on, are also impacting the traditional value systems of rural society.

The second change involves the policy environment. In the course of reform, the State has issued a whole series of public policies and adjustments to policies that relate to the three agricultures. On the one hand, policies relating to agriculture and rural areas have been completely overhauled in the early 21st century. Whole policy systems have been launched that aim at comprehensive urban/rural development and that have the ultimate goal of integrating urban and rural aspects of the country. Because of this, the government has extended unprecedented support to the development of rural society. On the other hand, the policies and systemic arrangements that center on land issues have had an immense impact on rural society, particularly given the pace of urbanization. Huge numbers of farmers who have lost their land are now being urbanized involuntarily. They are becoming a whole new segment of the population. Meanwhile, some farmers are taking action via fierce resistance to the requisitioning of land and involuntary transfer of local populations. Such land taking has become the main source of conflict in rural society in recent years.

Changes in the policy environment include how policies are implemented and not just changes in the content of policies. To take environmental policies as one example: despite stringent State requirements regarding environmental protection and repeated commands to obey those requirements, local governments generally look on the issue from the standpoint of their own economic development. Given the very real interests at stake, they disregard the environmental impact of industrial production. Right now, roughly one-sixth of the arable land in China is threatened by heavy metal contamination, as well as other forms of pollution. This puts new constraints on agricultural production, not to mention how it affects the lives of local farmers. This has been another key factor stirring up conflict in rural society.

The third change involves the "values" environment. In the wave of reform characterized as "marketization," social environments in both urban and rural settings are more fluid and more open, leading to changes in the value concepts of rural communities. To take the idea of the family as one example: in traditional society, the ties between father and son dictated that families did not split up and live separately, to the extent that if three generations were alive, the three all lived together under one roof. Today, the norm in the countryside is a nuclear family that has split up, which has led to a smaller size of families.

The change in values is also expressed in the "next-generation" of rural migrant workers. One can define "first-generation rural migrant workers" as those in the labor force who were once engaged in agriculture but who then shifted away from rural production. In contrast, those who grew up after the start of reform and opening up can be regarded as "next-generation rural migrant workers." They never engaged in farming prior to coming to work in cities. From the very start of their employment, these next-generation rural migrant workers have engaged in nonagricultural sectors of the economy, and their sense of values is distinctly different from that of the "traditional" rural migrant workers. In contrast to the generation that preceded them, a generation that was easily satisfied and willing to work hard, this generation is redefining social roles and status. They are newly asserting their rights (Zhao Shukai, 2012).

All of these changes in rural society are now being expressed in a concentrated fashion in rural social governance. As large numbers of young people move into cities to work, those left behind are older people or younger children, so an increasing percentage of the rural population lacks much enthusiasm about participating in elections for villagers' committees or in engaging in rural self-governance activities. Meanwhile, as the best and brightest of towns move into cities to work, the "back-up force" that is available to serve as Party cadres at the grassroots level is also losing people or is aging. It is hard to maintain organized public initiatives. Managing and protecting public facilities means raising the funds to do so, but local farmers are not willing to contribute. The policy of raising funds for public cases on a one-by-one basis is a mere formality in many places. In the course of large-scale population movement between cities and the countryside, changes in rural society are presenting governance with major new challenges.

3. Problems in rural governance at the present time

In recent years, agricultural production, the rural economy, and farmers' incomes have steadily improved, but the social and political situation in the countryside has not matched those improvements. Rural society is basically stable overall, but there are prominent problems in the governance of rural society that demand our attention.

Social conflicts are intensifying

The conflicts currently seen in rural society are mainly caused by conflicts of interest. As marketization proceeds, rural occupations are diversifying. Problems between farmers and other groups in society, as well as conflicts among farmers and among different classes of people, are leading to more and greater conflicts of interest.

In specific terms, social conflicts in rural areas fall in the following three main categories.

The first relates to land disputes. Conflicts surrounding the requisitioning/taking of land and compensation for that land have already become the main cause of mass incidents. The allocation of income derived from the gain in land values is the core issue here, given the way land is appreciating as urbanization takes place. Meanwhile, China's existing laws and regulations have gray areas when it comes to rural land property rights, which has led to fights over the rights and interests relating to land. The main issues have been brought on by land that was forcefully or illegally requisitioned. Surveys on rural land disputes indicate that forceful or illegal taking of land constitutes 33.1 percent of all land disputes (Yu Jianrong, 2005). Even if land has been lawfully requisitioned, however, a variety of concerns can lead to farmers' "resistance," that is, taking a stand against the action. These include dissatisfaction with the amount of compensation or with the resettlement provisions of people who had been living on the land. They also include the way governments sometimes do not come through with resettlement or compensation promises. They include brutality and violent behavior on the part of grassroots governments in the process of requisitioning land.

The target of farmers' resistance is generally focused on grassroots governments that are below the county level and focused on land developers. According to surveys, farmers still maintain a level of trust in and support for the central government, when it comes to issues of land requisitioning and land transfers. Farmers feel that policies of the higher levels of government are favorable to them, but the compensation and resettlement funds have been embezzled or misappropriated by local officials and developers in the process known as "collusion between officials and businessmen." More than 80 percent of farmers regard grassroots officials and developers as the target of their resistance. Meanwhile, methods of such resistance are trending toward extremes. In addition to simply submitting petitions to higher-up levels of government, farmers are taking such major actions as surrounding government offices, occupying and blocking highways so that transport is affected, and so on. They are even erupting into direct conflict with public security forces that have come to disperse crowds and preserve public order. In contrast to the activities in opposition to taxation that were occurring prior to the agricultural tax reform, actions by farmers in protesting land disputes are at a higher level in their degree of collective action, organization, and violence.

The second relates to environmental issues and safeguarding people's right to a clean environment. Farmers are increasingly aware of environmental issues and of their rights with respect to preserving the environment. Large-scale projects that severely pollute the environment have become a major cause of social conflict at the grassroots level. Surveys indicate that the frequency of major, large-scale environmental incidents is increasing in recent years. "Since 2005, the Ministry of Environmental Protection took direct action on 927 incidents. Among these, 72 incidents related to severe large-scale environmental issues, and the incidence of such issues in 2011 increased by 120 percent over the previous year" (Yang Dongping, 2012). In addition to pollution caused by such specific projects, the "historic debt" owed to the rural environment has been growing for a long time and is now becoming a major source of incidents. Such incidents are often triggered by the issue of garbage collection and waste treatment. Existing laws, regulations, and environmental-protection standards mainly are aimed at cities. They were formulated to prevent and deal with pollution in urban areas including single-source industrial pollution. Some of these laws and regulations are applied to the countryside in principle, but they are insufficiently specific and therefore hard to put into effect. Standards relating to emissions and discharges have loopholes that allow for abuse. Standards are unable to deal effectively with environmental problems in the countryside that are getting more severe and more complex by the day. Given the lack of adequate laws and regulations, it is difficult for farmers to resort to the judicial system in order to protect their rights. Instead, more farmers are choosing the path of mass resistance.

The third relates to conflicts arising from public engineering projects. Basic infrastructure projects in the countryside are closely related to how farmers make a living and how they live in general. These include construction projects relating to water, electricity, roads, housing, and natural gas. Recently, however, these have become a major inducement for rural social conflict. On the one hand, the supply of rural basic infrastructure is inadequate to meet the needs of local people, leading to dissatisfaction. On the other hand, in the course of implementing infrastructure projects, irregular practices are used in tendering and overall management so that the oversight of funds is neither open nor transparent. Farmers suspect collusion between public officials and businessmen, resulting in the embezzlement of public funds for private gain. The common practice these days is to subcontract out parts of major public projects. This can mean that contractual terms are unclear, and it can mean that there is not only little regulatory oversight of funds but also little safeguarding of quality. After quality issues arise later, when things are being used, it is impossible to trace back who is responsible and who should be held accountable. This then leads to conflict between the local people and the grassroots government.

Public security issues are extremely severe

In recent years, public security in rural communities has notably deteriorated. As people have migrated to cities, the problem of so-called hollowed-out villages has become more and more pronounced, and villagers' committees have become less able to conduct self-management and self-servicing of local affairs. In certain areas, the number of criminal incidents remains high. In some regions, crimes involving the taking of property are on the rise, including robbery and fraud.

Moreover, authority in local areas has "morphed" into new forms with the appearance of organized crime [what in English would be called "mafia power" and that, in Chinese, uses the composite term for "black" and "evil"]. Given the violent change in rural society during the period of transition from one economic system to another, some areas have found it hard to build up grassroots organizations and grassroots political authority that can deal with such rapid change. This has resulted in a kind of administrative vacuum. In areas of the country that do not have a strong presence of national authority, mafia power has taken advantage of the situation and moved in. Through the use of force, this new kind of authority takes over control of an area and does serious harm to normal social order. In addition to the ways in which organized crime inflicts damage on society at large, however, mafia forces are also infiltrating and corrupting grassroots government. This has led to the morphing of grassroots political authority and grassroots organizations into something that has "gone off," or gone bad. Through such manipulative practices as bribing people during elections, particularly at the local level of elections for villagers' committees, these forces gain control of local political power. People who have been successful in business either nurture their own mafia forces or hire others. They then enter grassroots-level government themselves, or, using the lure of economic gain, they rope in cadres who are already in government so that grassroots-level cadres then become their tool in achieving their own interests.

Meanwhile, illegal organizations continue to be active in China [as they were in a previous era], while activities of underground religious organizations are commonplace due to the ongoing prevalence of feudal superstitions. The lack of alternative cultural or public events has created a vacuum that is being filled by the activities of such illegal organizations. Some investigations into so-called religious organizations in recent years indicate that these use proselytizing as the pretext under which to carry on illegal activities in rural areas. This goes on over an extended period of time. Underground religions and activities that use fallacious ideas to rope people in are expanding rapidly in China's countryside. They are becoming a serious challenge to social order in rural areas.

Suicide is a major problem

Suicide has become a major social problem in China's countryside. In the thirty-some years since 1980, the suicide rate has continued to go up, as seen by the relevant data. Figure 8.1 shows a clear increase in the rate in the 1990s as opposed to the 1980s; after 2000, not only has the rate continued to rise as compared to the 1990s, but it is at its highest point in history. More recent surveys after 2009 indicate that the suicide rate in rural parts of China has continued a slow increase and is remaining high.

Conflict within a family is the primary cause of suicide. Surveys show that conflicts prior to a person committing suicide are primarily related to intergenerational disputes or to problems between husband and wife. The percentage of

(1/100,000)

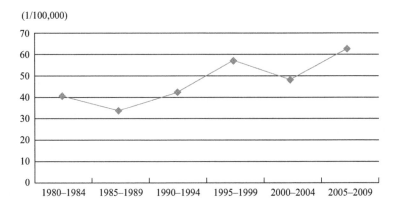

Figure 8.1 Changes of the suicide rate in the countryside (1/100,000)

Source: Liu Yanyu, *Study of Suicide in Rural Areas: A Qualitative Survey of 24 Villages in Six Provinces* (Background Report).

suicides involving intergenerational disputes is as high as 47.05 percent. Within such disputes, problems between a grandmother or grandfather and a son-in-law or daughter-in-law constitute 33.15 percent of presuicide conflicts. Problems between parents and children constitute 13.9 percent of all suicide incidents. Problems between husband and wife constitute 35.29 percent of suicide incidents.

The gender and age differences of people who commit suicide in rural areas are quite apparent. The rate of suicides among women and among older people is high. Surveys indicate that the female suicide rate is 1.4 times the male suicide rate in the age group 15 and older. In recent years, however, surveys also indicate that the rate of suicide in some rural areas and particularly among women is clearly declining; researchers attribute this to urbanization. As the population moves into cities and a middle class begins to emerge, many younger women from rural areas are able to escape the pressures put upon them by parents, unfortunate marriages, and poverty. They also are farther away from the "most convenient" method of committing suicide in rural areas, which is drinking pesticide.

In terms of the age of people who commit suicide, the rates are fairly high for older people: as many as 230.94 per every 100,000 suicides. In contrast, the rate for younger people is 48.27 per 100,000 suicides, and the rate for middle-aged people is 26.18 per 100,000 suicides. Since 2000, the rate of suicides among older people in rural areas has been rising rapidly. Surveys indicate that the main cause is simply making ends meet in order to stay alive, which involves two separate issues. One is inadequate daily intake of the requirements of living, for example food. The other is inadequate caregiving and particularly daily caregiving on a long-term basis. Even if older people can get enough to eat, therefore, they may not be able to survive simply out of the lack of caregiving. As the extent of the aging population rises in rural areas, this problem will require intervention on the part of the government in order to find solutions.

A rigid approach to maintaining stability is damaging social management

The term *rigid approach* as applied to maintaining stability in China's rural areas refers to the ways in which the government controls social organizations and social consciousness as a way to maintain political stability. By using State organs of force as a "backup," these methods seek to maintain a rigid, superficial, form of stability (Yu Jianrong, 2012). As a method of political control, this kind of "rigid approach to maintaining stability" is not in fact appropriate to modern society. It is not very effective, and its costs are high. It has a number of negative side effects that impinge upon the normal functioning of political systems. At present, there are two main ways in which this kind of rigid approach to maintaining stability is expressed in China's rural areas.

The first involves an emphasis on dealing with crises as a way to maintain stability. To a great extent, the current very severe situation with regard to rural stability is the result of underlying social problems. It is the result of problems that grassroots governments have created themselves through improper handling. The great majority of mass incidents in the countryside are things that did not erupt suddenly without any prior warning. Instead, they are due to latent social contradictions that have not been given the proper attention and proper handling. This has allowed small problems to grow until they evolve into large-scale incidents. Emergency control measures seek to keep things from escalating and reaching a point of no return. They achieve a superficial form of "rigid stability," but in doing so they generally adopt forceful and repressive measures. As a result, they can stir up greater resistance, which then requires the use of greater force. After conflicts erupt, grassroots-level officials then generally adopt cover-up measures and deceptive excuses that "trick those above and deceive those below," mainly due to the pressure of performance evaluations. This kind of crisis management, with its postevent salvage attempts, puts officials in a passive position when it comes to truly maintaining social stability. They are not in a position to take the initiative in controlling events but are rather led along by the events themselves.

The second involves the use of "central-authority pressure" as a way of managing situations. The way in which government is involved in too broad a spectrum of affairs has led to dissipation of governing resources and has created a situation in which government cannot deal with what it should be handling, while it creates a myriad of problems by getting into what it should not be handling. Meanwhile, the public at large has been accustomed to looking upon government as omnipotent. The prevailing attitude is that, if a problem arises, the government should fix it. This has led to grassroots government becoming the target of attack whenever a social problem comes up. Not only are governments exhausted, but they have to deal with things as though they are constantly walking on thin ice.

The current use of pressure as a way to manage situations comes from upper levels of government and is passed sequentially down through to grassroots levels. First, it is the upper levels that apply various forms of pressure on levels below them to maintain stability within their jurisdictions. Upper levels of government set performance targets that relate to the maintenance of stability, and the performance of officials is then rated according to how well they did. One particularly stringent requirement is the "one vote can reject" rule – the one-vote veto power – which puts enormous pressure on grassroots governments to come up to performance requirements. Second, under the enormous pressure that the higher levels of government place on grassroots governments, grassroots governments adopt high-pressure methods themselves to achieve "stability-maintenance goals." They attempt to control society in general as a way to head off any *potential* incident that might damage performance ratings. Grassroots governments take the attitude that swift repressive measures over potential incidents and potentially dangerous organizations are necessary, and the effect of this is to prevent the normal expression of local people's rights and interests. Grassroots-level officials have even used "labor reform" as a method of applying pressure, as well as hiring people from the underworld, that is, organized crime, to achieve objectives through force. This has the effect of further inciting resistance among farmers. It leads to a worsening of the relationship between cadres and the people. It creates a vicious cycle in which grassroots governments apply ever more pressure and then face ever more unrest.

4. Policy recommendations for creative ways to enable governance by rural communities

The Third Plenary Session of the 18th National Party Congress incorporated the following phrase in its overall goals for deepening reform: "Push forward the modernization of the nation's governance structures and governance capacities." The Fourth Plenary Session of the 18th Central Committee of the Party went a step further in stipulating:

> We must make better use of the standardizing and guiding role of the *rule of law*. We must do this so as to have better overall coordination of social forces, to balance the interests among society, regulate social relationships, and standardize social behavior. We do it so as to enable Chinese society to be both vital yet also orderly as it undergoes acute change. We do it so as to achieve economic development, clean politics, vibrant culture, social equity, and a sound ecosystem.

This statement of the Fourth Plenary Session also provides the guiding principles and goals of reforming social governance and creating new modes of social governance. At present, we are confronting new challenges in rural society and acute changes in economic and social forms. Because of this, we must consolidate the basis of the State's political authority, which is at the grassroots level. We must create a social environment in rural areas that is vibrant yet also peaceful and orderly. We must create the conditions whereby resources and people from both urban and rural areas can flow in both directions and indeed the conditions whereby urban and rural are unified into one system. We must integrate the historical legacy of China's traditional way of governance in rural areas with the innovative mechanisms of modern social governance. The aim is to find common measures that combine "governance by government" with "self-governance by the public itself." In creating a positive feedback loop between grassroots political authority and rural society, the aim is to put into effect a modernized form of rural social governance.

Strengthen the building of grassroots political authority

With respect to "governance by government," the core issue relates to the reform of townships. The questions are, "Should townships become mere organs of the level of authority above them? Should the authority of townships be incorporated into the level above, so that it wields stronger control over township governments? Or should townships themselves be a full-scale level of political authority, with a portion of powers currently held by the level above granted to them so that they can perform grassroots governance functions more effectively?" [The answer lies with the second of these two options.] Strengthening grassroots political authority at the township level and raising the capacity of governance at this level is a major way to address the current problems in rural social governance. At the same time, however, we must avoid the conundrum faced repeatedly in reform efforts in the past, namely, "If you pull back too much authority toward central control, all initiative dies, while if you grant too much authority, things become chaotic." In releasing authority down to the level of townships, we must ensure that authorities granted at each level of government are properly handled and that grassroots society has full power to participate in local government and full power to exercise supervisory oversight.

The first thing in this process is to clarify the standing of townships in legal terms. That involves defining their responsibilities and accountabilities, as well as raising the institutionalized levels of their governance. Right now, the national-level policy environment for resolving rural and agricultural issues has gradually been improving, as industrialization and urbanization move forward. However, the specific ways in which the central government and higher levels of government actually implement their policies must rely on grassroots governments. Because of that, the key still lies in enabling grassroots government to play a role in resolving rural and agricultural issues. Grassroots governments are the locations at which the policies for a "socialist new countryside" and "overall comprehensive development of urban and rural areas" actually get put in place.

This involves making very sure that we do actually transform the functions of township governments. As the financial powers and corresponding governing responsibilities of the central government versus local governments are gradually defined, we must define the functions of township governments in explicit ways. The priorities of townships must relate to rural social management and the provision of public services. Preserving public security in rural areas should indeed be a basic function of these governments, which they must take firm control over. In places where public security has serious problems, we can adopt such additional measures as instituting police stations to handle security in villages. In contrast, the responsibility for economic development of townships and authority over economic development should be handed up to the next higher level of government for overall arrangements so as to reduce the conflicts of interest between townships and people. At the same time, we must go further in improving the mechanisms that both incentivize and constrain behavior. We should launch performance ratings of townships that measure performance with respect to "governance" results.

With respect to raising the levels at which grassroots levels of government are institutionalized, we should improve the capacity of governments to operate by a formally defined code of ordinances. This is to improve the relationship between grassroots government and rural society but also to ensure that central-government political commands have a clear passage through to grassroots rural areas. In specific terms, this means improving the capacity of governments to deal with a highly fragmented and complex modern society and its political environment. It means improving the internal structures of government organizations by a division of labor in terms of functions. It means raising the professionalism of government departments in order to implement various functions and tasks, improving the systems that regulate a code of behavior, and improving levels of standardized [regulated] behavior.

With respect to improving the capacity of governments to operate according to specified rules, we must first set up effective and reasonable rules. Given the new problems being generated by changing social structures and diverging interests as the country goes through this transitional period, we must also constantly improve upon those rules and their relevant procedures in order to dissipate grassroots conflicts. Secondly, we should combine increased participation in local government and strengthened grassroots democracy with the establishment of efficient administrative systems. We should clearly define the boundaries of what the government is responsible for and what society at large is responsible for, so as to avoid the problem of "governments not doing what they should do while making a mess of getting into doing what they should not do," as well as to avoid the age-old practice of wrangling for turf among departments.

The second thing in the process of granting more authority to townships is to push forward the establishment of a system of township people's congresses and actually realize a situation in which people themselves are masters of their own house. Township people's congresses have a major role to play. In being directly elected by voters, they are a cornerstone of the entire people's congress structure. They are organs of the nation's power at the township level and critical in the process of strengthening and improving the leadership of the Party. They are the expression of how people become masters of their own house. Right now, one of the most outstanding problems is the lack of communication between government and society in that farmers lack any mechanisms through which to express their own rights and interests. To change this, we must improve the township people's congress system. This means that, within the already existing framework of people's congresses, we must strengthen the ability of people's congresses to exercise control over township governments in order to standardize and constrain their behavior as well as to uphold the authority of the Party and the State within rural society.

In this regard, we must establish institutionalized mechanisms by which the people's congresses can provide supervisory control over governments. The core issue here is that people's congresses must have the authority to oversee finances if they are going to be effective in supervising government work. This is also a necessary part of our reform of the system of public finance. Right now, the costs of disciplinary supervision within the Party at the township level are high, as well as the costs of such mechanisms as administering the performance evaluation system. What's more, having performance targets determined by each level of government in a top-down manner cuts the enthusiasm with which local governments try to apply appropriate solutions to their own specific issues. It incubates the practice of doing things for form's sake alone and allows for a perfunctory approach to work. To address these problems, it is necessary to set up institutionalized mechanisms that enable people's congresses to conduct such supervisory control and to expand grassroots public participation in grassroots governance.

Box 8.4   The "participatory budgeting" in the township people's congresses of Wenling

The participatory style of budgeting that is being done in the Wenling municipality provides for substantive monitoring and regulatory oversight of the finances of Wenling. It refers to the way in which citizens participate in discussions about the annual budget, mainly through the form of democratic deliberation, and the way in which people's congresses review the finances of the government and, moreover, decide upon any revisions and adjustments to the budget. Based on democratic deliberation, each township within the Wenling municipality has formed its own way of doing things, with its own unique features. The main ways are as follows.

1.   The "Xinhe" way of doing things that mainly uses review and regulatory oversight of the budget by the people's congress

The main feature of this method involves initial review prior to the people's congress, then examination during the people's congress, and finally supervisory oversight after the congress.

Initial review prior to the congress: Xinhe convenes "democratic deliberation meetings" to carry out initial review of the budget. It divides the budget into three small-group meetings for the purposes of this review, covering industry, agriculture, and social endeavors. In addition to representatives of the people's congress, all citizens and other organizations are free to participate if they wish, including associations, social groups, and representatives of other entities. After the meetings, each small group prepares a report on its initial review.

Examination during the people's congress: During the congress, representatives carry out intensive scrutiny of the budget, while responsible persons in the township government answer questions that representatives put

---

to them. After this, the chairman's group of the township people's congress and the township government hold a joint meeting. They make amendment proposals to the budget depending on the responses put forth by the representatives. After the budget is again reviewed by representatives' groups, it is voted on by the overall people's congress. Five or more people who agree on a particular point can recommend revisions to the budget. If more than half of the number of votes in the people's congress supports the revision, then it becomes a part of the new budget.

Supervisory oversight after the congress: The "finance small group" of the township people's congress is the standing committee organization that oversees township finances. It conducts regulatory oversight of the actual implementation of the budget by the government. It also participates in formulating the next year's budget.

2. The "Zheguo way of doing things," that involves democratic deliberation for construction projects

Zheguo has citizens participate directly in the decision-making process on finances and budgeting for township construction projects, through a form of consultation. The first step is to discuss a given project and propose a draft budget. The government selects a group of potential projects that lie within the administrative scope of that level of government and that relate to the people's well-being. It then organizes a group of professionals to carry out a feasibility study on each project and draw up a budget for each. The results are printed in a survey questionnaire for soliciting opinions from the public. The second step is to conduct democratic deliberations on the projects. This involves a random "ping-pong ball" method of selecting 2 percent of citizens above the age of 18 in the township as a whole. These people, selected by random process to be "citizen's representatives," fill in the questionnaires and participate in the democratic deliberation. They rank the projects in the order of funding that they feel is best. After many rounds of discussions and consultations, the citizen's representatives then again fill in questionnaires and rank projects. The third step is to have the people's congress examine the results and give approval. The township government convenes a meeting of its General Office to discuss the results of the representatives' recommendations and the survey results of the second questionnaire. It then makes sets out the outstanding projects in order ranking depending on the actual finances of the township, and it submits this final list to the people's congress, which reviews it and then votes on it.

3. Other innovative practices that are based on the Xihe and Zheguo models

These include such things as increasing the opportunities for debate in the people's congress in Xinhe prior to voting on the revised budget. They include the way Zheguo township, starting in 2008, expanded the scope of items under review by the democratic deliberation process to include the entire fiscal budget and not just specific projects. In the township of Ruoheng, the power over formulating the government budget has been given to the people altogether: prior to the people's congress, the forty-five villages (or neighborhoods), as well as the cutting-tool guild in the town, hold forty-six democratic deliberation activities. Based on the opinions of all concerned, they formulate an initial budget, which is then again divided into specific line items for democratic deliberation again.

4.   Injecting participatory methods into the budgetary oversight of departments

In 2010, the budgets of fifteen municipal-level departments accounted for 70.26 percent of the entire spending of the Wenling municipality.

The first participatory innovation developed with respect to the departments was democratic deliberation prior to the budgeting session of the people's congress. Ten days in advance, the finance and economics committee of the standing committee of the municipal people's congress sends draft budgets of these government departments to deputies of the congress and representatives of local citizens. Group discussions and deliberations are then carried out once the budgets have been reviewed and relevant departments have reported on their preliminary reviews.

The second was review of the departmental budgets, "one by one," by representative groups. In the month prior to the people's congress, each departmental budget is sent to the entire body of representatives. Different groups are asked to conduct in-depth research into the departments with which they are involved, so the first round of review is carried out by representatives themselves. At the people's congress, a session is held in which departments defend their budgets. Representatives then take another half day to review each budget on a one-by-one basis.

The third participatory method undertaken by Wenling is the promotion of openness in budgeting. Starting in 2008, the standing committee of the people's congress of Wenling publishes all information on supervisory oversight regarding the budget in public media so that the public can be absolutely crystal clear on how that year's budget is to be spent by different levels of government, as well as by departments. It also makes public the budgetary review processes, which now proceed in a completely open and transparent manner. Moreover, the full-text auditor's report on the budget is made available on the internet, so that any problems disclosed by the auditor are accessible, without any deletions, to the public.

Source: Wenling Participatory Budget, the website of the Standing Committee of the People's Congress of Huangyan District. http://www.zjhyrd.gov.cn/index_655.html.

Improving grassroots self-governance mechanisms

The key to transitioning from a mode of social management that is performed solely by the government to one that involves rural self-governance lies in creating effective ties between "grassroots Party organizations and grassroots governmental authority" on the one hand, and "villagers' self-governance organizations and rural economic and social organizations" on the other hand. It lies in creating a new pattern that allows for positive synergies between the two.

This involves two things. First, it means building up and strengthening rural self-governance organizations as a key way for people to exercise their democratic rights and interests as per law. Village self-governance organizations are entities within rural communities that carry out self-management of public-welfare endeavors and grassroots-level public affairs. They are self-educating and self-monitoring organizations. They are an important vehicle for people to exercise their democratic rights directly, as per law. We should establish vital mechanisms for grassroots self-governance under the leadership of grassroots organizations of the Communist Party of China. In doing this, we must properly handle the allocation of power between Party entities and self-governance organizations at the grassroots level. We must clarify their respective functions and the methods by which they expend funds, so that the strategic plans, guidelines, and policies of the Communist Party of China are effectively implemented in rural areas. We must ensure that the enthusiasm, initiative, and creativity with which and by which farmers participate in social management are fully engaged, so as to improve social self-governance and self-servicing capacities. Local governments should be encouraged to improve the relationship between village branches of the Communist Party of China and villagers' committees. Both should strive to achieve mutually beneficial results. We should make every effort to increase the engagement of farmers in rural self-governance and to turn the management and supervision of self-governance organizations into institutional channels by which farmers can participate in self-management and self-supervision. We should constantly improve the transparency of how villages are administered. We should promote information disclosure, strengthen deliberation procedures, and gradually establish effective village-level democratic supervision mechanisms with clearly defined responsibilities and smoothly integrated functions.

Second, it involves developing platforms to achieve results. This means cultivating rural economic and social organizations and sound rural governance as a platform for enabling the delivery of public services. Changing the way in which all affairs having to do with rural development rely solely on government will require organizing local people to provide community services for themselves through their own organizational systems. Not only will this lessen the burden on government, but it will increase channels of participatory social management among rural people. This also involves setting up effective dispute-resolution mechanisms in rural society. It means empowering rural traditional social networks and authority relationships to resolve conflicts on-site and in a timely manner. It involves setting up effective connections between rural social organizations and self-governing organizations, as well as operating mechanisms that support one another. The aim is to put in place a pattern of interaction between rural social organizations and self-governance organizations so that each can complement and strengthen the other.

We must focus on the task of cultivating rural social organizations as the priority. This means lifting the levels by which farmers are organized and upgrading the ability of farmers to undertake collective action. In recent years, the central government issued a series of policies supporting activities of farmers' cooperative organizations. In 2007, moreover, it issued the *Law on specialized farmers' cooperatives of the People's Republic of China*. The resulting development of rural economic organizations was quite apparent. In contrast, the development of social organizations handling such things as rural caregiving for the elderly, healthcare services, education, culture, and so on has clearly been inadequate. Social services in the countryside remain underdeveloped. Sole reliance on the transfer payments from central-government budgets as well as the budgets of other levels of government is not going to work. It cannot effectively deal with such problems as an aging countryside. Given the lack of social organizations in the countryside, however, rural social endeavors and public services have mainly been the responsibility of villagers committees and Party cadres at the grassroots level. There has been no alternative, no other social organization on which to depend. The organizational strength of grassroots governmental authority is limited, however. Meanwhile, many public services should not in fact be supplied completely by the government. It is imperative, therefore, that we set up a system of rural economic and social organizations that has broad coverage, is comprehensive, and is multitiered.

We must then fully enable this system to play a role in rural governance, this "comprehensive rural economic and social organization system." At present, many parts of China are already testing the waters in doing this. They are experimenting with comprehensive, multifunctional farmers' organizations. One example is the rural cooperative association of Rui-an city in Zhejiang province. Another is the Puhan village community of Yongji city in Shanxi province. The central government should actively guide and support the efforts of local governments to come up with creative ideas for rural social organizations. It should accelerate the reform and restructuring of grassroots agricultural departments to avoid redundancy and lack of clarity about who is responsible for what. It should establish institutional links between rural social organizations and State power.

Note

1   Yearbooks of Statistics of China. See also Qu Yanchun, "Thirty Years of Township Institutional Reform – A Review of Practices and Theories," *Donyue Tribune*, Issue 8, 2014.

9 Strengthening controls over resources and environmental protection, building an "ecological civilization" in the countryside

- Main problems facing the building of an "ecological civilization" in the countryside
- The serious impacts of environmental degradation in rural areas
- Countermeasures aimed at strengthening management controls over agricultural resources and at rural governance as it relates to the environment

Developing a more ecologically minded civilization is a necessary requirement for China's goal of building a moderately prosperous society in an all-round way. One of the key tasks in this process is to strengthen "ecological civilization" in the countryside. Agriculture is the fundamental industry in this regard: making agriculture more sustainable is the very heart of the process of building a modern agricultural production system. It is a primary part of building a society that conserves resources and has a healthy environment. China's rural areas constitute the main battlefield for building such an ecological civilization. By improving the environment in which rural people live and the environment as a whole, we push forward the strategic task of building a more beautiful countryside and a more beautiful China. Farmers are the primary components of this whole process, so engaging their positive participation is a fundamental requirement. Having them share in the results is essential to accelerating the creation of ecologically minded systems.

This chapter analyzes the primary issues confronting the building of an ecological civilization in the countryside, and it analyzes the severe impacts that are being brought on by a worsening environment. On that basis, it then recommends specific countervailing policies, as well as ways to strengthen the management of resources in rural areas, protect the environment, and build an ecological civilization.

1. Main problems facing the building of an "ecological civilization" in the countryside

In the thirty years since reform and opening up began, China's rural areas have been through dramatic social transformations as well as rapid economic growth. In this process, environmental pollution and the destruction of rural ecosystems have become daily more severe, to the extent that rural ecosystems are the most vulnerable part of China's "national environmental security." They are also a constraining factor when it comes to further rural economic and social development. In recent years, China has constantly improved its approach to protecting rural ecosystems, and the situation in certain areas has indeed improved. With respect to the deterioration in rural ecosystems, the government has passed a series of environmental protection policies that include returning farmland to forestry and returning overgrazed lands to grasslands, [that is, planting trees on farmland and planting grasses on grazing land]. With respect to the rampant despoiling of rural surroundings due to sewage and garbage disposal, it has passed policies that provide incentives rather than subsidies and policy measures that aim at remediating contiguous areas. The available data shows that the central government allocated RMB 19.5 billion for rural environmental protection projects between 2010 and the end of 2013. It mobilized all levels of government below the central level to invest more than RMB 26 billion in support of environmental remediation in 46,000 towns. As a result, more than 87 million rural people benefited directly. Nevertheless, the situation with respect to rural ecosystems is still extremely grave. The idea of building an ecological civilization is up against dealing with major problems. Not only do these hold back further agricultural production, but they are severely impacting people's health. They are aggravating efforts to safeguard social harmony and stability in rural areas, not to mention efforts to create "all-round" prosperity.

Constraints on the underlying resources of agriculture are getting worse

First, China's per capita amount of arable land and the quality of that land are low, while pollution of China's farmland is severe

According to key statistics of the *Second National Land Survey*, conducted by the Ministry of Land and Resources Department in December, 2013, China's arable land came to a total of 2.031 billion *mu* on December 30, 2009 [334.51 million acres]. On a per capita basis, that equals 1.5 *mu* on average, which is roughly 40 percent of the global per capita average. Since the start of the 21st century, the amount of land going to construction uses has gradually increased it went from 2.455 million *mu* in 2001 to 2.795 *mu* in 2010 – and as time goes on, constraints on available land resources in China will intensify. According to the goals set forth in the *National Plan for a New Form of Urbanization*, China's urbanization rate should reach over 60 percent by 2020. With massive numbers of rural people moving into cities, the amount of land needed for construction of housing, roads, hospitals, schools, cultural facilities, and other basic infrastructure requirements will grow, further limiting the amount of arable land available to the country. Meanwhile, authorities project ongoing population growth in the country until at least the year 2030 (Cai Fang, 2010). This will further exacerbate the scarcity of per capita farmland. In addition, the overall quality of China's arable land is not very high. According to a report issued by the National Land and Resources Department in December, 2009, *Survey of China's Land Quality by Grades, and Assessment*, land quality that is ranked as "low to middle-low" constitutes 67.4 percent of all arable land in the country. Moreover, the condition of the soil in the country as a whole does not allow for optimism. Some soil is heavily polluted, and land being used for farming has soil conditions that are worrying. Residues from industrial and mining waste in soils are a major problem. According to a report jointly issued by the Ministry of Environmental Protection and the Ministry of Land and Resources Department in April, 2014, *Report on a Survey of National Soil Pollution Conditions*, 16.1 percent of soil exceeded allowable limits for contamination, while 19.4 percent of surveyed arable exceeded the allowable limit.

Second, China's water resources are inadequate, water is used both excessively and inefficiently, and water pollution is severe

China is one of the most water-scarce countries in the world. In 2012, its total volume of water resources came to 2.95269 trillion cubic meters. That equaled a per capita volume of just 2,186.1 cubic meters, which is roughly one-quarter of the average worldwide. Since China's total water resources will not be increasing in the future, the problem of water-resource constraints is going to plague the country for some time to come. It is a problem that will be hard to resolve in any fundamental way. Agriculture is the largest of all water-consuming industries. Since the 21st century, the total amount of water used by China's agriculture has stabilized overall (see Figure 9.1). In 2012, agricultural use of water came to 388.03 billion cubic meters, which constituted 63.2 percent of all water use in the country. Given the scarcity of water resources, some places have drawn excessive amounts from underground aquifers over a long period of time, which is leading to ongoing declines in the water table. The extent of "funnel areas" [subsiding land] due to lowered water tables in the eastern part of northern China now covers an area of 70,000 square kilometers. In addition, the efficiency with which Chinese agriculture uses water is low. The coefficient of effective water use in irrigation systems is 0.5, which is 20 percentage points lower than it is in developed countries. Water pollution further exacerbates the shortage of water resources. On a nationwide basis, surface water is "mildly polluted" overall, but in 2012, the percentage of IV-type and V-type water quality in ten major drainage basins including the Yangtze River, the Yellow River,

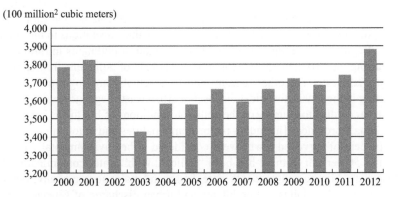

(100 million^2 cubic meters)

Figure 9.1 Agriculture-related water consumption in the 21st century

Source: *China Statistic Yearbooks*, Beijing: China Statistics Press.

and the Pearl River, came to 31.1 percent. In key lakes and dams that are State controlled, the percentage of IV-type and V-type water quality came to 38.7 percent. The situation with respect to polluted underground water is quite serious. According to a survey conducted by the Ministry of Environmental Protection in 2009, data derived from 641 wells in eight provinces and municipalities showed that 73.8 percent were producing IV- to V-type water quality. (The wells were located in Beijing, Shanghai, Liaoning, Jilin, Jiangsu, Hainan, Ningxia, and Guangdong.)

Environmental pollution in the countryside is severe

First, pollution from industry and urbanization is spreading into the countryside

Industrial pollution in the countryside began after rural areas began to industrialize in the 1980s. From the 1980s to the mid-1990s, China experienced the very rapid growth of town-and-village enterprises. Most of these entities were small and used outdated technology. Lacking any necessary pollution-control facilities, they simply discharged large quantities of waste material into their surroundings, which had an extremely deleterious effect on the rural environment. According to the 1997 Report *National Investigation of Pollution Sources of Industry in Towns and Villages*, the amount of pollutants that town-and-village industries discharged increased rapidly between 1991 and 1995. The main pollutants from these industries increased substantially as a percentage of total industrial pollutants emitted into the environment. Between 1984 and 1995, the percentage of liquid pollutants [wastewater] discharged by town-and-village industries went from 0.58 percent of the total to 21 percent of the total. The percentage of industrial solid pollutants went from 11.84 percent of the total to 88.7 percent of the total. In contrast to the survey on pollution from town-and-village industries that was conducted in 1989, pollution from industries had increased tremendously by 1995. Specifically, CO_2 emissions had increased by 23 percent, smoke-particle emissions increased by 56 percent, and industrial fine-particle emissions increased by 182 percent (Hong Dayong, 1999).

As pressures mount to protect the environment in urban areas and as some local governments have lowered the environmental requirements in their rural areas, a large number of polluting enterprises are moving their operations to the countryside. Regulatory oversight is minimal. The spread of pollutants in rural areas is occurring via two methods. One is from the spread of pollutants from urban and industrial waste. The other is from industries actually moving into rural areas. Starting in the 1990s, the wider disposal of urban waste began to impinge on rural areas. According to a survey on the pollution conditions of 141 towns in twenty-six of China's provinces [including major municipalities and autonomous regions], 76 percent of surveyed towns were considered to be environmentally polluted. Nearly 50 percent of these had been "inflicted with" water contamination from elsewhere. Mining contaminants were the second major source of environmental pollutants, while industrial pollutants and urban discharge of sewage were the primary source of water contamination (Tang Lixia et al., 2008).

Second, Chinese agriculture uses an excessive amount
of chemical fertilizers as crop inputs

Usage of chemical fertilizers continues to increase, while the efficiency of its use remains quite low (see Figure 9.2). In 2012, China used a total of 58.388 million tons of chemical fertilizer. The amount used per hectare came to 479.71 kilograms, which is two times the safe level of application under international standards. According to estimates, the uptake [absorption] of chemical fertilizers as applied in the same season is around 35 percent. Every year, 17 percent of the applied nitrogenous fertilizer and 2.4 percent of the applied phosphatic fertilizer goes directly into rivers, streams, and lakes. This has become the single major cause of the eutrophication of water (Zhu Zhaoliang et al., 2006).

Usage of pesticides also continues to increase, and the efficiency with which these are used is also quite low (see Figure 9.3). China's agriculture is subject

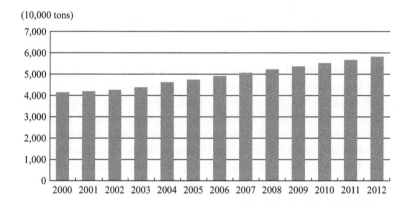

Figure 9.2 Chemical fertilizer application (net quantity) in the 21st Century
Source: *China Statistical Yearbooks*, Beijing: China Statistics Press.

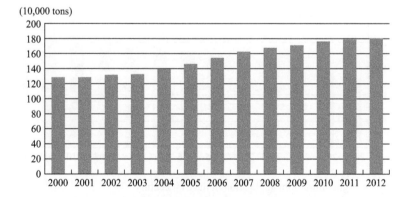

Figure 9.3 Chemical pesticide application in the 21st century
Source: *China Statistical Yearbooks*, Beijing: China Statistics Press.

to a great variety of pathogens and pests, which can indeed be controlled effectively when pesticides are used in a scientific manner. In 2013, China had a tenth consecutive bumper harvest, and the contribution of pesticides to this achievement should not be overlooked. However, pesticides are a double-edged sword. Inappropriate use can create such negative side effects as ongoing residues and environmental pollution, and they can seriously damage human health. The efficiency with which pesticides are used in China is only around 35 percent. The great majority of pesticides flow into nontargeted crops, the soil, and water (Shao Zhenrun, 2014). Another aspect of pesticide use relates to its packaging. In recent years, it is estimated that more than 3.2 billion bags are thrown away every year. The weight of these bags alone exceeds 100,000 tons, but in addition there is a residue of pesticides in every bag that averages between 2 percent and 5 percent of the original amount (Jiao Shaojun et al., 2012). Both the excessive use of pesticides and the problem of discarded packaging do direct damage to bodies of water, to soil, to human health, and to the surrounding ecosystem.

Meanwhile, use of plastic sheeting in agriculture continues to rise in China (see Figure 9.4), and with it the extent of plastic residues in the soil. The introduction of plastic covering as a technology used to grow vegetables sparked the leapfrogging growth of China's agricultural productivity in that sector. It enabled what has been called the "white revolution." However, the tremendous increase in the use of plastic sheeting is now gradually turning the white revolution into a calamity of white pollution. Residues of this sheeting prevent the normal passage of moisture content in the soil. This reduces the soil's capacity to handle drought, leading to secondary salinization. The fragments of sheeting also modify the soil structure, preventing the normal flow of oxygen, nutrients, and heat. This prevents root systems from communicating with the surrounding soil microbiome, which in turn lowers agricultural yields.

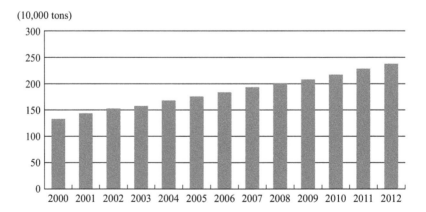

Figure 9.4 Agricultural film application in the 21st century

Source: *China Statistical Yearbooks*, Beijing: China Statistics Press.

*Third, the quantity of waste material being disposed
by agricultural systems is enormous*

Here, the worst problem is excrement-type pollution from animal and poultry breeding. In February 2010, the Ministry of Environmental Protection, the National Bureau of Statistics, and the Ministry of Agriculture jointly issued the *Report on the First National Survey of Sources of Pollution*. According to this report, in 2007, the volume of solid and liquid excrement produced by the country's poultry and animal-breeding industries came to 243 million tons. The quantity of urine alone produced by the industry was 163 million tons. Discharge of COD [chemical oxygen demand] came to 12.6826 million tons; nitrogen came to 1.0248 million tons; total phosphorus came to 160,400 tons; cuprum came to 2,397.23 tons; and zinc came to 4,756.94 tons. The COD discharged by the animal and poultry-breeding industry constitutes 96 percent of the total discharged by agriculture and 42 percent of the amount discharged by China altogether. Meanwhile, as artificial aquaculture becomes ever more common, large amounts of excess fish food and the medicines used in aquaculture are also discharged into water systems, creating a problem of eutrophication in bodies of water.

The utilization ratio of crop stalks and the residual organic matter of crops in China remains low. Burning this material has intensified the problem of air pollution. A report issued in 2014, *Annual Report on Comprehensive Usage of Resources in China*, notes that the quantity of retrievable stalk matter in China, nationwide, came to 830 million tons in 2013. The comprehensive usage rate was 77.1 percent, while the comprehensive usage amount was 640 million tons. The rest has become a source of land and water pollution, as well as pollution in the atmosphere. The prevailing attitude has become one of "deal with it by burning it," which is one of the major factors causing smog in the country. According to a report by Xinhua news agency, in the summer of 2013, remote sensing in the Beijing area showed that particulate matter of the PM2.5 size could go from 110 grams per cubic meter to 460 grams per cubic meter in the space of a few hours due to this kind of burning of crop residues.

*Fourth, garbage and waste disposal from rural communities
is discharged at random*

According to data compiled from a joint investigation of the "Patriotic Health Campaign Committee" and the Ministry of Public Health that looked at rural drinking water and environmental hygiene, in 2006 alone, the total amount of garbage generated by rural areas approached 300 million tons. This meant that each rural person generated 0.86 kilograms of garbage every day. Of this amount, one-third was simply thrown out at random. Sewage being generated in rural areas came to close to 9.9 billion tons. This meant that each person generated 29.3 liters every day. Of this total, 44 percent was discharged at random.

*Fifth, the worsening trend of environmental pollution in the countryside
cannot be reversed in a fundamental way in any short period of time*

On the one hand, industrial pollution and the pollution coming from urban residents is a problem that has been forming over a long time. Despite improved treatment processes, it already exists, and the situation cannot be improved very quickly. On the other hand, methods of agricultural production in the countryside and methods of disposing of the waste from daily life are also not things that can be changed quickly. The use of chemical inputs in agriculture will continue to exacerbate the problems. Disposal of garbage and sewage will continue to generate more pollution. The final verdict, based on these two causes, is that the worsening trend of environmental pollution in the countryside will not be improved in any substantive way over the short term. Environmental protection in rural areas is a long-term arduous task.

Deterioration of ecological systems

First, the ecosystems of China's grassland areas continue to get worse

Grasslands constitute the largest land-based ecosystem in China in terms of total area. They cover 41 percent of China's land area. Large portions of this area are now in a deteriorating state due to inappropriate agriculture, mining, and excessive grazing. This is seen in the continued decline of the production of grasses and the coverage of and severe decline in pasturage for livestock grazing. The worst cases show the process of desertification. The State has been implementing various projects to protect grasslands, including withdrawing land from livestock grazing and returning it to steppe, as well as the project meant to decrease sandstorms in Beijing and Tianjin. All these have done is to curb the rate at which grassland ecosystems are deteriorating, however. On a national basis, the ecosystems of grasslands are "improving in individual areas but declining overall" (Ministry of Agriculture, 2011).

*Second, the desertification of land and general degradation
of land are severe*

Results of the *Fourth Investigation on Wasteland and Desertification* in China show that initial steps in curbing the situation are positive to the extent that the total area of such land continues to diminish, although it is still increasing in certain areas. However, this extremely severe problem has not yet changed in any fundamental way. Land that has been made barren and land that has been desertified continues to be the most severe ecological problem facing China today (State Forestry Administration, 2011). By the end of 2009, land that has "been made barren" covered a total area of 2.6237 million square kilometers. This constituted 27.33 percent of China's total land area. Land that has been "desertified" covered 1.7311 square kilometers, which constituted 18.03 percent of China's total land area (see Figure 9.5).

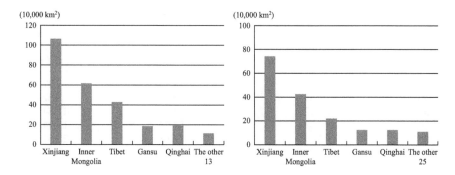

Figure 9.5 Land desertification and sandy lands in China

Source: State Forestry Administration, *Report on the Survey of Desertification in China*, January 2011.

Third, soil erosion is severe

According to remote-sensing surveys undertaken by the Ministry of Environmental Protection, in 2012, the area affected by soil erosion came to 2.9491 million square kilometers. This was 31.12 percent of the area surveyed. Of this total, the land area affected by water erosion came to 1.2932 square kilometers, while the area affected by wind erosion came to 1.6559 square kilometers. China is one of the world's most severely affected countries when it comes to the erosion of farmland due to wind and water erosion. The amount of topsoil lost to erosion every year comes to around 3.3 billion tons, which is 14.35 percent of the world's total (Liu Changming et al., 2001). In the northwestern part of the country, the topsoil layer has gone down from 80 to 100 centimeters in the 1950s to 20 to 30 centimeters at present (Wei Chao'an, 2011).

2. The serious impacts of environmental degradation in rural areas

Environmental degradation is limiting agricultural production

First, soil and water pollution, as well as the declining amount of grassland, is leading to a decline in agricultural productivity

Soil and water pollution are causing a decrease in the amount of irrigated land and is impoverishing soils to the extent that crop yields are declining. An investigative report from Inner Mongolia indicates that farmers are becoming unable to plant spring crops as usual due to wind erosion. They are being forced to plant varieties that mature in a shorter time and that can be planted in late spring. This is causing a decline in total production and is compromising their income (Wang Xiaoyi, 2009). A study done in Shandong province has indicated that irrigating with water contaminated with sewage has led to agricultural losses in the tens of billions of RMB from this one cause alone (Yang Danhui and Li Hongli, 2010) (see Table 9.1).

Table 9.1 Damage to crops due to soil contamination by sewage irrigation, 2000–2005

Year	Area of contaminated irrigation (10,000 hectares)	Damage to food crops (RMB 100 million)	Damage to vegetables (RMB 100 million)
2000	249.08	18.19	4.27
2001	373.61	30.02	7.22
2002	560.42	41.30	11.34
2003	840.63	84.74	15.44
2004	1260.94	172.03	28.64
2005	1891.41	267.46	57.52

Source: Yang Danhui and Li Hongli, "'Accounting for Environmental-Related Losses Based on Damage and Cost': Taking Shandong Province as an Example," *China Industrial Economics*, Issue 7, 2010.

Water pollution is having an extreme impact on the animal-breeding and fish-raising industries in particular. Fish farmers in many areas, particularly around Lake Taihu, are no longer able to continue to raise fish because of the pollution. Illegal discharges from industry are pouring large quantities of pollutants into the bodies of water that practice aquaculture, leading to major die-offs of fish and shrimp. According to the analysis of one survey that looked at pollution around Lake Taihu, the die-offs were occurring downstream due to the large quantities of pollutants being discharged upstream. Farmers who relied on this kind of aquaculture for a living were heavily impacted (Chen Ajiang, 2008).

The retreating steppe is posing a severe challenge to the sustainability of the animal husbandry industry. First, the diminishing amount of grassland and the reduction in its grasses directly affect the carrying capacity of the steppe. Second, given the lack of this kind of fodder, herders rely on buying hay or other feed to maintain their herds, which is leading to an enormous rise in the cost of raising animals. Data from one survey shows that the costs of production are indeed rising to cover the purchase of hay. Herding families that were interviewed said that two-thirds of their spending was now used on the purchase of hay. Moreover, one-third of those interviewed said that their costs are now more than their income due to the increase in production costs (Wang Xiaoyi, 2013).

Second, improper use of chemical inputs in farming is threatening the supply of agricultural goods due to food safety issues

Right now, the overuse of chemical inputs, particularly chemical fertilizers, is equivalent to an overdraft on the future productivity of the land. Chemical elements that have not been absorbed into crops enter the soil, bodies of water, and atmosphere, damaging soil health but also polluting the entire context for agricultural production. They are causing a comprehensive drop in agricultural resources and environmental quality, severely impacting the effective supply of agricultural goods.

The improper use of pesticides and animal-feed additives has led to a host of issues relating to food quality and food safety. Not only has this aroused widespread concern among the public, but it has led to a kind of terror about food safety. One incident in 2010 involved "poisonous red beans" from Hainan Island. The beans had been grown with chemicals that are prohibited in China for growing crops, including highly toxic isocarbophos and acephatemet. In 2013, an incident erupted in Shandong province concerning "poisonous ginger," which similarly used materials that are prohibited in crop production in China such as the pesticide generically known as "Shen-nong pills." [Shen-nong was the god of agriculture in Chinese legend. The pills are composed of aldicarb, a prohibited agricultural chemical in China.] Other incidents have been widely reported by the media, including the use of melamine, clenbuterol hydrochloride [known generically in China as "lean-meat hormone"], and Sudan Red. These all involve the improper use of additives in the process of raising animals and affect food quality and food safety.

The worsening environment has reached a point of damaging the health of rural residents

First, both agricultural waste and the disposal of garbage and sewage in towns are impacting the health of rural residents

The great majority of towns do not have systems for collecting and disposing of either garbage or sewage. Large quantities of both are simply discharged directly into the surrounding environment, which has a major impact on local health. Since the waste pollutes the sources of drinking water, and since the garbage is piled up at random, towns have become a "blind spot" when it comes to public hygiene. The refuse breeds quantities of mosquitos, insects, and microbes, which severely threaten the health of local residents.

Second, industrial pollution and garbage disposal from cities are both spreading out into the countryside, damaging the health of rural residents

Industrial pollution and the garbage of cities contain even greater amounts of pollutants that do even greater damage than locally generated pollution. Their spread into neighboring rural areas is having an even more severe impact on rural health. Relevant research indicates that the water-born pollutants of industrial production in particular are the chief culprits in the cancer villages around China, villages that have clusters of a high incidence of cancer (Gong Shengsheng and Zhang Tao, 2013). By the end of 2011, there were 351 such villages in China.[1] Prior to 1988, the increase in the number of cancer villages was slow. It accelerated after 1988, particularly in the period between 2000 and 2009, when a total of 186 new cases appeared. This later set of cancer villages constituted 53 percent of the total discovered up to that time (see Figure 9.6). The geographic distribution of China's cancer villages shows that they are mainly concentrated along the banks of rivers and inland water basins, including the mid- to lower reaches of the Yellow River, the Huaihai River, the mid- to lower reaches of the Yangtze River, and in the delta area of the Pearl River. In general, the eastern part of the country has more than the central part, but within the central part, cancer villages tend to be toward the west (see Figure 9.7).

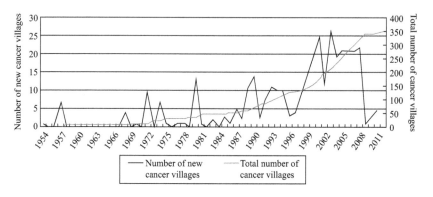

Figure 9.6 Annual increment and total number of "cancer villages" in China

Source: Gong Shengsheng and Zhang Tao, "Study on the Changes in Time and Spatial Distribution of 'Cancer Villages' in China," *China Population Resources and Environment*, Issue 9, 2013.

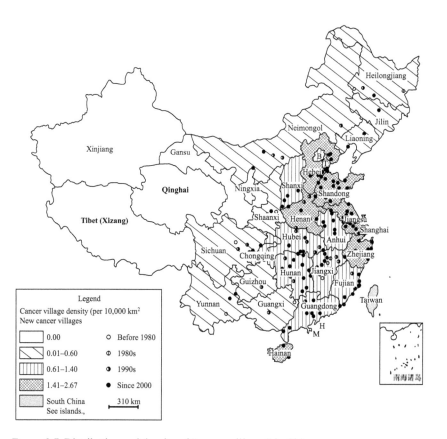

Figure 9.7 Distribution and density of "cancer villages" in China

Source: Gong Shengsheng and Zhang Tao, "Study on the Changes in Time and Spatial Distribution of 'Cancer Villages' in China," *China Population Resources and Environment*, Issue 9, 2013.

The worsening environment is increasing the frequency of incidents involving conflict of interests

First, rural residents express general dissatisfaction about the quality of their local environment

Environmental pollution is having an increasingly large effect on peoples' lives in rural areas, so rural people are more aware of issues than before. The Ministry of Environmental Protection conducted a survey of 6,000 residents in urban and rural areas in 2009 in order to ascertain the "degree of satisfaction with the environment." Rural people were clearly less satisfied with the environment than urban people, particularly on such issues as garbage disposal and access to drinking water. As for the extent to which environmental quality had improved, rural residents were also far less satisfied than urban residents. In cities, 65.8 percent of those interviewed said that they were "satisfied" or "fairly satisfied," while in rural areas, 57.9 percent of those interviewed said they were satisfied or fairly satisfied. In 2010, the results of a separate survey that the Ministry of Environmental Protection conducted by interviewing 6,000 rural and urban residents found that air pollution, water pollution, and physical garbage pollution were the environmental issues of greatest concern to the public. Within these environmental factors, garbage handling was the thing about which both urban and rural people were least satisfied. In comparing the 2010 results with the 2009 survey, urban residents who were "more satisfied or moderately satisfied" increased by 9.5 points, while the figure for rural areas was 2.2 points.

Second, mass incidents in rural areas that are sparked by environmental pollution are increasing in frequency

Economic losses and health issues that are caused by environmental pollution are now a frequent occurrence, leading to a constant increase in conflict-of-interest incidents. Examples that can be cited are the cadmium contamination incident in Liuyang, Hunan province, in 2004; the discharge of industrial pollution incident from a company producing chemicals in Dongyang, Zhejiang province, in 2005; the Fengwei sewage treatment plant incident in Quanzhou, Fujian province, in 2009; the aluminum plant contamination incident in Qingxi county, Guangxi province, in 2010 (Ren Bingqiang, 2011). According to a report disclosed by the Southern Metropolis Daily in 2007, environmental issues cause as much as one-fifth of all mass incidents. Environmental issues are the third largest cause of rural mass incidents in China. Another statistic that is widely quoted by now is that, in recent years, mass incidents relating to environmental pollution are increasing at an annual rate of 29 percent (Jia Feng et al., 2012). As environmental awareness grows among rural people and some companies irresponsibly discharge pollutants, mass incidents due to the resulting conflicts then begin to involve government departments. What began as a conflict between local people and a company evolved into conflict between local people and the government.

Moreover, mass incidents caused by environmental pollution frequently transcend the town or village and blow up into regional incidents. They begin to involve a fairly wide swath of area and to exert considerable influence. Not only do they bring on heightened attention as a result, but it becomes harder to find solutions. This is detrimental to the investment environment and economic development in a given region, but it also has long-term effects on social stability and on the attempt to build moderate prosperity.

3.   Countermeasures aimed at strengthening management controls over agricultural resources and at rural governance as it relates to the environment

Agriculture is the source of food and clothing for humankind. It is also the primary connection between humans and their natural environment in ways that require mutual harmonization. In looking broadly at the history of agriculture, as well as the situation today, agricultural production can cause serious ecological damage, but it also can be the source of advances in ecological improvement. To a substantial degree, an agriculture that "conserves resources and is friendly to the environment" can reduce the amount of damage done to the ecosystem by other sectors of the economy. Within a certain scope, agriculture can improve the ecological environment. Moreover, rural areas harbor the watersheds and green areas that provide an ecological screen [filter] for cities. "If China is to be beautiful, its rural areas must be beautiful." A beautiful countryside is both the cornerstone of and an organic component of a beautiful China. The development of a beautiful countryside and beautiful cities must be coordinated in one overall process if we are to build a beautiful China. It is highly significant, therefore, to put effort into pushing forward the "two forms" of agricultural development, namely resource conserving and environmentally friendly. It is important to foster the functions of agriculture in terms of providing ecological system goods and ecological system support. Building a beautiful countryside and improving the eco-environment of rural areas are highly significant for the policy goal of building an ecological civilization as a whole.

In recent years, as concerns about the problems of rural environments have increased in all segments of the population, and as all levels of government in China and the relevant departments have increased efforts to protect and rehabilitate the environment, the worsening of the rural environment has moderated somewhat. Certain limited areas are beginning to show improvement. However, the overall trend of a worsening situation in rural ecosystems has not yet been halted in any fundamental way. For this reason, we must concentrate the work of building an ecological civilization in rural areas on specific things as we aim at the worst existing problems. We should focus on the ongoing constraints on agricultural resources and on the fact that it will be hard to reverse the situation of a worsening rural environment in any fundamental way. Specifically, our focus should be on curtailing the spread of industrial and urban pollution toward the countryside, preventing and controlling broad-based agricultural pollution, and remediating soil pollution with a particular emphasis on heavy metals contamination. We must adopt measures that are truly effective by using such things as systems building, technical services, planning guidance, policy support, and greater funding.

***Establish sound structures and mechanisms to manage
the "rural ecological civilization."***

*First, set up sound structures to manage agricultural resources
and to protect the rural environment*

After thirty-five years of reform and progress, China has done the initial work in forming the leadership structures and actual work mechanisms for resource management and the handling of environmental protection. These are under the unified leadership of the State Council. Functions are handled by the division of labor and responsibility among different departments. Management and the actual work of implementation are coordinated. Large projects are dealt with by setting up dedicated line item projects, and the central government and local governments all have their accountabilities.

Nevertheless, at present, the management of resources and environmental protection in China is still beset by a host of problems. Multiple bodies are responsible for managing the same processes, there are overlapping functions and accountabilities, and the actual execution of functions is less than ideal (see Box 9.1). In terms of organizational structure, agricultural resources and rural environmental protection are the responsibility of numerous entities including the Development and Reform Commission, the Ministry of Environmental Protection, the Ministry of Agriculture, the Ministries of Forestry and Hydroelectric Power, the Ministry of Land and Resources, and so on, to the extent that many different entities handle any given endeavor. It is hard to differentiate and clearly define what each department is responsible for doing. Many functions are duplicated by overlapping jurisdictions while the regulatory objectives of different departments may be conflicting. In terms of actual execution of functions, there are no professional managers or technical people on the spot in local towns and villages to get things done.

**Box 9.1 The "nine dragons" situation with respect to
handling environmental protection in China**

Responsibility for handling water resources in China could be described as nine dragons all trying to manage affairs. According to the plans for departments as issued by the State Council, which address size, positions, and functions, nine separate departments are actually responsible for water-resource functions: the Ministry of Environmental Protection, the Ministry of Water Resources, the Ministry of Housing and Urban–Rural Development, the National Development and Reform Commission, the Ministry of Agriculture, the State Forestry Administration, the Ministry of Transport, the Ministry of Health, and the Ministry of Land and Resources. Among these, the Ministry of Water Resources is responsible for managing and protecting water resources, for water use and water conservation, for monitoring water quality, and so on. The Ministry for Environmental Protection is in charge of controlling water contamination, for monitoring water quality and discharges of pollutants, and for implementing and supervising environmental policies. The Ministry of Housing and Urban–Rural Development is responsible for sewage treatment in cities and the planning of water treatment projects, as well as for building and managing water treatment plants. The Ministry of Agriculture heads control of agricultural pollution that is on a widespread basis [not single-point sources]. The Ministry of Forestry is responsible for protecting the watersheds of water resources and for managing wetlands. The Ministry of Land and Resources is responsible for monitoring, regulating, preventing, and stopping the excessive drawing out of and also polluting of underground water resources. The Ministry of Health is in charge of drinking water and regulatory supervision of anything to do with aquatic products. The Ministry of Transportation controls pollution that comes from ships. The National Development and Reform Commission participates in the planning process of anything related to water-resource management and development, as well as the formulation of policy.

Source: Jin Shuqin, *Designing Policies for Water Contamination Control in River Basins: External Conceptual Innovation and Application*, Beijing: Metallurgical Industry Press, 2011 Edition

In terms of systems building, the existing structure for managing water resources and environmental pollution is aimed mainly at cities and at industrial pollution. It has relatively little to do with rural areas and agricultural considerations. Systems relating to agricultural resources and environmental protection have been particularly neglected (see Table 9.2).

Addressing these issues noted will require establishing sound institutions that are focused on agricultural resource management and environmental protection, but it will also require intergovernmental mechanisms and a unified approach. At the central government level, we recommend that China set up organizations dedicated to agricultural resource management and rural environmental protection and that we go further in explicitly defining these functions. At the local government level, we must strengthen the creation of institutions that handle grassroots-level agricultural resource management and rural environmental protection. We must nurture and encourage the further development of private service organizations at the grassroots level that provide for management of agricultural resources and environmental protection, and we must gradually improve the level of public services in the countryside. We must strengthen the ability to execute tasks in these two areas, which means consolidating the responsibilities and accountabilities that

Table 9.2 The eight environmental management systems

System	Main content	Management object
Environmental impact assessment	Survey, estimate, and assess the negative impacts of project location, design, and operation on neighboring environment before commencement of construction activities; propose prevention and control measures for approval through legal procedures	Mainly target at new industrial projects, also include those above designated size Animal farming projects
"Three simultaneous"	Environmental protection facilities must be designed, constructed, and put into operation simultaneously with the main part of a construction project	New projects
Registration and permit of pollutant discharge	Registration of pollutant discharge: enterprises and institutions shall register with and apply to environmental protection authorities for pollutant discharge. Permit of pollutant discharge: entities or individuals must apply to competent authorities for permit before discharging pollutants.	Enterprises and institutions
Quantitative assessment on comprehensive urban environmental control	Identify quantitative indicators to assess the effect of comprehensive environmental control and urban environmental quality and rate the overall level of urban environment efforts and environment management	Cities
Target responsibility system for environmental protection	Governors of provinces, cities, and counties sign contracts to specify their environment-related objectives and tasks as the basis of performance assessment and awards or punishments accordingly	Focusing on regional environmental quality and pollutant discharge reduction
Fee-based pollutant discharge	Pollutant discharge, direct or indirect, is subject to payment to the government based on the quantity and type of discharged pollutants	Entities and individual businesses that discharge pollutants
Correction within set time limit	Existing pollution sources that damage the environment shall make corrections within the time limit set by authorities specified by law	Mainly target at industrial enterprises
Centralized pollutant control	Within a specific scope and in line with pollution control planning, sewage, exhaust gases, and solid wastes are mainly disposed of in a centralized manner, in order to maximum environmental, economic, and social benefits at the minimum cost	Mainly target at industrial and urban pollution, such as urban sewage treatment plants

Source: Song Guojun, *Analysis of Environmental Policies*, Beijing: Chemical Industry Press, 2008 Edition

are currently spread over a number of different departments. We must unify the implementation of functions that conserve agricultural resources and protect the environment. This includes setting up land rehabilitation mechanisms and pollution control mechanisms that operate from an overall urban–rural perspective and that operate in concert with one another across different regions. We should also improve performance evaluation mechanisms that relate to the management of agricultural resources and environmental protection. Things like using up agricultural resources, discharging pollutants, and destroying the ecosystem should be included in local-government performance-rating systems, particularly the ratings that apply to the leadership teams at the county and township levels of governments. We should establish targets for the "building a rural ecological civilization" program, together with methods for judging how well targets have been met, which includes both incentive and punishment mechanisms. We should strengthen regulatory oversight over the performance evaluations, as well as incentives and constraints. We must mobilize the full enthusiasm of county and township governments for managing agricultural resources wisely and for protecting rural ecosystems.

Second, improve the legal system that applies to management
of agricultural resources and rural environmental protection

After thirty-five years of reform and development, China has basically succeeded in forming a legal system that is composed of more than fifty laws, regulations, and rules in this area. These cover such things as management of land and water resources, use of chemical inputs in farming, pollution control and prevention in rural areas, protection of farmland, protection of water and soil, protection of rural ecosystems, comprehensive rural environmental control, and so on (see Table 9.3).

Nevertheless, key laws and regulations are still lacking or ineffective, while problems with enforcement and regulatory oversight are fairly obvious. Because of this, we now need to move a step further in strengthening our legislation relating to agricultural resources and rural environmental protection, as well as enforcement of the laws. We must speed up the process of formulating a *Law on Preventing and Controlling Soil Pollution*, and we must revise the *Law on Preventing Water Pollution* and the *Articles on Charging and Collecting Fees for Discharging Pollutants*. In order to make the enforcement structures for environmental control more effective, we should strengthen regulatory oversight of enforcement and also strengthen protections that the judiciary system is supposed to provide. We should set up sound systems that allow for whistle blowing, and we should strengthen regulatory oversight by the public at large.

Third, set up property rights systems that govern natural resource
assets, as well as control systems that govern the use of those assets

At present, the "ownership" of the nation's natural resource assets is indeterminate. To address this and the fact that regulatory management of collectively owned natural resources is not in place, we must launch an effort to identify and define

Table 9.3 Laws and regulations on agricultural resource management and environmental protection

Laws

Environmental protection	Natural resource management	Related laws
Environment Protection Law [2014]	Water and Soil Conservation Law [2010]	Constitution [2004]
Marine Environment Protection Law [1999]	Mineral Resources Law [1996]	Criminal Law [1997]
Water Pollution Prevention and Control Law [2008]	Energy Conservation Law [2007]	Civil Procedure Law [1991]
Law on Appraisal of Environment Impacts [2002]	Flood Control Law [1997]	Administrative Procedure Law [1989]
Law on the Prevention and Control of Environmental Pollution by Solid Waste [2004]	Forestry Control Law [1998]	Public Security Administration Punishments Law [2006]
Law on Promoting Clean Production [2002]	Land Administration Law [2004]	Law on Administrative Penalty [1996]
Circular Economy Promotion Law [2008]	Agriculture Law [2013 Revision]	State Compensation Law [1994]
Water and Soil Conservation Law [2010]	Fisheries Law [2000]	Urban and Rural Planning Law [2007]
	Law on Desert Prevention and Transformation [2001]	Tort Law [2010]
	Grassland Law [2002]	Administrative Compulsion Law [2011]
	Water Law [2002]	
	Renewable Energy Law [2010]	
	Energy Law [2005]	

Regulations

Regulations on the Prevention and Control of Pollution from Large-scale Breeding of Livestock and Poultry [2014]	Regulations on Pesticide Administration [2001]
Regulations on National General Survey of Pollution Sources [2007]	Regulations on Environmental Impact Assessment of Planning [2009]
National Environmental Emergency Response Plan [2006]	Regulations on the Administration of Medical Wastes [2003]
Regulations on the Administration of Construction Project Environmental Protection [1998]	Detailed Rules for the Implementation of the Water Pollution Prevention and Control Law [2000]
Interim Regulations on the Prevention and Control of Water Pollution in the Huaihe River Valley [1995]	Regulations on Wild Plants Protection [1996]

(Continued)

Table 9.3 (Continued)

Regulations on Ocean Environment Protection against Pollution Damage Caused by Land-sourced Pollutants [1990]	*Regulations on Natural Reserves* [1994]
Regulations on the Administration of Construction Project Environmental Protection [1990]	*Regulations on the Administration of the Taihu Lake Basin* [2011]
Regulations on the Safety Administration of Dangerous Chemicals [2011]	*Regulation on the Safety Management of Radioactive Wastes* [2011]

Source: Han Dongmei and Jin Shuqin, "Analysis on the Agricultural Policies of China for Environmental Protection in Rural Areas," *Review of Economic Research*, Issue 43, 2013

ownership rights and then certify those rights with respect to such agricultural natural resources as water, forests, grasslands, barren lands, tidal areas, and so on. We must set up an effective natural resource property rights system that clearly defines whom assets belong to, that explicitly sets out both rights and account-abilities, and that provides for effective regulatory management. Based on clear zoning of the areas determined to be for production, for living, and for ecological purposes, we can then put in place a control system that handles the usage of agri-cultural resource assets. We must establish sound systems that conserve agricul-tural resources and use them more intensively, including water, land, and inputs. We must put in place a system that conserves farmland effectively and that uses it more intensively, a system that governs water resources and a system that provides for the protection of the rural environment. We must also establish a system for managing agricultural natural resource assets, which means explicitly defining the rights and accountabilities of the owners of those assets. We must improve the regulatory oversight of agricultural natural resources by explicitly defining the rights and accountabilities of those who use the resources.

Fourth, implement a system that requires compensation for usage of agricultural resources and a system that provides for ecological compensation

In this regard, we should deepen reforms that relate to the pricing of agricultural natural resources, as well as the taxes and fees that relate to these resources. This means setting up systems that reflect the scarcity of resources and that comply with market supply and demand. It means having systems that require compensation for the costs of restoring damaged ecosystems and restoring them to beneficial use, as well as systems that require compensation for use of such resources. We must be firm about requiring fees for the use of resources, which also means that we adhere to the principle of "whoever damages the environment is the one who pays." This requires setting up systems that allow for holding people accountable [including tracking them down and bringing suit against them] and systems that require com-pensation for damage due to environmental pollution. We should stabilize and also expand the scope of the pilot projects underway that return farmland to forested land

and that return pastureland to steppe. We should make adjustments in the extent to which farming is being carried out on land that is highly polluted [and not farm on highly polluted land], as well as on land that is being overly mined for underground water resources. In orderly fashion, we should restore such farmland, as well as affected rivers and lakes. We must adhere to the principle of "the one who benefits is the one who pays." This means improving the compensation mechanisms in key ecological-function parts of the country, and it means pushing forward compensation systems that are coordinated across different regions (see Box 9.2). We should promote systems that allow for trade in energy conservation, including the trade in carbon-emissions and pollution-emission rights. We should set up mechanisms that can guide private capital [social as opposed to governmental funds] in the direction of investing in environmental protection in rural areas.

Box 9.2 The application of compensation requirements to the process of controlling water contamination

Jiangsu province began to implement a trial project on October 1, 2014, called *Jiangsu Province's Methods for Protecting Water Environments on a Regional Basis through the Use of Compensation (draft)*. This was in response to the requirements put forth by the Party's Third Plenary Session of the 18th CPC Central Committee regarding setting up a "horizontal type of compensation system to address ecological issues, to strengthen accountabilities for protecting water environments, and to improve the quality of water environments." This plan contained the following stipulations.

1 Implement "two-way compensation" after monitoring performance and confirming results, as per the principle of "compensate those who reach targets." That is, apply penalties to cities and counties that do not come up to targeted mandates for water quality, compensate downstream cities and counties that have been affected by upstream pollution, and grant compensation to those cities and counties that do come up to targets.

2 When monitored water quality that leaves the boundaries of upstream cities and counties is below required standards, make upstream cities and counties pay compensatory funds to the provincial government for that portion of water quality that is below provincially determined standards. The provincial finance department then provides compensation to downstream cities and counties.

3 When monitored water quality that leaves the boundaries of upstream cities and counties is above mandated standards, have downstream cities and counties pay compensatory funds to the provincial finance department for that portion of water quality that is above provincially determined standards. Provincial finance departments then provide compensation to upstream cities and counties.

4   When water that directly enters streams, rivers, lakes, and the ocean is below monitored water quality standards for bodies of water as determined by the province, make the relevant cities and counties upstream pay compensatory funds to the provincial finance department at rates determined by the provincial government.

5   When water that directly enters streams, rivers, lakes, and the ocean is above monitored water quality standards for bodies of water as determined by the province, have the provincial finance department compensate the relevant cities and counties upstream at rates determined by the provincial government.

6   In sections of rivers where cities and counties share boundaries and where the water flows directly into rivers, lakes, and the ocean, if water quality in the section is up to mandated water quality standards for three years in a row or is better at outlet than in the section of the river by a targeted amount, the provincial finance department will compensate the cities and counties along that stretch of river.

7   In sections that the State has confirmed are of key significance and is monitoring as part of performance targets, if monitored water quality reaches targets for two years in a row, the provincial government will provide appropriate compensatory rewards to the cities and counties that are within the relevant area.

8   For those areas that the provincial government has confirmed to be watershed sources for the concentrated use of drinking water, if monitored results, as confirmed by the Environmental Protection Office, are above water quality targets for two years in a row, any city or county within that watershed will receive appropriate compensatory rewards from the provincial finance department.

Source: General Office of the Government of Jiangsu Province, *Circular of the General Office of the Government of Jiangsu Province on Distribution of the Measures for Implementing the Regional Water Environment Compensation (trial) Issued by the Department of Finance and Department of Environmental Protection of the Province* [S.Z.B.F (2013) No. 195], December 31, 2013

Be innovative in creating technological systems and servicing methods for a "rural ecological civilization"

At present, China has already set forth a list of model projects that the country is funding with respect to environmental protection, called *List of Key State Environmental Protection Applied-Technologies and Model Projects*. However, a glance at this list shows that very few items relate to agricultural resource management or rural environmental protection. Even fewer items are targeted at promoting technologies, services, and servicing methods in rural areas to deal with agricultural resource management and rural environmental protection. Because of this, we must speed up the process of finding servicing methods and technological systems that really do push forward our stated policy goal of establishing a "rural ecological civilization."

First, create sound technology systems that allow for managing agricultural resources and protecting the rural environment

We must commit R&D efforts to developing highly effective applied technologies for managing agricultural resources and protecting the rural environment, and these must be targeted at the specific requirements of the entire process of agricultural production, as well as rural living conditions. In terms of each link in the process of farming, we must apply such R&D efforts to creating resource-conservation-type technologies prior to production, environmentally-friendly-type technologies in the course of production, and pollution-control-type technologies in postproduction. In terms of the management of factor inputs, and the demands of environmental protection, our emphasis should be on creating applied technologies for intensive-type use of land, water, fertilizers, pesticides, and plastic sheeting. We should focus on technologies that use the excrement of animal and poultry production, both urine and solid wastes, and the organic residues of crop farming as resources themselves. We should focus on technologies that preserve land and water and that treat sewage and manage garbage disposal. We should promote the bundling of these technologies into systems that protect rural environments and preserve agricultural resources (see Table 9.4).

As soon as possible, we must prepare a list of technologies that relate to managing agricultural resources and protecting rural environments, and we should speed up preparations for an information platform that allows dissemination of such information. The aim is to enable the great numbers of people who are working on agricultural technologies, actually operating farms, managing agricultural resources, and protecting rural environments in order to have access to technical information as a way to understand it and make practical use of it.

Second, be innovative in creating technical service mechanisms that allow for better management of agricultural resources and protection of rural environments

This process should rely on the township or regional level of organizations that can promote agricultural technologies. It involves improving the facilities and overall conditions of technical service organizations dealing with farming, forestry, water power, science and technology, and weather. It involves strengthening their capacity to provide services and strengthening safeguards to ensure payment, exploring new ways to promote services, and being proactive in launching technical services that help farm operators themselves protect rural environments and manage agricultural resources.

Support and develop all kinds of "socialized" service organizations including farmers' cooperatives, professional technical associations, companies that provide technical service, and so on. Adopt a variety of methods to provide farm operators

Table 9.4 Technological systems for agricultural resource management and rural ecological protection

	Before production	*During production*	*After production*
Land	Improving soil organic matters	Land preparation, crop rotation, intensive land preparation by machines, fallow	Mitigation of heavy metal pollutants in cultivated land
Water resource	Developing water-saving crop varieties, readjusting industrial structure	Highly effective irrigation	Sewage treatment, control over underground depression caused by excessive water exploitation
Chemical fertilizer	Developing fertilizer-saving crop varieties	Slow-release fertilizer, organic fertilizer	Water eutrophication treatment, control over nonpoint sources of agricultural pollution
Chemical pesticide	Developing pest-resistant and disease-resistant crops, inter-cropping, bio-control over pests	Slow-release pesticide, biocontrol over pests and diseases	Pesticide pollution and residue control
Agricultural film	Soil moisture preservation	Biodegradable film, high-standard film	Film recycling
Utilization of animal excrements	Spatial design, integration of cultivation and breeding	Zero-emission breeding enclosure, bioferment feeds	Recycling of methane and organic fertilizers, animal excrement treatment
Crop straw utilization			Returning straw to fields
Waste disposal			Biosafe disposal
Sewage treatment			Centralized treatment of domestic sewage
Water and soil conservation	Water source conservation		Saline-alkali field control

Source: Compiled by Song Hongyuan.

with the technical services needed for lower-cost, more convenient, comprehensive ways to manage agricultural resources and protect the environment. Make use of government actions to guide for-profit service organizations into doing the kinds of business that are in the public interest. Such government actions might include government procurement, targeted consignment rewards and subsidies, tenders, and so on.

Be creative in devising new methods and ways to provide services. Set up technical service platforms that are regional and comprehensive as ways to manage agricultural resources and protect rural environments. This means drawing resources together and setting up comprehensive service associations and service centers in towns and villages. Promote the service model that links specialized technology companies + cooperatives + rural-household companies and agricultural companies + experts + rural households. Promote the integration of technologies in the material being produced, along with a "technology contract" method that applies to technical services as a way to improve management of agricultural resources and protection of rural environments. Expand the scope of coverage of technical services for managing agricultural resources and protecting rural environments. Ensure that technologies are able to reach down into every field and into every farm household.

Enhance planning and policy support for a "rural ecological civilization"

First, put a sense of urgency behind formulating and implementing plans

Accelerate the process of coming up with plans for sustainable agricultural development. This effort is aimed at the problems facing agricultural resources that are getting worse by the day, at a mode of increasing agricultural production that is extensive as opposed to intensive, and at the inability to sustain agricultural development. Its priorities include raising the efficiency with which agricultural resources are utilized, accelerating a transformation in the mode of agricultural growth, and setting up systemic mechanisms that allow for sustainable agricultural growth. We must put a major effort behind the creation of a "modernized form of new-style agriculture" that conserves resources, is environmentally friendly, and protects the ecosystem in which agriculture operates.

Accelerate the process of coming up with plans for dealing with the most outstanding environmental issues concerning agriculture. This is aimed at the most formidable and grim problems – increasingly severe agriculture-related environmental pollution, heavy destruction of the ecosystems required by agriculture, the unsustainability of agricultural development, and food safety concerns about agricultural products. Priorities here involve environmental rehabilitation, protection of ecosystems, promoting sustainable agricultural methods, and improving the quality standards that apply to food safety. In this respect, we must promote "green development," "clean development," "low-carbon development." We must also put a major effort into creating a more beautiful countryside.

We should adhere to several basic principles as we compile plans for sustainable agricultural development and plans for handling its most outstanding environmental issues. These are to combine the "red-line" management process [the red line calls for not falling below a minimum quantity of arable land in the country] with adherence to reasonable usage of resources; to give equal consideration to keeping harvests growing at a stable and steady rate while also doing ecosystem restoration and environmental rehabilitation; to ensure that the geographic distribution of agricultural production is appropriate to the carrying capacity of that area's environmental resources; and to approach domestic production and the use of international resources from an overall planning perspective. Priority tasks here include putting explicit protections on farmland, promoting long-term farmland usage of land, protecting water resources, developing agriculture that is highly efficient at using and conserving water, strengthening environmental pollution controls, building an environmentally friendly type of agriculture, launching ecosystem restoration projects, and upgrading the servicing capacity for agricultural ecosystems. We should divide agricultural production areas in the country into several key regions depending on whether they are already outstanding, developing at an appropriate rate, or need protection. We should launch key projects relating to protection of soil and water resources, remediation of agricultural as well as rural environments, restoration and protection of agricultural ecosystems, scientific and technical support systems, and regional development projects. We should strengthen such safeguarding methods as laws and regulations, assistance policies, supporting technologies, institutional structures and mechanisms, and leadership organizations.

Second, create sound systems for plan management and sound mechanisms for plan implementation

Strengthen management of planning coordination. At the national level, this means strengthening the connections among the plan for sustainable agricultural development, the plan for remediation of outstanding agriculture-related environmental issues, and the plan for zoning uses of State-owned land. It means clarifying the positioning of each plan and its functions. At the local government level, the nationwide plans should be used for primary guidance and should be integrated with the actual situations in local areas in coming up with sustainable-agriculture plans specifically for that area and remediation of outstanding environmental issues in that area. In terms of the specific target goals and tasks that are to be completed by the plans, annual goals and tasks should be formulated that conform to the development goals and key tasks set forth in the sustainable-agriculture plan and the remediation of outstanding environmental issues plan. The goals for the year should be broken out by each plan.

Improve mechanisms to ensure the implementation of plans. This means explicitly setting forth the responsibilities of the primary entities involved. Primary tasks to be accomplished by the relevant departments should be assigned to those departments for each plan. The main pathway to achieving objectives and safeguarding measures to ensure compliance should be studied and incorporated in the plan for sustainable agriculture and the plan to deal with outstanding agriculture-related environmental problems. There should be comprehensive performance evaluations relating to implementation of the plans. We should speed up the formulation of results-oriented performance-evaluation systems that are conducive to implementing the plan, as well as methods for actually conducting the evaluations. We should strengthen comprehensive performance evaluations that cover all stages of the plan, the implementation process, the results, and the effectiveness. Results of the performance evaluations should be used in deciding on promotions at all levels of leadership groups and leadership cadres. They should be considered a major part of the material used to decide on bonuses as well as punishments. We should strengthen the monitoring and evaluation of plan implementation by improving monitoring and evaluation systems and the capacity of institutions to do such monitoring and evaluation. We should be creative in finding ways to monitor and evaluate progress, including analysis of follow-up procedures and results. We should make sure that the results of analysis, including plan implementation and monitoring and evaluation data, are not only reported to relevant departments but published openly for the general public.

Third, push forward the strategic restructuring of agriculture

This involves continuing to implement the policy of restoring agricultural fields to woodlands and wetlands and restoring pastureland to steppe, among other measures. It must be done in line with the principles of voluntary participation by farmers, guidance by government, respect for order, appropriate solutions for local situations, and stable and secure proceedings. It is aimed at the most egregious situations of loss of soil and water and deterioration of ecosystems in rural areas. It requires adjusting the spatial structure [land use] of areas in which farming, fishing, and animal husbandry is currently in place.

Pushing forward the restructuring of agricultural production and the structure of crop and other plant production is targeted at the problems of excessive use of resources and intense pollution. It is done to meet the needs of protecting farmland and water resources, to use resources in ways that are both intensive and conservation oriented, to increase the effectiveness with which resources are used, and to improve the functioning of ecosystem services. In areas where both surface water and underground water are being overused, such as in the Yellow River and Huaihai River basins, we should reduce the area planted to winter wheat to the appropriate degree, while increasing the area planted to low-water-use crops and grasses. In areas that have intense heavy metal pollution, we should substitute alternative plants to gradually extract and lessen the pollutants in the soil. We should set up greenbelts and moderating-impact belts as necessary. In areas that have livestock-raising facilities along the edges of rivers and streams and near bodies of water that discharge relatively large quantities of pollution, we should set limits via zoning procedures to distinguish areas that forbid such livestock raising and areas that limit it, and we should determine the appropriate sizes for such facilities. In areas where fish farming is concentrated, we should determine reasonable sizes for the operations as well and reduce the amount of antibiotics and other medicines and feedstock additives used as inputs. We should promote "clean and healthy animal raising," and we should strictly control the catch of the fish industry. We should also put a major effort into such constructive activities as model farms for raising crops for horticulture and gardening, as well as model [or demonstration] areas for healthy fish farming and animal breeding.

Fourth, extend greater policy support to this whole effort

Our priorities surrounding the overall effort of improving the conditions surrounding agriculture and the ecosystem that supports agriculture are remediation of the pollution caused by heavy metals in the soil of farm fields, handling of excrement pollution caused by animal and poultry breeding, controlling excessive mining of underground water, and protecting the topsoil of northeastern China. Our spending should be increased on these areas. We must put in place policies that require fees for additional "construction-use land" and use those fees on protecting farmland and restructuring farmland. In this regard, we must gradually increase the percentage of the fees charged for newly added construction-use land that is spent on improving land quality and agricultural production capacity.

To meet the demands posed by conflicting objectives (increasing production, raising farmers' income, and using resources while still protecting the environment and the ecosystem), we should make adjustments in the current system of agricultural subsidy policies. We should increase subsidies for restoring and protecting environmental ecosystems as they relate to agriculture. We should improve subsidy policies for agricultural machinery and continue the pilot projects that allow for replacing old equipment with new. We should increase subsidies for new-style farming equipment that conserves on gas and has fewer emissions. We should improve the subsidies that allow fishing boats to use diesel fuel and launch a subsidy program that pays fish farmers not to farm during certain periods and that provides them with fishing-industry insurance. We should continue to offer subsidies for the release of fish into natural waters from hatcheries. We should improve the whole program of subsidies for withdrawing farmland from farming and putting in trees and grasslands. We should expand the scope of pilot projects in this regard, while also increasing the amount of subsidies. Through such public-finance-funded methods as subsidies and awards, we should support the use of high-results organic fertilizer, the use of high-results but low-residue pesticides, and the use of high-quality plastic sheeting but combined with a program to ensure that it is removed from fields after use. We should use financial support to encourage restructuring of agricultural production in areas that have heavy metals pollution and where underground water has been overly extracted. We should promote broader use of rotations in terms of grains and then grass, grains and then soybeans, and so on. We should increase subsidies in order to upgrade the organic matter in soils, subsidies to strengthen the ability of farmers to withstand calamitous risk, and subsidies for technology that enables stable production and increased yields.

Increase the force of building up a "rural ecological civilization."

Since the start of the 21st century, China's spending on environmental remediation has increased every year. As a percent of GDP, however, it has hovered at around 1.5 percent, which is far lower than the levels of major developed countries. Meanwhile, China's spending goes mainly to cities and to the industrial sphere. National spending on agricultural and environmental issues in rural areas is extremely limited. Since 2008, central finance has allocated funds for specific environmental protection projects in rural areas, and the amount increases every year. Despite this, however, the total amount of spending is still quite small – compared to the vast reaches of China's rural areas, it is no more than a token, like trying to use a thimble of water to put out a fire. We urgently need to set up mechanisms for ongoing stable increases in spending on the ecosystems of rural areas.

First, this means using government spending as the dominant force

Environmental protection is a public good that is strongly in the public interest. It involves a multiplicity of "responsible parties," among whom it is hard to distinguish who is most at fault. It requires a long spending cycle with low returns. All of these things make it necessary to employ the government's primary role in providing funds. Improving the policy of "public-finance support for agriculture" means increasing spending on environmental protection in rural areas. The central government's investment into basic infrastructure must continue to lean in the direction of the "three agricultures," that is, it must give priority to ensuring the steady increase of funding for basic infrastructure in rural areas. This means increasing funding but also improving the management of projects, consolidating funds that relate to agriculture, and applying them from an overall planning perspective. It requires increasing the force of environmental protection in rural areas. We should increase controls over agricultural resources and build up new "platform bases" that enable ecosystem remediation and environmental protection. We should promote the establishment of "demonstration model areas with admirable farming ecosystems," including "civilized ecosystem counties" and "civilized ecosystem towns." We should launch comprehensive and integrated technology models that demonstrate what a "livable" countryside should be.

Second, this means opening up more channels by which to fund rural environmental protection

Ecosystem remediation and environmental protection require massive amounts of financial investment. To take the restoration of polluted soils as just one example: if we were to restore just the soil that has been most heavily polluted, which is an estimated 50 million *mu* of land [8.2 million acres], the minimum cost would be RMB 20,000 per *mu* or a total of RMB 1 trillion – and that is by using the least expensive method, which is plant remediation. Yet the total amount of central finance spending put to polluted soil remediation during the entire 12th Five-Year Plan period came to just RMB 300 million. This is a pittance compared to the more than RMB one trillion needed to remediate China's polluted soils. There is a monumental gap between the amount of funds needed to restore the country's polluted soils and the funding being put into that effort. We recommend, therefore, that in addition to making full use of the guiding role of State spending, we use such incentive policies as discounted interest, rewards, compensation for risk, exemption and reduction in taxes and fees, and so on to mobilize the financial system and funds from society at large. We want to encourage other sources of funds to invest in agriculture and in protecting the environment of rural areas. We should guide R&D institutions to set up alliances with corporations to develop pollution remediation technologies and to develop agriculture, as well as to strengthen technical systems that allow for better management of agricultural resources and better protection of the environment. We should explore the market for developing rural environmental protection and promote "third-party handling" of rural environmental pollution.

Third, implement projects that engage in rural ecosystem rebuilding and environmental remediation

We should continue to implement development projects that relate to the country's development goal of building a "rural ecosystem civilization," including the key tasks that are involved. We should also launch new projects that relate to the protection of agricultural resources and highly effective utilization project (see Box 9.3), on the basis of already existing "construction" projects in this regard. These should be targeted at the most extreme problems: the tight supply of agricultural resources that are getting scarcer by the day, the problem of low utilization rates of resources that we do have, and the problem of severe pollution discharges coming from agriculture. The aim of these projects should be to make the most concerted efforts to protect farmland and water resources, to raise the degree to which resources are used intensively, to put effective controls on chemical inputs such as chemical fertilizers, pesticides, and plastic sheeting, to raise the efficiency of resource usage, and to improve the comprehensive use of wastes coming from agricultural production, including stalks from crops and excrement and urine from animal and poultry raising.

Box 9.3   Projects to protect agricultural resources and achieve more efficient use of resources

1.   Projects to protect farmland and use it more intensively and to remediate land damaged by pollution

Put greater effort into building up higher-quality farmland. Continue to launch projects that put more organic matter into the soil: constantly improve soil quality [health] by using soil testing and appropriate application of fertilizers, returning stalks to the fields, and using soil amendments and organic fertilizers. Launch projects that rehabilitate soils polluted with heavy metals; the focus here should be on rehabilitating acidic soils in the rice fields in southern China that have been polluted with metals. Focus on promoting and making better use of technologies to rehabilitate polluted soils. Launch projects to protect the topsoil of northeastern China.

2. Projects to protect watersheds [water sources] and water-conservation works for farming

Continue to promote projects that help agriculture conserve water, including the use of pipes in irrigation systems, the use of irrigation underneath plastic sheeting, and other effective conservation methods. Support base areas that are producing drought-resistant crops as demonstrations. Speed up the pace of reforming areas that are currently medium-size to large irrigation areas and build up more core demonstration areas that are exemplary in conserving water. Launch projects to deal with the worsening of "funnel areas" that have subsided due to overdrawing underground water. With respect to the Yellow River basin, the Huaihai River basin, and portions of provinces in northwestern China where there is excessive use of surface water as well as overdrawing of underground water, develop water-conserving irrigation projects and expand water diversion projects, reduce the amount of water under irrigation, adjust crop structures, and reduce the planting of crops that require more water.

3. Projects to control area-wide pollution from farming

Promote the use of low-toxicity and low-residue types of pesticides, as well as more advanced equipment for applying pesticides. Advance the use of such pest-prevention measures as using "green" pest-prevention and control in order to reduce pollution from pesticides and to improve the effectiveness of application. Improve soil testing and appropriate application of fertilizers. Publicize and promote the use of slow controlled-release biological and organic fertilizers and other new types of fertilizers. Support the building of livestock and poultry-breeding farms that are regulated and comply with standards, and reform those that are not. Promote low-carbon technologies in the raising of livestock and poultry, and promote the use of their waste material. Implement projects that reduce the polluting effects of aquaculture.

4. Projects to make use of agricultural waste materials

Continue to promote projects that make comprehensive use of all crop material [stalks] and centralized methane supply projects; support the turning of livestock and poultry manure into a resource.

Source: Compiled Song Hongyuan.

With respect to the poor housing, lack of public facilities, and poor hygienic conditions in rural areas, launch projects to remediate environmental problems and to provide environmental protection (see Box 9.4). Accelerate the formulation of standards for rural areas with respect to housing, drinking water, travel, and other basic living conditions. Rectify the overall environment of towns and villages so that the countryside is a more beautiful and livable place.

**Box 9.4   Projects to remediate environmental problems
in rural areas and to protect the environment**

1.   Projects to improve the living environment of residential areas

The focus here should be on garbage disposal and sewage treatment. Construct facilities for sewage treatment and garbage disposal; speed up the rebuilding of dangerous housing. Continue to advance projects to provide safe drinking water to villages. Implement projects to pave roads within towns. Put a major effort into county-wide rural electrification and water supply projects as per the "new countryside" policy.

2.   Projects to protect traditional villages

Traditional towns and villages that hold historic and cultural value should be put on a list of protected places. We should increase spending to preserve and protect such places.

3.   Projects to protect cultural legacy aspects of farming

We should gather data on and protect agricultural legacies that are contained in knowledge about how to do things, that is, the experience contained in traditional farming technologies. We should conduct the systematic collection and preservation of this cultural legacy.

4.   Projects to rectify rural ecosystems in general

Move steadily and systematically in building up a more livable countryside. This includes such things as putting effort into cleaning up the ecosystems of small watersheds, separating districts that raise livestock and poultry from residential areas in a scientific way, gradually building up systems for the safe disposal of sick or dead animals, accelerating the building of composting stations, launching projects to recover and reuse plastic sheeting used in farming, as well as the plastic packaging used for pesticides. Promote cleanup projects in the countryside, and strengthen the "rectification" of public areas in towns and villages.

Source: compiled by Song Hongyuan

To cope with the long-standing problem of soil erosion from destruction of watershed vegetable and land degradation and to deal with such ecological problems as soil erosion due to the felling of trees and removal of vegetation, we should launch and properly implement projects to restore and protect rural ecosystems (see Box 9.5). Increase spending on the protection of forests and on the forestry industry. Promote protection of steppe ecosystems and improve protections over water ecosystems. Stabilize ecosystems, and improve their ability to provide eco-system services.

Box 9.5   Projects to restore and protect rural ecosystems

1.   Projects to protect forests and support the forestry industry

Continue to launch as well as properly implement projects that protect natural forests. These include such reforestation projects as those in the northeast, north, and northwestern parts of China, the national project to prevent and control desertification, the Beijing-Tianjin project to control sandstorms, and so on. Implement a new round of efforts to withdraw farm-ing from grasslands and forested areas and restore the land to steppe where it should be steppe and to forest where it should be forest. Follow the laws of nature in determining what industry should follow the previous practice of farming.

2.   Projects to protect steppe areas

Continue to strengthen restoration of the steppe ecosystems in the three main watersheds of China, as well as the Qinghai Lake watershed, and the water sources of the Yellow River in southern Gansu province. Launch projects to set up "natural steppe protected areas." Place "priority protec-tion" on steppe areas that are of unique significance in terms of having rare plants and animals, key ecosystem functions, and economic or scientific value. Continue to strengthen efforts to protect steppe areas that are subject to the wind, soil, and water erosion. Provide subsidies and incentives for all parts of China in which animal husbandry is practiced in order to protect the ecosystem of grasslands. Launch reclamation projects in intermediate steppe zones that have already been plowed up for farming. Improve pas-ture mixes on the grassy hills and slopes of southern China.

3.   Projects to protect water ecosystems

Launch projects to restore wetlands in key [priority] parts of the country, and develop overall plans for how these areas can be used. Strengthen pro-tections over "protected ecosystem areas," "watershed protection areas," "the sources of rivers," and wetlands in general. Push forward the resto-ration of fragile ecosystems, and accelerate comprehensive rehabilitation of riparian systems and rural ditches and canal banks. Set up protection zones to protect wild plants in their native habitat, and set up national level biological protection areas to protect animal species in both natural-resource-protected areas and aquatic protected areas.

4. Projects to establish environmental monitoring networks

Accelerate the building of systems that do routine monitoring of the environment, increase funding for the building of environmental monitoring stations, and improve the advance warning network on environmental issues.

Source: Compiled by Song Hongyuan.

Note

1 A so-called cancer village is a reflection of high cancer morbidity rate at the spatial dimension of a village and refers to villages of high morbidity rate and mortality from cancers. No official statistics in this regard are available in China because of different identification standards, different times of statistics, and different numerical statements. Please refer to Gong Shengsheng and Zhang Tao, 'Study on the Changes in Time and Spatial Distribution of "Cancer Villages" in China.' *China Population Resources and Environment*, Issue 9, 2013.

10 Clarifying the responsibilities and accountabilities of governments and increasing support from public finance

- The evolution of the relationship between the State and farmers since the founding of the PRC
- Overall situation with regard to public spending at the current time
- Main problems with public spending at the present time
- Policy recommendations with respect to increasing public-finance spending

Under the planned-economy structure, urban and rural areas were kept isolated from one another, and economic and agricultural resources of the country flowed from the countryside toward the cities and industry. Moreover, this situation persisted over an extended period of time. Since the 1990s, the situation has improved as rural migrant workers move toward cities for jobs. Nevertheless, basic infrastructure and public services in the countryside are still far behind the situation in cities. In the 21st century, given increasingly apparent problems with farmers, farming, and the rural economy, the central government finally proposed the idea of having public finance actually cover the countryside as well. Policy goals for public finance shifted from a focus on agricultural production to a broader mission: "increase agricultural production, improve farmers' incomes, and develop endeavors that contribute to rural society." The overall approach to "extracting resources" from farming, farmers, and the rural economy went from the previous "extract less or do not extract at all" to "give more." Spending support began to increase on a consistent basis, while the scope of things that were being supported was also broadened. Results of these changes have been remarkable.

Given the unique nature of agriculture and its importance to national policy, all countries provide greater public financial support for agriculture once they reach a certain stage of development. Since the supply of public goods and services in most countries is the same for both urban and rural areas, however, public-finance policies mainly focus on ensuring that there is sufficient investment in agricultural production, as well as sufficient profits and people engaged in the business. The intent is to make sure the country has an adequate supply of agricultural goods. China's situation is somewhat different. Due to the extent of the country's "historic debts" and the constraints of its dualistic urban–rural system, not only does public finance in China need to address problems of agricultural production, but it needs to address the difference in the supply of public goods and services between the urban and rural parts of the country. In this sense, it needs to redefine the responsibilities and accountabilities of government. If we are to achieve a "moderately prosperous society in an all-round way," we must properly recognize the government's role in rural development. We must continue to increase support from public spending, but we must also make sure that public spending plays a larger role in reducing the disparity between urban and rural areas and a larger role in providing public services in rural areas. This chapter first looks back at the evolution of the relationship between the State and its rural population since the founding of the PRC. It then analyzes the general situation as it stands today, as well as the main problems. On that basis, it proposes policy recommendations for greater public-spending support for farmers, farming, and rural areas.

1. The evolution of the relationship between the State and farmers since the founding of the PRC

The relationship between the State and farmers has evolved through time since the founding of the PRC [1949]. Prior to the "tax and fees reform" [which started in 2001 and resulted in full tax exemptions for farmers in 2006], public services in rural areas were subject to the principal of "spending by each level of government, and decision-making [management] by each level of government." As a result, farmers themselves mainly provided their own public services. Local governments spent most of the nontax income that they took in from the local populace on salaries and benefits for government employees, as well as on routine administrative functions. Anything left over went to rural public endeavors. Meanwhile, unreasonable funding demands, improper apportioning of costs, and fees of various kinds began to put a heavy load on farmers. In 1994, the "division of tax revenues reform" [which assigned tax revenues to different levels of government] determined that agricultural taxes should be defined as local-government revenue. Nevertheless, revenues at the township and village levels of government came primarily from what were known as the "three deductions [from money owed] [*ti*] and the five general levies [*tong*]," as well as other levies required of farmers. In terms of public endeavors, the fiscal system allowed for the fairly complete division of authority. Most public goods and services were supplied according to the mantra "spending by each level of government, and management by each level of government." Such things as education, public health, roads, water conservancy projects, and so on upheld that principle. Since the nation's total fiscal budget was inadequate to cover everything, and the relationship between the State and farmers was "extractive," governments in rural areas went heavily into debt, and pressures on farmers to pay for everything intensified. After the "tax and fees reform" of the early 2000s, public finance gradually began to cover the "three agricultures" as well [farmers, farming, and the rural economy], and the State gradually took on greater responsibility in paying for rural public services. The scope of State spending was also broadened to include social welfare, public services, and basic infrastructure, in addition to economic development. The relationship between the State and farmers fundamentally changed from one that extracted resources to one that extended resources.

The State policy under the People's Commune system, in which the State "took more" from farmers and "gave less"

Under the planned-economy system, the State controlled all economic and social activity of its citizens. Agriculture provided the capital accumulation for the country's industrialization. Farmers were called upon to contribute to the development of cities. The State paid for the employment and welfare benefits of urban residents, while employment and welfare benefits in the countryside were mainly covered by the People's Commune system.

In terms of administration, People's Communes exhibited two key features. First, they combined the handling of both governing and social affairs ["society"] in one entity. Second, they followed the principle known as "First: big, Second: public." That is, the larger they were, the better, and the more their ownership was collective, the better. The country exercised direct control over the economic behavior of farmers through policy decisions relating to production. Via the People's Communes, the State also exercised direct uniform management of all social activity of farmers. Only between 6 percent and 7 percent of total national spending on capital construction [basic infrastructure] went to the agricultural sector. The supply of public goods and services in rural areas therefore basically came from the "self-reliance" of production brigades. State spending or assistance was supplementary (see Table 10.1).

Under the People's Commune system, funds for the supply of public goods in rural areas came mainly from three sources: the fiscal budgets of the commune, the public reserve fund and the public benefits fund, and farmers' "work points" [*gong fen*, a unit indicating the amount of work and quality of work performed, and the value of that work]. Under conditions that prevailed at the time, People's Communes could actually pull together fairly substantial resources, so their ability to allocate resources was considerable. They could provide public goods in a fairly effective way, and they could provide protection for the most vulnerable groups of people. During this period, such things as water conservancy projects, public education at the basic level, and rural cooperative healthcare made a certain degree of progress.

Grassroots organizations under township governments and self-governance entities practice the policy of "extracting more [from farmers] and giving less"

Once reform and opening up began, and with it the start of the household contracting system, the government withdrew from its previous interference in decisions regarding agricultural production. Farmers themselves now had the right to make decisions about their own farming operations. They became independent

Table 10.1 Supply of public products and services in rural areas in the People's Commune period

Service	Source of supply
Farmland irrigation and water conservancy	The communes took care of water affairs within their jurisdictions. The country did not provide subsidy for small irrigation and water conservancy projects affordable by production teams or gave necessary subsidies to those teams vulnerable to drought, with low income, weak in collective economy, and financially incapable.
Commune health center	Health centers run by communes were mainly supported by the collective economy. The country gave subsidies according to the economic status of the health centers.
Rural cooperative medical service	Subsidies from the central finance were mainly used to train medical staff and support poor production teams.
Primary and middle schools established by educational authorities	The main part of financial source came from national budget appropriation, and the rest was school fees, revenue from school-run businesses, and self-raised funds arranged by local finance.
Schools established collectively by production teams	Supported by state subsidy, collectives, school fees, and revenue from school-run businesses
Expenses for cultural activities, communication, and radio broadcasting	Expenses for staff, books, purchase of equipment and business costs of such institutions as cultural centers, broadcasting centers, and movie play teams were covered by state subsidy and funds of the communes.
Social relief and welfare	In addition to special-care allowance and social relief funds allocated by national budget, communes covered parts of the welfare expenses such as social relief and old-age homes.
Commune administrative management	The country decided the staff scales of communes according to their sizes and allocated administrative management funds; communes had to pay extra employees on their own

Source: Based on *Finance and the Financial Management of People's Communes*, Hangzhou: Zhejiang People's Publishing House, 1981 edition.

entities engaged in agricultural production. The original administrative system by which People's Communes had operated now dissolved; it had been a "three-tiered system of ownership based on the production brigade" [national level, People's Commune, production brigade]. What replaced it was a rural governance system composed of "township governments" and "villagers' self-governance organizations." This basic framework for governance implemented a system in which "government" and "society" were now separate from one another. It established township governments, and set up "villagers' committees" and "villagers' small groups." The primary functions of the township governments were threefold:

Table 10.2 Fund sources of public products and public services in rural areas

Supplier	Fund source
Commune finance	State budgetary revenue, including enterprise income, agricultural tax, industrial and commercial tax, animal slaughter tax, etc., and fines and confiscations Local extra-budgetary revenue, namely shared revenue distributed by superior finance that was not included in local budget, such as shares from agricultural surtax, industrial and commercial surtax, and industrial-commercial income surtax Commune revenue, namely internal accumulation of collective economy, such as income from commune-run enterprises and institutions, accumulation fund, etc.
Production brigade	Accumulation fund, welfare fund, and management fee (mainly the former two), directly set aside from revenues of production brigades Manpower used in farmland irrigation and water conservancy, training of militias, and management of production teams for which work point subsidies were received to participate in revenue distribution

Source: Qu Yanchun, *Evolution and Restructuring: Study on the Public Product Supply System in Rural China*, Beijing: People's Publishing House, 2012 edition

develop the local economy, provide public services, and maintain social stability. As these township governments were established and as the definition of the township as a proper level of government with a corresponding budget was clarified, revenue sources and expenditure requirements also became more clear (see Table 10.3). The funding sources of a township were threefold: (1) funds "inside the budget," which supported agricultural production, the building of basic infrastructure, the provision of public services, wages and salaries for administrative personnel, and public expenses; (2) funds "outside the budget" [or extra-budgetary], the spending of which mainly went to support normal operations of government departments, including office supplies, travel and communication costs, and entertainment; (3) self-generated funds, the spending of which mainly went to rural public construction projects, public services, education, and the rural collective's welfare benefits. Meanwhile, at the ultimate grassroots level, towns and villages adopted a "villagers' self-governance system." Revenues for financing the village collective came mainly from taxes and fees [defined as *ti-cheng*, deductions from money owed to farmers for their production] and from direct levies on farmers of three kinds: for the public accumulation fund, for the welfare benefits fund, and for "management fees." In addition, village collectives directly assessed a variety of other taxes and fees on farmers (see Table 10.4).

Under this kind of governance system and fiscal system, revenues coming into the "inside-the-budget" part of the system were able to keep the budget mainly in balance. Outside-the-budget funds were used to support the daily operations of grassroots government and to provide public goods for the township, which

Table 10.3 Incomes and expenditures of township governments

Financial revenue	State budget	Income tax and bonus tax from township enterprises, animal slaughter tax, urban maintenance and construction tax, open fair transaction tax, domestic animal trade tax, license tax of vehicles and vessels, deed tax, and other incomes
	Extra-budgetary funds	Agricultural surtax and rural education surtax appropriated to township finance by superior governments, extra-budgetary income managed by administrative institutions, and public utilities surtax collected by towns in line with State rules
	Self-raised funds	Public utilities surtax levied for rural schools, family planning, special care of families of soldiers, training of militia and road transport
Financial expenditure	State budget	Administrative management fee appropriated to township finance by superior governments, expenditure on culture, education, science and health, expenditure on agriculture, forestry and water conservancy, and other expenditures
	Extra-State budget	Expenditure on arrangement of preceding additional incomes and extra-budgetary incomes of administrative institutions
	Expenditure using	Township and village schools, family planning, special care, training of militia, building village roads,
	Self-raised funds	Five-Guarantee work and other causes run by local people with state subsidy

Source: Based on *Trial Measures for Township Financial Management*, issued by the Ministry of Finance in 1985; "Self-raised Funds" and Expenditure Using Self-raised Funds" are based on *Regulation on Administration of Fees and labors Born by Farmers*, issued by the State Council in December 1991.

Table 10.4 Incomes and expenditures of villages

Income source	Expenditures
Appropriation from superior	Fixed assets
Direct production	Production
Handovers from enterprises	Internal/external investment
Property sales and leasing	Public utilities
Paid use of house sites	Public welfare
Family planning fines	Handovers to superior
Deduction of farmers' payment and fund raising	Administrative management fee
Levies on behalf of superior	Other expenditures
Other incomes	

Source: Based on survey results of *Study on Rural Finance and Public Administration in China* taskforce; Song Hongyuan et al., *Study on Rural Finance and Public Administration in China*, China Financial & Economic Publishing House, 2004 edition

included such things as maintaining farm fields, repairing school buildings, repairing local roads, and so on.

Out of the need to maintain government operations and the local economy, however, grassroots governments also began to extract additional taxes and fees from farmers, and these demands became ever more onerous. During the period of the People's Communes, this burden had mainly been borne by the rural collective and mostly by the production brigade. Individual farmers had not felt its impact. Although the burden was heavy at that time as well, it did not become an intense social problem. Now, however, farmers themselves have become the primary entities bearing the burden on behalf of the local collective as well as the State, so they are beginning to have a direct visceral understanding of how that feels. According to relevant statistics, in 1985, farmers had to pay the following aggregate amounts in taxes: agricultural tax, RMB 4.7 billion; "people-funded" education, RMB 1.6 billion; support for the "five-protected types of households," RMB 1 billion; care for dependents of military heroes, RMB 500 million; culture and public health, RMB 2 billion; highway maintenance by civilian workers, RMB 2 billion; family planning programs, RMB 3.2 billion; subsidies for grassroots cadres and cadres not engaged in active duty, RMB 7 billion; assorted other fees, RMB 4 billion. The total came to RMB 25.7 billion, or RMB 31 per member of the rural population. Given that the per capita net income of a farmer in 1985 was RMB 397.6, this sum represented 8 percent of net income (Yu Depeng, 2007). By 1990, the tax burden levied on farmers had reached RMB 149, and by 1991 the burden came to 13 percent of a farmers' net per capita income (Chen Huadong et al., 2007).

The excessive burden now being borne by farmers is leading to an increased frequency of *in extremis* incidents of a horrific nature. According to statistics, in 1992 alone, seventeen incidents in nine provinces involved people who were hounded to death as a result of excessive tax burdens. (The provinces were Jilin, Hubei, Hunan, Sichuan, Hebei, Henan, Jiangsu, Anhui, and Gansu.) In 1993, there were more than thirty incidents nationwide of "very large" incidents including large-scale mass conflicts between cadres and people, people hounded to death [forced to commit suicide], and people beaten to the extent they were crippled. In 1994, there were nine incidents of deaths involving excessive burdens on farmers (Li Maolan, 1996). In order to decrease the load on farmers, in December of 1991, the State Council issued a document that explicitly regulated the items that were taxable and the amount of funds that local governments could extract from farmers. This was called *Regulations on fees borne by farmers and the administration of labor requirements*. It said that the units representing rural areas, namely rural collective economic organizations and township governments, could not extract more than 5 percent of the net per capita income of farmers in any given year, in the form of either "deducted amounts" [*ti-liu*] collected by the rural collective economic organizations or "comprehensive fees" [*tong-chou fei*] collected by township governments. It added that the "accumulation fund" was to be spent on farmland irrigation and water conservancy projects, reforestation, purchase of production-related fixed assets, and start-up collective enterprises. The "welfare benefits fund" was to be spent on the Five-Guaranteed Households, relief for families in distress, collective medical services, and other public-welfare causes. The management fees alone were to be spent on compensation for cadres and management expenses.

Rural public finance faces a dilemma. On the one hand, the rampant and capricious levying of fees and allocations as a way to generate funds has no standing in law, it increases the burden on farmers, and it is leading to increased conflict between the people and the government. On the other hand, not only does the State have insufficient funds to cover all spending, but a large percentage of township governments are at the mercy of unstable revenue sources. Over half of the "administrative villages" in the country are "hollowed-out villages" with no stable income. Meanwhile, rural governments are heavily indebted (see Box 10.1). Many villages are just bringing in enough fiscal revenue to survive. The ability of grassroots organizations to provide public goods and services is going down to such an extent that the most basic requirements are not being met, things like repairing ditches, paying for basic education, and providing healthcare. A comparison with the prereform period of the People's Communes is instructive: the coverage of rural cooperative healthcare went from the previous 90 percent of the rural population to 4 percent in 1989 (Zhang Yuanhong, 2006). During the People's Commune period, agricultural technology was promoted and supplied by four levels of organizations, namely county, commune, production brigade, and production small team. It is now supplied by two levels, namely county and township.

Box 10.1   Rural debt

The problem of rural debt arose in the latter part of the 1980s and became widespread by the late 1990s. Indebtedness came about as a result of five factors: first, launching public-welfare endeavors; second, "blind" investment in rural enterprises [investing with no regard for what the market might be since costs were covered by public funds]; third, paying costs up-front on the expectation of taxes and fees to be collected in the future; fourth, extremely high interest rates on loans; and fifth, daily costs of operating the town or village.

1.   From the early 1980s to the early 1990s

Debt that formed during this period was often the result of investing in township enterprises that had unclear property rights associated with them [the "absent owner syndrome" with no accountability when assets or funds went missing]. They also came about because township assets were used as collateral for town-and-village enterprise loans. During this period, all levels of local government issued policies encouraging the establishment of such town-and-village enterprises as a way to drive the economy and increase local public revenues. Town-and-village enterprises flourished as a result. Later, when business did not develop as expected, localities were left with large amounts of debt. This period represented the first high wave of rural indebtedness. Interest rates on the debt were quite high. The usual bank or credit union charged more than 18 percent, but some rural loans were charging 30 percent. The high interest rates put an increasingly heavy debt burden on towns and villages.

2. From the mid-1990s to 2005

Since the mid-1990s, in addition to the formation of a second high wave of enterprise debt, the main cause of rural indebtedness was the attempt to cover budgetary deficits by increasing debt loads. The gap in spending for education was one of the primary reasons for taking in loans during this period.

3. Since 2006

Since 2006, the rural indebtedness of China has entered what could be called a "post–taxes and fees era," an era in which the central government has begun to be more proactive in resolving rural debt issues. Three reforms have been most closely tied to this process: one relating to rural debt and township institutions, one relating to rural compulsory education, and one relating to county and township fiscal management systems. In the course of the tax-and-fee reform of the previous stage, indiscriminate collecting of fees in rural governance led to exposure of the rural debt problem. In 2006, the State Council issued an Opinion called *Opinion on work to be done in order to clean up rural debt.* This said that priority should be given to "dissolving" debt that had been incurred for the purpose of paying for rural compulsory education. In 2007, the General Office of the State Council put out *Notification for transmitting on to the State Council's "rural comprehensive reform small group" regarding cleaning up and dissolving rural debt incurred to pay for nine-year compulsory education in rural areas: pilot-program recommendations."* This recommended dissolving this portion of the rural debt. In 2009, a Number One document proposed that in dissolving rural debt in "an active but stable way," with the aim of completing the task of dissolving compulsory-education-type debt in rural areas, the country should continue to pursue pilot projects that dissolve rural debt formed for the purpose of paying for public-interest endeavors that are directly related to farmers' interests.

Given three new policy approaches, safeguards to shore up the capacities of county and township finances gradually improved the situation. The three new policy approaches were the "three rewards and one subsidy" policy and the two reforms of the public-finance management system, namely "provinces directly manage county finances" and "counties directly manage township finances." Considerable progress was made in resolving rural debt, with nine-year compulsory education being the main breakthrough area. Nine-year compulsory education debt was completely eliminated in some areas.

Source: Du Shuang, *Study on Rural Debt*, Zhengzhou: Henan People's Publishing House, 2008 edition; Song Hongyuan, *Review and Evaluation of Agricultural and Rural Policies during the 11th Five-Year Plan Period*, Beijing: China Agriculture Press, 2010 edition.

The burden on farmers increased after implementation of the 1994 "division-of-tax reform"

Once township organizations had been set up throughout China, the increased functions of these organizations led to a rapid increase in their personnel. The burden of paying for the employees therefore also increased, to the extent that a fair percentage of township organizations were unable to continue normal operations by the mid- to late 1990s. In 1994, the division-of-tax reform resulted in weakened financial authority on the part of township governments. Nevertheless, the tasks that township governments were responsible for constantly increased, given that this governing level was on the low end of the entire spectrum of government. In 1993, the ratio at which total fiscal revenues were assigned to central and local governments was 22:78; that is, 22 percent went to the central government, while 78 percent went to local governments. By 1994, the ratio became 56:44; that is, 56 percent went to the central government, while only 44 percent went to local governments. Meanwhile, the term *local governments* includes four separate levels of government including province, municipality, county, and township. The amount of fiscal revenue actually reaching grassroots-level governments therefore became minimal. The finances of county and township governments were now in very dire straits. At the same time, the amount of public finance that the State spent on supporting agriculture not only did not go up but actually went down (see Table 10.5).

With inadequate public spending coming from the central government, such public endeavors as basic infrastructure, basic education, and healthcare in rural areas now relied mainly on local governments. These expenses local governments paid by levying taxes on farmers. The taxes were encapsulated in the terms "three deductions [*ti*] and five levies [*tong*]." Local governments paid via "raising funds," "apportionments" [apportioning costs over the population], accumulating labor credits, and "voluntary labor." The general situation was summed up by the saying, "the first tax (agricultural) is manageable, the second (township levies and village deductions) is tough, and the third (additional ways of "raising funds" and apportioning costs) is a bottomless pit" (see Table 10.6). In addition, there were fees on everything and arbitrary additional costs, so that the burden on farmers grew

Table 10.5 Revenue and expenditure of central and local finance, 1993–1999

Year	National financial revenue (RMB)	Financial revenue of the central government (RMB)	Financial revenue of local governments (RMB)	Central financial revenue vs. local financial revenue (%)	
1993	4,348.95	957.51	3391.44	22.02	77.98
1994	5218.1	2,906.5	2,311.6	55.7	44.3
1995	6242.2	3,256.62	2,985.58	52.2	47.8
1996	7,407.99	3,661.07	3,746.92	49.4	50.6
1997	8,651.14	4,226.92	4,424.22	48.9	51.1
1998	9,875.95	4,892	4,983.95	49.5	50.5
1999	11,444.08	5,849.21	5,594.87	51.1	48.9

Year	National financial expenditure	Financial expenditure of the central government	Financial expenditure of local governments	Central financial expenditure vs. local financial expenditure	
1993	4,642.3	1,312.06	3,330.24	28.3	71.7
1994	5,792.62	1,754.43	4,038.19	30.3	69.7
1995	6,823.72	1,995.39	4,828.33	29.2	70.8
1996	7,937.55	2,151.27	5,786.28	27.1	72.9
1997	9,233.56	2,532.5	6,701.06	27.4	72.6
1998	10,798.18	3,125.6	7,672.58	28.9	71.1
1999	13,187.67	4,152.33	9,035.34	31.5	68.5

Source: *China Statistical Yearbook.*

Table 10.6 Financial revenue and fund-raising of townships in China, 1996–2000

Year	Total financial revenue of townships (RMB 100 million)	Fund-raising and charges of township (RMB 100 million)	Percentage of fund-raising and charges in township financial revenue (%)
1996	802	272.9	34.03
1998	869.9	337.31	38.78
1999	969.8	358.86	37
2000	1026.65	403.34	39.29

Source: Data for 1996, 1998, and 1999 from *China Fiscal Yearbook 2000*; data on total township financial revenue in 2001 from *China Fiscal Yearbook 2001*; data on fund-raising and charges of townships from *China Fiscal Yearbook 2001*.

increasingly onerous (see Table 10.7). According to a survey done in a particular county-level municipality, by 1999, these various *ti-liu* and *tong-chou* fees had gone up by more than ten times what they had been in the mid-1980s. The total sum of fees took up between 10 percent and 15 percent of a farmer's per capita net income. In addition to the taxes prescribed by law, however, which included

Table 10.7 Burdens on farmers, 1994–1999

Year	Agriculture-related taxes		Deductions and charges		Social burdens		Accumulation labor and voluntary labor	
	Total	Per capita (RMB)	Total	Per capita (RMB)	Total	Per capita (RMB)	Total	Per capita (RMB)
1994	231.49	25.3	365.8	40.0	70.5	7.7	71.1	16.4
1995	278.09	30.3	487.0	53.2	114.9	12.6	68.1	15.5
1996	369.46	40.2	605.9	65.9	131.2	14.3	105.7	23.7
1997	397.48	43.4	645.5	70.5	134.9	14.7	81.7	18.2
1999	423.50	45.9	602.0	65.3	256.0	27.8	84.4	18.0

Note: "Agriculture-related taxes" include agricultural tax, animal husbandry tax, farmland occupation tax, special agricultural taxes, and deed taxes. "Social burdens" include fund-raising, administrative charges, and fines and confiscations.

Source: Ma Xiaohe, *Study on Rural Tax Payment Reform in China*, Beijing: China Planning Press, 2002 edition
Unit: RMB100 million

the agricultural tax and the *ti-liu* and *tong-chou* fees, this particular county-level municipality in the survey also apportioned "costs" to farmers that totaled RMB 40.85 million. This amount came to RMB 87.3 per farmer. The "extra" burden was a full 40 percent of the normal tax burden. In this place, farmers were being taxed for more than thirty separate items (Xiao Yang, 2000). With the intensification of tax-related conflicts between farmers and grassroots governments, mass incidents have become more common. The *in extremis* kind of "horrific" mass incident has also become more frequent.

The State's policy of "extending more to farmers and taking less" after the rural tax-and-fees reform

In 2000, the central government initiated rural "tax-and-fees reform" in order to relieve the tax burden on farmers and resolve the problems of rural grassroots governance in a more fundamental way. From 2001, the central government implemented pilot projects in certain provinces and municipalities and then gradually extended those experiments to other areas. By January 1, 2006, the central government had completely abolished the agricultural tax, which greatly reduced the burden on farmers. In contrast to the situation in 1999, prior to the rural tax-and-fees reform, the total reduction of that specific part of farmers' "burden" came to over RMB 100 billion every year. In per capita terms, that came to around RMB 120 (Ministry of Agriculture, 2007).

These reforms resulted in massive changes in rural finance, in the sources of funds, in the method of taking in funds, and in the primary entities responsible for supplying rural public goods. The changes came about from the elimination of the "four agriculture-related taxes" (the agricultural tax itself, the special agricultural tax, the animal husbandry tax, and the animal slaughter tax), the elimination of township levies (for rural schools, family planning, special treatment for the families of military personnel, militia training, and road building), and the elimination of the village management fee. Except for certain items that villagers themselves felt should be funded via pooled money or pooled labor, each of which was subject to specific review, the State, at the national level, now became responsible for providing public goods that previously had been the responsibility of township governments and villages. State spending on the fiscal needs of rural areas therefore gradually increased. Between 2006 and 2012, the amount of central-government spending dedicated to farmers, farming, and the rural economy went from RMB 317.3 billion to RMB 1.23876 trillion. Central-government spending on these three agriculture-related areas rose from 7.9 percent to 9.8 percent of total fiscal spending.

Rural tax-and-fee reform was able to shift the State's policy toward farmers, in the direction of what now could be characterized as "extend more and extract less." Meanwhile, the central government quickly took the opportunity to push forward a major policy initiative on "comprehensive rural reform" (see Box 10.2). This represented an attempt to "straighten out" and improve the allocation of interests in the relationship between the State and farmers. This comprehensive reform aims to reform township organizations, rural compulsory education, and county and township fiscal management systems. It aims to set up operating mechanisms and rural administrative structures that are more professional and effective, public finance systems that cover both urban and rural areas, and government guarantees for compulsory education in rural areas. It includes further efforts to reduce the tax burden on farmers, increase their incomes, and push forward rural social endeavors. The assistance that State finance is now providing in support of farmers, farming, and the rural economy has resulted in a major transformation of priorities, to the extent that farmers are beginning to see the light of a new dawn in terms of more equal distribution of basic public services.

Box 10.2 Comprehensive rural reform

In October 2006, the State Council issued a Notification, *Notification on various work issues surrounding comprehensive rural reform.* This called for the basic completion of three primary tasks within the 11th Five-Year Plan period or at least within a slightly longer period. The three primary tasks are reform of township organizations, reform of rural compulsory education, and reform of the fiscal management structures of counties and townships. Each is now described,

1. Reform of township organizations

The overall requirements of this reform are the following. First, adhere to principles of appropriate solutions for local conditions, greater simplification and efficacy, and authorities that are in line with accountabilities. With respect to those principles, the aims were to transform government functions, streamline staff in organizations, improve administrative efficiency, establish a code of behavior, coordinate operations, and create operating mechanisms and grassroots administrative management structures that are clean [noncorrupt], efficient, open, and transparent.

Priorities for township governments are to strengthen the following functions:

First, stabilize the "basic operating system" in rural areas, preserve and protect the rights and interests of farmers and confirm their status as a mainstay of the country, organize the building of basic infrastructure in rural areas, and improve social service systems for agriculture. Second, speed up rural social endeavors in order to provide greater public services to farmers. Third, strengthen social management, which includes launching efforts to alleviate poverty and provide emergency relief, ameliorating rural social conflicts, and maintaining rural social stability. Fourth, promote the building up of democratic governance in rural areas and self-governance by villagers, raise awareness and understanding of the democratic rule of law among farmers.

In so doing, restructure township government organizations in ways that strictly limit the number of employees in leadership positions, reform and restructure "township stations," and create innovative new ways to provide services. Draw up a list of the actual names of people on staff, set up mechanisms to coordinate among departments, including the organization department [*bian zhi*] and personnel and finance departments. Ensure that within five years the number of people on the payroll of township organizations has gone down, not up. Comply with State regulations in ensuring that social security is provided for personnel working in township units, and make sure that those people who are taken off the payroll are resettled properly.

2.   Reform of rural compulsory education

The overall requirements of this reform are as follows. Set up mechanisms that safeguard the funding of rural compulsory education by strengthening government investment in schools, ensuring that responsibilities are explicit at each level of government, ensuring that each level of government spending bears a portion of the costs and that spending consistently goes up. Push forward comprehensive reform of rural education by raising the quality of education and the equal ability of all to get an education. Deepen reforms that have to do with educational personnel, and ensure that a qualifications system is applied to people who become teachers. Find innovative ways to provide subsidies to teachers, establish a monitoring and performance evaluation system with respect to teachers and courses, and improve the caliber of rural teachers overall. Improve staff management in primary schools and middle schools, and be firm about dismissing any staff or teachers who are not qualified. Allocate urban versus rural education resources in a reasonable way, set up a system that encourages teachers and college graduates from cities to teach in rural areas and set up specific positions for such people.

Set up modern long-distance learning systems in rural grade schools and middle schools. Create a reasonable geographic distribution of schools in rural areas. It is strictly forbidden to build schools in excess of those that are necessary [as an excuse to get public funds or land-use rights] or to undertake activities that are impractical just to reach performance goals. Raise the effectiveness with which educational resources [i.e., public funds] are used.

3.   Reform of county and township fiscal management structures

The overall requirements of this reform are the following. First, abide by principles as required by a form of public finance that operates under a socialist market-economy system. Set up improved fiscal management systems under the provincial level that match up sources of funding with governing responsibilities. Explicitly define and differentiate the spending responsibilities of county and township governments. Adjust the distribution of revenues among different levels of government in a reasonable way. Increase the amount of transfer payments that go to county and township governments and go further in improving fiscal policies that provide rewards and subsidies in order to be absolutely sure that grassroots governments have the ability to pay the costs of governing. Improve the distressed financial situation of counties and townships by putting into effect the policy to provide subsidies to the town level of governments, while at the same time ensuring that township institutions and rural organizations operate as they should. Readjust the structure of public-finance spending. This means constantly increasing the amount spent on agriculture and rural areas and putting any incremental budgetary increases into education, healthcare, and culture in rural areas. Incremental increases in State funds for basic infrastructure should mainly be spent in rural areas. Considerably increase the percentage of government revenue from land transfers that is spent on rural areas. Go further in increasing the amount of funds spent on support of farmers, farming, and the rural economy in general. In places that have the appropriate conditions, continue to push forward the fiscal management-system reform known as "provinces manage counties directly," while "counties govern township finances, but the funds are used by townships." Set up the fiscal reward-and-subsidy policy that is subject to specific review for each item. Gradually create a diversified investment system whereby government spending plays the leading role while farmers are active in fund-raising as well and social forces [private enterprises] also participate on a broad basis. Speed up the process of reforming the system of property rights that defines who owns public-interest endeavors in the countryside. Ensure the sound development of basic infrastructure in rural areas and the sound growth of endeavors that are in the public interest.

Source: Based on the *Report on Agricultural Development of China* (2007–2013).

2. Overall situation with regard to public-finance spending at the current time

Government transfer payments to rural areas have consistently increased in recent years. Meanwhile, a number of considerations are gradually enabling the formation of ways to provide better public services in rural areas. These include the establishment of systems that can provide public-finance coverage in rural areas. They include major improvements in the financial situation of rural areas. They include improvement in the level of guarantees for public services in the areas of agriculture, education, healthcare, transportation, water conservancy, and social security. The scope of things that public finance now covers continues to expand, and we continue to improve public-spending mechanisms and structures.

The amount of State fiscal support for farmers, farming, and rural areas continues to increase at a stable pace

State funds for support of farmers, farming, and rural areas have increased quickly in recent years. From RMB 175.45 billion in 2003, they went to RMB 1.23876 trillion in 2012. Spending on "agriculture" altogether [farmers, farming, and rural areas] has gone from 7.1 percent of total spending to 10.5 percent (see Figure 10.1).

Since 2006, when comprehensive efforts to "promote a socialist new countryside" were launched, the State has further increased its spending on social and

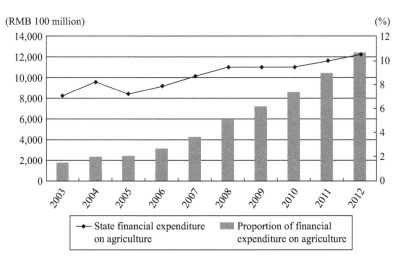

Figure 10.1 Financial expenditure on agriculture and percentage, 2003–2012

Note: Since 2007, statistics on state financial expenditures on agriculture differ from previous years because of readjustment to the financial statement system. Data after 2007 is about central financial expenditures on Sangong.

Source: Department of Rural Surveys, National Bureau of Statistics, *China Rural Statistical Yearbook (2013)*, Beijing: China Statistics Press, 2013 edition.

economic development in rural areas. Spending on agricultural production and related endeavors accelerated between 2007 and 2012, going up at an average annual rate of 21.6 percent. The four subsidies for agriculture (see Box 10.3) and spending on social endeavors in rural areas went up tremendously, at an average annual rate of 26.2 percent and 30.4 percent respectively. Meanwhile, interest-rate subsidies and spending on the reserve for agricultural products also continued to increase at a stable pace (see Table 10.8).

Box 10.3   The "three subsidies" for agriculture goes to "four subsidies"

Many countries use direct subsidies for agriculture as a policy tool to provide financial support for farming. Internationally, developed nations such as the United States and countries in Europe readjusted such policies in the mid- to latter part of the 20th century in ways that allowed for direct subsidies as the primary way to support agriculture. These were aimed at enabling agriculture to withstand various kinds of risk, helping farmers stabilize and increase their incomes, and also protecting the rural environment. China's direct-subsidy policies have been late in coming, but they have developed fairly quickly.

Prior to 2002, the fiscal support that China provided to farmers in the form of direct subsidies was limited to things like paying for withdrawing land from agriculture in order to carry out reforestation. It also was limited to just some parts of the country and just some farmers within those areas. Fiscal support was not applied nationwide, nor was it on a large scale. During the 10th Five-Year Plan period, however, direct spending of central finance funds to farmers was increased in terms of both the type and number of subsidies. The three main types of subsidies that went to farmers directly were for grain production, improved seed varieties, and purchase of farming equipment. The grain subsidy had previously been an indirect subsidy paid out at the "grain circulation" link of the process; this now became a direct subsidy paid directly to those farming grain. The improved-varieties subsidy referred to a program of setting up "demonstration areas" that used improved seed varieties and paying financial subsidies to farmers who then used those improved seed varieties and accompanied their use with the adoption of better technologies. The farm-equipment subsidy referred to a partial subsidy that the State paid directly to those who either purchased or renovated large-scale farming equipment. Recipients included farming individuals, employees of farms, professional farming entities, and institutions and service organizations that were directly engaged in agricultural production.

Between 2000 and 2005, the central government spent a total of RMB 32.02 billion to implement the "three subsidies" policy. Starting in 2006, the State added a fourth subsidy that was called a "comprehensive subsidy for materials used in agricultural production." In 2006, central government spending on these four subsidies came to RMB 30.95 billion. This increased to RMB 162.8 billion by 2011. Over the six-year period, the State spent a total of RMB 593.94 billion on the four subsidies.

The fact that funds for the four subsidies were provided directly to farmers helped realize the intent of the policy, which was to provide assistance to a basic industry that was in a very weak condition. While stimulating increased production of grain, the policy also enormously enhanced the degree to which farmers directly benefited, and it raised the degree to which farming is becoming mechanized.

Source: Han Jun, *Rural Reform of China – Systemic Innovations to Boost the Development of Farmers, Farming, and The Rural Economy (2002–2012)*, Shanghai: Shanghai Far East Publishers, 2012 edition.

Table 10.8 Central financial expenditure on Sangong, 2007–2012

Year	Central financial expenditure on Sangong,	Percentage in State financial expenditure	Growth over previous year	Of which			
				Expenditure on rural production and agricultural projects	Four subsidies	Expenditure on rural social undertakings	Expenditures on reserve of agricultural products and interest
2007	4,318.3	8.70	36.10	1,801.7	513.6	1,415.8	587.2
2008	5,955.5	9.50	37.91	2,260.1	1,030.4	2,072.8	592.2
2009	7,253.1	9.50	21.79	2,679.2	1,274.5	2,723.2	576.2
2010	8,579.7	9.50	18.29	3,427.3	1,225.9	3,350.3	576.2
2011	1,0497.7	9.60	22.35	4,089.7	1,406.0	4,381.5	620.5
2012	12,387.6	9.80	18.00	4,785.1	1,643.0	5,339.1	—

Source: Department of Rural Surveys, National Bureau of Statistics, *China Rural Statistical Yearbook (2013)*, Beijing: China Statistics Press, 2013 edition.

Unit: RMB100 million

Efforts to build basic infrastructure in rural areas have been greatly strengthened

Massive increases in the amount of State public-finance spending on basic infrastructure in rural areas have had a notable effect on improving living conditions for rural residents, as well as on improving agricultural production. Spending has gone for safer drinking water for rural people as well as animals, for renovating the rural electricity [power] grid and roads, and for dealing with methane disposal and the dangerous housing situation (see Box 10.4). Between 2006 and 2013, on a nationwide basis, funding for safe drinking water projects came to RMB 207.53 billion, of which central government spending was RMB 129.7 billion. This improved the safe-drinking water situation for 470 million people. Between 2003 and 2012, a total of 2.92 million kilometers of rural roads across the country were either newly built or rebuilt. Since 2009, the renovation of dangerous housing has gone from pilot projects to becoming a nationwide program; by 2012, it covered all rural areas in the country. The spending on this effort has provided renovations of dangerous housing to more than 10.334 million impoverished households.

Box 10.4   Basic infrastructure development in rural areas

In this new period, the building up of basic infrastructure in rural areas has received enormous support. According to a 2013 survey undertaken by the Rural Economy Research Center in the Ministry of Agriculture, major improvements have come about as a result of the enormous support of State public finance. This survey covered 140 counties and 1,700 farming households in fifteen provinces across the country. Its results showed the following.

Of 126 counties with valid data, a total of 1,200 households now had access to safe drinking water, which was 67.5 percent of all surveyed households. In thirteen of the surveyed counties, all households were completely able to get safe drinking water.

Of 135 counties with valid data, 97.6 percent on average had "constructed villages" that were accessible by roads. Among these, in 113 counties, all "constructed villages" were connected by roads.

In 123 counties with valid data, an electricity grid reached 83 percent of counties on average. In sixty-seven counties, the rural electricity "renovation rate" was 100 percent, which constituted 54.5 percent of the total. On average, 83 percent of households were connected to the grid, and there were sixty-four counties that had a 100 percent rate of renovation of the grid. These sixty-four counties constituted 52 percent of the total. Meanwhile, in 134 counties with valid data, 99.9 percent of villages had a power supply, which meant that basically every town had electricity. The rate of power supply in the households in these villages was 99.9 percent, which meant that basically every household had electricity.

In 127 counties with valid data, 1.97 million households were making use of methane. 101 counties with valid data had 1,342 large and medium-sized methane-utilization plants. Forty-four counties with valid data had 507 plants for centralized biomass gas supply projects.

In 123 counties with valid data, sixty-three had been chosen by higher levels of government as pilot projects for renovation of dangerous housing, or 51.2 percent. Of these, by 2013, higher levels of government had actually conducted the renovations in fifty-seven pilot counties, and an average of 1,274 households had been renovated in each county.

Source: Rural Economy Research Center of the Ministry of Agriculture, *Report on Implementation of Rural Policies (2009–2013)*.

Of particular note is the environmental remediation being undertaken via various methods in China (see Box 10.5). This is due to the increased priority that central finance has placed on improving the rural ecosystem. Starting in 2008, China's central treasury set up a dedicated fund for rural environmental protection. By the end of 2011, this had allocated RMB 8 billion to be used on comprehensive environmental remediation in rural areas. This sum had in turn mobilized RMB 9.7 billion from local government levels. With this funding, 16,300 towns and villages had undertaken environmental control measures, and 42.34 million people had benefited (Li Lihui, 2012). This dedicated fund used such methods as "rewards to replace subsidies" and "rewards to motivate action" as ways to support comprehensive rural environmental controls and to support the creation of "ecological demonstration areas." Starting in 2010, the central government passed a three-year plan of action to rehabilitate contiguous areas of the environment in rural areas and allocated RMB 12 billion in dedicated funds for this initiative. It adopted the method of "rewards to motivate action" in order to improve local rural environments. By the end of 2012, the central government had invested a total of RMB 20 billion into environmental protection projects,[1] which in turn had mobilized RMB 16 billion in funding from local governments as well as the private sector.

Box 10.5   Policy options for using public finance to fund comprehensive rural environmental remediation

Public-finance policy is an effective way to support rural environmental remediation. Quite a few policy tools can help in this effort, including taxes and fees, different kinds of investment, subsidies, and the use of China's financial system structure, as is now described.

1.   Taxes and fees as policy tools

This policy option mainly includes ways to use tax and nontax revenue. Goals to achieve rural environmental remediation can be achieved by formulating tax policies that are selective and graduated, as well as nontax revenue policies, and by using such measures as tax increases or decreases, creation or elimination of taxes, and preferential tax treatment through reductions or exemptions of taxes.

2.   Investment types of policy tools

This policy option mainly includes public spending and government procurement. Public spending is mainly done to provide financial backing, while government procurement is mainly to provide policy guidance and to incentivize social [private-sector] funding to enter into the sphere of rural environmental remediation.

3.   Subsidy types of policy tools

This policy option mainly includes subsidies and government guarantees. Such measures can provide substantial incentives. Current subsidies being used include those for withdrawing land from farming and putting it into either trees or grasslands, subsidies for "ecosystem public-interest [not-for-profit] reforestation," and so on. Up to now, China has not provided many government guarantees in the sphere of rural environmental protection, and such guarantees should be increased. First, the government should use the flexibility and manageability of public-finance subsidies to support environmental-protection behavior on the part of rural residents. Second, it should use the "guidance effect" of public-finance guarantees to enable market mechanisms to play a role in environmental protection. That is, it should take advantage of corporate forces in the effort to push forward comprehensive rural environmental remediation.

4.   Institutional ways to structure finance, as policy tools

This policy option is mainly based on the "division-of-taxes" public-finance system in China and the system of transfer payments. The public-finance system aspect mainly provides institutional support for comprehensive remediation, that is, it emphasizes structural elements. The transfer-payment aspect is a reflection of the way funds are allocated among levels of government. This policy option is currently the most important policy tool being used with respect to environmental remediation. The existing transfer-payment system has set up a variety of dedicated types of transfer payments that are specifically to be used on rural environmental protection. In applying this policy instrument, the government must ensure smooth financial relationships among government levels; it must ensure that the financial authorities of each level are properly matched to the functional authorities. On the macro level, this means providing institutional support for comprehensive rural environmental remediation; on the micro level, this means meeting the funding needs for comprehensive rural environmental improvement.

Source: Liaoning Research Institute for Public Finance, *Financial Policies for Comprehensive Rural Environmental Remediation*, website of the Ministry of Finance, November 28, 2011.

Major efforts are being put into supporting the development of social endeavors in rural areas

The nation's spending on social endeavors in rural areas has been substantially increased. Areas that are now covered include the following: guarantees for costs of compulsory education, training of farmers for nonfarming jobs, rural healthcare, the establishment of a rural social security system, cultural and sports programs, work to do with rural demographics and family planning, poverty alleviation and disaster relief, among others. As a result, rural basic education, healthcare, and levels of social security have notably improved. By 2012, close to 130 million students were enjoying the results of the policy that eliminates school fees and that allows for the free use of textbooks. In addition, more than 30 million boarding students had their boarding fees waived. In the central and western parts of the country, more than 12 million boarding students from economically distressed families were being given living allowances. By the end of 2012, the great majority of rural areas across the country were implementing a policy of free lunches for students, a policy that was benefiting 26 million children. In 2014, the central government passed the *National Plan for Early Childhood Development in Impoverished Areas*. This provides certain guarantees for the children of vulnerable families who live in impoverished zones; the guarantees begin at birth and end only after the age of compulsory education. In healthcare, pilot projects for the "new countryside rural cooperative healthcare" program were launched in 2003, with funding of RMB 10 per year per person which came from central and local public finance; in 2010, the subsidy amount was raised to RMB 120 per person per year, and coverage of the "new countryside cooperative healthcare program" was extended to all residents in rural areas. In 2012, the subsidy amount was again raised to RMB 240 per person per year. In 2013, it went to RMB 280, and in 2014 it went to RMB 320. Meanwhile, the percentage of hospital costs that could be reimbursed went up to around 75 percent, while safeguards against major illnesses also were increased. In the second half of 2009, the country launched pilot programs in "new countryside social pension insurance." By 2012, within the short space of three years, this program basically provided coverage for all. In 2014, the country began establishing a nationwide, unified, basic pension insurance system for residents of both urban and rural areas. Meanwhile, the minimum living allowance system that had begun in 2007 for rural residents will now be incorporating all eligible rural impoverished families. In 2012, the average amount of this minimum living allowance was RMB 2,067.8 per person per year. In 2012, the program was directly benefiting more than 53.4 million impoverished farmers.

Using a variety of channels to help increase agricultural production

Public finance has played an extremely important role in improving the conditions that relate to agricultural production and in supporting the development of agriculture in general. The central treasury has put more funding into agricultural sciences and the training of agricultural professionals. It has put funding into supporting R&D projects and into transforming science into agricultural results. Through the use of such nationally funded approaches as the 863 Program, the 973 Program, the Key Technology R&D Program, and the National Natural Sciences Foundation, the central treasury has selected projects relevant to agriculture for special support. Starting in 2005, it set up a fund for activities to "enrich people and strengthen counties, and to support the regional development of specialty products." In 2007, it set up a fund for developing modern production systems in agriculture, which then launched improved production technologies for some fifty primary agricultural products including wheat, beef cattle, and bulk vegetables. In 2009, the Ministry of Agriculture and Ministry of Finance jointly launched a reform to improve grassroots agricultural technology and a project to establish "model" counties in this regard. By 2011, 800 model counties had been set up nationwide, and the central treasury had invested RMB 800 million in the project. Each county received RMB 1 million in subsidies, which were used on the use and dissemination of agricultural technologies.

Another priority area in which public finance has extended support to farmers and farming has involved banking and finance. This has aimed at developing rural finance and rural insurance. First, in recent years, the central government has launched pilot projects at the county level to encourage banks to extend loans for agriculture. This has been done through an incentivized rewards program. In 2009, county financial institutions that had increased their agricultural loans over the previous year by more than 15 percent were given a 2 percent incentive payment on the portion of loans over that 15 percent. This incentive payment was paid for by both central and local public finance according to an established percentage. In 2009 and 2010, central finance invested RMB 1.729 billion in this program, which mobilized a total amount of loans for agricultural purposes that came to RMB 86.5 billion. Second, subsidies have been allocated to financial institutions that target the "new countryside" initiative. Starting in 2008, central finance dispersed these subsidies to rural financial institutions such as town and village banks and rural credit cooperatives, if they met requisite conditions. This had the effect of guiding "social" [nongovernmental] funds in the direct of the three agricultures [farmers, farming, and the rural economy]. By 2010, subsidies from the central treasury for this program had reached RMB 261 million. Third, public finance launched pilot programs to provide subsidies for agriculture-related insurance. These agriculture-related pilot sites were launched in 2007, and by 2011, the total subsidies that central finance had put into insurance premiums came to RMB 26.21 billion. The resulting insurance covered risks valued at over RMB 1.5 trillion.

3. Main problems with public spending at the present time

In recent years, the increase in total public spending on farmers, farming, and the rural economy has played a tremendous role in providing basic public goods and services and in strengthening infrastructure in rural areas, as well as in furthering agricultural development. Results have been apparent. Nevertheless, due to obstacles caused by historic "debts" and the dualistic urban–rural system, provision of public goods in rural areas is still highly inadequate. Indeed, the unequal situation between public services in urban and rural areas is still extreme. Not only are public-finance inputs not yet enough, but problems still exist in methods of spending and the mechanisms by which funds are used.

Inadequate public-finance spending

First, the quantity of public funds that go to rural areas is inadequate

The degree of inadequate spending by China on rural areas is extreme. The international experience shows that the turning point in a national economy comes when agricultural value-added becomes less than 10 percent of GDP. That is, when agriculture goes below 10 percent of an economy, the government needs to put more into agriculture to develop it. Developed economies have one aspect in common: the smaller the share of the agricultural sector in the economy, the more the government supports agriculture in order to keep it going. By 2013, China's agricultural value-added had already come down to being 10.01 percent of GDP (see Table 10.9), which means that China is now in the position of having to put more into its agricultural sector.

Between 2007 and 2009, OECD countries subsidized agriculture at a rate of 22 percent, that is, 22 percent of total agricultural revenues came from subsidies. In South Korea, the figure was as high as 52 percent; in Japan it was 47 percent, in Canada 17 percent, and in the European Union 23 percent. In China, it was a mere 9.1 percent. Meanwhile, in South Korea and Japan, the total amount of agricultural subsidies came to roughly 64 percent of the value of each country's total

Table 10.9 Percentages of agricultural added value in GDP in some countries

Year Country	2004	2005	2006	2007	2008	2009	2010	2011	2012	2013
Argentina	10.41	9.4	8.39	9.39	9.84	7.5	10	9.09	10.05	6.68
Australia	3.48	3.27	3.09	2.37	2.44	2.37	2.28	—	—	2.4
Brazil	6.91	5.71	5.47	5.56	5.91	5.63	5.3	5.46	5.24	5.71
Germany	1.1	0.87	0.85	0.96	0.9	0.82	0.88	—	—	0.78
Republic of Korea	3.73	3.33	3.16	2.88	2.68	2.78	2.56	—	—	2.34
Russian Federation	5.62	4.97	4.52	4.41	4.4	4.68	4.04	—	—	3.94
France	2.46	2.29	2.11	2.22	2.06	1.76	—	—	—	1.8
Canada	2.17	1.84	1.66	1.69	1.91	—	—	—	—	—
Mexico	3.85	3.72	3.67	3.64	3.65	3.95	3.91	3.73	4.07	3.48
United States	1.35	1.21	1.04	1.13	1.22	1.1	1.18	—	—	—
South Africa	3.11	2.67	2.88	3.37	3.22	3.04	2.48	2.4	2.57	2.39
Japan	1.32	1.22	1.18	1.15	1.14	1.16	1.16	—	—	—
Saudi Arabia	3.96	3.24	2.95	2.78	2.3	2.93	2.49	—	2.24	—
Turkey	10.92	10.8	9.52	8.68	8.61	9.35	9.6	9.16	9.02	8.53
UK	1	0.67	0.66	0.69	0.79	0.72	0.72	—	—	0.64
Indonesia	14.34	13.13	12.97	13.72	14.48	15.29	15.31	16.88	12.82	14.43
India	19.03	18.81	18.29	18.26	17.78	17.72	17.74	17.22	17.39	18.2
Italy	2.51	2.19	2.11	2.05	2.01	1.89	1.89	—	—	2.15
China	13.39	12.12	11.11	10.77	10.73	10.33	10.1	10.04	—	10.01

Source: "Global Macro-economic Data", sina.com (http://finance.sina.com.cn/worldmac/indicator_NV.AGR.TOTL.ZS.shtml).

Unit: %

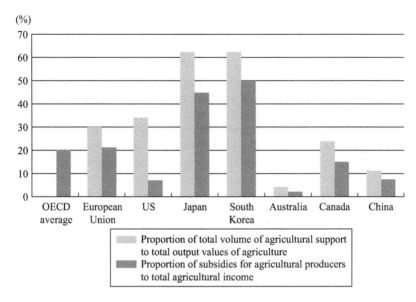

(%)

Figure 10.2 Agricultural support and protection levels of major countries

Source: Han Jun, *Rural Reform of China (2002–2012)*, Shanghai: Shanghai Far East Publishers, 2012 edition.

agricultural output. In the United States, the figure was 36 percent. In the European Union, it was 32 percent, and in Canada, it was 26 percent. In China, the figure was a mere 13 percent (see Figure 10.2). Compared to developed countries, the level of China's support for its agricultural industry is low. At present, China is not at the same stage of development as Organisation for Economic Co-operation and Development countries and therefore cannot reach the subsidy ratios of those countries in any event. Nevertheless, it should be recognized that as China does enter the ranks of middle-income countries, it should constantly increase its public-finance spending on agriculture and certainly should not reduce it.

Second, the supply of public goods in rural areas is lagging behind supply in urban areas

This problem is quite pronounced and can be seen particularly in the severe inadequacy of water-related facilities on farmland [ditches, tiling, drainage, irrigation systems], in problems with drinking water for both humans and animals, in the lack of roads, and in the lack of services to promote new farming technologies.

In terms of water conservancy facilities, 40 percent of large-scale backbone irrigation projects, 50–60 percent of small and medium-sized irrigation projects, and 50 percent of small-scale farm field water conservancy projects are either in disrepair or lack equipment. The problem of irrigation projects "not making it the last kilometer to the actual field" is widespread [that is, the money is spent before the final work gets done].

The situation with regard to safe drinking water is revealed by a survey done by the Rural Economic Research Center in the Ministry of Agriculture in 2013. Among 126 "effectively surveyed counties" [with valid data], 33.5 percent of households did not have safe drinking water at all; another 113 counties did not provide safe drinking water for all households. The situation with regard to roads is similar: at present, 13.5 percent of "constructed villages" are not interconnected with hardtop roads. Meanwhile, rural roads are low-standard, narrow, poorly maintained and cannot stand up to any kind of natural disaster. Some public roads in rural areas have even been "let go" in terms of any maintenance at all.

With respect to basic public services in rural areas, grassroots service organizations that can help promote agricultural technologies have not been developed. The great majority of townships do not have any safety monitoring equipment to test the quality of agricultural products, nor do they have the conditions, ways, and means for regulatory oversight. The country's firefighting system does not operate in most of the countryside. Garbage handling, waste disposal, and other such environmental and hygienic services are simply lacking.

Third, the provision of public services to urban and rural areas is unequal

The unbalanced allocation of public resources between the urban and rural parts of China has led to inequality of basic public services. This is seen most dramatically in the areas of basic education, healthcare services, and levels of social security. All of these lag far behind in the countryside.

Public-finance spending on rural education is one example (see Table 10.10). In 2011, the average per student cost to the government of a normal grade school in cities was RMB 7,037.4. This was RMB 1,271.9 more than government spending per student on a normal grade school in the countryside. The per student cost to the government of a normal middle school in cities was RMB 9,371.7, which was RMB 1,874.5 more than government spending per student on a normal middle school in the countryside. In terms of the caliber of teachers, far fewer teachers in rural areas have college degrees. In 2010, the percentage of teachers with college degrees or above in rural grade schools was 27.9 percentage points lower than it was in urban schools; the percentage of teachers with college degrees in rural middle schools was 19.2 percent lower than it was in urban middle schools.

In the healthcare arena and among available technicians, the situation is similar. In 2012, there was an average of 2.5 medical technicians for every 10,000 people in cities. In rural areas, the figure was just 1 for every 10,000 people. With respect to professional or assistant physicians, the urban-rural ratio was 2.3 to 1. The ratio for registered nurses was 3.4 to 1. In terms of the number of beds in medical clinics, the ratio of availability in cities versus the countryside was 2.2 to 1 in 2012 (see Table 10.11).

Table 10.10 Financial input in urban and rural primary and middle schools

	Regular primary school			Regular middle school		
	School students (10,000)	Financial expenditure per capita (RMB)	Proportion of teachers with college (or above) background (%)	School students (10,000)	Financial expenditure per capita (RMB)	Proportion of teachers with college (or above) background (%)
Urban	2,891.3	7,037.4	49.6	1,783.6	9,371.7	82.0
Rural	6,460.7	5,765.5	21.7	2,975.6	7,497.2	62.8

Note: 1. Data on financial expenditure per capita comes from *China Statistical Yearbook on Educational Expenditure (2012)* on 2011 information; data on proportion of teachers with college (or above) background comes from *China Statistical Yearbook on Educational Expenditure (2011)* on 2010 information. 2. Data on school students is estimated based on the proportion of educational expenditure of educational institutions (national education and other departments) to educational expenditure per capita (national education and other departments) and are respectively 3,050,000 and 5,743,000 lower than the numbers of primary and middle school students in *China Statistical Yearbook*. 3. Data on financial expenditure per capita is estimated based on the revenues of educational institutions from state educational expenditure and the numbers of school students.

Table 10.11 Medical technicians and hospital beds, urban vs. rural, 2012

	Number of medical technicians per 10,000 persons	Number of professional or assistant physicians per 10,000 persons	Number of registered nurses per 10,000 persons	Number of hospital beds per 10,000 persons
Urban	85	32	37	68.84
Rural	34	14	11	31.14

Source: Website of National Bureau of Statistics.

In terms of fund-raising for urban and rural basic medical insurance, in 2012 the payment for new rural cooperative medical insurance was 13.5 percent of that for medical insurances of urban employees. In terms of compensation, in 2012 the average reimbursement of new rural cooperative medical insurance was RMB138 per claim, 34.9 percent and 36.2 percent of that of medical insurance of urban employees and that of urban residents respectively (see Table 10.12).

Table 10.12 shows the gap between urban and rural areas in medical insurance in 2012.

The large urban–rural gap is also found in subsistence allowances. In terms of standard and expenditure, in 2012 the subsistence allowance granted to urban residents was 1.9 times that to rural residents, and the expenditure on subsistence allowance in urban areas was 2.3 times that in rural areas (see Table 10.13).

Table 10.12 Urban–rural gap in medical insurance, 2012

	Urban basic medical insurance		New rural cooperative medical insurance
	Urban employees	Urban residents	
Number of insured (100 million persons)	26,486	27,516	8.05
Fund revenue (RMB100 million)	6,062	877	2,484.7
Number of claims (100 million)	12.3	2.3	17.45
Fund expenditure (RMB100 million)	4,868	877	2,408.0
Proportion of reimbursed hospitalization cost	81%	64%	—

Source: Data on urban basic medical insurance is based on *2012 Status of Social Insurance of China* issued by Ministry of Human Resources and Social Security; data on new rural cooperative medical insurance is based on *2013 China Health Statistics Summary*.

Table 10.13 Urban–rural gap in subsistence allowance, 2012

		Unit: RMB/person/month
	Average subsistence allowance	Average expenditure on subsistence allowance
Urban	330.1	239.1
Rural	172.3	104.0

Source: Ministry of Civil Affairs, *China Civil Affairs Statistical Yearbook (2013)*, Beijing: China Statistics Press, 2013 edition.

Public-finance spending in rural areas is not very effective

At present, the management of public-finance funds in rural areas is dispersed among various entities, since various entities use the funds. There is no systematic way to coordinate fund use overall, which leads to low efficiency in terms of results.

First, management of project funds is not scientific. The authority to allocate State public-finance funds for "agriculture" resides in many different governmental departments. Each does its own allocating and management depending on the size of the project, and there is no overall plan for coordinating projects that are large, medium-sized, or small. Meanwhile, there is no logical and effective way to measure how well a project has been executed in order to evaluate results. The problems of "redundant funds allocation" and "waste of money" are fairly severe.

As a result, it is hard for funds to get down to the ultimate target; the problem of not reaching "the last kilometer" is not infrequent. In addition, departments select and confirm projects on a top-down basis. It is hard for farmers' demands to be transmitted up in the other direction, so that decision making about projects is not well connected with information on what is actually needed. Local governments are also generally looking after their own interests and seeking to gain points in performance ratings. They are not highly motivated to put resources into rural public goods. When they do invest in such things, they have a short-term, quick-results mentality and put their efforts into projects that will gain merit points. As a result, public goods and services that farmers truly need are not provided in any effective way.

Second, the structural allocation of public funds is irrational. Local governments put a substantial portion of the funds into human resources and overhead. Very little is left over that can actually be used to supply rural public goods. According to surveys conducted by relevant institutions, right now around 70 percent of public-finance spending that is to be used on support for farmers goes to paying for administrative overhead, including staff costs. There are inadequate safeguards to ensure that a sufficient portion of limited public-finance funds is used for fundamental, strategic, public-interest-type projects that support agriculture. Spending is particularly insufficient for the parts of the agricultural process that relate to socialized services, industrialized operations, and testing and monitoring of agricultural goods. Instead, more funds tend to go to building new basic infrastructure. The amount spent on revamping and upgrading already built infrastructure is rather little. Meanwhile, the degree to which public-finance funds should be supporting and mobilizing the injection of social [or private] funds into the provision of rural public goods is inadequate. The structures and mechanisms that enable public funds to play a role in guiding and incentivizing private-sector funds are not yet in place. Such types of funds are still at a preliminary stage of "feeling their way forward."

The transfer payment system needs to be improved

First, transfer payments simply cannot make up for the deficits that exist on the balance sheets of grassroots governments. Starting in 2006, the central government began allocating more than RMB 100 billion every year in support of the rural tax-and-fees reform. Of this amount, the central government supported the finances of local governments by transferring RMB 78 billion to their accounts. The aim was to resolve deficits that were being generated by the loss of tax revenue due to reducing and exempting agricultural taxes. However, the central treasury's disbursement of funds was not enough to make up for the financial gap between revenues and expenditures at the township level of government. For example, in 2002, township accounts went down by around RMB 30 billion on a nationwide basis as the result of the loss of revenue from the rural tax-and-fees reform. The amount of transfer funds disbursed by the central government came to RMB 24.5 billion, leaving an ostensible gap of more than 5 billion. However, the actual disparity between revenues and expenditures of townships was more on the order of RMB 90.5 billion. It is estimated that *de facto* total township revenues in 2002 came to around RMB 160 billion, of which the agricultural tax was not quite RMB 45 billion. The rest of the revenues came from the agricultural "specialties" tax, the "three *ti* and five *tong*," the extra rural educational fees as well as indiscriminate other fees. Although the central government allocated RMB 24.5 billion in transfer funds, that still left a huge deficit in township finances. In order to alleviate the shortfall, the State adopted a whole series of measures such as the "three rewards and one subsidy policy," the "provinces directly manage counties policy,"[2] and the "counties manage township finances policy."[3] Despite efforts to transform the functions of governments as a part of the tax-and-fees reform, however, and despite the fact that revenues of grassroots governments declined enormously and consequently also spending, problems did not go away. Fiscal-management structures at government levels below that of provinces still were not matched to functional responsibilities of governments. Nor were the spending requirements and responsibilities of county and township governments well-defined, along with how revenues should be split up between those two governments. A disconnect remained between grassroots-level revenues and governing responsibilities. A major gap remained between revenues and expenditures.

Second, the effectiveness with which transfer payments are utilized is rather low. Administrative responsibilities for handling agriculture and rural affairs in China are divided among a host of departments, including agriculture, forestry, water conservancy, meteorology, the development and reform commission, finance, commerce, science and technology, and the environment. Funds disbursed by the central treasury are divided up into line-item projects, and these are then allocated by the departments at each governmental level, which disburses the funds on down to rural grassroots units. The development goals and plans that each department formulates for its own purposes are not coordinated, however, so that project funds cannot be pooled. This leads to enormous redundancy and wastage. Meanwhile, there is intense competition to get funds from line-item projects, while the process of deciding on how to allocate them is subjective and open to individual discretion. This means that local governments must spend considerable effort to court the people deciding on project funds, leading to a large amount of rent-seeking behavior. After funds for line-item projects are disbursed down to lower levels, communications between central and local levels of government are highly imperfect. Regulatory oversight over the use of funds is split up among many departments, making effective control very difficult. The result is that such practices as embezzlement, interception, "squeezing," and general waste are prevalent. The State Auditor's Office issued a report on the handling of the 2013 budgets of thirty-eight central-level departments stating that there are 363 line-item projects relating to transfer payments and that the problem of overlapping and duplication of efforts is extreme.

Third, with respect to general transfer payments, these funds appear to be misinvested. In recent years, the total sum of general transfer payments to local governments has gone up enormously. The use to which such general payments are put is decided by local governments, however, who generally do not decide to invest them on rural public goods. In addition to the fact that local governments take their own interests and merit points into consideration, one of the main reasons for the improper investment of general transfer payments is that there is a mismatch between the fiscal authorities of central versus local governments and the governing responsibilities of each. Things that should be the responsibility of the central government and provincial governments have been foisted off on lower levels of government. Supply of public goods is a primary example. The burden for providing public goods gets passed all the way down to grassroots governments, who simply cannot handle the load.

Suppliers of public goods in rural areas do not enjoy financial authority that is in line with their functional responsibilities

In providing public goods, the central government should mainly cover things that are national in nature while local governments should carry the burden of handling local-type public goods. However, there has never been a clear demarcation of who is responsible for what among all levels of government – central and provincial, provincial, county, and township – and between townships and the governments of towns and villages. After the division-of-taxes reform in particular [1994], authority over finances was increasingly consolidated at higher levels of government. At the same time, responsibility for carrying out the functions of government was increasingly passed down to lower levels of government. This led to imbalances between the amount of money allocated for government and tasks required of government at both the central and local levels. Since township governments are at the very end of the line in the hierarchy of governments, and since higher levels of government wield control over the hiring and firing of personnel, as well as how to allocate funds, township governments are put in a vulnerable position. They are at the mercy of the commands of those above them, and they are obliged to do tasks that have been "passed down." Not only has this added to the difficulties of grassroots governments, but it has made the burden on farmers themselves much harder to bear.

Table 10.14 details the items that constitute this "burden on farmers" on a nationwide basis. It shows that major problems still exist, such as the 72.2 percent of all family-planning fees [in Chinese, "fees for planned birthing"] that farmers themselves must bear, the total national sum of which comes to RMB 12.12 billion. The actual ways in which this money is spent, however, have never been made publicly available. There is no way to ascertain where this money is now or what resulted from its use. Family planning is in fact a national-level responsibility, a public good that relates to the national well-being. It is unreasonable to ask farmers to pay these fees.

Table 10.14 Farmers' burdens in 2013

	Amount (RMB 100 million)	Proportion (%)	Growth rate (%)
I. Money handed in to collectives	120.1	100	1
1. Land contract	101.8	84.8	2.1
2. Coproduction	5.6	4.7	−13.6
3. House building	3.5	2.9	4.9
4. Miscellaneous	9.2	7.6	−1.8
II. Fund-raising and fund-for-labor by villagers	131.0	100	−20.7
i. Fund raising through specific review	75.0	57.3	−23.9
1. Road	48.7	37.2	−26
2. Water projects	13.0	9.9	−26.8
3. Afforestation	1.2	0.9	−1.9
4. Miscellaneous	12.1	16.1	−12.1
ii. Fund-for-labor through specific review	56.0	42.7	−16
III. Agricultural production fees	149.2	100	−5
1. Water for irrigation	66.8	44.8	−3.8
2. Electricity for irrigation	77.9	52.2	−5
3. Miscellaneous	4.5	3	−19
IV. Administrative charges	167.8	100	15.2
1. House building by farmers	7.3	4.4	−6.8
2. Migrant workers	7.1	4.2	−8.1
3. Agricultural machine, motorcycle, three-wheeler and low-speed lorry	26.2	15.6	−10.7
4. Family planning	121.2	72.2	28.6
5. Miscellaneous	6.0	3.6	−7.4
V. Rural compulsory education fees	15.1	100	−17
1. Exercise book	5.8	38.3	−20.8
2. Agent service	5.7	37.5	−16.2
3. Miscellaneous	3.7	24.2	−11.3
VI. Fines	3.3		−3.4
VII. Fund raising apportionment	1.0	100	−30.6
1. Road	0.6	62.3	−36.7
2. Water projects	0.2	19	−13.2
3. Power projects	0.0	2.6	−52.9
4. Miscellaneous	0.2	16.1	−12.1
VIII. Labor force through specific review	10.5	100	−27.1
1. Road	6.4	61.2	−25
2. Water projects	2.1	20.4	−42.9
3. Afforestation	0.4	3.5	−10.5
4. Miscellaneous	1.6	14.9	−6.5

Source: Department of Rural Economic System and Management, Ministry of Agriculture, *Statistics on Rural Operation and Management (2013)*.

4.   Policy recommendations with respect to increasing public-finance spending

The inadequacy of public spending and the lack of public goods and services in rural areas can be attributed to two things: structural causes and the mechanisms for actually providing public goods. If we are to improve the actual ability to provide public goods by spending public-finance funds, we must look for solutions in the structures and mechanisms by which government operates and public goods are supplied. On the one hand, this means changing government functions and improving the existing structures by which public finance in rural areas operates. On the other hand, it means enabling market mechanisms to play an effective role. That involves exploring multiple channels for providing public goods to rural areas in an effective way.

Set up sound public-finance structures that are conducive to providing public goods in rural areas

In implementing the policy of developing rural and urban areas via an overall plan, one important consideration will be establishing a system of public finance that covers both urban and rural areas alike and that benefits all people in the country. This includes setting up systems for providing public goods that receive support from public finance.

First, we must establish mechanisms that provide for stable increases in spending on farmers, farming, and the rural economy. Given the prevalence of "historic debts" as defined by inadequate rural basic infrastructure and the ongoing inadequate supply of public goods, we should clarify the responsibilities of the central government versus local governments. We should specifically define the percentage that each is to spend out of the total budget and how fast that should increase every year. This must be in the context of a total amount that increases yearly, as well as a percentage for the central government that increases yearly. In line with the needs of unifying urban and rural development into one process, we must increase the pace of building up rural basic infrastructure and rural social endeavors. We must accelerate the speed at which rural conditions are improving, both in terms of living conditions and in terms of production.

China's *Law on Agriculture* explicitly says that the rate of public spending put to agriculture must increase at a pace that is faster than the pace at which government revenues increase. We must continue to put this regulation into effect in a thorough way. At the same time, taking the very practical considerations of the public finances of each level of government into account, we should go further in exploring alternate sources of funding. We recommend that we keep raising the percentage of income from land transfers that goes to the building of rural basic infrastructure. We also recommend that land remediation be incorporated into the scope of activities supported by line-item projects funded by public finance. When operating income is taken in by the central and all levels of government, we recommend that a fixed percentage be applied to spending on farmers, farming, and the rural economy and that we guarantee a stable increase in the amount of budgetary expenditures spent on agriculture. A fixed percentage of the excess budgetary revenue should be allocated to spending on farmers, farming, and the rural economy, so as to supplement insufficient public budgetary funds in those fields.

Second, we must improve the system by which the central government makes transfer payments to local governments. Transfer payments are a way to guarantee that local governments have the capacity to provide public services on an equal basis, as well as being a way to resolve the financial difficulties of local governments themselves. In targeting the existing major problems that plague this whole system, we recommend starting with the following measures in order to create a transfer system that is regulated, impartial [fair], and effective.

First, increase the total amount of funds that are distributed via transfers. This also involves improving the structure of the funds that are transferred. While abiding by the principle of "making adjustments that are appropriate to existing capital, while focusing on key priorities when in any incremental additions," we should increase the percentage of central-government funds that are spent on rural areas. We should improve the transfer-payment system that transfers money from provincial- and municipal-level governments toward counties and township governments. We should increase the strength of support for line-item transfer payments as well as "general transfers." We should optimize the structure of usage, and use general transfer payments to make up for deficits in local-government finances. We should gradually lower and eventually eliminate the percentage of tax-refund projects, which currently constitute a large percentage of all projects. We should carry out transfers that are reasonable and in line with different levels of development in different parts of the country, so that public services are equalized among regions. In the more economically developed parts of eastern China, the percentage of central-government contributions in the form of transfer payments can be somewhat lower; in the central and western parts of the country, it can be higher. The aim is to ensure the supply of public goods as needed in rural areas.

Second, improve methods by which transfer payments are made. We should use the "factor method" instead of the "base-figures" method. In determining and confirming the figures for transfer payments that the central government makes to each local area, we should take a variety of factors into overall consideration. These should include the population in the relevant area, its land area, its per capita amount of arable land, per capita GDP, the living conditions of any ethnic minorities, the natural resources, level of social development, and so on. Then we should make a reasonable estimation of what weighting each of these factors should be given or what numerical value each should be given. We then calculate the total marks that each province, municipality, and autonomous region is qualified to receive in coming up with an ultimate figure of the amount of support each should receive.

Third, place greater emphasis on the performance evaluations that should accompany each transfer-payment project and improve the way we do those evaluations. At present, the central government has already begun to incorporate agriculture-related objectives in performance evaluations, as have some provinces. Nevertheless, the system governing performance evaluations is imperfect. The quality of information relating to evaluations, the validity of results that are cited, and the actual application of funds are all questionable. Projects relating to agriculture are generally broadly based, numerous, and dispersed among departments. They also have differing time cycles. From now on, we therefore should explore a more scientific, logical, and practicable way of evaluating the performance of these projects by improving databases of information and evaluation methods, setting up systems for monitoring results and "assessment-based funds allocation," and influencing the allocation of funding by making the results of such evaluations open and transparent. Through strengthening the application of a performance-evaluation system, we should aim to change the current way people contend to get a project but then shirk on implementation. We should change the way they emphasize initial construction but then neglect the follow-on management. Through these methods, we should aim to improve the effectiveness with which public funds are used, so that limited funds can play a greater role in achieving results.

Fourth, create a sounder structure of laws and regulations so that public-finance transfer payments are carried out within a regulated framework. This means conscientiously implementing the newly revised *Budget Law*. It means defining the fiscal authorities, as well as governing responsibilities of the central government versus local governments. It means formulating stand-alone laws and regulations that have to do with public-finance transfer payments, creating explicit regulations on the policy goals of transfer payments, the sources of funds, the auditing standards that apply, and so on. It means ensuring that there is a body of law on which public-finance transfer payments may rely for their validity and proper execution.

Third, we must create better management mechanisms or policy making on the supply of public goods in rural areas. Current mechanisms decide on policies via a top-down approach, which leads to imbalances in the supply and demand of public goods, as well as simply to inadequate supply. At the earliest possible time, we must set up mechanisms that can reflect the needs of farmers and that allow for bottom-up decision-making processes. We must allow the great mass of farmers to come into and participate in the process of policy formulation with respect to the supply of public goods. This should be done through improving villagers' self-governance mechanisms and setting up not only decision-making and management mechanisms but also regulatory supervision mechanisms. We should improve levels to which farmers are organized so that they can consolidate their own needs and wishes and better participate in policy formulation. We should establish democratic supervisory mechanisms with respect to rural public goods. This means setting up ways of ensuring that information is open and transparent with respect to plans and budgets and that the execution and final results of plans are also open and transparent.

Fourth, we must clarify the responsibilities of each level of government with respect to supplying rural public goods. This involves defining the responsibilities of each major entity involved at each level of government and restructuring the supply system for rural public goods. At present, the primary governmental entities involved in supplying public goods are divided into five levels: central, provincial, municipal, county, and township. Following the principle of a division of governmental authority among governments, those things that are national in character should be funded by the central government, as well as purely public goods; goods that are regional in nature or quasi public should be supplied depending on the scope of the beneficiaries and may be supplied by more than one level of government. Rural social security, rural cooperative healthcare, and so on should mainly be supplied by the provincial level of government with the central government also sharing responsibility. Regional types of disease prevention, promotion of agricultural technologies, rural electrification, and so on should be the responsibility of the municipal or county government. Such things as the building of water conservancy projects, running water facilities, and other such basic infrastructure facilities should mainly be the responsibility of the township, with the next higher level of government providing financial support, while the village committee is responsible for actual implementation. The externalities of rural compulsory education are very significant; for a long time now, the central government and provincial-level governments have not taken enough responsibility in this regard so that grassroots-level governments and farmers themselves have carried the burden. Therefore, the central government and provincial governments should take more responsibility for paying for rural compulsory education.

Fifth, we must change the management functions of grassroots-level governments and organizations. Right now, township governments put too much effort into economic activities while neglecting the task of supplying farmers with public goods. The reason this problem exists, in addition to the fact that it helps reduce financial problems for townships, is that it is created by pressure to perform and meet targets from upper levels of government. We therefore should transform the township duties as defined, that is, change the substance of performance objectives. In designing specific performance goals, we should emphasize the priorities of rural basic education, rural healthcare, rural social security, the education and training of farmers, building up rural basic infrastructure, rural science and technology services, management of family planning, and so on. Second, we should improve the methods by which performance is evaluated. This means setting up decision-making mechanisms that "combine upper and lower," which means not only enabling higher levels of government to constrain the behavior of grassroots governments but enabling farmers themselves to constrain the behavior of grassroots governments.

In addition to executing the duties assigned to them by the villager's self-governance system, the villagers' committees should focus on gathering together, organizing, and reporting on farmers' needs and desires in a timely manner. They should assume responsibility as appropriate for fixing roads, preserving water conservancy facilities, protecting social order, and other such "supplying rural public goods responsibilities" that mainly require labor as opposed to money.

Sixth, we must improve the fund-raising methods and labor-raising methods that are done through specific review, that is, through review of individual propositions, and we should streamline their operating procedures. While firmly adhering to the principle of being on a voluntary basis, having direct benefit, done depending on abilities, democratic decision making, and reasonable limits, we should launch fund-raising and labor-raising public-benefit projects at the village level. Projects that raise funds and labor forces through this specific review process should be rewarded by public finance – which should extend both rewards and subsidies. We should then raise the percentage of public-finance rewards and subsidies and also improve policies so as to strengthen targeted guidance, regulatory oversight, and inspections. We should unify both fund-raising and subsidies and create new mechanisms that allow for a diversity of entities to invest in the building up of village-level public-interest endeavors.

Push forward marketization reforms that involve the supply of rural public goods

In order to enable public finance to be effective in providing public goods in rural areas, we must combine stronger governmental support and government protection with the abilities of the market to make decisions about how to allocate resources. We should enable market-driven forces to participate in supplying public goods.

First, this requires defining the goals of reform, and it means strengthening the government's responsibilities. The government has the primary responsibility for supplying rural public goods in those areas of agriculture and rural development in which the market is ineffective. The government must shoulder that responsibility in a conscientious manner. Then, as per the principle of "the one who pays is the one who benefits, and the one who invests is the one who reaps the rewards," it should also introduce market mechanisms. Via such means as payment of fees, subsidies, or procurement, the government should guide and encourage communities, cooperative organizations, farmers themselves, as well as enterprises, to supply public goods. The government's role should be to set up sound regulatory mechanisms to ensure that the market functions properly; it should be the one to regulate the behavior of communities, cooperative organizations, farmers, and enterprises.

Second, this requires defining "rural public goods" in a more fine-grained way and clarifying the boundaries of responsibilities. In strengthening the ability of public finance to provide rural public goods, the government must truly transform its own functions. It must streamline government and relinquish certain authorities to others, not serve as the end-all and be-all and not interfere as if it were. Any activities that the market can handle should be passed over to the market, and anything that "society" [the private sector or nongovernmental entities] can handle should be passed over to society. Generally speaking, local governments can pass responsibility for quasi public goods over to the market. In order to reduce the burden on government, a diversified supply network should be formed that includes government but also includes rural communities, privately run organizations [businesses], not-for-profit organizations, and private individuals. More specifically, the central government should be the primary supplier of purely public goods in rural areas; these things include environmental protection, large-scale backbone water conservancy projects, basic R&D in agriculture, the prevention and control of agricultural pests that affect the entire country, and so on. These things have significant externalities, and the beneficiaries are not limited to rural areas. The government may cooperate with the private sector in mixed forms of supply entities dealing in quasi public goods. This includes things that have fairly high costs, such as medium-sized water-conservancy projects, rural roads, rural electricity, communications, rural science and technology education and promotion, market development, provision of market information, and so on and that also have external ripple effects. People-operated [private] organizations may be the primary suppliers of things like processing and circulating agricultural goods, technical services, and information guidance [advising]. It may be possible for large agricultural households that have sufficient financial means to construct and repair small-scale water conservancy facilities.

Third, pushing forward market-oriented reforms in the area of rural public goods means promoting the development of market mechanisms that can supply public goods in rural areas. we need to explore effective methods for doing this – create multitiered supply mechanisms, such as a fee-based scheme for quasi public goods, competitive systems and contractual systems, auctioning of special permits, outsourcing via contracts, and so on. We must use a variety of channels for fund-raising – adopt such diverse methods as issuing bonds and industry investment funds, with the money coming from overseas as well as BOT (Build-Operate-Transfer). In doing this, we must always respect the principle of "the one who invests is the one who benefits." The aim is to realize a diversification of property rights and to realize privatization in the course of supplying public goods in rural areas. To the greatest degree possible, we should seek to reorganize and use existing resources and revitalize our existing fixed assets so that we can make use of them.

Notes

1 Please refer to http://www.huanjingchanye.com/html/trend/num-market/2014/0623/1542.html
2 See *Opinions Concerning Promoting the Reform of Direct Management of County Finance* (C.Y. [2009] No. 78), Ministry of Finance, 2009.
3 This is a financial management method whereby townships are independent accounting entities, but county financial authorities directly manage and supervise township financial revenues and expenditures via the form known as "uniform budget and accounts, centralized revenues and expenditures, uniform procurement and bill management."

11 Accelerate reform of the household registration system and promoting the unification of urban and rural development

- Accelerate reform of the system that manages household registrations
- Push forward the process of ensuring that basic public services are provided to all long-term residents in cities
- Push forward mechanisms that enable the transitioning agricultural population to become "urbanized"

The way all countries develop suggests that dualistic structures generally move in the direction of unified systems. Urban and rural economies and societies become one functioning system. Labor, technologies, capital, and other resources that contribute to production combine in ways that jointly contribute to sustainable development of the country as a whole, as well as its various regions. In China, pushing forward efforts to consolidate urban and rural development is highly significant for a variety of policy objectives. These objectives include developing a modernized agriculture, pushing forward a "new form of urbanization," reducing the disparity between urban and rural areas, and promoting a moderately prosperous society in an all-round way. In terms of what this requires, at present there are two outstanding problems in China's dualistic urban–rural structure. One is the enormous disparity between urban and rural. Despite the trend toward lessening the income gap between rural and urban residents, a huge gap still exists between urban and rural realities. This is especially seen in the difference in the quality and quantity of public services. The second is the difficulty of enabling the transitioning rural population to become true urban citizens, enabling them to become truly "urbanized." Right now, there is a pronounced difference in the availability of compulsory education, healthcare, housing, and social security for rural migrant workers in cities, as opposed to the availability of those things for urban residents.

At China's current rate of urbanization, the country will be 60 percent urbanized by the year 2020. At that time, there will be around 400 million people who have transitioned out of agriculture and are living in cities. In addition, however, there will still be 500 million people living in the countryside. Pushing forward the consolidation of urban–rural systems and creating a moderately prosperous society will require using the advantages of both, so that they rely on one another and propel one another forward.

On the one hand, we must find ways to enable the transitioning population, formerly in farming, to become truly urbanized. If this problem is not resolved, not only will it impact the sustained and healthy development of urbanization, but it will hold back the development of agriculture and the countryside. First, it will be detrimental to the flow of production factors in rural areas and their optimum allocation. When rural labor moves into cities for jobs yet cannot "settle down there" and enjoy local public services, this keeps rural people from giving up their land back home. Moreover, it leads to their building housing on that farmland, which then holds back the use of economies of scale in farming. It also generates an enormous amount of waste in the form of empty housing. Second, not resolving the problem of truly urbanizing former farmers generates the problem of "older people, women, and children who are left behind." This poses tremendous risks and latent problems for future social and economic development.

On the other hand, urbanization will not be able to come up with solutions for *all* "agricultural" problems, including those of farmers, farming, and the rural economy. In 2020, there will still be 500 million people living in the countryside. Along with the process of urbanization, therefore, we must consider how these people can live better and more productive lives. To that end, we must implement the two policy goals of "building a new countryside" and "modernizing the countryside." We must urge labor, technologies, capital, and other resources to flow in a reasonable way toward the countryside. The aim is to create moderately prosperous rural communities that have food security, increasing incomes, social security guarantees, upgraded capacities, social harmony, a wholesome environment, and sound systems.

Pushing forward the unification of urban and rural in China means reducing the disparity between urban and rural, promoting the "urbanization" of the transitioning population, and pushing forward the building of a new countryside (the priorities for which are raising the level of public services in rural areas and raising the level of social security). In terms of urbanizing the transitioning population, the most critical aspects are going to be reforming the system that governs household registrations and ensuring that public services provide coverage for the entire population. Chapter 7 of this volume has already discussed the issue of developing rural public services and raising the level of social security in rural areas, so this chapter will focus instead on reform of the household registration system. It will look at how to deepen reforms and push forward urban public services that cover all long-term urban residents. It first reviews and sums up the reform of the household registration system to date, then analyzes its ongoing problems. Finally, it makes policy recommendations on innovative ways to manage populations and policies that deal with a transitioning population. It recommends pushing forward total coverage of basic public services for all long-term urban residents in five specific areas: compulsory education, employment and job-creation services, healthcare, social security, and housing guarantees. After analyzing the challenges and problems faced by the effort to truly urbanize the transitioning rural population, this chapter recommends setting up mechanisms that link public-finance transfer payments to the process of urbanizing this population. It recommends setting up ways to ensure that jurisdictions have spending authorities that are in line with their governing responsibilities. It also presents policy recommendations that aim at guaranteeing that people in the transitioning rural population have secure ownership of their own assets.

1. Accelerate reform of the system that manages household registrations

The dualistic household registration system is still the ultimate obstacle when it comes to pushing forward the unified development of urban and rural parts of China. First, the dualistic household registration system prevents the transitioning rural population from becoming truly urbanized. This makes it hard to realize the critical-mass effect of cities, and it also makes it hard to develop economies of scale in agriculture. It delays the process of modernizing agriculture and the process of urbanization. Second, the dualistic urban–rural household registration system further entrenches the way in which urban and rural development moves along separate tracks. This intensifies disparities. In 1985, urban incomes were only 1.86 times rural incomes. In 2004, the figure had gone to 3.21 times rural incomes. Third, the dualistic system affects social fairness and justice –perpetuating income inequality, which has the effect of setting up opposition between groups of people as the process of urbanization goes forward.

The experience of trying to reform the household registration system in different ways

Since the start of the 21st century, reform of the management system governing household registrations has consistently moved forward. The central government, as well as all levels of local government, has carried out a variety of exploratory activities that have achieved some progress. At the top-tier level of designing reforms, household registration reform has moved ahead with substantive steps. In January 2011, the General Office of the State Council issued, *Notification on Pushing Forward Reform of the Management System of Household Registrations, in a Deliberate but Proactive Way*. In 2014, the State Council issued *Opinion on Going Further in Promoting Reform of the Household-Registration System*. This set forth a comprehensive plan for carrying forward reform, and it also made the following three major breakthroughs. First, it created the overall framework for a "new-type household registration system" and strengthened the functions of registering and managing populations and household registrations within that system. Second, it carried out overall readjustments to the current system and instituted auxiliary reforms, and it began to disengage the household registration system from the welfare benefits system. Third, with respect to the requirements

Table 11.1 Landmarks of the reform of the household registration system

Year	Policy
July 16, 1951	*Provisional Regulations on Management of Urban Households* issued by the Ministry of Public Security was the first regulation of its kind after 1949.
1955	*Directives of the State Council on Setting up Regular Households Hierarchic System* required that households registration system should be established in cities, townships, and villages across China and statistics be made once a year.
January 1958	The NPC Standing Committee adopted the *Regulations of the People's Republic of China on Household Registration*, which for the first time clearly divided urban and rural residents into Agricultural Households and Non-agricultural Households.
August 1964	*Rules of the Ministry of Public Security on Transfer of Household Registration* specified tough control over transfer of household registration from villages to cities and towns and from towns to cities.
October 1984	*Circular of the State Council on Issues concerning Settlement of Farmers in Towns* lifted the bar of household control.
July 1985	*Provisional Rules of the Ministry of Public Security on Management of Temporary Population in Cities* symbolized perfection of management of temporary population in cities; in September, the ID card system was launched as the basis for modernized population management.
June 1997	*Circular of the State Council on Approving and Distributing the Plan of the Ministry of Public Security on Pilot Reform of Household Registration System in Small Towns and Opinions on Improving Rural Household Registration Management System* specified that rural people who had been working and living in small towns and who met the preconditions may apply for registration as local permanent households.
July 1998	*Circular of the State Council on Approving and Distributing the Opinions of the Ministry of Public Security on Certain Prominent Problems of Household Management* further lifted the bar of household registration system.
March 2001	*Circular of the State Council on Approving and Distributing the Opinions of the Ministry of Public Security on Advancing the Reform of Household Registration System in Small Towns* marked thorough implementation of the reform in small towns.
February 2012	*Circular of the General Office of the State Council on Actively and Steadily Promoting the Reform of the Household Registration System* pointed out that nonagricultural industries and agricultural population should be guided to transfer to medium-sized and small cities and administrative towns in an orderly fashion to gradually satisfy the demands of the eligible agricultural population for settlement in urban areas and gradually achieve urban–rural equity in access to basic public services.
December 2013	*Resolution of the CPC Central Committee on Key Issues concerning Overall Deepening Reform* indicated that efforts should be made to "innovate population management and accelerate reform of household registration system; the settlement restrictions shall be lifted completed in administrative towns and small cities and gradually in medium-sized cities, settlement preconditions shall be appropriately defined in large cities and population of metropolises shall be strictly controlled."
July 30, 2014	The O*pinions of the State Council on Further Promoting the Reform of the Household Registration System* was officially released after a one-year preparation.

Source: Based on relevant documents.

for "settling down" in a given city, it went further in making those requirements more socially equitable, and it lowered the requirements for settling in cities with sufficient carrying capacity.

Exploratory trials on the part of local governments have also made certain breakthroughs. First, each area has been pushing forward the ability of rural migrant workers to get job training in cities, to get education for children they have brought with them, and to get such public services as healthcare and social security. Second, most provinces throughout the country have eliminated the differentiation between a "rural household registration" and a "nonrural household registration." They have set up a uniform system in terms of applying for a household registration. Third, some places have implemented a points system, including Guangdong and Shanghai, among others. If the points of a rural migrant worker come up to a certain figure, the person can apply to get an urban registration for that city. By now, the reforms of the household registration system are already impinging upon deep-seated problems and contradictions in the urban–rural dualistic system. This is highly significant for pushing forward unification of urban and rural systems in China and for building a moderately prosperous society in an all-round way.

The latest advance in reform came on December 3, 2014. The Legislative Affairs Office of the State Council put out a public request for opinions on a Draft called, *Draft Version Asking for Opinions on "Management Methods for Residence Certificates.* This explicitly stated that those people holding so-called Residence Certificates would be able to enjoy the same equal rights as those with a household registration, including the right to compulsory education, equal employment, and so on. In addition, they would gradually be able to enjoy equal financial assistance for occupational training, employment support, housing guarantees, old-age pensions, social welfare benefits, social emergency relief, and the ability of children to participate in exams for middle school and college in the city in which they are actually living.

Box 11.1   Draft version asking for opinions on "Management Methods for Residence Certificates"

On December 4, 2014, the Legislative Affairs Office of the State Council solicited opinions from the public concerning the *Management Measures for Residence Permit (exposure draft)*, which specifies that permit holders are equal with registered households in access to such rights and interests as compulsory education and employment and will gradually have access to equity in assistance in intermediate occupational education, employment support, housing guarantee, old-age care, social welfare, social relief, and their children will be entitled to local school entrance examinations.

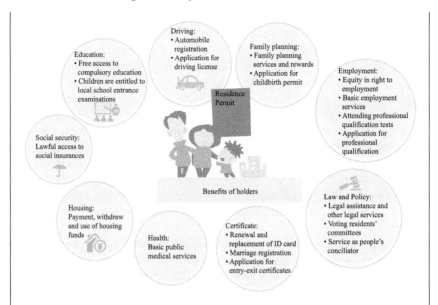

Figure 11.1 Public opinions were solicited concerning the *Management Measures for Residence Permit (exposure draft)* to specify the rights and interests of permit holders

Source: "Public opinions were solicited concerning the *Management Measures for Residence Permit (exposure draft)* to specify the rights and interests of permit holders," xinhua.net, December 5, 2014.

Existing problems with reforming the household registration system

First, the conditions for "settling down" in small towns are basically already "open," but progress in reforming systems in larger cities has been slow. After nearly thirty years of reform of the household registration system in smaller cities, problems in being able to "settle down" there are basically resolved. This is especially true of long-term residents of small cities in the central and western parts of China. In large and medium-sized cities, in contrast, cities have carried out reforms, but their emphasis is on how to select people that they themselves need among immigrants from elsewhere. Larger cities do their utmost to attract people with higher skills and who are fairly wealthy. It is still extremely difficult for rural migrant workers to settle down in such cities. Cities set up barriers to entry in the form of technical requirements, investment requirements, and income levels, or they put quotas on the numbers of people allowed to settle within their jurisdictions.

Second, it is easier for farmers to get public services in a given city if they are of the same region, whereas it is much harder for people coming in from elsewhere. Many places have already incorporated farmers into those getting urban public services if they come from the same locality, as part of their progress in unifying development of urban and rural areas. However, they still put a variety of restrictions on those who want to come in from outside their areas. For example, Guangdong has stipulated that rural migrant workers from Guangdong province will receive the same treatment as long-term urban residents with respect to pre-school education for their children and compulsory education, if they have lived in that city for a consecutive five years, have paid social security premiums for five years, have a stable job, and comply with family planning policies.

Third, places that have not completely severed the tie between a household registration and welfare benefits now are also allocating new welfare benefits to people with urban household registrations, and they are managing such benefits accordingly. Since the priority for household registration reform is to scrape away the tie between benefits and household registrations, this kind of "reform" is not an advance. For example, several years ago some cities provided rewards and subsidies to companies that hired employees who had permanent household registrations in the city. Another example: many cities are not allowing people without local household registrations to purchase housing in the city, amid other kinds of restrictions.

Fourth, the single largest problem is figuring out how to apportion the costs of household registration reform. Reform of the system involves very substantial public costs. Meeting the need for extra public services will take a massive amount of capital. Where is this money going to come from? This is the dilemma for household registration reform. As reform proceeds and a very large number of farmers migrate into cities, allowing them to enjoy the same urban public services and social security, giving them the same equal treatment in welfare benefits as urban residents requires money. The core issue is who is going to pay the costs? Given this backdrop, if we aim to push forward household registration reform in a quick, effective way, we must construct mechanisms that allocate costs and share the burden in a reasonable way. We must break up the massive costs of reform into discrete portions carried by diverse entities if we are to have adequate funding for full public-service coverage of all residents and if we are to build the necessary basic urban facilities.

Policy recommendations on how to speed up reform of the household registration system

First, by the year 2020, basically establish a "new-style household-registration system" that is aligned with establishing a moderately prosperous society in an all-round way, that provides effective support for social management and public services, that safeguards the legitimate rights and interests of citizens, that takes the human being as central, and that is regulated and orderly. Work hard to ensure that roughly 100 million transitioning rural people and other long-term residents of cities can actually "settle down" in those cities as urban citizens.

Second, speed up the implementation of policies that operate on a graduated scale, that is, take into consideration the carrying capacity of each city in coming up with differentiated solutions. Divide the types of cities and groups of people into categories. When cities have a greater carrying capacity than there is demand to settle down in that city, lower the conditions for being able to settle there. Completely open smaller cities with respect to residency requirements. When cities have only a modest carrying capacity, set up minimum requirements for being allowed to settle there, but do not make them overly rigorous, or they will undercut the goal of reforming the system overall. The 2014 State Council's *Opinion on Going Further in Promoting Reform of the Household-Registration System* went into finer detail in differentiating cities with regard to implementing household registration policies (see Table 11.2).

Third, innovate in finding ways to improve the population management system in both cities and rural areas

First, set up a uniform urban–rural household registration system for registering people in general. Setting up such a unified system for registering people in both cities and the countryside not only will strengthen management of the population and household registrations, but it will go further in deepening the basis for reform of the household registration system. This means eliminating the distinction between "agricultural household registration" and "nonagricultural household registration," as well as the "blue stamp household" categories that were derived from that distinction. This means unifying registration such that it is an all-round "citizenship [residents] registration." It allows for functions that relate to managing a population that is registered. At the same time, we must set up statistical systems that correspond to the unified registration system having to do with education, public health, employment, social security, housing, land, and population data.

Second, establish a system of "residency certificates." This system should incorporate two different considerations. The first defines the conditions for residency certificates. These should be as simple and as broad as possible. According to the *Opinion on Pushing Forward Reform of the Household-Registration System*, citizens who leave their long-term residence and live in a city at the "municipality" level or above for more than six months may apply for a residency certificate in the new place. Those holding residency certificates who then meet further requirements and are eligible may apply for *permanent* residency status. The second consideration sets up mechanisms that allow for provision of public services, by using the residency certificates as a vehicle and by linking the number of years of residency and other such conditions with provision of public services. In the initial period, it will not be possible for people to enjoy all welfare benefits and rights to public services right away. Nevertheless, the barriers to entry for *basic* benefits and public services should be set as low as possible and should be as simple as possible. According to the *Opinion on Pushing Forward Reform of the Household-Registration System*, those holding residency certificates are entitled to the same rights as local households [people already in the register] to such things as labor employment, basic public education, basic healthcare services, family planning services, public cultural services, and certificate handling services. Then, using the length of time lived in a place, a person can gradually

Table 11.2 Preconditions for settlement in cities

Types of cities/towns		Preconditions for settlement				
		Legal and steady domicile (including rental)	Legal and steady job	Years of payment for urban social insurance	Years of consecutive residence	Settlement score system
County-level cities, towns serving as the seat of county governments, other administrative towns		Yes	No	No	No	No
Cities with 0.5–1 million urban population	With small burden on comprehensive bearing capacity	Yes	No	No	No	No
	With heavy burden on comprehensive bearing capacity	Specific requirements may be set on the scope and conditions, not on the area and value.	Specific requirements may be set on the scope and number of years.	No more than 3 years	No	No
Cities with 1 million urban population		Yes	Reaching certain years	Yes	No	No
Cities with 3–5 million urban population		Tough requirements may be set on the scope and conditions.	Tough requirements may be set on the scope and number of years.	No more than 5 years	No	Approved
Cities with 5 million urban population or more		Yes	Yes	Yes	Yes	Yes

Source: *Opinions of the State Council on Further Promoting the Reform of the Household Registration System*, promulgated in 2014.

access other benefits and rights at the same level as the population already in the population register. Those things would include financial support for professional education, job support, housing guarantees, caregiving services for the elderly, social welfare benefits, social emergency relief, and so on. At the same time, children would gradually become eligible to participate in the entrance exams for high school and college, based on (a) the number of consecutive years they have attended school in the city and (b) the qualifications that allow them to participate in the entrance exams. In line with the principle of equal treatment, those who hold residency certificates must participate in military service, must join militia organizations, and must engage in other such citizens' duties as required by the State and the locality.

Third, establish an information system that covers demographic data in a sound and well functioning way. The outstanding problem with the current population-registering system is that information is incomplete since registering is not thorough. First, given the way populations are shifting around, registering is haphazard. In principle, anyone who has lived in a place for over three months is supposed to register in the new place. In reality, it is very hard to track people who are moving between different parts of the country and even within a certain area. Second, different government departments have data on people for whom they are responsible, such as departments governing education, social security, housing, and so on. This information is not effectively consolidated and shared with others, however, so that it is hard for the data to support population-development strategies and policies. This also makes it hard to decide on how to provide population services and management. We therefore must set up a sound and well functioning system that registers populations who are actually living in a given place. That means strengthening statistical surveys and getting a complete and accurate hold on the size of populations, their structures, geographic distributions, and other data. It means setting up a national population information data bank at the fundamental level, which incorporates all people in the country and has the "citizens' personal certificate number" as the sole indicator to represent that person and which includes only the most basic data on the person as the criteria for defining that person. As time goes on, we then must improve upon the information systems relating to this databank in the various categories of employment, education, income, social security, housing, credit, healthcare and family planning, taxation, marriage, ethnicity, and so on, such that information can be coordinated and shared across different parts of the country and among different departments.

Fourth, set up mechanisms that allocate the costs of paying for this reform, and make sure the mechanisms function in a sound way. This involves setting up public-finance transfer payment systems that allocate funds among different levels of government. These must be based on the household-register registration of people and must rely mainly on the actual carrying capacity of cities. On that basis, we then must also establish mechanisms for distributing the costs among a diversified set of participants, including government, enterprises, and society at large. The central government should provide financial assistance to those areas most affected by rural migrant workers who have crossed provincial jurisdictions to settle in cities, when such migration incurs particularly onerous burdens and has strong externalities. The emphasis here should be on financial support for areas into which populations are migrating with respect to public hygiene [e.g., toilet facilities], family planning, compulsory education of children, job support, and social security. In particular, financial support should be increased for the building of guaranteed-housing-type facilities in areas where migrating populations are concentrating. At the provincial level, the priorities should focus on providing financial support for public services for populations who are migrating within the province but also between different cities or counties. Municipal governments that have an inflow of people should mainly bear the costs of paying for the process of turning rural migrant workers into actual urban citizens by expanding the functions and facilities of the city to incorporate them. This includes the costs of basic municipal facilities and public facilities. It includes spending on public services for "urbanizing" rural migrant workers within the jurisdiction of the given government. The emphasis here should be on paying the main portion of the costs of building guaranteed-type low-cost housing. Enterprises, meanwhile, must respect the principle of equal pay for equal work and of equal rights for equal work. They must improve the work conditions of rural migrant workers, upgrade skills by providing training, and gradually help strengthen the ability of rural migrant workers to become actual urban citizens. Individuals themselves who have migrated into cities must bear costs and responsibilities as well by upgrading their own individual capacities and paying their portion of the costs of social security (National Development and Reform Commission, 2013).

2. Push forward the process of providing basic public services to all long-term residents of cities

By the goals set forth in the *National Plan for a New Type of Urbanization (2014–2020)*, by the year 2020, the country should have incorporated roughly 100 million rural residents into cities as settled urbanites. The "transitioning rural population" includes far more people than just 100 million, but it will not be possible to provide all urban facilities for more people by that time. The migration of rural labor between the urban and rural parts of the country is going to be a long-term phenomenon. Based on the principle of carrying out a sequential and incremental process that provides basic safeguards, we should approach the process in stages. First, actively promote a shift in providing basic public services that are now mainly aimed at the population already in urban household registers to providing services for those people who have been long-term residents of a city but who are not in the permanent registry. Then gradually begin to provide basic municipal public services for people who have jobs in cities but are not "settled down" in those cities on a permanent basis.

Safeguarding the equal rights to education for families who have brought children with them from the countryside

Starting in the mid-1990s, a large amount of rural labor began surging toward cities in more developed parts of the country. The numbers of rural migrant workers who brought families with them also began to increase, and school-age children who then "left school" when they arrived in cities became a prodigious problem. In order to address this problem, in May 2001, the State Council issued "*Decision on the reform and development of basic education.*" For the first time, this set forth a policy on the "main entities" responsible for compulsory education of rural migrant workers' children: the government jurisdictions into which people have migrated are responsible, and the public primary schools and middle schools that operate on a full-time basis are responsible. These entities were to safeguard the rights of the children of the "floating population" to education by adopting various methods to do so.

Since 2001, the central government and various levels of local government have issued a number of policy measures in this regard, and notable accomplishments have indeed been made with respect to enabling such children to study at public schools. Despite this, however, a great number of children are not in fact able to go to school once their parents migrate to cities, for various reasons. They then are "left back" in the countryside, or they come to cities but enter what are called "schools for the children of laborers," or they simply drop out of school. The main reasons for this include the following.

First, the financial resources of public schools are simply insufficient. Relative to the scale of the problem, financial resources of publicly operated schools in cities are limited particularly with respect to basic facilities, teachers, and overall

Table 11.3 Public school enrollment of migrant children since 2011

City	Percentage of public school enrollment	Qualification	Difficulty	Latent rules
Shanghai	70	5 certificates, including immunity	Relatively hard	Social relation
Guangzhou	40	Residence for no less than 6 months, steady job and income, graduation from local kindergarten	Very hard	High sponsor fee
Kunming	55	3 certificates, including childbirth	Hard	Social relation or high sponsor fee
Beijing	70	5 certificates, including that explaining nobody looks after children in place of household registration	Relatively hard	High sponsor fee for good schools

Source: China Development Research Center of the State Council, World Bank, *China: Toward Efficient, Inclusive and Sustainable Urbanization*, Beijing: China Development Press, 2014 edition.

costs. Under the current system of public finance, allocation of public spending on schools is based on the number of people in the household registry of the given school district. The great majority of municipal government budgets do not include education expenses for children of rural migrant workers.

Second, the entry requirements for studying at public schools are quite restrictive. Many cities have set up stringent access requirements for children who have accompanied their parents into cities and who want to apply to public schools. These generally require that the parents hand over their certificates confirming "proof of occupation and residence" to education departments, which confirm they are allowed to work in the jurisdiction and have an actual place to live. The requirements of some cities are more severe. What's more, many places require that parents pay fees of various kinds to support their child's education in public schools, such as "sponsoring fees" and "school selection fees." This places an enormous burden on families.

Third, there are privately operated "schools for the children of laborers," which provide teaching that is very low quality. Teachers at such schools are under-qualified, facilities are primitive, and education is minimal. This means that such schools cannot get permits from local education departments to function as a "public" school and so cannot get financial support and services. Some of these schools have actually been closed down altogether due to lack of adequate qualifications and lack of safety measures.

Fourth, in some cities, it is still very hard for children of rural migrant workers to sit for higher-education exams in the city where they are permanently residing. [They must go back to their home town if they want to take exams.] Municipal governments in these cities are generally concerned that once they allow such children to take exams *in situ*, such allowance will lead to a large influx of other children from the floating population who will be encouraged to come in and take exams too. This will then place an enormous burden on the public services and public finances of the municipality. Beijing's restrictions serve as one example. Beijing's municipal government stipulated the following rules starting in 2014: children of migrant laborers may register for taking exams for vocational schools of higher education if the parents have a valid certificate of residence in Beijing, if they have a stable and legally approved residence, if they have paid social security in Beijing for six or more consecutive years, and if their children have registered properly in the Beijing municipal school registry for a consecutive three years of high-school education. Once these fairly restrictive provisions have been met, the children are allowed to participate only in exams for vocational schools; they still cannot participate in the regular college entry exams.

We must safeguard the right of the children of the transitioning rural population in China to receive an education. First, this means expanding the size and number of public schools in order to ensure that the "accompanying children" of rural migrant workers in particular receive an education. Second, it means having the government purchase educational services for those children who are not able to attend public schools in order to ensure that they do receive at least an education at privately administered schools. By extending financial support, assistance to teachers, and so on, the government should raise the quality of education being provided by such schools. Third, we should gradually improve upon policies that exempt students of high-school vocational education from paying fees, if they are the children of rural migrant workers, and preschool education that is of a "public welfare" nature. Fourth, we should push forward with ways to ensure that children of rural migrant workers can participate in exams for higher education, once they have received education at the compulsory level. This includes allowing them to participate in exams for high school after graduating from middle school. Fifth, we should improve upon ways to finance the education of accompanying children of rural migrant workers. That means incorporating the education of such children into the scope of educational planning at all levels of government and into public-finance guarantees for education.

Box 11.2   Shanghai's solution for the problem of education for children of rural migrant workers: public education that is driven by a "double-axle," namely public and private

As of 2009, Shanghai had roughly 400,000 floating-population children in the city. The great majority of these are the children of rural migrant workers. Shanghai's policy goal is to enable all of the children of rural migrant workers to get a free education. Starting in September 2008, Shanghai simplified the procedures for getting into schools for such children to the extent that they only had to provide the identification certificates of their parents and either their residency permit from Shanghai or proof of their employment. Children of rural migrant workers who then were able to attend public schools were given the same treatment as Shanghai's own students. They were not obliged to pay transient school fees or "miscellaneous school fees." They could register in public schools and be evaluated according to the same criteria as everyone else. Entry into such things as the Communist Youth League and the Communist Party of China was handled in equal fashion.

The Shanghai municipality's handling of education for children of rural migrant workers is driven by a double-axle process. Starting in 2004, efforts were increased to incorporate such children into public schools. Through a variety of forms, including specially designated schooling sites or extracurricular classes, at present more than 60 percent of such children are receiving public education.

At the same time, Shanghai increased the extent of its support for the schools that specifically teach children of rural migrant workers. It gradually began to incorporate these into privately run schools whose management is overseen by the government. Starting in 2005, the government has dedicated an annual sum of money specifically to improving educational conditions at such schools. In 2007, it spent an enormous sum of money to improve school cafeterias and toilets and to provide such things as schoolroom chairs and tables, computers, and books, none of which required compensation. Starting in 2008, the government gradually began to incorporate these schools into the privately managed school system. The overall goal is to have 70 percent of the children of Shanghai's rural migrant workers enrolled in public grade schools by 2010 and the other 30 percent in privately managed grade schools that are overseen by the government. By middle school, all children should be going to public schools.

Source: "Children of Migrant Rural Workers in Shanghai May Go to Both Public And Private Schools." www.cnr.cn, June 19, 2009.

Improve job-placement services and business start-up service systems in cities

Since both the central government and all other levels of government are extremely concerned about the employment problems of rural migrant workers in terms of both employment and job creation, they have issued a series of policy measures on these issues. These mainly can be categorized as follows.

Gradually implement an employment system that provides equal treatment for urban and rural [people]. Go further in sorting through and eliminating any discriminatory regulations and unreasonable restrictions that are targeted at rural migrant workers who come into cities to find work. Improve services that allow rural migrant workers to shift employment. This includes opening up any public-service job opportunities to rural migrant workers that are being provided to urban residents. It means providing free consultation services on policies, employment information, employment guidance, and job prospects. Strengthen professional skills-training for rural migrant works.

Doing all this, in addition to constantly improving job-creation services targeted at the transitional population moving out of agriculture, is highly significant when it comes to meeting our policy goals. Specifically, it is significant in transitioning rural labor into new jobs, improving the incomes of farmers, and stimulating economic growth in both the urban and rural areas.

However, in looking at the actual situation, major problems still need to be addressed. These relate specifically to employment and business start-up services for the "transitional population that is moving out of agriculture." First, certain industries in a portion of cities still maintain discriminatory regulations against "outsiders." Beijing's taxi drivers are one example. Beijing still does not allow people who have come in from outside the city to work as taxi drivers. Meanwhile, some government institutions and public institutions as well as State-Owned Enterprises put household registration restrictions on their job announcements when they are recruiting college graduates. Second, there is a substantial surplus of vocational education resources in some large cities, yet these cities do not open their doors to the children of rural migrant workers. For example, intermediate occupational schools in Beijing cannot find enough students, yet they shut their doors to the children of migrant workers. Third, the results of existing governmental programs to provide occupational skills training are lackluster at best. On the one hand, resources are dispersed so that the efficiency with which funds are used for training is low in such departments as the Ministry of Human Resources and Social Security, the Ministry of Agriculture, and the State Council's Office of Poverty Alleviation. On the other hand, there is often a disconnect between the kinds of training that rural migrant workers need and the kinds that are supplied. Training tends to be generic, with little variation, so that results are minimal. Fourth, occupational safety responsibilities have not yet been clarified, so training for safety in certain jobs is not being paid for by enterprises.

With respect to improving the systems for employment and business start-up services in cities, the first thing we must do is improve the management procedures that register employment and unemployment, so that the transitioning population is incorporated in these figures. The second thing is to provide government subsidies to this population for occupational skills training. We must launch projects to encourage schools, vocational institutions, and training organizations to be proactive in providing skills training and occupational training for rural migrant workers. We should push forward the building of occupational training bases. Third, the government should increase its support for start-up companies. It should support start-ups by rural migrant workers whether they return to their home towns to do this or do it where they are currently living.

Box 11.3   Night school for rural migrant workers

Rural migrant workers are the primary force in China's construction industry. One of the larger companies to make use of this force is Beijing's Zhu-zong Group, in English called the Beijing Uni-construction Group Co., Ltd. (BUCC). In March 2007, this company set up the first night schools for rural migrant workers in over one hundred of its construction sites. It carried out training of these people by setting up schools right on the spot, using materials specially prepared by experts in various professional categories. These experts compiled documentation on such subjects as *The BUCC Manual on Safety Procedures in Construction Projects, The BUCC Quality Control Standards in Construction Projects, Safety Procedures Manual in Fire-fighting Procedures, Temporary Use of Electricity Safety Procedures and Standards to Be Used on Construction Sites, Management Standards for Scaffolding and Occupational Safety Information Handbook*, and so on. In addition, the rural migrant workers were provided with courses on relevant laws and regulations, such as the *Labor Law, Occupational Safety Law,*

Law on Labor Contracts, and the *Beijing Occupational Safety Regulations*. Each night school is staffed with professional teachers based on the subject matter. The "president" of each night school is the project manager at the given construction site.

Between 2007 and 2011, this training platform provided training for 510,000 rural migrant workers, and 6,331 rural migrant workers received a national certificate confirming professional qualifications as a result of attending night school. This had a tremendous effect on upgrading the professional caliber of these workers.

Source: Department of Housing and Urban–Rural Development of Fujian Province, "*Upgrading Professional Quality through Night School for Migrant Rural Workers*," February 27, 2013.

Improve basic medical care conditions and hygienic facilities for the transitioning rural population

According to relevant regulations, some basic medical services and hygienic facilities are to be provided at no cost to all residents living within a given jurisdiction. These things generally include eight specific items: medical [health] files, medical [health] education, free inoculations, prevention and control of infectious diseases, child healthcare, women's and old people's healthcare, treatment for chronic disease, and management of severe cases of mental illness. Later, certain other items were added to this list, including immunizations for Hepatitis B, checkups for women aged 15 to 59 for breast cancer and uterine cancer, and operations on cataracts for people who cannot pay for this service. These services are to be provided by the community health services center. They are to be provided for the entire urban population in a given jurisdiction, including the floating population. The costs of covering these things is to be paid by the central government and local government, with subsidies that are determined by the number of permanent residents in the area, including the floating population.

In actually implementing these regulations, however, the current reality is that quite a few places do not include certain things within the scope of health services for rural migrant workers. Control and prevention of illnesses among rural migrant workers, checkups for prevention of infectious disease, and immunizations for women and children who are at certain ages are generally not included. For one, it is hard for planned immunizations and health services to reach women and children in the migrant worker population. Inoculations of children "who come in from elsewhere" are particularly rare. For another, there are still lacunae in the services provided for he control and prevention of illness among rural migrant workers in general. The government provides no-cost or subsidized treatment for such things as AIDs, tuberculosis, and schistosomiasis, but these policy measures are hard to put into effect due to the mobility of rural migrant workers, as well as their lack of understanding about how to maintain good health. Third, rural migrant workers are in strong need of governmental protection with respect to occupational diseases. This is a particularly urgent problem. In developed industrial nations, occupational health services cover 70 percent to 90 percent of laborers. In China, the figure is around 20 percent. The situation with officially hired employees is somewhat better; the situation with people hired on a contractual basis is not as good, while the floating population of rural migrant workers has basically no occupational health services whatsoever.

If we are to improve the basic medical care and health conditions of rural migrant workers, the first thing is to ensure that resources are available to incorporate all permanent residents into urban basic healthcare services. That means incorporating the transitioning rural population, as well as other permanent residents, into the systems that provide community healthcare and family planning services. It means providing basic medical healthcare for these people. The second thing is to encourage localities that have the means to pay for it to incorporate rural migrant workers and their dependents into the scope of medical assistance programs in their jurisdictions. The third is to increase publicity about policies relating to prevention and control of serious infectious diseases and to improve prevention and control services for rural migrant workers. Fourth, we must ensure that enterprises take primary responsibility with respect to occupational safety by increasing regulatory oversight of occupational safety conditions and truly improving the prevention of and protection from occupational diseases among rural migrant workers.

Box 11.4   The health of the floating population and its situation with respect to medical treatment

In 2012, the China Development Research Foundation did a survey in the largest "village" in the municipality of Kunming in Yunnan province, which is called the Chuanfang Community. The survey discovered that, among five different types of insurance, the one of most concern to the floating-population residents was medical insurance. (The five are insurance for job-related injury, unemployment, medical insurance, social pension insurance, and housing public-fund insurance.) When people get sick among this floating population, 45.38 percent go to a "proper hospital" for treatment, 28.08 percent go to a private clinic, and 28.08 percent simply go to a pharmacy to buy medicine, depending on the illness. As to the main reasons for not going to a proper hospital, 68 percent say that the fees are too high, and 18 percent say that the procedures are too much trouble. As for why people have no social pension insurance [old-age pensions], 72 percent say "they are not clear about how it works," 16 percent say "the company won't do it," while 27 percent say, "I myself am not willing to do it" (see Figure 11.2).

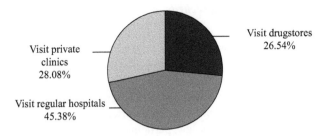

Figure 11.2 Pie chart showing how the floating population in Chuanfang Community accesses medical assistance

The two-week rate of getting sick, that is, the "morbidity rate" among the floating population of Chuanfang, is much higher than among the normal population; it is eight to ten times the rate of villagers in the neighboring areas. Colds, coughing, and diarrhea are the three most common symptoms described. Given that the health conditions of this floating population are not good, the need for public healthcare services is high. At present, Chuanfang has just one community health center, around twenty-eight privately operated clinics, and four pharmacies. The privately operated clinics are what the floating population uses most frequently. Compared to people who come from the locality, these "outsiders" are not able to be reimbursed for hospital costs. Indeed, they have essentially no medical safeguards at all, while their low incomes prevent them from paying for proper services. (The rural people from the locality not only have regular work income, but they get dividends from their collective, as well as rent income from renting out their properties.) When "outsiders" get sick, they either do not see a doctor at all – they self-diagnose and buy their own "medicine" from a clinic – or they go to a "black clinic" [an unlicensed one] to be treated.

In terms of the health of pregnant women: 100 percent of women who come from the locality itself, that is, local residents, have frequent prenatal checkups and go to a hospital to have their child. In contrast, "outsiders" mostly have their child in a rented room. They also receive no prenatal checkups whatsoever. Their health conditions are extremely disturbing. In terms of the health of children of the floating population in Chuanfang, around one-quarter have never had any kind of inoculation against disease. Only 79.5 percent of those who have an "immunity card" actually get inoculation services on a regular basis. The great majority of floating-population children are not covered by the municipality's health insurance, nor do they even have health insurance from the new countryside cooperative healthcare system.

Source: China Development Research Foundation, Task Force on Integrating Children of the Floating Population into Society, 2013.

Expand the coverage of social security in cities

China began to set up a social security system that is aligned with a market-economy system in the mid-1990s, in urban areas. Policy regulations in this regard did not exclude rural migrant workers who live in cities, and they particularly did not exclude those who have formal [proper] jobs in "units" (see Box 11.3). According to the *Labor Law*, any laborers who have "a labor relationship" with any enterprise, or *ge-ti* business organization [sole proprietorship], or other entity within the boundaries of China must, by law, participate in social security and enjoy the benefits of such social security. In order to raise the extent to which rural migrant workers are in fact safeguarded under this system, in 2006, the State Council put forth the *Opinion on Resolving Various Issues to Do with Rural Migrant Workers.* This stated that social security issues having to do with rural migrant workers were to be resolved in a proactive but stable manner and that rural migrant workers were to be included in the scope of "occupational injury insurance" as per the law. Those places that were qualified to do so could also incorporate rural migrant workers who had stable jobs into the "urban basic medical insurance for employees" system, as well as the social pension insurance for urban employees. In addition, rural migrant workers were free to participate in the new countryside cooperative medical insurance of their home towns, if they chose to do so.

However, the actual situation shows that the percentage of rural migrant workers actually participating in urban medical insurance programs is low. In 2013, among all rural migrant workers who were working outside their hometown base, only 15.7 percent participated in social pension insurance, 2.5 percent in work injury insurance, 17.6 percent in medical insurance, 9.1 percent in unemployment insurance, and 6.7 percent in maternity insurance. These rates were far lower than participation rates of people holding an urban household registration. The critical issue here is institutional obstacles that still prevent rural migrant workers from participating in urban social security systems. First, rural migrant workers without official jobs (since they are temporary workers) cannot participate in urban social insurance. They are not company employees and so cannot be a part of urban employee health insurance or social pension insurance programs. Meanwhile, cities do not provide coverage for anyone who is not "properly employed" [that is, for anyone who is employed on a temporary basis]. Their medical insurance is for "residents," and their social pension benefits are for residents. Second, it is fairly hard to transfer social insurance and to continue it in a new place. Right now, social insurance is organized and managed at a fairly low level of government. Social [old-age] pension programs for municipal employees are managed in an overall way at the provincial level, but most of the *healthcare* insurance of municipal employees is handled at the county level. It is quite hard to issue pension payments outside the area in which they were initially registered. It is hard to pay medical costs outside as well. When rural migrant workers travel outside the area of their original plans, they mostly choose to pull out of insurance. Even if they travel within a jurisdiction, it is hard for many places to handle the pooled accounts of pension insurance; they can transfer the individual's account, but they cannot transfer the amount saved in the pooled account. Third, it is impossible to link up urban forms of social insurance with the new countryside cooperative healthcare system and the new countryside old-age pension system. The new countryside cooperative healthcare system is generally managed at the county level. Expenses can be reimbursed within that jurisdiction, but rural migrant workers who travel elsewhere cannot get reimbursed for medical expenses.

We must address three issues in order to expand coverage of urban medical insurance to the transitioning rural population as well as other permanent residents. First, we need to allow the transitioning population to participate in urban residents' medical insurance and urban residents' social [old-age] pension insurance. Second, we need to improve the linkage between urban and rural social security. This means enabling the insurance programs that the transitioning rural population had in the countryside to merge with the urban social security system in a standardized way. It means both improving and consolidating the urban–rural basic medical insurance system for all residents and speeding up the unification of a medical assistance program for urban and rural residents. Third, we should raise the government level at which programs are planned and managed. This requires setting up a nationwide basic social pension fund that is managed at the national level. It means speeding up the unification of the basic social pension system for urban and rural residents and putting in place policies that enable employees to transfer and carry on their social [old-age] pension funds when they move.

Box 11.5   The systemic arrangements for enabling rural migrant workers to participate in social insurance

At present, China regards those people who work mainly in nonagricultural jobs but whose household registration remains rural as "rural migrant workers." In terms of actual jobs, these people can be divided into three main categories. One category works in locally based town-and-village enterprises. The second works in cities for all the different entities that hire people. A third works in part-time or temporary jobs either locally or by travelling elsewhere for the work. Depending on the nature of their employment, insurance policies treat these categories differently.

1. Old-age pension insurance

The three main policy documents relating to China's social [old-age] pension insurance for rural migrant workers were put out in 1997, 2001, and 2005. The 1997 document was issued by the State Council and called *Decision on Setting Up a Unified Basic Social Pension System for Employees of Enterprises*. The 2001 document was issued by the Ministry of Labor and Social Security and called, *Notice on Issues Relating to Policies Intended to Improve the Basic Social Pensions of Urban Employees*. The

2005 document was issued by the State Council and was called, *Decision on Improving the Basic Social Pension Insurance System of Enterprise Employees*. These three documents set forth mandatory provisions on the participation of all employees in all kinds of enterprises located in cities. Although the documents did not specifically refer to rural migrant workers, they obviously covered them within the scope of "all employees of enterprises." The methods currently in force are explicit with respect to how urban enterprises must pay a certain percentage of the social pension insurance of rural migrant workers, how accounts must be transferrable, payment terms with respect to timing, and benefits of the pensions. Meanwhile, requirements of rural migrant workers are the same as for people with an urban household registration: they must pay 8 percent of their total wages in premiums, and they have to have been working continuously and paying that for a full fifteen years before retirement before they can receive pension payments. If rural migrant workers move within the jurisdiction of the same social pension program, their individual accounts can move along with them. If they cross jurisdictions, they can either have the individual accounts sealed for later, or they can pull out of the insurance.

2. Medical insurance

At present, there are two main types of medical insurance aimed at meeting the needs of rural migrant workers. One is the "medical insurance for employees of urban enterprises." The second is the "new-type rural cooperative medical insurance." Two policy announcements set forth mandatory provisions with regard to the medical insurance for employees of urban enterprises. One was in 1998, when the State Council issued its *Decision on Establishing a Basic Medical Insurance System for Urban Employees.* The second was in 2003, when the Ministry of Labor and Social Security issued *Notice on Further Improving upon and Expanding the Coverage of the Basic Medical Insurance for Urban Employees*. Since rural migrant workers who work for urban enterprises are one component of "urban employees," naturally it is also mandatory that they participate. The premiums for this employee insurance are generally 2 percent of the wage income of each person. Around 30 percent of the portion paid by the employer goes into the personal account of the individual. The rest is used to set up a pooled fund. With respect to the second type of insurance, on October 2002, the *Decision of the State Council and the Central Committee of the Communist Party of China on Further Strengthening Work on Rural Health and Hygiene"* set forth the plan for gradually setting up a "new-type rural cooperative medical insurance system" that was focused primarily on pooled funds to cover major illness. This system began with pilot projects in 2003. As of 2016, it provides coverage for all residents in rural areas. All rural migrant workers are incorporated into the system if the location of their household registration is still rural. The current policy regulations are that rural migrant workers must pay a portion of premiums, while both central finance and local-government financial departments subsidize the other portion.

3. Occupational injury insurance

Two documents have set forth explicit regulations requiring all rural migrant workers to participate in occupational injury insurance if they have any kind of "labor relationship" with an employer. *Rules on Occupational Injury Insurance* was issued in 2003; the *Notification on Issues to Do with Rural Migrant Worker Participation in Occupational Injury Insurance* was issued in 2004. The premium is to be paid entirely by the employer. Individual rural migrant workers are not required to contribute. It should be noted that the State does not differentiate between rural migrant workers and urban employees when it comes to participation in this insurance. The State also makes no distinction between urban and rural in the application of the regulations; all rural migrant workers who are "hired" by anyone must be incorporated into the program. However, at present the premiums for the insurance must be covered entirely by the employer, and it is *de facto* quite difficult for rural migrant workers who are employed on a part-time or temporary basis to be incorporated in the system.

4. Unemployment insurance and maternity insurance

At present, China has no specific regulations with respect to the participation of rural migrant workers in unemployment and maternity insurance. Participation by rural migrant workers in these two kinds of insurance must rely on two more general documents: the *Regulations on Unemployment Insurance*, promulgated by the State Council in 1999, and the *Provisional Measures for Maternity Insurance for Enterprise Employees*, issued by the Ministry of Labor in 1994. Both of these types of insurance are aimed at companies and institutions in cities and their employees. Because of this, any rural migrant worker properly employed by such an employer is incorporated into these insurance programs, but the issue of insuring those employed on a part-time basis has not yet been addressed.

Source: Song Hongyuan (2012).

Expand the coverage of housing guarantees in cities

In recent years, the various relevant departments in the central government and local governments have passed policies and measures aimed at improving the housing conditions of rural migrant workers. A notable example is the document put forth by the State Council in 2006, called, *Various Opinions on Resolving*

Table 11.4 Housing of rural farmers in 2013

Indicator	Dormitory provided by employer	Work shed in construction sites	Business sites	Joint rental	Rental	Buy house where he works	Work outside and live at home	Others
Total	28.6	11.9	5.8	18.5	18.2	0.9	13	3.1
Municipality and provincial capital	30.4	14.9	5.9	21.6	20.4	0.7	3.2	3
Provincial city	33	10.9	5.8	20.5	19.9	0.9	6.4	2.7
Small town	23	10.4	5.6	13.9	14.9	1.2	27.3	3.8

Source: National Bureau of Statistics, *Report on 2013 National Monitoring Survey on Migrant Rural Workers*, May 12, 2014.

Unit: %

Rural Migrant Worker Issues. This clearly called for improvement in housing conditions for rural migrant workers by working through a number of different channels. While there may have been some improvement as a result, the actual situation is that rural migrant workers who travel outside their home base for work still mainly rent accommodations, and these are in very unfavorable surroundings (see Table 11.4). It is of particular note that many rural migrant workers rent space in underground basements. They live on the outskirts of cities, at the interface of rural and urban, or they live in what are known as "villages within cities." Hygienic facilities are either poor or lacking, fire prevention is minimal, and living conditions are substandard. Reasons for this include the following. First, rural migrant workers are not sure they will put down roots in the place they are working, so they do not feel it necessary to try to buy a place for themselves and try to register locally. Many, instead, purchase housing back in the county seat of their home place. Second, urban housing prices keep rural migrant workers from buying. Between 1999 and 2010, housing prices in cities doubled overall, but in Shanghai and Beijing they went up by five times. The more developed the city in which rural migrant workers gather to find work, the higher the housing prices, so that prices far surpass buying power. Third, the costs of renting are also rising rapidly. In order to save money, rural migrant workers generally rent space in cheap and undesirable places. Fourth, rural migrant workers lack any public housing safeguards. Most cities do not incorporate them within the scope of the public housing system. They are excluded, and this is particularly true of incoming rural migrant workers who are not long-term local residents.

In order to improve the housing conditions of rural migrant workers, we first should incorporate them into the urban housing safeguards system. It is worth pointing out, however, that some cities do indeed promote "public housing" and declare it to be for people coming in from elsewhere. However, although housing is paid for by government programs, it is then used to attract professional talent instead of the intended recipients. Those most in need of housing safeguards – low-income people and the impoverished population – are unable to benefit.

Second, rented accommodations are going to continue to be the primary solution for some time to housing rural migrant workers. Because of that, we should strengthen controls over the environment in which such accommodations exist, particularly the underground rooms, the villages within cities [slum neighborhoods], and the interface areas at the edges of cities. We must regulate how rents are charged, improve sanitary conditions, and provide subsidies for rents. By setting up a legitimate and well functioning market for rentals, we should seek to improve the housing conditions in which rural migrant workers currently live.

3.   Push forward mechanisms that enable the transitioning agricultural population to become "urbanized"

The key to ensuring that the transitioning agricultural population becomes urbanized lies in the following: strengthening the accountabilities of all levels of government, allocating the costs in a reasonable way, and thoroughly mobilizing the forces of "society at large" [nongovernmental funding]. This involves crafting mechanisms that are government guided, open to participation by nongovernmental entities, and have costs that are born jointly. It involves coordinating the process.

Key problems

First, some *nong-min* [farmers/rural people] are worried that they will lose their former benefits once they become urbanized. By relevant laws and regulations, once rural residents become urban residents, it is indeed possible that their contractual rights to operate land, their rights to use "residential land" in the countryside, and the dividends from income made from collective assets may indeed be drawn back into the collective. Meanwhile, rural land has gone up considerably in value, particularly in the more developed parts of China. If the "agricultural" population transitions to becoming a "nonagricultural" population, it may indeed lose a major part of the compensation when land is requisitioned for other use. Moreover, after rural residents transition to becoming urban residents, regulations on having a second child become more stringent. All of this dampens the enthusiasm of rural people for moving their registration status to cities. In some areas, we are even seeing the phenomenon among people who had already transitioned to being nonagricultural of wanting to go back to having a rural household registration.

Second, some urban residents worry that their own level of benefits will decline once outsiders are incorporated into their city. A survey of residents in Guangzhou found that more than half of the city's residents felt that immigrants coming in from elsewhere should have the right to medical care, compulsory education, the right to join labor unions, as well as the right to participate in local elections. About the same percentage, however, were opposed to having the immigrant population apply for unemployment compensation, the minimum living allowance, or low-cost housing (Liu Linping, 2008). Another study, completed in 2010 but using the data from a 2005 nationwide comprehensive social survey, discovered that the better the public services of a given place and the higher the quality of those services, the more its urban residents were unwilling to take in the immigrant population. Meanwhile, cities facing high unemployment pressures had very much the same attitude. In some cities, there were also incidents when the parents of schoolchildren demonstrated against allowing the dependents of rural migrant workers into their schools.

Third, local governments are not enthusiastic about pushing forward household registration reform. They worry that if there is a dramatic increase in the demand for services, the quality of their existing services for current urban residents will decline, and this will exacerbate social problems. In addition, they fear that the floating population may well come into their cities just to take advantage of the public services. They will not come in to avail themselves of the opportunities to get a job. Moreover, they see the benefits of household-registration reform as being national in nature, while most of the costs of social services are actually provided by local governments (see Figure 11.3). Since the costs of reform will mainly be funded by local governments, there is little incentive for local governments to provide free services or subsidies to rural migrant workers.

Fourth, expanding the coverage of public services in cities will put considerable pressure on public spending. The inadequacy of public facilities is already quite apparent, given ongoing increases in the size of the "outsider" population. If the availability of public services is expanded, even more people will pick up and leave their rural homes for cities. It will speed up the flow of incoming people and raise the need for public services even more. Expanding coverage of public services means building new schools, having more community health centers, and increasing social security subsidies. This will put an enormous burden on public spending that many cities will simply be unable to handle.

The estimate is that it will cost roughly RMB 80,000 to 140,000 in public services for every rural migrant worker who is "urbanized." That sum includes the

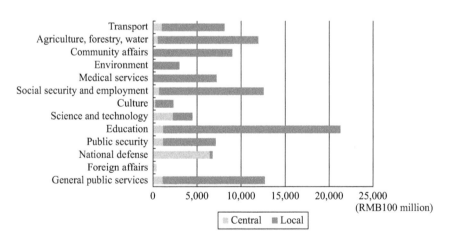

Figure 11.3 Central and local expenditure structure, 2012

Source: National Bureau of Statistics, *China Statistical Yearbook (2013)*, Beijing: China Statistics Press, 2013 edition.

costs of compulsory education, basic public health services, social security (medical as well as pension), social emergency relief, and guaranteed-type housing (China Development Research Foundation, 2010; The State Council's Develop Research Center and The World Bank, 2014). According to the *Opinion on Going Further in Reforming the Household Registration System*, China intends to achieve the goal of transitioning roughly 100 million people into urban status by the year 2020, including both former residents of rural areas and the population already living in cities but not recognized as urban citizens. This therefore will require public spending on the order of roughly RMB 8 trillion to RMB 14 trillion. In terms of the total, this seems a monumental figure. It should be pointed out, however, that the total will be invested over a period of six years, which means that the average in any single year will be between RMB 1.3 trillion and RMB 2.3 trillion. This is roughly 2.3 percent to 4 percent of China's GDP in 2013. What's more, the total for every year will be spent on a variety of things for which public spending is already being invested, including basic infrastructure, public services, and housing. Therefore, given the current state of the country's economic development and its finances, this goal of urbanizing 100 million people is realistic and financially feasible.

Recommendations on policy measures to deal with the problems

First, establish a system in which spending responsibilities are aligned with governing authorities. Most important in this regard is to make sure that the responsibility for providing social security and compulsory educated is matched with the ability to fund these things, as we push forward the process of urbanizing the "transitional agricultural population." Right now, social insurance programs fall within the purview of municipal- and county-level governments. They are managed by independent social security funds of each local government. Funds come from both social insurance premiums and government subsidies. If we are to realize a situation in which social security can be transferred when a person moves and in which social welfare benefits come under nationwide pooling and management, we must increase the force of central funding and overall planning. At present, education is mainly the responsibility of local governments in China. Given the mobility of the population, however, and the very substantial externalities involved in education, local governments are not highly enthusiastic about putting resources into it. The international experience is that the central government should in fact bear the majority of educational costs.

Second, set up linkage mechanisms that tie transfer payments to the urbanization of a transitioning population, and set up linkage mechanisms that tie the use of land for urban construction to the urbanization of a transitioning population. "Money goes where the people go." This means that spending pressures will gradually go down on the budgets of jurisdictions into which people are flowing, as will the opposition of city people and their governments to providing public services to incoming populations. In recent years, transfer payments already reflect the percentage of long-term residents in a place that exceeds the registered population of that place. Transfer payments are calculated accordingly to take account of more

people; the factor of urbanizing the transitioning population is already being fig-
ured into the balancing of transfer payments. Nevertheless, the weighting of this
factor is still too low. Guangdong is a good example, since it has more "outsiders" than anywhere else. In 2011, the central government subsidized compulsory
education to the extent of RMB 126.51 billion on a nationwide basis, which came
to RMB 874 per child on average. In Guangdong, however, the subsidies came
to RMB 2.625 billion. If one figures a total number of schoolchildren at 13 million in Guangdong, that equals RMB 201 per child, not even one-quarter of the
national average (Lin Shining and Li Xiaoxia, 2013). We must increase the weighting applied to the actual resident population in terms of general transfer payments,
as well as transfer payments for education, social security and employment, and
medical services.

In addition, set up linkage mechanisms that tie land to people, that is, increase
the amount of land quota allowed to a given city depending on the number of
rural migrant workers it has incorporated into its urban systems. Increase the
quota every year according to the city's absorption of people, so that the city can
deal with land-usage issues once those people have become urbanized. The land-
usage quotas should be determined by the size of the population absorbed into the
city. Those cities that absorb more people get more land. Those that absorb fewer
people get less land. Those that do not take in people at all get no quota. There
also should be a linkage that relates to the land between urban and rural areas.
Increasing urban construction-use land should be done only to the extent that
land defined as "rural construction-use land" is decreased, and decreasing urban
construction-use land should be done only to the extent that rural construction-
use land is increased. People in the zone between urban and rural areas could be
linked in the same way. When the construction-use land in a given jurisdiction is
increased, that should be tied to the number of outsiders who are urbanized in that
jurisdiction. The aim is to create a balance in compensating for the occupation of
farmland (China Development Research Foundation, 2010).

Third, create safeguards that ensure that farmers [rural people] who settle down
in cities as registered urban citizens do not lose their rights to their assets back
home. In this recent period, some areas have conducted pilot programs that involve
requiring farmers to give up their farmland as a condition for getting an urban
household registration (this includes both their contracted farmland and the land
under their residences – their "residential-use land"). In evaluating the results of
these pilot programs, it is clear that the majority of rural people are unwilling to
give up their own land. According to surveys undertaken by relevant institutions,
in 2010, 86.3 percent of rural migrant workers who were willing to take up permanent residence in cities hoped to be able to keep their contracted land, while
66.7 percent of them also hoped to be able to retain their residential land and any
buildings on it (Task force of the State Council's Development Research Center,
2011). In light of all these concerns, the General Office of the Central Committee of the Communist Party of China and the General Office of the State Council
recently issued an Opinion called *Opinion on Guiding the Process of Orderly
Circulation [Buying and Selling] of Operating Rights to Farmland in the Direction*

of Developing Greater Economies of Scale in Agriculture. This explicitly called for adhering firmly to the property rights [ownership] of rural land held by the collective. It called for stabilizing farmers' contracted rights to operate land. Finally, it called for "invigorating" those operating rights [that is, releasing controls that prevent them from being "circulated" or sold]. This allows farmers to move into cities for work without worrying that they are going to be forced to lose their land, but it also enables them to enjoy the economic benefits if and when their land is transferred [i.e., sold] to others. On the basis of confirming these rights, the next step is to speed up the process of identifying, registering, and certifying operating rights to land. It is to nail down land-contracting relationships through the use of legal documentation.

Concluding remarks

The most fundamental points that this report makes can be summed up as follows.

China has already entered the most critical period for achieving moderate prosperity in an all-round way. After going through three successive policy shifts over the past decades, the "invigorating" policies of the 1980s, the "stabilizing" policies of the 1990s, and the "repay the countryside" policies since 2000, China's rural development has entered a new stage. Based on the interaction of urban and rural, the goal now is to integrate urban and rural systems into a unified whole.

The success or failure of building moderate prosperity in an all-round way will depend on progress in achieving moderate prosperity in the countryside. The success or failure of that effort will in turn depend on unwavering determination to continue reforms, and it will depend upon correct decisions about development strategies and policy options. In the context of much deeper reforms in today's China, the two most important forces behind the process of building moderate prosperity in an all-round way are urbanization and the modernization of the countryside. Urbanization and the modernization of the countryside are interdependent. Without smooth progress in urbanization, it will be impossible to modernize rural areas. Without the foundation of a modernized countryside, urbanization will encounter a host of obstacles and will not proceed as it should. Four priority areas will need funding as we make policy decisions to push forward on both urbanization and modernization. These are agriculture and the building of basic infrastructure in rural areas, investment in rural human capital, investment in the rural ecology and environment, and the building up [and better governance] of rural society. These four are critical to creating moderate prosperity in rural areas, and they provide important handholds in the process of integrating urban and rural development. China's policy aim is to double per capita rural incomes by 2020 over the year 2010. As we pursue that, we must place even greater priority on preventing further disparities in income, including those between urban and rural incomes and those within rural incomes. Instead, these income gaps must decrease. We must ensure that living standards of the three most vulnerable groups of people – the elderly, the sick, and the poor – are not allowed to fall below China's national poverty line.

In specific terms, we must start with the following ten spheres of activity as we build moderate prosperity in an all-round way in China's rural areas. (1) Take proactive steps to deal with changes in how labor resources are now allocated and in how the rural population is geographically positioned around the country. (2) Deepen reform of the land system, and ensure that farmers have greater rights with respect to their own assets. (3) Realize a greater balance between the supply and demand for grain [for food security], and safeguard the quality and safety of food. (4) Generate innovative new ways to handle agricultural operations, and accelerate the modernization of agriculture. (5) Increase farmers' income and improve fairness in how income is distributed. (6) Improve the social security system and provision of public services. (7) Push forward innovations that improve social governance in rural areas. (8) Strengthen management over resources, and improve environmental protection, and establish a "rural ecological civilization." (9) Define government responsibilities and accountabilities in clear fashion and increase support from public spending. (10) Speed up reform of the household registration system, and push forward the unification of urban and rural development. These areas constitute strategic priorities in China's future rural reform. They must be promoted in coordinated fashion, using a comprehensive framework that looks at "rural" and "urban" from an overall point of view.

As compared to the situation prior to reform and opening up, the productive capacity of China's rural areas is now far greater, and the level of farmers' incomes has notably improved. The countryside has already gone through earthshaking changes. Although the current task of creating moderate prosperity in an all-round way in rural areas is monumental, as we implement policies that support, strengthen, and nurture agriculture, farmers, and the rural economy, we should be able to achieve this grand goal within the prescribed time.

Background reports that were incorporated in this volume

Zhang Xiaoshan: *Prominent Problems and Countermeasures concerning Current and Future Rural Economic and Social Development*

Zhang Hongyu: *Summary and Analysis on the Rural Economic and Social Policies of the Past Decade*

Lv Qingzhe: *Assessment on the Progress of Rural Affluence and the Standard and Indicator System of Rural Affluence in a New Era*

Li Zhou: *Study on the Industrial Development of Agriculture*

Cai Fang and Wang Meiyan: *Study on Issues concerning Rural Labors*

Liu Shouying and Shao Ting: *Rural Land System and Construction of the Affluent Society*

Wang Sangui and Zhang Weibin: *Rural Poverty Alleviation Policies and Farmers' Income Growth*

Zhou Feizhou, Fu Wei, Jiao Changquan, Wang Shaochen, and Tan Mingzhi: *Report on the Development of Rural Public Finance and Public Services in China*

Li Yuanxing: *Study on Social Problems in Rural Areas*

Wang Xiaoyi: *Environmental Problems in the Progress of Rural Development*

Yu Jianrong: *Dilemma and Breakthrough in Current Social Administration in Rural Areas*

Liu Yanwu: *Study on Suicides in Rural Areas: Based on the Qualitative Survey of Twenty-four Villages in Six Provinces*

Jin Sanlin: *Status of Food Supply–Demand and Food Safety*

Wu Zhigang and Li Jie: *Intensifying Rural Infrastructural Construction*

Zhang Hongkui and Gao Ming: *Boosting the Integrated Urban–Rural Development*

Zhao Hai and Ma Kai: *Innovation of the Agricultural Operation System*

Jin Shuqin and Zhang Canqiang: *Building the Eco-civilization in Rural Areas*

Hang Jing and Gao Qiang: *Defining the Roles of the Government*

Feng Wenmeng: *Prediction of Changes in China's Rural Population by 2020*

Yu Jiantuo: *How to Understand the Affluence Indicator System and Its Design Principles*

Feng Mingliang: *Challenges and Countermeasures concerning Rural Governance in China*

References

I. Chinese

Archives of Rural Policy Research Office, Secretariat of the CPC Central Committee, *A Collection of Rural Policies since the 3rd Plenary Session of the 11th Central Committee of the Communist Party of China*, Beijing, Central Party School Press, 1985

Blue Book of China's Society 2013, Beijing, Social Sciences Academic Press, 2012

Build a Well-off Society in an All-Round Way and Create a New Situation in Building Socialism with Chinese Characteristics (Report to the Eighteenth National Congress of the Communist Party of China, 2002)

Cai Fang, "Population Transformation, Population Bonus and Lewis Turning Point," *Economic Research Journal*, 2010 (4)

Cai Xiaoli, Liu Li, "Provision of Rural Public Products: Roles of Joint Organizations," *Comparative Economic & Social Systems*, 2006 (2)

Cai Yumei, Zhang Wenxin, Liu Yansui, "Multi Objective Prediction and Analysis on China's Demands for Farming Lands," *Resources Science*, 2007 (7)

Cao Chunyan, Wu Qun, "Difficulties and Breakthroughs of Soil Contamination Control in China," *Guangming Daily*, 2014–10–12

CCCPC Party Literature Research Office, *A Collection of Important Literatures since the 18th CPC National Congress*, Beijing, CCCPC Party Literature Press, 2014

Chen Ajiang, "Analysis on Stakeholders in Water Contamination Accidents," *Zhejiang Academic Journal*, 2008 (4)

Chen Ganquan, Xin Chaohui, Yan Fangcai, *Challenges and Countermeasures for Old-Age Care Services in Rural Anhui*, website of the Development Research Center of the Government of Anhui Province (http://www.dss.gov.cn/News_wenzhang.asp?ArticlelD=326168)

Chen Huadong, et al., "Evolution of Township Governments and Their Roles since 1949," *Social Science Front*, 2007 (2)

Chen Jianhua, Li Jie, "A Research on "Who Are Cultivating Lands'," *Research Report of the Research Center for Rural Economy of the Ministry of Agriculture*, 2013

Chen Xiaoan, "Decision-Making Mechanism for Supply of Rural Public Products: Status Quo, Challenges and Countermeasures," *Journal of Southwest University for Nationalities*, 2005 (4)

Chen Xiwen, "Environmental Problems and Rural Development of China," *Management World*, 2002 (1)

Chen Xiwen, Zhao Yang, Luo Dan, *60-year Evolution of China's Rural System*, Beijing, People's Publishing House, 2009

Chen Xiwen, et al., *Study on China's Food Safety Strategy*, Beijing, Chemical Industry Press, 2004

China Development Research Center of the State Council, World Bank, *China: Toward Efficient, Inclusive and Sustainable Urbanization*, Beijing, China Development Press, 2014

China Development Research Foundation, *New Urbanization in China: For a People-Centered Strategy*, Beijing, People's Publishing House, 2010

China Development Research Foundation, *China Development Report 2011/12: Changes of Demographic Conditions and Resulting Policy Adjustment*, Beijing, China Development Press, 2012

China Development Research Foundation, *Parametric Insurance and Reform of Natural Disaster Relief System in China*, Beijing, China Development Press, 2014

"China Livelihood Indicator Research" Task Force of China Development Research Center of the State Council, "Analysis and Advices on Soil Contamination in China," *Survey Report of China Development Research Center of the State Council* (abstract) No. 105, 2014-8-5

China State Finance Magazine, *China Fiscal Yearbook* (2000–2011)

A Collection of the Documents No. 1 of the State Council of the CPC Central Committee on Agriculture, Rural Areas and Farmers (1982–2000), Beijing, People's Publishing House, 2014

Cui Fang, "Nutrition Bag: A Good Start to Lifelong Health," *Jian Kang Bao*, 2010-8-31

Deng Xiaoping, "China's Goal Is to Achieve Comparative Prosperity by the End of the Century," *Selected Works of Deng Xiaoping*, Vol. II, 2001

Department of Housing and Urban-Rural Development of Fujian Province, *Upgrading Professional Quality through Night School for Migrant Rural Workers*, 2013-2-27

Department of Price, NDRC, *A Collection of Material on the Cost and Benefit of Agricultural Products in China (2000–2012)*

Department of Rural Economic System and Management, Ministry of Agriculture, *Statistics on Rural Operation and Management*, 2013

Department of Rural Surveys, National Bureau of Statistics, *China Rural Statistical Yearbook*, Beijing, China Statistics Press, 2013

Du Shuang, *Study on Rural Debts*, Zhengzhou, Henan People's Publishing House, 2008

Du Yang, Lu Yang, "Labor Supply Trends and Policies in the New Stage of Economic Development," *Report on China's Population and Labor No. 14: From Demographic Dividend to Institutional Dividend*, Beijing, Social Sciences Academic Press, 2013

Du Yang, Lu Yang, "China's Natural Unemployment Rate and Its Implication," *The Journal of World Economy*, 2014 (4)

Du Yang, Wang Meiyan, "Total Employment and Employment Structure in China: Re-Estimation and Discussion," *Report on China's Population and Labor No. 12: Challenges during the 12th Five-Year Plan Period: Population, Employment and Income Distribution*, Beijing, Social Sciences Academic Press, 2011

Fei Xiaotong, *Childbirth Policy in a Rural China*, Beijing, Peking University Press, 1998

Feng Haiying, Liu Yonggong, "Environmental (Land) Degradation and Poverty: From the Perspective of Literature Review," *Qinghai Social Sciences*, 2012 (3)

Firmly March on the Path of Socialism with Chinese Characteristics and Strive to Complete the Building of a Moderately Prosperous Society in All Respects (Report to the Eighteenth National Congress of the Communist Party of China, 2012)

Gao Wen, "Clean Water for Farmers: Review of Rural Drinking Water Safety Work in Past Ten Years," *Farmers' Daily*, 2014-8-19

General Office of the State Council, *12th Five-Year Plan for State Food Safety Regulatory System*, 2012

Gong Shengsheng, Zhang Tao, "Study on the Changes in Time and Spatial Distribution of 'Cancer Villages' in China," *China Population Resources and Environment*, 2013 (9)

Gong Weicai, Xue Xingli, "New Concept on Rural Insurance: Public-Benefiting Gradient Pension," *Shandong Social Sciences*, 2012 (8)

Guo Ping, Chen Gang, *Analysis on the Data from the Follow-up Survey on the Conditions of the Aged Urban and Rural Population of China in 2006*, Beijing, China Society Press, 2009

Han Dongmei, Jin Shuqin, "Analysis on the Agricultural Policies of China for Environmental Protection in Rural Areas," *Review of Economic Research*, 2013 (43)

Han Jun, "Guidelines for Sangong Works in the New Phase," *Survey Report of China Development Research Center of the State Council*, No. 151, 2014–10–28

Han Jun, et al., *Rural Reform of China (2002–2012)*, Shanghai, Shanghai Far East Publishers, 2012

He Yupeng, Chen Sicheng, *Analysis on China's Rural Development Status and Trends under the Urbanization Background*, Washington, DC, DRCnet

Hold High the Great Banner of Socialism with Chinese Characteristics and Strive for New Victories in Building a Moderately Prosperous Society in All Respects (Report to the Seventeenth National Congress of the Communist Party of China, 2007)

Hong Dayong, "The Eight Social Characteristics of Environmental Problems in Contemporary China," *Teaching and Research*, 1999 (8)

Hu Xiaoping, Guo Xiaohui, "Analysis and Prediction of China's Food Supply and Demand Structure in 2020: From the Perspective of Nutrition Standard," *China Rural Economy*, 2010 (6)

Hu Xiaoyun, Huang Liangui, *Mode Wins: Analysis on the Leading Enterprises of Agricultural Industrialization*, Zhejiang, Zhejiang University Press, 2013

Hua Sheng, *Transformation of Urbanization and Land Traps*, Beijing, Oriental Publishing Center, 2014

Huang Xiaohu, "Review and Analysis on the Land Acquisition System," *Shanghai Land & Resources*, 2011 (2)

Huang Yanxin, Yu Kui, Shi Gaokang, Wang Gang, Li Yang, Hu Shunping, Wang Anqi, "Analysis on Issues Concerning the Reform of the Rural Collective Ownership System," *Issues in Agricultural Economy*, 2014 (4)

Hui Liangyu, "Further Diversify and Expand the Road of Agricultural and Rural Development with Chinese Characteristics, Carefully Summarize Rural Experiences to Boost Innovation of Theories and Policies," speech at 2012 China Rural Development High-Level Forum, *Farmers' Daily*, 2012–6–11

Jia Feng, Niu Lingjuan, Luan Caixia, Fu Jun, "Environmental Protection in China: Situation, Status Quo and New Issues," Lu Xueyi, Li Peilin, Chen Guangjin (eds.), *Analysis and Prediction of China's Social Situation*, Beijing, Social Sciences Academic Press, 2012

Jiang Gaoming, "Solving Rural Environmental Pollution with Ecologically Recyclable Agriculture," *Environmental Protection*, 2010 (9)

Jiao Shaojun, Shan Zhengjun, Cai Daoji, Xu Hong, "Be Alert to "Wastes from Farmlands': Advices on Control over Pollution by Abandoned Chemical Packages," *Environmental Protection*, 2012 (8)

Jin Feng, Li Qun, "Evaluation and Optimization of Financial Expenditure for Supporting Agriculture," *Journal of Taxation College of Yangzhou University*, 2010, 15 (6)

Jin Shuqin, *Designing Policies for Water Contamination Control in River Basins: External Conceptual Innovation and Application*, Beijing, Metallurgical Industry Press, 2011 Edition

Lan Hong, Ma Yue, "Governmental Funds for Soil Restoration Are in Urgent Need," *China Environmental News*, 2014–4–10

Li Bengong, *Estimation on the Centennial Trend of Population Ageing in China*, Beijing, Hualing Press, 2007

Li Feng, Zhang Shangwen, Zhang Yulong, *Reflections on Promoting Rural Old-age Care Service System of Xiangzhou District*, portal website of Xiangzhou District (http://www. hbxy.gov.cn/publish/cbnews/201210/26/cb21324_1.shtml)

Li Jiange, "Enhance Rural Infrastructure, Improve Rural Public Services," *Qunyan*, 2006 (9)

Li Lihui, "The Central Government Allocates RMB5.5 Billion Special Funds for Improvement of Rural Environment," *People's Daily*, 2012–02–14

Li Liqing, "Probe into Enhancing China's Rural Public Service Channels," *Agricultural Economics*, 2005 (8)

Li Maolan ed., *Study on Farmers' Burdens in China*, Taiyuan, Shanxi Economics Press, 1996

Li Ping, *Illustration of Financial System*, Beijing, China Financial & Economic Publishing House, 2010

Li Shi, "Status, Trends and Influencing Factors of Income Gap in China," China Development Research Foundation (ed.), *Income Distribution in the Transitional China: Assessment on the Impact of Policies for Income Distribution* (pp. 11–39), Beijing, China Development Press, 2012

Li Shi, Hiroshi Sato, Shi Taili, *Research on Income Distribution in China: Analysis on the Changes of Income Gap in China*, Beijing, People's Publishing House, 2013

Li Shi, Luo Chuliang, "Re-Estimating the Income Gap between Urban and Rural Households in China," *Journal of Peking University*, 2007 (2)

Li Yurui, Liu Yansui, Long Hualou, "Spatio-Temporal Analysis of Population and Residential Land Change in Rural China," *Journal of Natural Resources*, 2010, 25 (10)

Liang Suming, *Rural Building Theory*, Shanghai, Shanghai People's Publishing House, 2011

Liao Hongle, Li Jian, "Assessment and Advices on the Implementation of the Policies for Identification, Registration and Certification of Rural Lands," *Rural Dynamics*, 2014 (14)

Liaoning Research Institute for Fiscal Science, *Financial Policies for Comprehensive Rural Environmental Improvement*, website of Ministry of Finance, 2011–11–28, http://www. mof.gov.cn/index.htm

Liu Minquan, Xu Zhong, Yu Jiantuo, "Irregular Finance in Credit Market," *The Journal of World Economy*, 2003 (7)

Liu Minquan, Yu Jiantuo, Xu Zhong, *Study on Rural Financial Market of China*, Beijing, China Renmin University Press, 2006

Lin Shining, Li Xiaoxia, "Over 3 Million Migrant Children Receive In-school Compulsory Education in Guangdong," *Yangcheng Evening News*, 2013–9–10

Liu Shouying, *Land Issue in the Transitional China*, Beijing, China Development Press, 2014

Liu Yansui, Liu Yu, Zhai Rongxin, "Geographical Research and Optimizing Practice of Rural Hollowing in China," *Acta Geographica Sinica*, 2009, 64 (10)

Lin Yifu, *System, Technology and Agricultural Development in China*, Shanghai, Shanghai Joint Publishing Corporation, 2005

Liu Changming, He Xiwu, et al., *Plan for China's Water Issue in the 21st Century*, Beijing, Science Press, 2001

Liu Jinwei, "Status Quo of Equity in Urban-Rural Basic Public Health Services in Beijing: Evaluation and Countermeasures," *Chinese Health Economics*, 2011 (2)

Liu Weijun, *Study on Food Safety Control in China*, Master's Dissertation of Northwest A&F University, 2006

Lu Bu, Wu Kai, Chen Yinjun, Xiao Bilin, Chen Xueyuan, Wang Xiaoping, Wang Yong, Wan Fushi, "China's Regional Food Productivity Potential in 2020 and the Way to Realize It," *China Soft Science*, 2009 (10)

Lu Mai, Du Zhixin, Cao Yan, "Pre-School Education Should Be Popularized in Villages," *Survey Report of China Development Research Center of the State Council* (abstract) No. 165 2014

Luo Zhendong, et al., "Analysis on the Characteristics of Equalized Development of Urban-Rural Basic Public Service Facilities: Based on Survey in Changzhou City," *Urban Studies*, 2010 (12)

Lu Xinye, Hu Feifan, "Estimation and Analysis on Supply and Demand of Food in 2020," *Issues in Agricultural Economy*, 2012 (10)

Ma Xiaohe, *Study on Rural Tax Payment Reform in China*, Beijing, China Planning Press, 2002

Ma Yuexin, Zhao Liyun, Zeng Guo, "Malnutrition of Children Aged 0–5 Year and Intervention Research Progress," *Foreign Medical Sciences* (Section of Hygiene), 2009

Ministry of Agriculture, *Report on Agricultural Development of China* (2007–2013)

Ministry of Agriculture, "2012 Report on National Monitoring of Grasslands," *Farmers' Daily*, 2011–4–13

Ministry of Agriculture, *Statistics on Rural Operation and Management (2013)*, 2013

Ministry of Civil Affairs, *China Civil Affairs Statistical Yearbook (2011)*, Beijing, China Statistics Press, 2011

Ministry of Education, *China Statistics Yearbook on Educational Expenditure*, Beijing, China Statistics Press, 2011–2012

Ministry of Education, *Statistical Communiqué National Education Development in 2013*, Beijing, China Statistics Press, July 2014

Ministry of Finance, *Opinions of the Ministry of Finance on Further Enhancing Management of Agriculture-Supporting Funds*, 2008 (28)

Ministry of Health, *National Report on Nutritional Status of Children Aged 0–6 Year (2012)*, website of MOH, May 2012, http://www.moh.gov.cn

Ministry of Human Resources and Social Security, *2012 Status of Social Insurance of China*, 2013

Ministry of Human Resources and Social Security, "Migrant Rural Workers Benefit Most from Urban and Rural Pension Insurances," *Beijing Daily*, 2014–2–27 (2)

National Bureau of Statistics, *China Environment Statistical Yearbook (1949–2011)*, Beijing, China Statistics Press

National Bureau of Statistics, *Data on National Census 2000*, Beijing: China Statistics Press, 2000

National Bureau of Statistics, *Data on National Census 2010*, Beijing: China Statistics Press, 2010

National Bureau of Statistics, *Report on 2012 National Monitoring Survey on Migrant Rural Workers, 2012*, Beijing: China Statistics Press, 2013

National Bureau of Statistics, *China Statistical Abstract 2014*, Beijing: China Statistics Press, 2014

National Health and Family Planning Commission, *2013 China Health Statistics Summary*, 2014

NDRC, *Outline of Mid and Long-Term Planning for Food Security (2008–2020)*, 2008

Nie Fengying, et al., *Analysis on the Food Safety and Vulnerability of Poor Counties in China: Based a Survey of Six Counties in the Western Region*, Beijing, China Agricultural Science and Technology Press, 2011

Nuo Yanqing, Zhao Liang, Jiang Yugui, "Comparison of Operating Social Service Modes and Analysis on Restrictions," *Management and Administration on Rural Cooperative Economy*, 2013 (4)

OECD, *Reviews of Agricultural Policies China*, Beijing, Economic Press China, 2005

Qian Shuitu, "Retrospect and Prospect of Thirty-Year Reform of China's Rural Financial System," *East Asia Papers*, 2008 (5)

Qin Hui, *Ten Expositions on Tradition: The System Culture and Its Change in Chinese Society*, Shanghai, Fudan University Press, 2003

Qu Yanchun, *Evolution and Restructuring: Study on the Public Product Supply System in Rural China*, Beijing, People's Publishing House, 2012

Qu Yanchun, "30-Year Reform of Rural Institutions: Review of Practical Evolution and Theoretical Study," *Dongyue Tribune*, 2014 (8)

"Reform of Household Registration System" task force, Institute of Economic System and Management, NDRC, *Major Challenges and Overall Plan for the Reform of the Household Registration System of China*, 2013

Ren Bingqiang, "Rural Environmental Conflicts and Governance Crisis of Local Governments," *Journal of Chinese Academy of Governance*, 2011 (5)

Research Center for Rural Economy of the Ministry of Agriculture, *Report on Execution of Rural Policies* (2009–2013)

"The Rural Environmental Protection Fund Has Invested a Total RMB20 Billion," website of (http://www.huanjingchanye.com, 2014–06–23)

Shao Zhenrun, "How to Effectively Improve Agricultural Chemical Efficiency," *Farmers' Daily*, 2014–1–16

Sheng Lamei, Wang Jiayou, "Economic Analysis on Integration of China's Agriculture-Supporting Funds," *Economic Research Guide*, 2011 (18)

Shi Yulin, *Study on Rational Allocation of Agricultural Resources and Improvement of Comprehensive Agricultural Productivity*, Beijing, China Agriculture Press, 2014

Song Guojun, *Analysis on Environmental Policies*, Beijing, Chemical Industry Press, 2008

Song Hongyuan, *Review and Evaluation of Agricultural and Rural Policies during the 11th Five-Year Plan*, Beijing, China Agriculture Press, 2010

Song Hongyuan, *Study on Contemporary Economic Transformation and Rural Development of China*, Beijing, China Agriculture Press, 2014

Song Hongyuan, et al., *Study on Rural Finance and Public Administration in China*, Beijing, China Financial & Economic Publishing House, 2004

"Special Fund for Migrant Rural Workers Suffering from Pneumoconiosis," *Workers' Daily*, Beijing, Information Office of the State Council, 2014–3–13

State Council, *National Program of Action for Child Development in China (2011–2020)*, July 2011

The State Council, "Report on Works about Drinking Water Safety," *Report to the 27th Session of the 11th NPC Standing Committee*, Beijing, Information Office of the State Council, 2012–6–27

The State Council Information Office, *The Grain Issue in China (White Paper)*, Beijing, Information Office of the State Council, 1996

The State Council Information Office, *Opinions of the State Council on Further Promoting the Reform of the Household Registration System*, Beijing, Information Office of the State Council, 2014–7–30

State Forestry Administration, "Communiqué on the Survey of Desertification in China," *China Green Times*, 2011–1–5

Sun Lei, *Explorations and Practices of Family Farm in Shanghai*, Shanghai, Shanghai University of Finance & Economics Press, 2013

Sun Yefang, "Why Criticizing Rural Reformism?", *Chinese Rural Area*, 1936, 2 (5)

Task Force of China Development Research Foundation, *Assessment Report on the Implementation Result of Policy for State Financial Support for Intermediate Occupational Education*, August 2014

Task Force of China Preschool Education Development Strategy, *Study on China's Preschool Education Development Strategy*, Beijing, Educational Science Publishing House, 2010

Task Force of Research Department of Rural Economy, China Development Research Center of the State Council, *A Study on China's Agrarian Institutional Change*, Beijing, China Development Press, 2013

Task Force of Section of Agriculture, Department of Finance of Xinjiang Uygur Autonomous Region, "Study on Construction and Application of the Performance Assessment System for Financial Support for Agriculture," *Review of Economic Research*, 2010 (10)

Task Force of Sichuan Academy of Social Sciences, "Practices and Exploration of Rural Land Joint-Stock Cooperatives," *West Forum on Economy and Management*, 2013 (3)

Task Force of Zhangzhou Bureau of Finance, "Analysis on Establishing and Improving the Performance Assessment System for Financial Support for Agriculture," *Rural Finance and Financial Affair*, 2013 (11)

The Third Plenary Session of the Fourteenth Central Committee of the Communist Party of China, *Decision of the CPC Central Committee on Certain Issues in Establishing a Socialist Market Economy System*, November 1993

The Third Plenary Session of the Fifteenth Central Committee of the Communist Party of China, *Decision of the CPC Central Committee on Certain Major Issues Concerning Agriculture and Rural Areas*, October 1998

The Third Plenary Session of the Sixteenth Central Committee of the Communist Party of China, *Decision of the CPC Central Committee on Certain Issues Concerning the Socialist Market Economy System*, October 2003

The Third Plenary Session of the Seventeenth Central Committee of the Communist Party of China, *Decision of the CPC Central Committee on Certain Major Issues on Rural Reform and Development*, October 2008

The Third Plenary Session of the Eighteenth Central Committee of the Communist Party of China, *Decision of the CPC Central Committee on Certain Major Issues Concerning Comprehensively Deepening Reforms*, 2013

Tu Shengwei, *Communities, Enterprises, Cooperative Organizations and Supply of Rural Public Products*, Beijing, Economic Science Press, 2011

UN Representative Office in China, *Promoting Food Safety in China*, 2008

UN Representative Office in China, *Environment and Health in China*, April 2009

UNDP China Office, et al., *China Human Development Report: Making Green Development a Choice*, Beijing, China Financial & Economic Publishing House, 2002

Wang Mei, "Eighteen Amendments to Seven Laws including the Prison Law," *The Beijing News*, 2012–10–27

Wang Mengkui ed., *Anti Poverty and Children Development in China*, Beijing, China Development Press, 2013

Wang Xianming, *Modern Gentlemen*, Tianjin, Tianjin People's Publishing House, 1997

Wang Xiaoyi, "Herdsmen's Life in Drought: A Survey of Baiyinhaga of Xing'an League," *Journal of Huazhong Normal University*, 2009 (4)

Wang Xiaoyi, "Grassland Drought under the Background of System Transformation: Settlement of Herdsmen, Grassland Fragments and the Impact of Marketization of Herding Areas," *Journal of China Agricultural University*, 2013 (1)

Wang Yamin, Lan Dingyuan, *Study on Concepts and Practices of Rural Governance: Review of Good Governance in the History*, Beijing, Guangming Daily Press, 2009

Wei Zhaoan, "Speech of Vice Minister Wei Zhaoan at the National Work Conference on Lands and Fertilizer," *Information Circular of the Ministry of Agriculture*, 2011 (47)

World Bank, *World Development Report 1992: Development and the Environment*, Beijing, China Financial & Economic Publishing House, 1992

World Bank, *Green Water and Blue Sky: Prospecting China's Environment in the 21st Century*, Beijing, China Financial & Economic Publishing House, 1997

World Bank, *China's Food Security: Long-Standing Problems and Optional Solutions*, Beijing, China Financial & Economic Publishing House, 1998

World Bank, *World Development Report 2008: Agriculture for Development*, Beijing, Tsinghua University Press, 2008

Wu Yongjian, "Marketization: An Alternative Supply of Rural Public Products: Crisis and Deviation in Current Supply of Rural Public Products," *A Collection of Papers of the Annual Symposium on Institutional Economics*, 2006

Xi Jianrong, "Half of the Pollutants Are from Rural Areas, Legislation Is in Urgent Need," *Legal Daily*, 2011–3–29

Xiang Jiquan, "Exploration and Method Transformation of China's Rural Construction in 100 Years," *Journal of Gansu Institute of Public Administration*, 2009 (2)

Xiao Tangbiao, "Governance of Rural Society and Evolution of Township System," *Journal of Party School of CPC Ningbo Municipal Committee*, 2002 (5)

Xiao Yang, "It Is Too Hard to Be a Modern Farmer," *Reform of China*, 2000 (6)

Xie Mingguang, Wen Jianwu, *Road to an Affluent Society*, Beijing: China Statistics Press, 2000

Xie Ping, Xu Zhong, *Gains and Losses of Rural Financial Reform in Last Ten Years*, website of China Finance 40 Forum (http://www.cf40.org.cn), 2013

Xiong Yibo, Chen Junyi, Xu Haitao, "Report on the Special Survey on the Evolution of Villages in Hubei Province," *China Rural Studies*, 2014 (30)

Xu Yong, *Unbalanced Politics of China: A Comparison between Urban and Rural Areas*, Beijing, China Radio & TV Press, 1992

Yang Danhui, Li Hongli, "'Accounting for Environmental-Related Losses Based on Damage and Cost': Taking Shandong Province as an Example," *China Industrial Economics*, 2010 (7)

Yang Dongping, *China Environmental Development Report (2012)*, Beijing, Social Sciences Academic Press, 2012

Yang Jianli, Yue Zhenghua, "Estimation on the Supply and Demand of Food and Major Agricultural Products in 2002 and Policy Advices," *Reform of Economic System*, 2014 (4)

Yu Depeng, "Analysis on Farmers' Burdens from Social and Legal Perspectives," *Twenty-First Century* (Online), 2007 (5)

Yue Ximing, Jia Xiaojun, "Status Quo and Problems of China's Transfer Payment System," China Development Research Foundation (ed.), *Income Distribution in the Transitional China: Assessment on the Impact of Policies for Income Distribution* (pp. 213–262), Beijing, China Development Press, 2012

Yu Jianrong, "Land Issue Has Become the Focal Point of Farmers' Right-Protection Conflicts," *The World of Survey and Research*, 2005 (3)

Yu Jianrong, "Dilemma and Solution of High-Pressure Stabilization: More on the Rigid Social Stability in China," *Exploration and Free Views*, 2012 (9)

Zeng Hongying, *Standards and Periodical Objectives of Equity in Access to Basic Public Services*, Beijing, China Planning Press, 2013

Zhan Jingwen, *Yunnan Plans to Launch Renovation of Unsafe Rural Houses and Build Houses for 300,000 Quake-Stricken Households*, xinhuanet.com (http://www.huaia.com/qcyn/ynyw/ynsx/2014/08/4036724. html)

Zhang Hongbo, "Analysis on the Age Structure of Labors in Rural Jiaodong," *Journal of Hebei Agricultural Sciences*, 2009 (10)

Zhang Jing, *Basic Level Governments: Problems in Village System*, Zhejiang, Zhejiang People's Publishing House, 2000

Zhang Kaiti, Guo Ping, *Blue Book on Population Ageing and the Condition of the Aged in China*, Beijing, China Society Press, 2010

Zhang Xiaoshan, Li Zhou, *Study on Thirty-Year Reform in Rural China*, Beijing, Economy and Management Publishing House, 2008

Zhang Yuanhong, "Supply and Fund Raising of Rural Public Health Services," Rural Development Institute of Chinese Academy of Social Sciences (ed.), *Focusing on Sangong: China Rural Development Research Report No. 5* (pp. 32–56), Beijing, Social Sciences Academic Press, 2006

Zhang Yunhua, et al., *Study on Improving and Reforming Rural House Site System*, Beijing, China Agriculture Press, 2011

Zhao Kezhi, "Accelerating Popularization of 15-Year Compulsory Education to Help Children with a Good Start Point," *Guizhou Daily*, 2014–3–5

Zhao Qiguo, Huang Jikun, "Development Trend of Agricultural Technology and Strategic Choice for the Year 2020," *Ecology and Environmental Sciences*, 2012 (3)

Zhao Shukai, *Rural Governance and Institutionalized Government*, Beijing, Commercial Press, 2010

Zhao Shukai, *The New Life of Farmers*, Beijing, Commercial Press, 2012

Zhao Wen, *Chinese Agriculture in a New Pattern*, Beijing, Economy and Management Publishing House, 2012

Zhao Zhanjun, Xie Mei, "Road to Market-Oriented Supply of Rural Public Products," *Rural Economy*, 2005 (12)

Zhou Qiren, *Urban and Rural China*, Beijing, CITIC Press, 2014

Zhu Zhaoliang, David Norse, Sun Bo, *Measures for Control over Non-point Sources of Agricultural Pollution*, Beijing, China Environmental Science Press, 2006

Zuo Ting, "Survey and Analysis on Rural Pollution in China: Data from 141 Villages," *China Rural Survey*, 2008 (1)

II.   English

Brown, L. R., *Who Will Feed China: Wake-Up Call for a Small Planet*, New York, W. W. Norton & Company, 1995

Cai, Fang, Lu Yang, "The End of China's Demographic Dividend: The Perspective of Potential GDP Growth," Ross Garnaut, Cai Fang and Ligang Song (eds.), *China: A New Model for Growth and Development*, Canberra, The Australian National University E-Press, 2013, 55–74

Drakakis-Smith, D. W., *Third World Cities*, Abingdon, UK, and New York, Routledge, 2000, 81

Harris, R., Todaro, P. "Migration, Unemployment and Development a Two-Sector Analysis," *The American Economic Review*, 1970 60 (1), 126–142

Knight, John, Lina Song, *The Rural–Urban Divide: Economic Disparities and Interactions in China*, Oxford, Oxford University Press, 1999

Norse, D., Z. L. Zhu, "Policy Response to Non-point Pollution from China's Crop Production," *Special Report by the Take Force on Non-point Pollution from Crop Production of* the China Council for International Cooperation on Environment and Development *(CCICED)* Beijing, 2004

Oi, Jean C. *Rural China Takes Off: Institutional Foundations of Economic Reform*, Berkeley, University of California Press, 1999

Ravallion, Martin, Shaohua Chen, "When Economic Reform Is Faster Than Statistical Reform: Measuring and Explaining Income Inequality in Rural China," *Oxford Bulletin of Economics and Statistics*, 1999, 61 (1), 33–56

Shi Li, Terry Sicular, "The Distribution of Household Income in China: Inequality, Poverty and Policies," *China Quarterly*, March 2014 (217)

Shue, Vivienne, *Sketches of the Chinese Body Politic*, Stanford, CA, Stanford University Press, 1998

Sicular, Teery, Yue Ximing, Bjorn Gustaffson, Li Shi, "The Urban–Rural Income Gap and Inequality in China," *Review of Income and Wealth*, 2007, 53 (1), 93–126

Wang Jinxia, Jikun Huang, Tingting Yan. "Impacts of Climate Change on Water and Agricultural Production in Ten Large River Basins in China," *Journal of Integrative Agriculture*, 2013 (6)

Zhong Linxiu, Hongmei Yi, Renfu Luo, Chang Fang Liu, Scott Rozelle. *The Human Capital Roots of the Middle Income Trap:The Case of China, Paper Presented at the 2012 LAAE Conference*, Brazil, August 18 to 24

Index

absolute poverty, eliminating 148, 157–63; *see also* poverty alleviation
administered towns 33, 80
administered villages: college students in 216; number of 26–7
age: agricultural labor force 33–4; rural migrant workers 34; suicide rate 225
aging society: caregiving dilemma 28–9; China's population 27–8; living conditions of elderly in Hubei province 173–4; security system for 170–5
agricultural labor force 30–2; age structures of 34; aging of 33–4; changing agricultural production 42n6; cost of 89; definition of 31–2; gross national income and agricultural employment 39
agricultural production: Anbang Company as model 125–7; domestic and international supply and demand 117; environmental degradation limiting 243–5; gap between supply and demand 90–1; impact of resource factors on yield 89; increase in costs 87–8; management processes 109; operations and organization management 142; organizational forms and operating methods 130–1; public finance for increasing 290–1; supply and demand for grain 88–91; supply and demand for meat and dairy 91; trade and net imports 89–90; water use 86; *see also* food security; grain production; new-style agricultural operating system
agricultural productivity: economic reform and 37–8; historical comparisons on 37; improving 149–52; soil and water pollution impacting 243–4
agriculture: added value in GDP by country 292; arable land quantity

and quality 236–7; challenges facing existing ways of 116–18; chemical fertilizer use 239–40; domestic and international markets 117; farmers and public service facilities 192; financial expenditure on 284; food security and 104–5; formulation and implementation of plans for 259–61; land system in 46, 47; micro-loans in 140–1; modernization of 113; modernizing production 40; operating income from 149–52; order-based 135; pesticide usage in 239–40; plastic sheeting/film use in 240, 258; pollution of farmland 236–7; public finance recommendations for 301; size of arable land by farming households 116; socialized service organizations in 125; strategic restructuring of 261; subsidies for 285–6; subsidy policies for grain production 107; using innovations and technology 136–7; waste disposal by 241; water consumption 237; water resources and pollution 237–8; Wens model for industrializing 123–4; *see also* new-style agricultural operating system
all-round, term 14
Anbang Company model for farming 125–7
animal excrements, technological systems for management of 258
aquatic products, supply and demand for 91
Argentina 292
Australia 292, 293

"beautiful countryside" initiative, Guizhou province 189–91
beef, supply and demand for 91
Beijing Municipal Bureau of Land and Resources 62

Beijing Uni-construction Group Co., Ltd. (BUCC) 322
benefit compensation mechanisms, grain production 107
Blackstone Group of America 57
board of directors, collective property rights 81–2
board of supervisors, collective property rights 81–2
Book of Rites (the *Li Ji*) 1
Book of Songs (the *Shi Jing*) 1
bourgeoisie, term 45
Brazil 91, 92, 292
budgeting: innovative practices of Xinhe and Zheguo models 231–2; participatory, in Wenling township 230–2; participatory methods in oversight 232; Xinhe way of doing things 230–1; Zheguo way of doing things 231
business start-up services, transitioning populations 321–2

Canada 292, 293
cancer villages 245, 246, 268*n*1
caregiving dilemma, China's oldest county 28–9
central-authority pressure: social management 226–7
certification: evolution of 51–2; land rights 52–4, 58; methods for issuing 54
Charter of the Chinese People's Political Consultative Conference (1949) 45
Chen Chunming 185
Chengdu Jifeng Industrial Corporation 122
Chen Jianhua 29
Chen Sicheng 27
China: agricultural support and protection 293; agricultural value in GDP 292; grain production 91, 92
China Development Research Foundation 110–11, 167, 180, 185, 324–5
China Disease Prevention and Control Center 110, 180, 182, 185
China Food Safety Convention 97
China's Agricultural Policy Simulation and Projection Model (CAPSiM) 88, 89, 112*n*1
China's water simulation model (CWSM) 85
Chuanfang Community, medical care of floating population 324–5
clenbuterol hydrochloride, lean meat powder 96–7, 245
collectively owned construction-use land: Guangdong province measures 69–71;

possibility of putting, on market 68–9; problems facing systems for 67–8; sale of property rights 68–9
collectively owned property rights: adjusting laws regulations and policies 82; defining qualifications determining membership for 77–8; methods of quantifying assets and issuing shares 80–1; Minhang district of Shanghai 80; opinions about quantifying assets 76–7; organizational forms reforming 81–2; pilot program in Pingluo county 78–9; progress in reform of system for 76; quantifying assets for distribution as shares 76–7; reform for system governing 75–82, 83*n*6–7; three levels of ownership of assets 79–80; *see also* property-rights system
college students, serving as county officials 215, 216–17
commercial-use land 49
communications infrastructure program, Guizhou province 190
Communist Party of China (CPC): 14th CPC Central Committee 11; 15th CPC Central Committee 114; 17th CPC Central Committee 111, 114, 164; 18th CPC Central Committee 19, 42*n*1; grassroots organizations of 233; hiring college students as town officials 216–17; organization of farmers 199; reform of 201; reforms in countryside 200–201
compensation requirements: agricultural resource usage and 254–5; water quality and 255–6
conflict resolution, town and village governance 209–11
Constitution of the People's Republic of China (1954), 45; land requisitions 72–3
construction projects, social conflicts 223
construction-use land 46, 49: agricultural-type 141–2; arable land turned to 89; *see also* collectively owned construction-use land
contracting system (*cheng-bao*) 200
contractual operating rights to farmland 55–60; basic features of existing system 55–6; developing market in Shanghai for transfer of 59; general principles regarding reform 57–60; industrial and commercial capital investments in 57; issues facing current system 56; secondary market in land-use rights 59–60

Conveyance of Rites (*Li Yun*) 1
corn: global production 92; projections of supply and demand 90; *see also* grain production
corruption, Wukan incident 212–14
Costa Rica 39
country gentleman [*xiang shen*] 199, 200
countryside construction project, funding 194
crop straw utilization, technological systems for management of 258

dairy products, supply and demand for 91
demographic dividend 42
Deng Xiaoping 2–3
Development and Reform Commission 249
Development Research Center of the State Council 14
Dili Group 57
diseases, mortality rate of rural residents 181
division-of-tax reform, burden on farmers 278–80
double-voting system, conflict resolution 209–10
dragon-head enterprises: financial and insurance systems 138; industrialized agriculture 135; new-style agricultural operation 118–19, 123, 135; operating methods of 131, 142
Du Shuang 278

eaglet project, local management 216–17
Earthbound China (Fei Xiaotong) 218
ecological civilization in countryside 20; agriculture-related water consumption 237; arable land quantity and quality 236–7; building up 262–7; deterioration of ecological system 242–3; environmental pollution in 238–42; fertilizers and pesticides in agriculture 239–40; garbage and waste disposal from rural communities 241; industrial pollution 238; planning and policy support 259–62; plastic sheeting in agriculture 240, 258; pollution from urbanization 238; problems facing the building of 235–43; projects to restore and protect ecosystems 267–8; resources of agriculture 236–8; soil erosion 243; waste material disposed in agriculture 241; water resources and pollution 237–8; *see also*

environmental degradation in rural areas; environmental protection in rural areas
"ecological migrants" assistance for impoverished 191
ecological systems: desertification of land 242, 243; deterioration of 242–3; grasslands 242; soil erosion 243
economic aggregate 4, 6n1, 14
economic development 1–4, 8–9: agricultural resources in 117, 123; collective economic organization 78–9; collective property rights 81–2; demand for water 85; food security and 101; grand goal of 38–9; poverty alleviation 144, 157, 159; public finance in 271, 285, 333; rural governance 220, 227–9; social and 22, 30, 45, 50, 56, 60, 77, 151, 164, 192, 202, 308; supply and demand for grain 93–4
economic growth: agricultural productivity in reform 37–8; cities as center of gravity of 192; stage-shift transformation 146; working-age population 39–40
"eco"tourism 57
education 12, 13: allocating resources for rural areas 165–70; children of rural migrant workers 318–21; enrollment rate of senior high schools 168; financial input in urban and rural schools 295; Hebei province 194–5; improving quality of rural labor force 41–2; migrants 149; night school for rural migrant workers 322–3; poverty alleviation and 169; preschool 166; public finance in rural areas for 289–90; rural compulsory 166, 170; rural compulsory reform 282–3; students attending vocational and high schools 168; task relating to 16–17; vocational 166–7, 169
Egypt 94
elderly people: living conditions in Hubei province 173–4; social security for rural 170–5
electricity program, Guizhou province 190
environment: environmental management systems 251; monitoring networks 268; rural social conflicts 222–3
environmental degradation in rural areas: agricultural production and 243–5; animal husbandry industry 244; cancer villages in China 245, 246, 268n1;

conflicts of interests and 247–8; food safety and chemical use in farming 244–5; garbage disposal and sewage in towns 245; health of rural residents 245, 246; industrial pollution 245; soil and water pollution 243–4; water pollution 244; *see also* ecological civilization in countryside

environmental protection of rural areas: building rural ecological civilization 262–7; compensation for controlling water contamination 255–6; compensation system for agricultural resources 254–5; eight environmental management systems 251; financial investment in 263–4; government spending in 263; laws and regulations on 252, 253–4; management controls for 248–67; managing agricultural resources 249–50, 252; managing agricultural resources and 257–9; nine dragons handing 249–50; planning and policy support for 259–62; projects for remediation of problems 266; projects for rural ecosystem rebuilding 264–7; projects to protect agricultural resources 264–5; projects to restore and protect ecosystems 267–8; property rights system 252, 254; technological systems and servicing methods for 256–9; technological systems for 258

environmental remediation, public finance for funding 288–9

European Union, agricultural support and protection 293

expropriations, future reform of 71–5

family: conflict and suicide 224–5; social governance of clans 199

family farms: experimenting in Shanghai 120–1; land transfer of 133–4; new-style agriculture system 115, 120; operating methods of 130, 142; status of 128

farmers: funding social endeavors for 289–90; grassroots organizations policy with 271–6; medical insurance security 182; People's Commune system and 271; public finance recommendations for 301–5; public spending burden on 299, 300; relationship with State after founding of PRC 270–81; safety of housing 187–8; social conflicts 222–3; State fiscal support for rural areas 284–5; State's policy after rural

tax-and-fees reform 280–1; tax burdens on 275–6, 278–80

farmers' cooperatives: alliances with 134; new-style agricultural operation 115, 121, 122; operating methods of 131, 142

farmers' incomes: comparing growth in 21st century 150; fiscal spending on policies benefiting 153–4; growth of per capita net 144; increasing operating income 149–52; minimum living allowance standards 156–7; new-style agricultural operation 118; preferential policies and transfer-type 152–7; price change of farm produce and agricultural business 151; setting up moderately prosperous society 144–8; shifting rural populations toward cities 148–9; social welfare benefits and social security 155, 157

farming: chemical usage in, impacting food safety 244–5; human resources for 142; projects to control pollution from 265; technology managing resources and protecting environment 257; water-conservation projects 265

farmland: arable land in China 86–7, 236–7; arable land turned to construction-use land 89; family farms 120; illegal land use 82n2; impact on agricultural production 89; projects to protect 264–5; quantity and quality of 85; size of arable land by farming households 116; *see also* contractual operating rights to farmland

Fei Xiaotong 218

fertilizers: agricultural usage 239–40; food safety 244–5; technological systems for management of 258

finance *see* public finance

financial services system: farming 137; vocational education 169

fiscal spending, policies benefiting farmers 153–4

floating population 13; education rights of children 318; medical care of 324–5

food: global production 92; quality 119; trade and net imports 89–90

food safety: agricultural production management 109; challenges facing China's 95–7; chemical usage in farming 244–5; demands for more 117–18; existing laws 99; information platform 109–10; lean meat powder 96–7; national institutions 98; nutrition of targeted groups of people 110; policies and measures for safeguarding 108–10; policy documents on management of 99–100; poverty and 97; regulatory institutions and oversight 108–9; regulatory system addressing 95–100; systems and policies in China 97–9

food security 15, 84; agricultural technology 104–5; core contents and requirements of national strategy 100–102; grain production and policies 107–8; implementing national strategy 100–10; measures to guarantee 102–8; price-formation mechanisms 106–7; productivity of labor and land 102–3; rice hybrids 105; rural modernization 18; term 84; urban-rural dichotomy 9–10; water conservancy 103–4

forestry industry 267

France 292

Fujian province, rice fields 85

gender: ratio of China's population 24, 42*n*3; suicide in rural areas 225

General Administration of Quality Supervision, Inspections and Quarantines 98

geographic distribution, population 40–1

Germany 292

Gisser, Micha 165

global supply and demand: grain production 91, 92, 93; impact on China 94–5; projected changes 93–4

governance: college students serving as town officials 215, 216–17; current pattern in rural communities 199–217; government structures managing rural areas 201–6; grassroots democratic self-governance 206–9, 211, 214; modernization of 198; reform of rural systems of 19; resolving conflicts between two committees 209–11; transformation in rural social, in modern era 199–201; *see also* rural governance problems

grain production: change in world grain markets and impact on China 94–5; food security and 102–3; geographic distribution of resources for 86–7; global supply and demand for 91, 93–4; improving subsidy policies 107; increase in costs 87–8; insurance coverage for 107–8; price-formation

mechanisms for 106–7; projections of supply and demand 90; quantity and quality of arable land 85; resource constraints limiting 85–8; security of 84; setting up benefit compensation mechanisms 107; supply and demand for 88–91, 118; threat of water shortages 85–6; trade and net imports 89–90; *see also* food security

grassroots organizations; governance of rural communities 228–30; management functions of 304; mechanisms for rural communities 233–4; policy with farmers 271–6; task relating to governance 17

Guangdong province: amount of construction-use land 67; rice fields 85; rights to collectively owned construction-use land 69–71

Guangdong Wens Food Group Co., Ltd. 123–4

Guangxi Zhuang Autonomous Region 110

Guizhou province, living conditions in rural areas 189–91

healthcare: availability of clean drinking water 178–9; child malnutrition 180, 182, 184; Chuanfang Community 324–5; for floating population 324–5; funding of rural insurance system 178–9; Hebei province 195; improving standards for rural people 182–4; infant mortality rate (1991–2012) 177, 178; insurance of rural residents 178, 179–80; maternal mortality rate (1991–2012) 176, 178; medical resources of township 196–7*n*6; mortality rate and diseases of rural residents 181; mortality rate of children under five (1991–2012) 177, 178; nutrition packets 185–6; public finance in rural areas for 289–90; rural citizens 175–86; sanitary toilets 179; task relating to 16–17; transitioning rural population 323–4; urban *vs* rural, medical technicians and hospital beds 295; *see also* new-style rural cooperative healthcare system

Hebei province, public facilities in villages and townships 194–5

He Yupeng 27

hollowed-out villages 40–1; public finance 276; public security issues 223–4

homestead land 41, 54, 61

homestead site: chaotic expansion of 64; future reform of rural system in

China 66–7; ownership rights 66–7; policy of tying together increases and decreases in land 65; term 60; transfer of 63–4; "usufruct rights" 64; *see also* residential-use land

Hong Ruichao 214

household contracting system: new-style agriculture 114–15; relationship of 132

household registration system 309–17; experience of reforming 309, 311; landmarks of reform of 310; opinions on management methods for residence certificates 311–12; policy recommendations on speeding up 313–17; preconditions for settlement in cities 315; problems with reforming 312–13; public-finance transfer payment system 316–17; recommendations for reforming 333–5; residency certificates 314, 316; rural migrant workers and housing 329–31; welfare benefits and 313

housing conditions: change in housing area and quality for rural residents 187; moderately prosperous housing 188–9; program in Guizhou province 190; proportion of rural families 188; rural residents 186–9, 265, 266

housing that enjoys limited property rights 62–3; *see also* residential-use land

Huang Liangui 124

Hubei province, living conditions of elderly in 173–4

human capital 19, 32, 144, 148, 166, 336

human resources 19: agricultural production 104; compulsory education 111; farming 142; public funds 297

Hunan Anbang New-agricultural Technology Co., Ltd. 125–7

Hu Xiaoyun 124

Hu Xingdou 62

hygienic facilities, transitioning rural population 323–4

illegal organizations 213, 224

illness, elderly people in Hubei province 173–4; *see also* healthcare

imperial examination system (*ke-jeu* system) 200

impoverished "ecological migrants" assistance 191

incomes 15–16: change of urban/rural income ratio 145; elderly people in Hubei province 173; ratio between top

and bottom 20 percent households 146; urban and rural growth 145; urban-rural disparities 9; *see also* farmers' incomes

incremental reform, market economy 10–11

India 91, 92, 292

Indonesia 91, 92, 292

industrialization, process of 3–4

insurance coverage: elderly in rural areas 170–5; farmers 182; grain production 107–8; rural financial system and 138–9; rural healthcare 178, 179–80

intergenerational relationships 174

Italy 292

Japan: agricultural labor force 42–3n7; agricultural support and protection 293; agricultural value in GDP 292; sideline occupations 43n9

Jiangsu province, rice field 85

Jin Shuqin 250

job markets: rural migrant workers 36–7; placement for transitioning populations 321–2

Kang Youwei 2

Kazakhstan 39

labor force *see* rural labor force

labor shortages, phenomenon 35–6

land: desertification and degradation of 242, 243; factor of production 218; land reserve system 73; quota and usage by transitioning population 334–5; social conflicts 222; soil erosion 243; technological systems for agricultural production 258; technological systems for management of 258; *see also* farmland; land system

Land Reform Act (1950) 45

land requisitions: amounts paid for 74; depending reform of 72–5; distributing benefits of gains in land values 74–5; future reforms of 71–5; limits on governments for 73–4; main issues related to 72; public infrastructure 73

land system: China's rural areas 18, 44–5; collectively owned construction-use land in Guangdong province 69–71; deepening reform of requisitions 71–5; evolution of 45–6; framework of management 46; general principles for future reform of 57–60; income from sale of land 49–50; industrial, commercial and residential purposes 49; main characteristics of 46–8; main issues in 48–50; market access 48–9; property rights 48, 50; reforming property-rights system 51–4; reforming rural homestead sites 60–7; secondary market in land-use rights 59–60; transferability of contractual operating rights to farmland 55–60; *see also* contractual operating rights to farmland; land requisitions; property-rights system; residential-use land

Law of Land Contracts (2002) 51

Law of Land Contracts in Rural Areas 45, 47, 48

Law on Food Safety 99, 100, 108

Law on Land Administration 45, 63, 67, 72

Law on Land Management (1986) 45–7, 50, 52, 67, 72, 79, 218

Law on the Quality and Safety of Agricultural Products 99, 108

laws and regulations, agricultural resources and environmental protection 252, 253–4

lean meat powder: food poisoning case, 96–7; food quality and safety 245

Lewis dual-economy model 8

Lewisian turning point 8–10

Liu Shouying 65

Li Yuanxing 174

Mao Zedong 2

market environment, rural society 220

Masayoshi, Ohira 2

maternity insurance, rural migrant workers 329

Mauritius 39

medical insurance: expanding coverage in cities 326–7; rural migrant workers 328–9; urban-rural gap in 296

medical system 12: transitioning rural population 323–4; treating of floating population 324–5; *see also* healthcare

mental health, rural older people 174

Mexico 292

micro-loans, agriculture 140–1

migrant workers *see* rural migrant workers

Million Summits Holdings Ltd. Company of Hong Kong 57

Minhang district of Shanghai, quantifying assets and paying shareholders 80

minimum living allowance standards 155–7; poverty alleviation and 161–2

Ministry of Agriculture 75, 97–8, 105, 120, 123, 125, 241, 249–50, 287, 291, 294, 322

Ministry of Commerce 98

Ministry of Environmental Protection 223, 237–8, 241, 243, 247, 249–50

Ministry of Forestry 250

Ministry of Health 250

Ministry of Housing and Urban-Rural Development 62, 249, 250

Ministry of Human Resources and Society Security 216, 322

Ministry of Land and Resources 63, 65, 85, 236–7, 249–50

Ministry of Transport 249

Ministry of Transportation 250

Ministry of Water Resources 249–50

moderate prosperity (*xiao kang*) 1–4, 7; concept of 14; four investments 19–20; land system 44–5; principles of 20; tasks and challenges of 14–18; three securities 20

moderately prosperous society: all-round way 14–15, 19–20, 143, 157, 160, 187, 236, 336–7; concept of 6; farmers' income in setting up 144–8; housing 188–9; pathway toward 18–21; poverty-alleviation policies 157–63; social harmony 198

mutual-aid funds: targeting poverty 162–3; Zhejiang province 139–40

National Agricultural Census 27, 187

National Bureau of Statistics 4, 14, 21*n*3, 30–1, 35, 158, 163*n*1

National Development and Reform Commission 14, 21*n*3, 249, 250

national environmental security 235; *see also* ecological civilization in countryside

National Health and Family Planning Commission 98

National Party Congress 2: 13th 3; 16th 5; 17th 5, 21*n*3; 18th 5, 12, 53, 113, 114, 147–8

National Planning for New-type Urbanization 2014–2020 23–4

National Population Census: Fifth 27, 30; Sixth 23, 27, 29, 30, 39, 186, 187–8; Third 29

National Student-Nutrition Office 111–12

National Women's Federation 186

new-style agricultural operating system 119–20; agricultural-type construction-use land 141–2; characteristics and problems of 128–9; components of, and their interconnections 114–15;

current status of 119–29; dragon-head
enterprises 118–19, 123, 131, 135;
economies of scale and productivity
132; evolution of 113–14; family farms
120–1, 133–4; farmers' cooperatives
121, 122, 133–4; financial support
from public finance 141; government
guidance and market forces 133;
handling important relationships
131–3; household contractual operating
system and 132; human resources
for 142; importance of establishing
118–19; innovations and technologies
136–7; key tasks of 133–7; measures
to resolve problems in 137–9, 141–2;
micro-loans 140–1; mutual aid
cooperative in Zhejiang province
139–40; necessity and urgency of setting
up 116–19; operations and managing
organizations 142; organizational forms
and operating methods 130–1; overall
framework of 113–15; rationale for
developing 129–33; rural financial
and insurance systems 138–9; rural
financial services organizations 127–8;
rural labor rate transitioning off land
132–3; rural land management system
137–8; socialized service organizations
in 125, 132, 135–6; specialized large
households 120; structure of 115;
types and development status of
119–23; Wens model for industrializing
agriculture 123–4
new-style household-registration system
313–17; *see also* household registration
system
new-style rural cooperative healthcare
system 175–6, 179–80; *see also*
healthcare
new-style social [old-age] insurance
system 171–5, 196*n*3–4
"new type of urbanization" 18, 19, 29
new-type urbanization planning 23–4
nonagricultural rural workers: labor force
32–7; sideline occupations 33, 43*n*9
Number One document 51, 53, 77, 82,
203, 277
Nutrition Improvement Program 111–12
Nutrition Improvement program for Rural
Compulsory Education Students 153
Nutrition Packet program: healthcare
185–6
nutrition program: principles of 110; rural
children 110–12, 184

occupational injury insurance: rural
migrant workers 329
"one-system that incorporates three
transformations" concept of 210–11
organized crime 224, 227
ownership rights: homestead sites 66–7;
rural land 137–8

Panama 39
participatory budgeting, township people's
congresses of Wenling 230–2
pension system 12, 20: rural old-age
insurance 171–5, 327–8
People's Commune 47, 79, 114: fund
source of public product and services
273; prereform period of 276; reforms
of 200–201; self-governance after
206; State policy under system of 271;
structures 203; supply of public products
and services in rural areas 272; taxes
and fees 275
People's Republic of China (PRC) 199:
Constitution of 201; relationship
between State and farmers since
founding of 270–81
pesticides: agricultural usage 239–40; food
safety 244–5; technological systems for
management of 258
Pingluo county in Ningxia, membership in
collective economic organizations 78–9
plastic sheeting, agricultural film usage
240, 258
policy environment, rural society 220–1
pollution: cancer villages 245, 246, 268*n*1;
chemical fertilizer and pesticide use in
agriculture 239–40; environmental 247;
environmental, in countryside 238–42;
environmental management systems
251; garbage and waste disposal from
rural areas 241; industrial 13, 238; mass
incidents in rural areas 247–8; rural
forms of 13; soil and water, impacting
agricultural productivity 243–4; task
relating to 17–18; waste disposal by
agriculture 241; *see also* environmental
degradation in rural areas
population: aging society of China 27–8;
demographic changes in rural 22;
demographic profile of China 39–40;
improving geographic distribution
of 40–1; mobility of 13; rural areas
218–19; structure of China's rural
27–30; working-age 39–40; *see also*
rural population

pork: lean meat powder 96–7; supply and demand for 91

poverty alleviation 12, 16: downward trend of rural population 158; eliminating absolute 148; food safety concerns 97; impoverished populations areas 158–9; incentive mechanisms of policies 160; and minimum living allowance system 161–2; modes of 159; monitoring survey 159; mutual-aid funds targeting 162–3; policies of 157–63; project-selection models for 161; strength of spending on policies 160; vocational education and 169

private-public partnerships (PPPs) 193

production brigade, fund sources of public products and services 273, 275

Project on Early Childhood Development in Impoverished Regions 185

property-rights system: evolution of rights confirmation and certification 51–2; methods for confirming and issuing certificates 54; process of confirming and certifying rights to land 52–4, 58; progress in reform of 76; pushing reform of 51–4; *see also* collectively owned property rights

public engineering projects, rural social conflicts 223

public finance: agricultural production increases 290–1; building infrastructure in rural areas 286–8; burden on farmers after "division-of-tax reform" 278–80; central and local expenditure structure 332; current spending 284–91; financial revenue and fund-raising of townships 279; fiscal support for farmers, farming and rural areas 284–5; grassroots organizations under township governance and self-governance 271–6; marketization reforms for rural public goods 305–6; People's Commune system 271; recommendations for spending 300–306; reform of county and township fiscal management 283; revenue and expenditure of central and local finance 279; rural debt 276–8; rural environmental remediation 288–9; rural modernization 19; State's policy after rural tax-and-fees reform 280–1; subsidies for agriculture 285–6; township governments 274; urban-rural system 269–70; villages 274; *see also* public spending problems

public products and services: fund sources in rural areas 273; supply in rural areas in People's Commune period 272

public security, rural governance problem 223–4

public service facilities: Hebei province 194–5; rural areas 191–3, 196

public spending problems 291–300; famers' burdens in 2013 299, 300; funds going to rural areas 292–3; inadequate 292–6; public goods in rural areas 299; recommendations for 300–306; rural areas 296–7; supply of public goods in rural areas 293–4, 299; transfer payment systems 297–9, 301–3; urban and rural gap of public services 294–6; urbanization 331–3

Qing-county model, conflict resolution 211

ractopamine, lean meat powder 96–7

regulations *see* laws and regulations

Renmin University 163

Ren Zhiqiang 62

Republic of Korea 292

reserved resettlement land 83n4

residence certificates 311; system of 314, 316; *see also* household registration system

residential-use land 44, 49; basic characteristics of system 60–1; "housing that enjoys limited property rights" controversy 62–3; occupation rights 61; ownership rights 61; problems with existing policies of 61, 63–4; reforming management system governing 60–7; transfer of homestead sites 61; usage rights 60, 61; *see also* land system

rice: fields by province 85; global production 92; hybrid development 105; projections of supply and demand 90; *see also* grain production

Ri Sheng Long Micro-Credit Companies, Ltd. 140–1

Rudong county, caregiving dilemma 28–9

rule of law, social governance 227–8

rural communities: changing dynamics in current era 217–21; comprehensive rural reform 281–3; current governance pattern in 199–217; garbage and waste disposal by 241; grassroots political authority for 228–30; grassroots self-governance mechanisms 233–4; infrastructure development in 286–8;

marketization reforms for supplying
public goods 305–6; mass incidents
by environmental pollution 247–8;
participatory budgeting 230–2; policy
recommendations enabling governance
by 227–34; public finance spending in
296–7; public-finance structures for
providing public goods to 301–5; public
funds in 292–3; public services in urban
vs 294–6; rural debt 276–8; supply of
public goods in 293–4, 299; supply of
public products and services 272
Rural Consumer Price Index 144, 163*n*1
rural development strategy: historical
perspective 10–14; relationship between
urban and rural areas (1993–2002) 11;
rural economy (1978–1992) 10–11; rural
income growth 145; rural modernization
18–19; three agricultures policies 12;
unifying urban and rural development
(post-2013) 12–14; urban areas "paying
back" to (2003–2012) 11–12
rural financial service organization:
characteristics of 129; current status
of 127–8; farmers and farming 137;
insurance systems and 138–9; new-style
agriculture system 115
rural governance problems 221–7; public
security 223–4; rigid approach to
maintaining stability 226–7; social
conflicts 222–3; suicide 224–5
rural labor force: agricultural labor
force 30–2; average length of time in
agricultural work 32; improving quality
of 41–2; nonagricultural 32–7; rate of
transition off the land 132–3; trends by
year 2020 37–40; year 2020 30–40
rural medical assistance 154, 178, 179–80,
182; *see also* healthcare
rural migrant workers: age structures of
34; education for children of 320–1;
employability of 42; employment and job
creation for 321–2; first-generation 42*n*5;
job markets 36–7; monthly income of
(2008–2013) 88; next-generation 42*n*5;
night school for 322–3; nonfarming
jobs 34–6, 38; numbers and types of 33;
orderly migration of 12; participation in
social insurance 327–9; social security
in cities 326–7; term 32–3; urban
employment and structure 35; urbanizing
317; wages and job situations of 36
rural population: change in housing area
and quality 187; changes by province

25; changes in age structure of 28;
demographic changes in 22; distribution
in 2020 24–6; housing conditions of
186–9; living conditions in Guizhou
province 189–91; modernizing
agricultural production 40; number of
administered villages 26–7; number
of rural residents in 2020 23–4; public
service facilities for 191–3, 196;
structure of China's, in 2020 27–30; *see
also* transitioning rural population
rural public service facilities 191–3, 196
rural social governance: governmental
structures managing 201–6;
transformation in modern era 199–201
rural society: changes and reforms in 220–
1; characteristics of 218–19; market
environment 220; policy environment
220–1; values environment 221
Russian Federation 292

Sangong, financial expenditure on 286
Sanjiu Enterprise Group (Three Nine) 57
scientific development, concept of 14–15
second-child policy 23, 42*n*1–2
self-governance: grassroots democratic
206–9, 211, 214; internal institutions
of 208–9; number and population of
administrative villages 207; problems
at grassroots level of 211; public goods
and services by organized mechanisms
214; recent explorations of 215, 217;
rural areas 219, 233–4; Wukan village in
Lufeng municipality 212–14
semiurbanization, process of 38
sewage treatment 247, 250, 251, 258, 266
Shandong province, rice field 85
Shanghai: education for children of rural
migrant workers 320–1; family farms in
120–1
Shanghai Municipal Agriculture
Commission 59
shareholders' meeting, collective property
rights 81–2
Sheng Hong 62
Shenzhen, amount of construction-use
land 67
Shouguang Agricultural Products Logistics
Park 57
social governance: role of rule of law
227–8; task relating to 17
socialized service organizations:
constructing new mechanisms for
135–6; current status of agricultural

125, 129; operating methods of 131; relationship of 132

social management: rigid approach to maintaining stability 226–7

social pension system *see* pension system

social security system 16: education in rural areas 165–70; farmers 155; Hebei province 195; housing for rural residents 186–9; improving the rural old-age 170–5; living conditions in rural areas of Guizhou province 189–91; maternity insurance 329; medical insurance 328–9; Nutrition Packet program 185–6; occupational injury insurance 329; old-age pension insurance 327–8; public finance in rural areas for 289–90; public service facilities 191–3, 196; rural healthcare system 175–86; rural migrant workers 327–9; unemployment insurance 329

Song Hongyuan 77, 80, 278

Songjiang district of Shanghai, family farms in 120–1

South Africa 39, 292

South Korea: agricultural labor force 42–3*n*7; agricultural support and protection 293; agricultural value in GDP 292

soybean: projections of supply and demand 90; *see also* grain production

specialized large households: land transfer of 133–4; new-style agricultural operation 120; operating methods of 130, 142

specialized services, new-style agriculture 115

spending *see* public finance

standard of living 15–16

State Administration for Industry and Commerce 98

State Administration of Quality Supervision, Inspections and Quarantines 98

State Council's Development Research Center 90

State Council's Food Safety Committee 97–8

State Council's Office of Food Safety 97

State Food and Drug Administration 98

State Forestry Administration 249

State-Owned Enterprises 10, 11; job creation 321–2; medical insurance for workers 183

State-owned land: allocating land resources 47; compensated requisitions of 73

steppe areas, projects to protect 267

subsistence allowance, urban-rural gap in 296

suicide, rural governance problem 224–5

Sun Lei 121

Sun Yatsen 2

Tao Ran 49

technical service, agricultural resources and environmental protection 257–9

technological systems: rural ecological civilization 256–9

three agricultures: farmers, farming and rural economy 164, 219; government spending in 263, 270; micro-loans in 140; nongovernmental funds in 291; policies 12; self-governance in 205, 219, 220; State fiscal support for 284–5

towns: Party branches 208–9; resolving conflicts between two committees governing 209–11; self-governance 206–9, 211, 214

townships 201: administrative jurisdictions 201–2; college students serving as officials 215, 216–17; financial revenue and fund-raising 279; governments of 202–6; incomes and expenditures of government 274; reform of fiscal management structures 283; reform of organizations 281–2; revenues of governments 202–6

transfer payment system: public finance 316–17; public spending 297–9; recommendations for 301–3; urbanization of transitioning population 333–4

transitioning rural population: business start-up services 321–2; expanding coverage of housing guarantees in cities 329–31; expanding coverage of social security in cities 326–7; job-placement services 321–2; mechanisms to urbanizing 331–5; medical care and hygienic facilities for 323–4; night school for rural migrant workers 322–3; providing public services to city residents 317–31; safeguarding education rights for 318–20; Shanghai's education solution 320–1; urbanization of 308–9; *see also* household registration system; rural population

Turkey 39, 292

two-committee system, conflict resolution 210

underground religious organizations 224
unemployment insurance, rural migrant
  workers 329
United Nations Development Program 14
United Nations Food and Agriculture
  Organization 93, 105
United States: agricultural support and
  protection 293; agricultural value in
  GDP 292; grain for ethanol production
  94; grain production 91, 92
urbanization: new form of 307; number
  of administered villages 26–7; of
  transitioning population 308–9, 331–5;
  urban income growth 145; *see also*
  transitioning rural population
urban-rural dichotomy: China 8–10;
  education 295; medical insurance 295,
  296; medical technicians and hospital
  beds 295; public services provision
  294–6; subsistence allowances 295, 296
Uruguay 39

values environment: rural society 221
Venezuela 39
villagers' committee 47, 79, 201
villages: cancer 245, 246, 268*n*1; fund-
  raising and labor-raising methods 304–5;
  incomes and expenditures of 274; Party
  branches 208–9; populations of 26–7,
  40–1; projects to protect 266; resolving
  conflicts between two committees
  governing 209–11; self-governance
  206–9, 211, 214; shrinking number of
  43*n*10; Wukan incident 212–14
villages-within-cities, phenomenon 64
vocational education/training 41–2, 154,
  166–7, 169
vulnerable populations, Guizhou province
  191

Wang Debang 63
Wang Hui 49
water: agriculture-related consumption
  237; availability of clean drinking
  178–9; comparing by use in economy
  86; compensation for controlling
  contamination 255–6; conservancy
  facilities in rural areas 293–4; food
  security and 103–4; geographic
  distribution of 86–7; goal of safe
  drinking, in countryside 184; impact on

agricultural production 89; prevalence
  of sanitary toilets 179; projects to
  protect, ecosystems 267–8; quality
  17–18; resources and pollution 237–8;
  restriction of 89; safety program in
  Guizhou province 189; technological
  systems for agricultural production 258;
  technological systems for management
  of disposal 258; threat of shortages 85–6
welfare benefits 81, 155, 271, 273, 275,
  309, 311, 313–16, 333
Wenling municipality, participatory
  budgeting in 230–2
Wens model, industrializing agriculture
  123–4
wheat: global production 92; projections
  of supply and demand 90; *see also* grain
  production
*Work Report of the State Council on
  Ensuring the Safety of Drinking Water*
  (State Council) 17
work responsibility system, new-style
  agriculture operation 136
World Bank 90, 94, 163*n*2, 180, 333
World Development Indicators (WDI)
  163*n*2
World Trade Organization 11, 94, 117
Wukan incident, Lufeng municipal
  government 212–14

xiao kang see moderate prosperity (*xiao
  kang*)
Xi Jinping 7
Xinhe, budgeting process 230–2
Xue Jinbo, Wukan incident 213–14

Yuan Longping 105

Zhang Jiancheng 214
Zhang Xiaoshan 57
Zhanqi Village Land Shareholding
  Company, Ltd. 122
Zheguo, budgeting process 231–2
Zhejiang Jiaxing Zhongmao Plastic
  Industry Co., Ltd. 97
Zhejiang province: mutual aid cooperative
  of Moslem population in 139–40; rice
  field 85; rural cooperative association of
  Rui-an city 234
Zhou Qiren 62
Zhuang Liehong 214

For Product Safety Concerns and Information please contact our EU
representative GPSR@taylorandfrancis.com
Taylor & Francis Verlag GmbH, Kaufingerstraße 24, 80331 München, Germany

www.ingramcontent.com/pod-product-compliance
Ingram Content Group UK Ltd.
Pitfield, Milton Keynes, MK11 3LW, UK
UKHW021021180425
457613UK00020B/1016